Unveiling Your Future

PROGRESSIONS MADE EASY

Maritha Pottenger & Zipporah Dobyns

ACS Publications

Also by ACS Publications

All About Astrology Series of booklets
The American Atlas, Expanded 5th Edition (Shanks)
The American Ephemeris 2001-2010
The American Ephemeris for the 21st Century [Noon or Midnight] 2000-2050, Rev. 2nd Ed.
The American Ephemeris for the 20th Century [Noon or Midnight] 1900-2000, Rev. 5th Ed.
The American Heliocentric Ephemeris 2001-2050
The American Midpoint Ephemeris 2001-2005
The American Sidereal Ephemeris 2001-2025
The Asteroid Ephemeris 1900-2050
Astrological Insights into Personality (Lundsted)
Astrology for the Light Side of the Brain (Rogers-Gallagher)
Astrology for the Light Side of the Future (Rogers-Gallagher)
Astrology: The Next Step (Pottenger)
The Book of Jupiter (Waram)
The Book of Pluto (Forrest)
The Book of Uranus (Negus)
The Changing Sky, 2nd Edition (Forrest)
Easy Astrology Guide (Pottenger)
Easy Tarot Guide (Masino)
Expanding Astrology's Universe (Dobyns)
Finding Our Way Through the Dark (George)
Future Signs (Simms)
Hands That Heal, 2nd Edition (Bodine)
Healing with the Horoscope (Pottenger)
The Inner Sky (Forrest)
The International Atlas, Revised 5th Edition (Shanks)
The Michelsen Book of Tables (Michelsen)
Millennium: Fears, Fantasies & Facts
The Night Speaks (Forrest)
The Only Way to...Learn Astrology, Vols. I-VI (March & McEvers)
    Volume I, 2nd Edition - Basic Principles
    Volume II, 2nd Edition - Math & Interpretation Techniques
    Volume III - Horoscope Analysis
    Volume IV- Learn About Tomorrow: Current Patterns
    Volume V - Learn About Relationships: Synastry Techniques
    Volume VI - Learn About Horary and Electional Astrology
Past Lives, Future Choices (Pottenger)
Planetary Heredity (M. Gauquelin)
Planets on the Move (Dobyns/Pottenger)
Psychology of the Planets (F. Gauquelin)
Spirit Guides: We Are Not Alone (Belhayes)
Tables of Planetary Phenomena, Rev. 2nd Edition (Michelsen/Pottenger)
Uranian Transneptune Ephemeris 1900-2050
Your Magical Child, 2nd Edition (Simms)
Your Starway to Love, 2nd Edition (Pottenger)

UNVEILING YOUR FUTURE

PROGRESSIONS MADE EASY

MARITHA POTTENGER
ZIPPORAH DOBYNS

Dedicated to **all** our students—with special mention to
Deb, Michaeleen and Cindy—with heartfelt thanks and appreciation.

International Standard Book Number 0-935127-65-8

Cover design by Daryl Fuller

Published by ACS Publications
5521 Ruffin Road
San Diego, CA 92123-1314

First Printing, August 1998
Second Printing, May 2002

Table of Contents

CHAPTER SEVEN
HARD ASPECTS TO THE ANGLES 178

CHAPTER EIGHT
ASPECT CONFIGURATIONS 201

CHAPTER NINE
MOON CHANGING HOUSES OR SIGNS 212

CHAPTER TEN
PROGRESSED ASPECTS BY SUN, MERCURY, VENUS AND MARS (PLUS THE "BIG FOUR" ASTEROIDS) 218

CHAPTER ELEVEN
ASPECTS OF PROGRESSED MOON 274

CHAPTER TWELVE
EXAMPLES 296

REVIEWS

Astrological peers are raving about Unveiling Your Future! Here's what **Raymond A. Merriman, President of International Society for Astrological Research**, has to say:

"How many times have you been asked by students: 'Can you recommend a good book on secondary progressions?' And how many times have you responded with something like, 'Well, I learned about progressions from ...., but as far as a book just on progressions, I don't really know.'

"Most of the literature on secondary progressions is contained in a single chapter within books on general or predictive astrology. However, now comes a new book called *Unveiling Your Future: Progressions Made Easy*, dedicated entirely to the subject of secondary progressions by two of the foremost professional astrologers today: Maritha Pottenger and Zipporah Dobyns.

"The expertise of the authors truly stands out. Anyone can write a reference book which interprets various astrological signatures, but Pottenger and Dobyns have their own unique style and insights. The crux of their analysis is psychological, but even within that they offer a generous grouping of events that are possible under each progression. And unlike most books on astrological forecasting, this one also includes delineations involving Chiron, the Moon's Nodes, and the four primary asteroids: Ceres, Pallas, Juno, and Vesta. Not only is this material different from other books, but the interpretations also just happen to be very good!

"There is a wealth of new material presented in this wonderful new book. The interpretations are clear, sensible, and insightful. The material is organized in a very practical way, which makes it easy to use as a reference work. And the later chapters include some case histories which demonstrate exactly how the authors apply their techniques.

"Astrologers looking for an excellent book on secondary progressions can't go wrong with *Unveiling Your Future: Progressions Made Easy.* **It is probably the best book written on the subject, and will likely become the standard for secondary progressions for many, many years to come. Highly recommended.**"

Jeanne Long, financial astrologer, author and international lecturer, has this to say:

"**Maritha Pottenger and Zipporah Dobyns have done the impossible...they've made looking into the future easy!** *Unveiling*

Your Future addresses the most mysterious and exciting area of astrological delineation – known as progressions, revealing it in such a way that looking into the future has never been more easy or clearly defined. The authors have pooled their vast astrological knowledge and compressed it into this valuable reference book. It is presented in a refreshingly clear and practical way, but more importantly, in a usable manner.

"Maritha and Zip never hold back astrological information; they always make a point of going to the limit in generously sharing their knowledge.

"Wonderfully, **this book has something for everyone**, from the student to the professional. It provides a solid foundation in a step-by-step format to keep the student on track. I especially like the keyword headings in many sections of the book, such as 'Sun in Leo or 5th House: Star Quality' and 'Venus in Aries or 1st House: Please Me!' I love it. A student will get the picture instantly.

"Advanced students and professionals will appreciate the wealth of information presented on "big four" asteroids and Chiron showing how they function in the progressed chart. Much of this is new information including the section on house rulerships. The Case Studies Section presents a simple formula which combines long-term and short-term cycles with lunar cycles and progressed aspects to put all of the pieces into perspective.

"Most importantly, *Unveiling Your Future* shows how to put all the fragments of conflicting information together in a clear-cut and concise way, allowing you to explore the future in a surprisingly easy fashion. Finally, Maritha and Zip not only take you on an adventure into your future, but counsel and guide you as to the best use of the energies involved.

"Because this book offers a whole new world of easy progressions, you will want to **keep it handy for constant reference**. Thank you Maritha and Zip for taking the time to share!"

Carol Tebbs, MA, astrologer, teacher, and UAC Board Chair has this to say.

"Page one of *Unveiling Your Future* leads off with meaty stuff—a prioritized list of what to look for to interpret a secondary progression. And then, the well-experienced astrological mother/daughter team, Maritha Pottenger and Dr. Zipporah Dobyns, follows through with the goods — a detailed, humane interpretation of the various combinations formed by angles, planets, nodes, and yes, "the big 4" asteroids and Chiron. **For student to professional, this book provides insight and depth to one of astrology's standard interpretive tools, the Secondary Progression. Consider it a must read.**"

CHAPTER ONE

BASICS

Astrology offers us a way to see the cosmic order. The Sun, Moon, planets and other astronomical factors are part of the cosmos and they are visible, permitting us to see and understand both worldly and personal issues at any given time. The patterns in the sky at the time of a birth—whether of a human baby, an animal, a business, a country or an idea—describe the psychological nature of the entity being born at that time.

In one of the most useful of many systems to help us understand the stages of growth of the new entity, a **day** in the sky has been found to picture a **year** of life. In this system, which is known as secondary progressions, the movements of planets in the sky in one day symbolize the issues (and a range of possible events) faced by the person during the equivalent year.

This volume will not cover the mathematics of progressions; that is amply covered in other texts or calculated by astrological services (see back of book). It would be helpful to be familiar with the individual speed of the planets so you can estimate (by checking an ephemeris) about how long an aspect will last.[1] (For example, aspects from the progressed Sun last about two years. Aspects from the progressed Moon last around two months. Aspects from progressed Mercury can last from about one and one-quarter years to almost eight years, depending on retrogrades. And so on.)

These pages will provide an easy entry to interpreting your personal progressions—and those of other people. To make the information accessible, we have convenient look-up sections for different kinds of progressions. For fullest understanding, however, we suggest you read the introductory material first.

---

1 Throughout this text, a one-degree orb is used for aspects. That means aspects are not considered to be "in effect" until they are within one degree of exact and aspects are finished when they move one degree beyond the exact aspect.

Priorities

A general "rule of thumb" in astrology is: the more often a pattern repeats in the sky, the less important a single occurrence is likely to be in your life. The rarer an astrological placement, the more significance should be given to it in your interpretations. Following is an outline which suggests priorities to follow when interpreting progressions. The chapters in this book will follow this outline and provide instant look-ups for the planetary placements discussed.

Look first for any **long-term (sometimes lifetime!) progressed aspects**. Aspects from outer planets to natal ones can last for many years in secondary progressions. Sometimes, with retrogrades, an aspect will hold (within a 1-degree orb) for a lifetime. These aspects are very significant! They indicate **enduring, character issues which will pervade the life**. (All aspects discussed within this book can be from progressed planets to progressed planets **or** from progressed planets to natal placements.)

Long-term aspects are interpreted in Chapter 2.

Look for any "one-time only" or "rare" progressed events. This includes **progressed planets changing direction** (retrograde to direct or direct to retrograde). Such changes are often keys to major new chapters in the life. Also look for the **Sun or any other planets (except the Moon) or angles changing house or sign**. The Sun only changes signs (after the first change) every 30 years or so. Any sign or house change suggests a new focus, a new emphasis. Also note any **progressed New Moon** (planting seeds for a whole new cycle) or **progressed Full Moon** (fulfillment stage; time to move to a new level, or begin another cycle). The entire progressed lunar cycle takes about 28-30 years.

Planets and angles changing house, sign or direction are covered in Chapter 3. The lunation cycle is covered in Chapter 4.

Conjunctions to the angles of the horoscope (Ascendant, Midheaven) **are important**. (Some astrologers find the auxiliary angles—East Point/West Point and Vertex/Antivertex useful as well.) Events are more likely to be involved when the angles are aspected and conjunctions are the strongest aspect. (Any conjunction to an angle is also, perforce, an opposition to the other end of the axis.) Think in terms of the symbolism of the angles involved, the planets themselves and the houses ruled by those planets. As with all aspects, look for **repeated themes**.

Give extra weight to all conjunctions (except, of course, outer planets to themselves).[2]

House rulership information pertaining to conjunctions is covered in Chapter 5. Conjunctions (planet/planet, planet/angle and angle/planet) will be interpreted in Chapter 6.

Hard aspects and quincunxes involving the angles are very significant. Hard aspects include conjunctions, squares and oppositions, along with octiles

---

2 Because the outer planets move so slowly in progressions, the progressed planets will be conjunct their natal positions for many years.

(also called semi-squares) and trioctiles (also called sesqui-squares or sesqui-quadrates). The latter two are like mini-squares. Think of hard aspects as keys to events rather than assuming "conflict." Consider the nature of planets, signs, and houses involved (including the houses ruled by planets making aspects). Quincunxes and oppositions are often associated with separations (voluntary or involuntary) and consequent new directions.

Hard aspects to the angles will be interpreted in Chapter 7.

5. **Aspects activating any aspect configurations** in the chart (T-squares, grand crosses, yods, grand trines, etc.) or a progressed planet or angle reaching a degree that activates several natal (and/or progressed) planets at the same time (including stellia). **Watch for networks!** (Astro's *360-degree Aspect Scan* can identify degrees in the zodiac which are particularly "sensitive"—make lots of aspects in your chart.) With an aspect configuration, it seems to be activated from the time the first aspect is made until the last aspect is finished. For example, a grand cross with $ at 18 4 and (at 19 7 and % at 20 0 and ^ at 21 1 would be activated when anything reached 17 degrees, and last through 22 degrees (1-degree orb both sides). When networks are activated, events often (but **not** inevitably) occur. Even without an event, the individual will be working hard on the issues depicted by that natal (or natal/progressed) network.

Aspect configurations are discussed in Chapter 8.

A change of sign or house by the progressed Moon. The progressed Moon is a major key to emotional needs, and where we seek safety. A new sign or house shows issues and needs in high focus for the next few years (average of 2-1/2 years per sign—time spent in houses varies due to size differences).

The Moon's changes of house and sign are interpreted in Chapter 9.

Hard aspects and quincunxes involving the Sun or any of the planets (or asteroids). Hard aspects and quincunxes are more associated with events. Watch for repeated themes in factors involved (*e.g.*, Venus, a planet in the 7th, the ruler of the 7th and Juno all involved puts high focus on one-to-one relationship issues). Watch for **aspect themes** (e.g., many squares). Soft aspects also help to describe the issues in focus, but are not as indicative of events.

Pairs of planets in aspect will be interpreted in Chapter 10.

8. **Month-by-month analysis of aspects to the progressed Moon**. The progressed Moon is often a "timing trigger." Since its aspects last only a month or two, events more often occur when the progressed Moon moves in to join an already-existing, longer-term pattern. Watch particularly for times when the progressed Moon feeds into hard-aspect patterns already present or makes aspects to planets symbolic of the background focus. (For example, lots of 7th house action and Midheaven involvement may suggest marriage, business partnership, etc. If the Moon conjuncts, squares, or opposes Venus, that would be a confirming aspect.)

The aspects of the progressed Moon are covered in Chapter 11.

Options

The interpretations offered here will show a range of possibilities. Since life is infinitely variable, astrology strives to reflect it. Each planet symbolizes many different potentials. It is possible to identify a set of core issues, but one cannot specify that exactly this or that event will take place. Much has to do with the personal choices of the individual involved. That, to us, is one of the reasons to look ahead with astrology.

If our fate were truly "set" by the stars, there would be little point in forecasting. It is because the patterns in the heavens speak to psychological principles—which can be manifested in many different events—that it is worthwhile to examine our possible futures. The better we understand the options available, the more wisely we can choose. The more fully we comprehend the needs and desires (including some subconscious ones) which are driving us, the more easily we can find actions which will satisfy "warring" parts of our psyche and bring us more fulfillment.

Although each interpretation focuses most strongly on the inner needs and desires which are depicted by the heavens, we will also include—where relevant—"mundane" (outer world) event possibilities, such as marriage, change of residence, having a child, etc. These are not intended to be inclusive (as they cannot be), but will include some of the more common expressions of the various aspects and placements which are interpreted and offer a foundation for brainstorming more options.

By looking forward, each reader can then work to create his/her favorite future—to feed and enhance the possibilities which are most attractive to that individual! The aim of this book is to help illuminate possibilities and pathways which lie before you.

We believe that growth is the "name of the game" of life and that growth is a long process. Self-awareness can be enormously helpful but we still have to work to make peace between our contradictory desires, to moderate our excesses, to further develop our talents. And even though growth takes time and work, do remember to enjoy the journey!

CHAPTER TWO
LONG-TERM ASPECTS

Due to stations and retrogrades, some planets will **hold** an aspect (within the one-degree orb) in secondary progressions for years and years. The outer planets, particularly, can maintain certain aspects for extended periods. Such aspects are keys to **central** issues in one's character. They point to **enduring themes** that last for years in one's life.

The following interpretations link outer planets with each other. In some cases, due to a retrograde period or because the aspect was applying at birth, a progressed outer planet (Jupiter through Pluto) will remain in aspect to a natal personal planet (Sun through Mars) for a number of years. (Thus, for example, progressed Pluto may remain within 1 degree of the conjunction to a natal Sun.) For those aspects, refer to the delineations in Chapters 6 and 10—and think long-term. For aspects involving the outer planets and the Moon, see Chapter 11 and think long-term.

As indicated by the headings, we do not find a difference in the planetary pairs between one planet applying in aspect to the second versus the second applying to the first. So, interpretations for Jupiter conjunct Saturn are the same as for Saturn conjunct Jupiter, etc.

The Question of Rulers

In addition to the basic interpretations offered here, consider the question of rulers. The houses which are ruled by the planets making a long-term aspect often are involved with the enduring themes and issues. When two rulers have a long-term conjunction, the matters of the two or more houses ruled tend to be merged. When the rulers have long-term harmony aspects (sextile or trine), the issues pertaining to those houses tend to complement one another. Where rulers have a long-term conflict aspect (square, opposition, or quincunx), the individual may have to work to make peace between, or take turns between, the competing needs of the different houses. Especially with oppositions and quincunxes, separations may occur between the people/ places/ objects concerned with the two (or more) houses involved.

As an example, following are some sample possibilities (brainstorm more of your own) for conjunctions between a first-house ruler and a ruler of each of the other houses:

SIGN	RULER	ANCIENT RULER OR CO-RULER
Aries (♈)	Mars (♂)	
Taurus (♉)	Venus (♀)	
Gemini (♊)	Mercury (☿)	
Cancer (♋)	Moon (☽)	
Leo (♌)	Sun (☉)	
Virgo (♍)	Mercury (☿)	
Libra (♎)	Venus (♀)	
Scorpio (♏)	Pluto (♇)	Mars (♂)
Sagittarius (♐)	Jupiter (♃)	
Capricorn (♑)	Saturn (♄)	
Aquarius (♒)	Uranus (♅)	Saturn (♄)
Pisces (♓)	Neptune (♆)	Jupiter (♃)

HOUSES LINKED BY CONJUNCTION OF RULERS

1st and 2nd: financial independence important; personally identified with what one earns, owns, and enjoys; strong sensual nature; grace in action (beauty in motion) with lovely sports, dancing, etc.; may be impulsive spending; assertive regarding resources and possessions.

1st and 3rd: identified with the mind; rapid thinking and (possibly) impulsive speech; sibling rivalry, a sibling or other relative as a role model of what to be or what not to be; forceful communications; rapid reactions; easily bored; good debater, extemporaneous speaker; quick hands; actions center around relatives, learning, or disseminating information.

1st and 4th: identified with home, family and/or nurturing parent; expresses self through protecting others or being dependent; assertive in the nest; lots of activity within the home; ambivalence (hot/cold reactions) about the parental role; seeks "my way" domestically.

1st and 5th: fun-loving spirit; identified with children and/or creativity; natural stage presence and dramatic instincts; dynamic and forceful; can be impulsive; generous; may instinctively gamble or speculate; can be aggressive about gaining attention; spontaneous with childlike enthusiasm.

1st and 6th: conscientious; identified with work; determination to work on one's own terms; entrepreneurial spirit; forceful on the job; lots of action (or strife) at work; personally active in regard to health; anger an issue in terms of well-being; can be self-critical; wants to improve self.

1st and 7th: torn between assertion and accommodation; working on balance between self and other; may be too other-directed or insist on own way in relationships; likely to attract active, exciting partners; graceful actions; passion for balance and fairness; sensitive to appearances.

1st and 8th: emotionally intense nature; could be volatile with mood swings; forceful in regard to joint resources and possessions (or gets involved with powerful people); instinctively looks beneath the surface; fascinated by death, ecology, sex; personal experience with addiction or self-mastery.

1st and 9th: seeker of the truth; restless, tends to travel; naturally philosophical; inclined to over generalize; can be extravagant; a risk-taker; may be aggressive about religion, morality or beliefs; lots of action in regard to education, the law, other countries, spiritual matters, etc.; very direct.

1st and 10th: identified with career and success; working on balance between personal will and limits of society; authority figure important (positive or negative) role model; wants to call the shots vocationally; early self-doubts and inhibitions possible; assertive about status, drive to accomplish.

1st and 11th: individualistic, freedom-loving; active with friends, groups, organizations, causes, and the cutting edge; assertive about justice and humanitarian principles; willing to break the rules; unusual; may be accident-prone (moving too fast or too intent on getting away); seeks the new, the nontraditional.

1st and 12th: working on balance between self-assertion and self-sacrifice; natural imagination; active on behalf of beauty, compassion, or escapism; instinctively idealistic; assertive pursuit of mystical experiences; illusory appearance; acting on intuition; subconscious images important.

One other variation can occur. When two planets aspect each other, the basic planetary meaning of one may apply to the (natal) house which is ruled by the other. For example, if progressed Uranus conjuncts Pluto long-term, the basic planet/planet interpretation (provided below) is relevant. In addition, if Scorpio is on the cusp of the 1st house (Ascendant) and Aquarius is on the cusp of the 4th house, the 1st and 4th houses are likely to be linked (through the conjunction) for this individual. (See above table.) Also, this person will tend to bring issues of intensity, life-and death, psychological probing, fascination with hidden matters, and power struggles (Pluto) into the home and family relationships (4th house ruled by Uranus). Similarly, the basic identity, action and appearance (1st house ruled by Pluto) of this person will probably have an overtone of individuality, uniqueness, weirdness, unpredictability or concern with the wider world (conjunction to Uranus).

Planet to Planet Long-Term Aspects
Jupiter, Saturn, Uranus, Neptune, Pluto, Chiron, Nodes

Remember that the harmony aspects, the sextile and trine, do not guarantee pleasant consequences since they can lead to excesses which create problems. On the other side, the challenge aspects of square, opposition, and quincunx can be handled by satisfying the conflicting desires alternately, or by compromising to permit some of both desires to be part of one's life. Conjunctions can be experienced as either harmonious or conflicted, depending on the nature of the factors involved.

CONJUNCTIONS (Check houses which are linked as well.)

Jupiter Conjunct Saturn or Saturn Conjunct Jupiter

This aspect points to a major theme involving the polarity of ideals (goals, values and faith) versus reality (pragmatism, survival needs, limits and rules). The planets involved are fire and earth, pointing to the potential of high productivity if combined well. One potential is advancement in the career, moving toward a position of power, gaining expertise, knowledge and mastery in life. Jupiterian careers are likely—involving publishing, the law, foreign countries, travel, philosophy, religion, education, or the wide dissemination of ideas and ideals.

If you experience a clash between these principles, it might be between faith versus fear; expansion versus contraction; optimism versus pessimism; freedom/openness versus structure; future versus past; or fun versus work. The most common extremes are (1) chronic disappointment due to wanting too much, too fast—or never being satisfied (because life is never ideal) and (2) idealizing power or control or authority figures or believing one has the right to run life (and other people)—according to a narrow set of values. If the beliefs, values, and principles (Jupiter) are too limiting and inhibiting (Saturn), the individual may constrain him/herself as well as others. On the up side, this points to people who test their metaphysics and religion in the crucible of real life, who combine enlightenment and wisdom (Jupiter) with pragmatism and reality-testing (Saturn).

This conjunction has been called a signature for the "Great Teacher" and can indicate the person who is able to make their dreams into a reality (usually through a career). However, questions of ethics, moral principles, and beliefs are still relevant. Some people's dreams are other people's nightmares. This combination can also represent solidifying beliefs, values and world views or conservative ethics or making "The Establishment" (status quo) into the ultimate value. Only you can decide how you will blend your beliefs, values, ethics and morals with the structure of society and the standards for success or "making it" in a career.

Jupiter Conjunct Uranus or Uranus Conjunct Jupiter

This aspect emphasizes freedom, individuality, progress and the mind. All might be important during the years the aspect is in orb. Often, the thinking is original and creative. You may enjoy trying on new ideas and changing your mind. Intellectual stimulation is probably the breath of life for you and your favorite friends. You are likely to value equality and the democratic process, to idealize tolerance, openness and equal opportunity for all.

If these themes are carried too far, you may be incredibly restless, always on the move (mentally and physically). You may relate well on a cool, intellectual level, but have challenges getting really close to people. You may seek variety and have trouble settling down to anything. Bluntness could be overdone.

If this side of your nature strongly conflicts with most of the rest of who you are, you may attract individuals into your life who are radical, erratic, unpredictable, who jump to conclusions, or are opinionated. They could express the freewheeling side which you are not comfortable with.

If the inventiveness represented here is positively channeled, you can literally change the world, moving it toward a better future.

Jupiter Conjunct Neptune or Neptune Conjunct Jupiter

This aspect focuses on the issue of faith: both conscious (able to be expressed in words) and subconscious (an emotional experience). Typically, you view life from an expanded perspective, aware of the overview. Idealism is likely to be marked; you would prefer to see the best in people and in life. You reach for the sublime. You may have the capacity to inspire others.

If not integrated, heart goals may be at odds with head goals. Your priorities may seem confused, as you try to sort out and make discriminations between a wide range of inputs. Rationality might battle intuition and you could feel torn between truth and compassion. If one side does not "fit" into the bulk of your nature, that side might be expressed by someone near and dear to you. Polarizing on issues sometimes helps us to see them more clearly.

The development of faith is vital in your life. A firm faith in the self (enough to risk, to try) is essential, without so much that one is foolhardy or arrogant. Faith in a Higher Power is also important—so that you can relax and let the Universe take over once you have done your part.

Jupiter Conjunct Pluto or Pluto Conjunct Jupiter

Intense emotions are possible with this fire/water blend. You may have powerful feelings about beliefs, values, ethics, religions, education or world views. You might idealize or overvalue sex, sharing, finances, resources or intimacy. You are learning to combine the desire for a deep, enduring commitment to another person with the restless drive to know, understand and explore to the ends of the earth in a quest for your ultimate values.

If freedom needs are set in conflict with closeness needs, you may play hot/cold in relationships, or get mixed messages from a partner. You might manifest one side, while a mate expresses the opposite. Long-distance relationships or falling in love with unavailable people are other options. Sharing goals, values, beliefs, hopes and the quest for understanding with a partner can help to bring you together. If intimate encounters are seen as an ultimate value, you might put a partner on a pedestal, give sexuality too much importance, worship money or see sharing as the most important thing in life.

Other potentials with this aspect could include skill at fund-raising, research, spiritual leadership or financial management. You may give priority to self-mastery and transformation.

Jupiter Conjunct Chiron or Chiron Conjunct Jupiter

This combination marks an intense passion for knowledge, including a need for freedom to pursue it wherever the quest takes one. Idealism is emphasized and needs to be expressed through some type of action that helps to create a better world. If the hunger for the Absolute is directed toward any fragment of life such as money, power, fame, especially if the goals are purely material, the person can never have enough and this pattern can lead to excesses. It is important to accept our humanness, do the best we can, and then trust a Higher Power to handle what is beyond our personal power. Look for ways to expand your knowledge and to share it with others. It is essential to be clear about your beliefs, values and goals, and to try to stay realistic in your expectations of yourself and others.

Jupiter Conjunct/Opposite Nodes
or Nodes Conjunct/Opposite Jupiter

This pattern indicates the possibility of tension between your search for ideals, including the freedom to go wherever they might be found, versus your need for emotional security in a nest or with close relationships. You might be expecting too much from relationships or other people might expect too much from you. We need to put our faith in the Absolute, the Whole, rather than in a home or a family or any other part of life. People who are important to you might have different beliefs and values, and you may need to focus more on the values which are shared while giving each other the right to hold some contrasting views. Ambivalence is possible over being independent versus being dependent. A working compromise calls for interdependence with both sides giving and receiving in their own area of strength. Reasonable expectations and sensitivity to mutual needs can keep the peace.

Saturn Conjunct Uranus or Uranus Conjunct Saturn

This aspect suggests that you are dealing with the contrast between the old and the new, the traditional and the unconventional, or stability and structure versus risk-taking and change. You can establish peace between the two by working for change within a structure (innovating within the rules) or by changing the structure (creating a new set of rules).

You are likely to prefer a career which involves freedom, technology, the new, the unusual, the different or the unique. Self-employment may appeal and erratic hours, pay or duties are quite possible. Uranian professions (science, the media, astrology, computers, anything unusual) are quite possible. If your need for variety and freedom remains subconscious, you might attract periodic changes or upsets in your work. If you are aware of your independent side, it can help you to be more original and inventive on the job. If Saturnian inhibitions, doubts and anxieties are overdeveloped, you could limit your individuality and hold back your natural inventive spirit. With the best of both, you can be innovative in a very practical, sensible way.

Your friendships and networking may assist your career and could be a stable factor in your life. You are likely to be serious about humanity, causes, groups and new-age knowledge. You may seek control or leadership in any of those areas.

Saturn Conjunct Neptune or Neptune Conjunct Saturn

This aspect suggests that you are striving to bring together ideals and reality, practicality and spirituality, the visible world and the invisible world, what is and what ought to be. In some way, you want to bring the beautiful dream down to earth and make it real, preferably through your professional role (career).

This combination can point to the professional artist, whose inspired visions of beauty and perfection uplift other people. It can indicate the practical mystic who applies the insights gained through nature, meditation, prayer, etc. to real life problems with useful results. Or, you might be the sensible idealist, who is translating utopian visions into practical accomplishments.

A less comfortable option is the professional victim—running away from an imperfect world, and his/her perceived lack of competence to do anything. Illness (physical, emotional, mental) could be a problem. Escapism could be sought through alcohol, drugs, fantasy, etc. Many victims have successfully switched to a savior role through self-help groups (e.g., Alcoholics Anonymous). An authority figure may have provided an example of handling or failing to handle ideals.

You may live out several of these possibilities in coming to terms with the mixture of yearning for cosmic consciousness while focusing on the practical necessities of a physical existence. Life needs both!

Saturn Conjunct Pluto or Pluto Conjunct Saturn

This combination suggests strong powers of endurance, concentration, organization, and perseverance. Willpower is likely to be strong. Although usually oriented toward stability and security, once you make a commitment (to a person, a project, an idea), you are likely to be unswerving in your determination to "make it work!"

Business skills are likely, and you might be drawn to any Plutonian professions: medicine, financial management, ecology, investments, psychotherapy, sex therapy, massage, detective work, research, corporate positions, etc. The trend is toward work that involves intense emotions, hidden matters, great control, power, issues of sharing, or transformations.

Power issues may emerge in close relationships. Fear (of being controlled, dominated, rejected) might lead to avoiding relationships or inhibitions around sex, intimacy, money, or facing psychological depths. Also possible is subconsciously choosing a "father figure" (male or female) who seems strong, responsible, reliable (but is likely to end up dominating, controlling and dictatorial). Or, you might attract someone who expects you to play "Daddy"—be the hardworking, dedicated one.   An equalitarian experience demands strength from both people—the ability to give and receive, to share fully with another human being.

Dominance is a likely issue with these planets conjunct. The challenge is to put your mark on the world through competitive sports, games, business, politics or causes—rather than trying to control people and life around you—or attracting power-hungry, intimidating control freaks into your life. Use the clout of this combination wisely.

Saturn Conjunct Chiron or Chiron Conjunct Saturn

This is a high success combination if you can integrate these two very different sides of life. You need to blend the confidence, creativity, and enthusiasm of Chiron, which loves to start new things, with Saturn's practical, productive capacity to work. If the aspirations are too high, it is possible to give up when the earthy demands (of Saturn) seem too boring or too much effort. Or the instinctive caution of the earth may clip the wings of the visionary Chiron and settle for smaller, safer goals. A successful blend of the principles can keep one eye on the sky and one foot on the ground.   Career choices could involve knowledge or healing.   You can reach the top, with courage, a clear vision, willingness to work and patience. You might also be working on practical ways to improve your own health.

Saturn Conjunct/Opposite Nodes
or Nodes Conjunct/Opposite Saturn

This pattern suggests tension connected to security needs and close relationships. The pressures may involve either material or emotional security. If material issues are central, it is important to be very realistic about work and responsibility. Guard against one person getting caught in the "Atlas" role, trying to carry more than his or her share. Central emotional issues call for sensitivity to mutual needs lest one person feel deprived, abandoned, or emotionally inhibited. With practicality, empathy, and mutual caring, security needs can be met. People can feel safe both in the "real world" and in the world of feelings.

Uranus Conjunct Neptune or Neptune Conjunct Uranus

This combination suggests a transpersonal focus. You may be adept at overviews. Collectivity, community and networking may be natural for you. Humanitarian ideals are likely. You are apt to think in terms of the greater good and long term. Ethical politics probably appeal. You may have an unusual approach to spiritual matters.

If idealism is carried too far, you could be deceived, confused or have rose-colored glasses in terms of knowledge, friends, groups, organizations, causes and humanity in general. Sacrificing yourself for equality is possible, as are rationalization and over generalization. Savior/victim interchanges are a potential, particularly in terms of friends and associates.

Intuitive talent is quite possible, and flashes of genius may occur. If the conscious and subconscious are set at odds with one another, or rationality and logic battle intuition, you may feel torn. Sudden insights are probable and you may be able to explain and articulate impressions and "vibes."

Uranus Conjunct Pluto or Pluto Conjunct Uranus

This aspect highlights the need to combine freedom urges with a drive for intimacy and attachment. The desire for security, stability and safety may also vie with risk-taking instincts and the urge for change.

Mate relationships work better when they include a strong element of friendship, openness and tolerance. If independence needs are not faced, they may be expressed (excessively) by partners. Or, you might attract relationships subject to sudden changes or splits (when subconscious needs to break loose and break free become overwhelming). If attachment needs are not faced, the mate could be excessively intrusive, controlling or intense. Financial matters and shared possessions are a likely arena for facing risk versus security issues, so you and a mate could play out opposite sides of that issue as well.

Emotional intensity may be directed toward friends, causes, the future or humanitarian principles. You may make a deep, emotional commitment to Uranian principles (freedom, tolerance, justice for all, democracy, etc.). Reforming zeal is quite likely. As time goes by, you may become more aware of hunches, intuition, the feelings of others, and more in touch with your own depths.

Uranus Conjunct Chiron or Chiron Conjunct Uranus

This combination marks an intense drive for knowledge and freedom. It may signal a period of immense creativity, of breaking loose from previous limits and exploring new horizons. New knowledge (gained or shared with others) may be very important. Concern with social causes is likely, but an increased social life with friends is also possible. Humor and optimism can be assets, in addition to strong intellectual curiosity. There is a basic urge to be open and expressive, sometimes to the point of bluntness. Remember that tact is sometimes useful. But do use this period to sharpen your mental skills and to liven up and inspire the world.

Uranus Conjunct/Opposite Nodes
or Nodes Conjunct/Opposite Uranus

This pattern points to tension involving some variation on freedom versus closeness, independence versus dependence, detached intellect versus sensitive feelings. If these motifs are not integrated, disruptions and breaks in relationships are likely. Either you or a partner may carry aloofness or the desire for liberty too far. A reasonable compromise can leave room for both sides of these polarities. With mutual tolerance, it is possible to have both friends and family, even if they have different tastes and interests. We can care deeply about close relationships but also be able to give time and effort to social causes, to service to humanity. We can increase our ability to be our unique selves while remaining aware of and responsive to the emotional needs of others, willing to help and be helped.

Neptune Conjunct Pluto or Pluto Conjunct Neptune

This combination of two water planets suggests deep, intense emotions that are often veiled. With a rich inner life, you may not reveal the many, swirling eddies beneath the surface of your personality. Intuitive talent is quite possible. Often, however, psychic abilities can manifest as a "knowing without knowing" where your impressions guide your life without conscious thought.

You are likely to deal with an idealistic theme where mates and intimacy are concerned. One option is to share artistic or spiritual or helping-healing activities with a partner. Another possibility is getting involved with someone who is beautiful, works with beauty, is idealistic—or just plain spacey! Savior/victim associations are possible as well. Fantasy relationships may occur if real life does not seem satisfying enough—or ordinary people don't meet perfectionistic standards. The urge for a soul mate is intense; you want a deep, merging experience.

Transcendent experiences can be a source of power for you. You may be drawn toward a "hermit" path at times, as a way to fully explore, control and master your spiritual insights and inspirational experiences. You need some alone time to probe your inner depths, to explore the many layers of your being. Ultimately, however, it is likely that you will want to merge with a mate as well as gaining a sense of Oneness with life.

Neptune Conjunct Chiron or Chiron Conjunct Neptune

This combination can mark a deeply spiritual period, including considerable openness to psychic awareness. It is important to be conscious of personal beliefs, values and goals, since they are shaping the direction of your life. An arrival at unintended destinations is usually an indication that many of your personal directing values have remained subconscious. Try to analyze what you trust, where you look for meaning in life, what you want for ultimate fulfillment. Then you can move toward what is really important to you while realizing that life is a long journey and remembering to enjoy the journey. Mystical experiences may occur and you may be drawn toward artistic activities. You can also contribute to the healing of the planet.

Neptune Conjunct/Opposite Nodes or Nodes Conjunct/Opposite Neptune

Sensitivity is highlighted with a yearning for cosmic grace in close associations. Rose-colored glasses (or unreachable dreams) could affect your relationships— or you may be blessed with great empathy and strong compassion for others. Underlying connections could seem obvious to you; perhaps you have talent for spotting patterns or taking a holistic view. Psychic openness is possible, but might sometimes mean picking up feelings or impressions you would rather not. Escapist activities could offer temptations. Your caring, idealistic side is best channeled toward sharing beauty with others, or into healing/helping activities.

Pluto Conjunct Chiron or Chiron Conjunct Pluto

This combination can mark a period of emotional intensity as Chiron's fire and Pluto's water produce steam. You may be idealizing marriage or looking for the ideal mate who shares your beliefs and values. You could also attract other people who are looking for perfection. Guard against putting too much trust in another person or in the material world. It is important to accept humanness in yourself and in your relationships. Shared power and pleasures can be valuable and important, but they are not Absolutes. An urge to explore the depths of the psyche is also likely during this period. You may be drawn toward research interests. Or you might become more involved in joint resources such as investments or have to deal with debts. You have the power to explore deeply, to understand yourself and others, and to move toward self-mastery.

Pluto Conjunct/Opposite Nodes or Nodes Conjunct/Opposite Pluto

Emotional and sometimes material security issues are highlighted by this pattern. Tension is possible between partners and other family members (parents and/or children). It may seem difficult to meet the needs of more than one generation. Dependency issues are also possible, and best handled by being able both to give and receive assistance. A high level of sensitivity may be another complicating factor. If openness to the feelings of others is too intense, it is possible to reduce it by focusing on personal action or on the analytic intellect. Knowing when and how to let go may be a challenge. It is important to be able to share on a very deep feeling level, yet be able to release when the time is right.

Chiron Conjunct/Opposite Nodes
or Nodes Conjunct/Opposite Chiron

This combination calls for integration in order to maintain the freedom to pursue wide ranging interests while still maintaining a secure base with a home and family or other close relationships. Compromises may be needed to make room for both freedom and commitments in the life. Tensions may stem from overly high expectations of others or we may feel constrained to live up to their expectations. Both the intellect and emotional warmth are needed in life. By staying aware of personal values and goals, and also staying in touch with the needs of others, it is possible to balance the seesaw.

HARMONY ASPECTS (Check houses linked by rulers also.)

Jupiter Sextile/Trine Saturn or Saturn Sextile/Trine Jupiter

Intellectual aspirations meet achievement needs and the optimal result is possible. You may be able to channel much faith, optimism, enthusiasm, confidence and zest into accomplishments. You could take tremendous strides in your career or building the basic structure of your place in society. Mentors might assist you in reaching toward your dreams. You must keep a balance between aspirations and common sense, between confidence and caution. Business matters are favored. You can combine faith in self and competence. When positively harnessed, this can be a time of major achievement.

Jupiter Sextile/Trine Uranus or Uranus Sextile/Trine Jupiter

Freedom needs may be strong as your sense of independence and free flow is highlighted. In some way, you need to fly, to soar above the crowd, to go further than you have gone before. Whether you explore physically, mentally, emotionally, or spiritually, the need is to try your wings and expand your possibilities. Intellectual restlessness is likely. You may go beyond traditional boundaries in search of knowledge, Friendships may seem sweeter and you are more open to life's multiple options.

Jupiter Sextile/Trine Neptune or Neptune Sextile/Trine Jupiter

This period indicates the potential of a smooth flow between your head and your heart. Your intellectual beliefs, goals and values can easily harmonize with what your heart desires. Thoughts back up yearnings and intuition can assist logic. A spiritual or religious focus is quite possible, including mystical experiences, but any action is appropriate that gives you a sense of being inspired and uplifted. Work with your dreams on every level.

Jupiter Sextile/Trine Pluto or Pluto Sextile/Trine Jupiter

You have the potential of raising a committed relationship to a higher level. You may be able to create a more perfect union. The focus is on furthering your dreams with others who share your life, seeing the best in each other and encouraging one another's highest potentials. Expectations can be a two-edged sword, but—positively handled—your belief in each other can spur you to greater and greater synergistic exchanges. If you are not yet involved with someone, now is the time to focus clearly and visualize strongly what you want in a mate while maintaining the awareness that we cannot expect perfection in human relationships.

Jupiter Sextile/Trine Chiron or Chiron Sextile/Trine Jupiter

This combination suggests harmony between different values and goals in your life. They tend to support and reinforce each other so you can achieve one without feeling that you have to sacrifice another. The quest for knowledge may be especially important, along with a desire for freedom to go wherever you choose to find your answers. New studies are possible, or teaching, writing, traveling. Distant horizons may tempt you. Try to stay somewhat realistic, since it is not always true that if some is good, more will be better. Idealism is emphasized. Clear goals and the confidence to move toward them can take you far. The future beckons.

Jupiter Sextile/Trine Nodes or Nodes Sextile/Trine Jupiter

This pattern suggests harmony between your beliefs, values and goals and your close relationships. Your family could help you gain an education or they might enjoy traveling with you or sharing the pursuit of common goals. Your personal faith could encourage relatives or might lead you to work for animal rights, ecological ideals, or the preservation of historic buildings if your nurturing instincts reach beyond personal relationships. In general, you should be able to make room in your life for both security needs and roots, and for the lure of far horizons and a quest for ideals.

Saturn Sextile/Trine Uranus or Uranus Sextile/Trine Saturn

This pattern suggests a good balance between the old and the new, the conventional and the unconventional. You have the capacity to bring together the best from each and to create a useful synthesis. New ideas, approaches, technology or friends may further your career. Your practicality, stability, sense of responsibility and willingness to work can assist your friendships, networking and openness to alternatives. With a willingness to test ideas, you can naturally choose the best among a variety of options.

Saturn Sextile/Trine Neptune or Neptune Sextile/Trine Saturn

This period can be one of manifesting beautiful dreams, great beauty or strong ideals. You have potential harmony between your visualizing, inspirational, artistic, spiritual side and your practical, achieving, work-oriented side. You can tune in to your visions and bring them to earth—through art, healing, helping, inspiring or other uplifting channels. However, even with a harmony aspect, if the expectations are too high, you might feel chronically dissatisfied at falling short of perfection or succumb to escapist paths. Inner peace is possible if you accept an appropriate share of the responsibility, keep your compassion practical, and trust a Higher Power when you have done your share.

Saturn Sextile/Trine Pluto or Pluto Sextile/Trine Saturn

Organizational skills are highlighted by this combination. You can be extremely thorough and exacting, with strong endurance. Skill with details shows potential talent in research, business or any fields requiring one to put together lots of pieces or to explore masses of data in a disciplined way. Self-control may be a personal concern, but you are able to have a healthy approach. Harmony is implied between your work and a mate (with whom you share an intense emotional involvement). You can balance commitments between your career and your personal life.

Saturn Sextile/Trine Chiron or Chiron Sextile/Trine Saturn

This pattern shows a potential for very great success, with harmony between your faith, ideals, and goals and your ability to be practical and productive. A clear sense of what you want, along with willingness to work, can keep you moving steadily up the mountain. You may move into a position of increased power and authority in your work. Expanded knowledge can also contribute to your career success, or your work may involve travel in some way. Your work could also make a contribution to society and could include a focus on healing.

Saturn Sextile/Trine Nodes or Nodes Sextile/Trine Saturn

This combination emphasizes security issues and suggests the ability to meet security needs for both yourself and others. Harmony is possible between you and parents or parent substitutes who help you, or you may be involved in playing parent to others. The primary focus could be on either material or emotional security, but you should be able to handle both successfully. You can keep a good balance between your domestic life and your career ambitions now. Remember to share the responsibility. It is important to be able both to give and receive.

Uranus Sextile/Trine Neptune or Neptune Sextile/Trine Uranus

Extra psychic insight is possible during this period. You have the potential of blending mental flashes with intuitive openness. Your inner wisdom may inspire changes. A transpersonal focus is likely, feeling drawn toward groups, causes, philanthropic works, mysticism, or some form of trying to enhance a greater Whole. Inspirations are possible, but do stay grounded too.

Uranus Sextile/Trine Pluto or Pluto Sextile/Trine Uranus

This period can be a time when your sense of individuality enhances your deep relationships, and vice versa. Intimacy can complement independence. You have the capacity to enjoy a sense of freedom within a committed partnership, to love with an open hand. Your intellect can support your gut-level intuitive impressions and vice versa. You can probe the deeper psychological levels of your being and of others to gain insight and understanding. Inventive approaches to shared resources and pleasures may prove rewarding. Willpower is usually strong and can be useful to facilitate desired changes. Healthy transformations are possible.

Uranus Sextile/Trine Chiron or Chiron Sextile/Trine Uranus

This pattern is a strong indication of intellectual ability, encouraging you to expand your knowledge and to share it with others. You might study, write, teach, or travel, but it is important to enlarge your horizons, to break new ground in some way in your life. A love of freedom is usually also present, whether you seek it primarily for yourself or work to achieve it for others. Excesses could be a problem at times, leading to scattering your energy in too many interests and projects, or to resisting necessary limits which are part of life in a material world. Stay open to your curiosity but also look for ways to apply your mental skills in the world.

Uranus Sextile/Trine Nodes or Nodes Sextile/Trine Uranus

This combination suggests that you have the capacity to integrate your desire for independence and equality with your need for closeness, which usually implies some dependency. You might enjoy sharing your innovative ideas and friends with your family. You might look to friends as your primary emotional support system. Your family may value openness and space yet still be there for you when needed. You should be able to function with the detached, objective intellect but also be comfortable sharing human warmth and feelings.

Neptune Sextile/Trine Pluto or Pluto Sextile/Trine Neptune

This pattern reflects the potential of your idealistic, compassionate, unifying side assisting and supporting your desire for a mate. Sharing a love of beauty, mysticism, spiritual quests or other inspirational activities can deepen the bonds between you. Seeing the best in each other allows you to share the physical, sensual and material world with basic respect and caring (avoiding power struggles). Too much idealism can lead to dissatisfaction in relationships. The possibility exists of some psychic openness to a mate. If perfection is expected, human beings will never measure up (you or a partner). If you share values and goals, the ties between you will be strengthened.

Neptune Sextile/Trine Chiron or Chiron Sextile/Trine Neptune

This pattern shows harmony between different beliefs, goals and values. The head and the heart, the conscious and the subconscious sides of the mind, can cooperate in guiding you toward your deepest wishes. There is a strong potential for inspirational guidance in this combination as you can access your inner wisdom. Dreams may be revealing. Work as a healer could be deeply fulfilling. Artistic talent is also very possible, often including a love of nature. This is a time for both your own spiritual evolution and for you to offer a spiritual gift to the world.

Neptune Sextile/Trine Nodes or Nodes Sextile/Trine Neptune

This configuration suggests the potential for heightened sensitivity, which may include psychic talent. Your capacity for empathy, compassion, and idealism can enhance your close, emotional associations. You may consistently see the best in those you love (or yearn for infinite grace and perfection in close relationships). Sensitivity might slip into escapism or passivity if not channeled into healing, assisting or artistic connections with others. Much mutual support is possible. You may inspire or be inspired by family or close others. You may have an intuitive grasp of patterns, naturally seeing connections and feeling the mystical Oneness of life.

Pluto Sextile/Trine Chiron or Chiron Sextile/Trine Pluto

This pattern suggests the capacity to harmonize your goals and ideals with your close relationships. You may seek knowledge together, or just enjoy moving in the same direction in life. You can increase your understanding of yourself and of others, and use the knowledge to help others. Increased psychic ability and empathy are also possible. You could become more involved in research or in the handling of joint resources such as investments and debts. If you have developed writing skills, publication and royalties are possible. Power issues may be important, and you may gain in wisdom by combining intelligence with ethical principles. Issues of freedom versus closeness or independence versus dependence may call for attention, but you have the ability to handle them. Use this period to deepen your self-awareness and self-mastery.

Pluto Sextile/Trine Nodes or Nodes Sextile/Trine Pluto

This combination emphasizes the importance of deep, caring relationships, usually with much mutual help. Security is normally connected to attachments, which can involve people or possessions. The home base and family and mate should be mutually supportive. Sometimes pets or possessions are a substitute for people, but a human support system is generally preferred. Much psychic openness and empathy are likely between you and close associates. If the sensitivity produces too much vulnerability, it is possible to reduce it by focusing on personal action or on detached analysis. It is important to be able both to give and receive.

Chiron Sextile/Trine Nodes or Nodes Sextile/Trine Chiron

This pattern points to harmony between your attachment to home, family or other emotional relationships and your urge to explore the wider world in search of an ideal. Your family might encourage your studies, or share your beliefs and goals, or you may just enjoy life together. Your faith may lead you to contribute to the security of others or you may receive assistance from others to help you reach your goals. A balanced life permits both intellectual stimulation and emotional warmth, and this combination supports your ability to enjoy both.

CONFLICT ASPECTS (Check houses linked by rulers also.)
[Include octiles (semi-squares) and trioctiles (sesqui-quadrates) as variants of the square if desired.]

Jupiter Square/Opposite/Quincunx Saturn (and vice versa)

Beliefs may clash with physical reality until integrated. Aspirations could be at odds with the rules of the game (of life) including natural law and cultural regulations—wanting too much or lacking faith and expecting too little, giving up too soon. The challenge is to aim high **enough** while avoiding overreach (seeking the impossible) and under evaluation (not trying for perfectly reasonable objectives). Clashes are possible with authority figures over moral, ethical, religious or philosophical issues. Your beliefs and goals are likely to be tested in the crucible of real-life achievements and ambitions. With the integration of faith and hard work, you can do much!

Jupiter Square/Opposite/Quincunx Uranus (and vice versa)

This pattern calls for open circulation and the ability to see many alternatives and possibilities. Your faith or belief system may be challenged or changed. Perfectionistic expectations (yours or theirs) could become an issue with friends. The desire for independence could be overdone or stifled. Look for ways to expand the freedom and openness in your life. Be willing to experiment, but try to also maintain your core stability, your ability to stay centered.

Jupiter Square/Opposite/Quincunx Neptune (and vice versa)

This period suggests the potential of tension between head goals and heart goals. Your mind may war with your intuition, your thoughts with your feelings. You may experience conflict between the truth and compassion. You need to make peace between your intellectual understanding of life and your emotional experience and **knowing** of it. You may deal with spiritual, religious, philosophical or mystical principles. It is important to clarify your values and long-range goals which determine your priorities.

Jupiter Square/Opposite/Quincunx Pluto (and vice versa)

This combination could point to tension between the desire for a committed relationship and the urge to be free to pursue a wider role in the world. Or the tension could be between what you want in a mate and what is possible in a human relationship. You and a mate can be inspirational to one another, spurring each other on to greater heights, but if expectations are too high, you may yearn for the perfect love that does not exist. You might also attract other people who want more than is possible. Differing beliefs, goals and values also could cause tension in close relationships. Issues of sensuality, sexuality, and shared resources may call for compromise. With mutual caring and willingness to give a little, to meet in the middle, this can be a time to deepen and strengthen emotional bonds.

Jupiter Square/Opposite/Quincunx Chiron (and vice versa)

This pattern shows tension between different beliefs, values or goals. You may want contradictory things from life or want to achieve more than is humanly possible. Analyze what you trust and try to set up a clear value hierarchy so you can make choices based on what is most important to you. Try to be realistic in your aspirations and to enjoy the journey toward your ideals. If we wait until we reach perfection to be happy, we have a long wait. Continue to pursue knowledge. It offers an important key to help you set reasonable goals and to successfully move toward them.

Jupiter Square/Quincunx Nodes (and vice versa)

This pattern indicates the possibility of tension between your search for ideals, including the freedom to go wherever they might be found, versus your need for emotional security in a nest or with close relationships. You might be expecting too much from relationships or people might expect too much from you. We need to put our faith in the Absolute, the Whole, rather than in a home or a family or any other part of life. People who are important to you might have different beliefs and values, and you might need to focus more on the values which are shared while giving each other the right to hold some contrasting views. Ambivalence is possible over being independent versus being dependent. A working compromise calls for interdependence, with both sides giving and receiving in their own area of strength. Reasonable expectations and sensitivity to mutual needs can keep the peace.

Saturn Square/Opposite/Quincunx Uranus (and vice versa)

The theme of this period is confrontation between the old and the new or the conventional and the unconventional. If you make an integration, you can have the best of both worlds. If not, there may be clashes with authority figures about new ideas, or a sense of frustration with groups or friends concerning what is necessary or essential to do. Networks, causes or new-age ideas might seem at odds with your work and vice versa. With compromise, it is possible to revolutionize some parts of your life while maintaining some stability in other areas, and to feel secure while changing. A testing, experimental attitude can be helpful. Some rules and apparent limits can be changed with time and realistic effort.

Saturn Square/Opposite/Quincunx Neptune (and vice versa)

This period calls for making peace between the ideal that you desire and what actually exists in your world. If you are able to reconcile the two, you can accomplish much in terms of art, healing, helping or other inspirational activities. We need to do our share toward making a more ideal world and then trust a

Higher Power to avoid the danger of getting lost in wishful thinking or escapist activities, or living frustrated over the imperfection of life, or being subject to generalized anxiety. You have the potential of putting together psychic insights and pragmatic realizations—turning inner wisdom into a physical reality. It will require disciplining your dreams and transcending your limitations. Analyze what you can do first to move toward your vision and then do it. All journeys start with one step followed by others.

Saturn Square/Opposite/Quincunx Pluto (and vice versa)

This combination carries much potential force. Ambition, will-power, intensity, tenacity are all included. It is important to channel your drive for power into your career where it is appropriate, and to be willing to compromise and share power in your intimate relationships. Self-control may be an important issue. Work demands may compete with close relationships, often due to time pressures. Separate careers for husband and wife can complicate life and require compromise. With realism and discipline, this period can be very productive. The capacity for organization and handling details is highlighted. If you have been avoiding dealing with details realistically, you may have to face them in this period. All Saturn aspects call for practicality. They mark times of feedback from the world when we receive the consequences of past actions that let us know how we are doing so we can decide whether we want to stay on the same path or change our handling of life.

Saturn Square/Opposite/Quincunx Chiron (and vice versa)

This pattern suggests tension between your handling of power (your own potency or dealings with power figures or with the "rules of the game") versus your aspirations and goals. It is important to be realistic in your expectations, both in what you want and in the ways in which you try to achieve it. It is possible to take on too much responsibility (and guilt when we cannot be super people), or to expect the world to give us what we want without much personal effort. Try to be clear and practical about your ambitions and your abilities. There are some things we can do, some we can't do, some we have to do. Wisdom involves knowing which is which and living within the rules of life voluntarily.

Saturn Square/Quincunx Nodes (and vice versa)

This pattern suggests tension connected to security needs and close relationships. Anxiety or pressure may exist in regard to material or emotional security. If limitations or fear are an issue on the material plane, it is important to be very realistic about work and responsibility. Guard against one person getting caught in the "Atlas" role, trying to carry more than his or her share. When emotional issues are central, sensitivity to mutual needs is essential. You or those very close to you could feel emotionally restrained or could fear abandonment or lack of love. With practicality, empathy, and mutual caring, security needs can be met.

Uranus Square/Opposite/Quincunx Neptune (and vice versa)

The tone of this aspect is transpersonal: concerned with the greater whole in some fashion. However, you may feel torn between an intellectual detachment and abstract overview versus an emotional empathy and understanding. You will be learning to comfortably blend individuality with Oneness. Savior/victim leanings could affect friendships, but compassion could also inspire new connections. If the conscious and subconscious parts of your mind work together, you can gain inspired insight and can make a contribution to humanity. Inspirational openness and great breadth of awareness are possible but it is also important to stay grounded.

Uranus Square/Opposite/Quincunx Pluto (and vice versa)

This aspect suggests tension between a drive for individuality, independence and personal freedom versus a drive for intensity, commitment and deep, psychological sharing. Detachment may vie with emotional passion. Security needs may war with risk-taking instincts and secrecy with openness. You could feel torn between going your own way versus sharing with another person. The solution lies in finding compromises, keeping some of each in your life. Will-power is usually strong and can be used to gain self-control as well as in resisting any external control.

Uranus Square/Opposite/Quincunx Chiron (and vice versa)

This combination suggests tension between different intellectual interests and values. There may be struggles over limits with an underlying urge to resist all limits. You want to get "out of the rut," to explore new horizons, but may need to clarify what you really want in life, to be able to make choices. We can't do everything. We can do one or two things well, and a variety of other things "lightly." We have to do some things if we want to survive in a physical world. This pattern shows high potential intelligence, creativity, ability to innovate, but you need to define your beliefs, values and goals in order to use your ability effectively in the world.

Uranus Square/Quincunx Nodes (and vice versa)

This pattern points to tension involving some variation on freedom versus closeness, independence versus dependence, detached intellect versus sensitive feelings. A reasonable compromise can leave room for both sides of these polarities. With mutual tolerance, it is possible to have both friends and family, even if they have different tastes and interests. We can care deeply about close relationships but also be able to give time and effort to social causes and service to humanity. We can increase our ability to be our unique selves while remaining aware of and responsive to the emotional needs of others, willing to help and be helped.

Neptune Square/Opposite/Quincunx Pluto (and vice versa)

During this period you will be challenged to integrate your intense need for intimacy and a mate with your desire for an ideal life connected to the wider world. Your mystical, compassionate, idealistic side may seem in conflict with your sensual, intense, power-oriented side. Control may vie with acceptance. Excessive idealism could create conflicts in relationships, or pull you away from other people. More psychic openness is possible. If you tune in wisely, particularly to those who bond with you on an intimate level, the potential is here for personal transformation through contact with your Higher Self and respect for another individual.

Neptune Square/Opposite/Quincunx Chiron (and vice versa)

This pattern shows tension between different beliefs, values or goals. Head goals may be in conflict with heart goals, or conscious values with subconscious ones. Try to access your subconscious, to determine the nature of the conflict. Dreams are often helpful for this purpose. Also, pay attention to events which are contrary to conscious desires since they are often due to subconscious conflict. Solutions usually require compromise. If we value both truth and kindness, we can try to be tactful. Some things can be left unsaid. Sometimes, the challenge involves aspirations that are just too high. If we were already perfect, we would not be here. It is important to have high goals, but we can also enjoy the journey toward them. Try to clarify what you trust and want the most, and after you have done what you can, give the rest to the Infinite.

Neptune Square/Quincunx Nodes (and vice versa)

Sensitivity is highlighted with a yearning for cosmic grace in close associations. Rose-colored glasses (or unreachable dreams) could affect your relationships— or you may be blessed with great empathy and strong compassion for others. Underlying connections could seem obvious to you—perhaps you have talent for spotting patterns or taking a holistic view. Psychic openness is possible, but might sometimes mean picking up feelings or impressions you would rather not. Escapist activities could offer temptations. Your caring, idealistic side is best channeled toward sharing beauty with others, or into healing/helping activities.

Pluto Square/Opposite/Quincunx Chiron (and vice versa)

This combination suggests the possibility of tension between freedom and closeness, independence and dependence. Life is interdependent, and compromise is necessary if we want a close, caring relationship with a mate as well as the space to explore wider horizons. Sometimes the tension involves values and beliefs which differ from the mate's and compromise is again necessary. Since this pattern points to considerable emotional intensity, learning to compromise may be a major part of the challenge. We need to know when is enough and when to let go. If marriage is over- idealized, or if we are seeking a perfect relationship, we need to accept humanness in ourselves and in others. Reasonable expectations and shared faith can heal both people and relationships.

Pluto Square/Quincunx Nodes (and vice versa)

Emotional and sometimes material security issues are highlighted by this pattern. Tension is possible between partners and other family members (parents and/or children). It may seem difficult to meet the needs of more than one generation. Dependency issues are also possible, and best handled by being able both to give and receive assistance. A high level of sensitivity may be another complicating factor. If openness to the feelings of others is too intense, it is possible to reduce it by focusing on personal action or on the analytic intellect. Knowing when and how to let go may be a challenge. It is important to be able to share on a very deep feeling level, yet be able to release when the time is right.

Chiron Square/Quincunx Nodes (and vice versa)

This combination calls for integration in order to maintain the freedom to pursue wide ranging interests while still maintaining a secure base with a home and family or other close relationships. Compromises may be needed to make room for both freedom and commitments in the life. Tensions may stem from overly high expectations of others or we may feel constrained to live up to other people's expectations. Both the intellect and emotional warmth are needed in life. By staying aware of personal values and goals and also staying in touch with the needs of others, it is possible to balance the seesaw.

CHAPTER THREE
MAJOR CYCLE CHANGES

Your natal horoscope remains a fundamental reflection of your basic nature. Therefore, it is a framework for the motion of the progressed planets and angles (e.g., Midheaven, Ascendant). When progressed factors move into new (natal) houses or signs, they suggest a shift in your expression of the parts of life symbolized by the planet or angle. This chapter focuses on the issues that are emphasized for many years of your life. Chapter Six considers shorter term issues (and possible events) when progressed planets conjunct angles or progressed angles conjunct planets.

Don't forget rulerships. When a planet changes house or sign, it may indicate a new chapter in regard to the house(s) ruled by that planet. In each of the following interpretations, assume that the last sentence reads: **Since [insert planet name] rules your [insert house number] house, you may begin a new cycle in regard to the issues of that house**. One example: when a woman accepted a new job in the field of astrology, her Sun and Venus were both changing sign. The job meant more money than she had been making and a change of residence. In the progressed chart, her Sun ruled the 2nd house (self-earned income) and her Venus ruled the 4th (home) and 11th (astrology, groups, new age knowledge, etc.). In her natal chart, the Sun ruled the third house (communication—the job involved much writing and many conferences) and Venus ruled the 5th (creativity) and the 12th (imagination, infinite resources).

Planets and Asteroids Changing House or Sign

SUN

Sun into 1st House or Aries: Personal Potency

With this combination, self-esteem issues become central in your sense of personal identity and personal power. Personal actions could bring attention, recognition, response, love and admiration from others (or infamy and shame). You need a moderate amount of healthy pride in yourself. Too much can lead to self-absorption at the expense of the rights of others; too little can lead to self-blocking and a danger of illness. Passions (sexual and otherwise) are likely to increase in the coming years. You may be more willing to take risks, or be attracted to challenges. Higher energy is common, but it could burn out quickly. Increased assertiveness, enthusiasm, initiative, spontaneity, creativity and humor are all possible developments as you find ways to manifest your inner fire.

Sun into 2nd House or Taurus: Sensuous Savoring

An increasing sense of luxury is likely with an attraction to nice things and potential extravagance. This is an excellent time for both the creative and the performing arts. Appearances and beauty may be important. Your sense of self-esteem could be connected to earnings, possessions, or artistic skills. Comfort and pleasure are apt to be central, possibly leading to self-indulgence. But you may also develop increased stamina, loyalty and persistence. Simplicity and reconnecting to the Earth could also appeal. In all your doing or getting or spending, remember to enjoy the process.

Sun into 3rd House or Gemini: Mental Magnetism

In the years ahead, mental or communication skills can bring positive or negative attention. Increased self-esteem as well as external recognition and rewards are possible through your use of your intellect, hand dexterity, and/or through family connections. Dramatic presentations of ideas are possible, with humor more marked. You may enjoy word play, puns or mind games. Persuasiveness and sales ability can be developing assets. Studies, teaching, writing and traveling are all good outlets for your expanding skills. Keep communication lines open and maintain mutual understanding and acceptance in dealing with the people around you.

Sun into 4th House or Cancer: Home is Where the Heart Is

The years ahead are likely to include more family focus, with a strong desire for love and attachments. Both giving and receiving emotional warmth will be important. Pride/shame are connected to home and family ties; you might want to enlarge or otherwise improve your home. The end of a cycle is possible in regard to family, home, career and status. You may swing from confidence to insecurity. These intense feelings could lead you to take things very personally.

There is a tendency to relate as a parent or as a child, so equality might be a challenge. You can be loyal, loving and sympathetic with increased intuition, the ability to tune in to the feelings of others. Some kind of emotional support system is essential. Don't cut yourself off from people or turn to food as a substitute reassurance. If close emotional ties are not available from home and family, you may satisfy some of the need with pets, by deepening friendships, or by helping people in your work.

Sun into 5th House or Leo: Shining Star

This combination represents an urge to do more than has been done before. You may channel it into drama, having children, creating things, taking risks, speculation. It is time for self-expansion, play and recognition The pride/shame polarity is highlighted, putting your self-esteem on the line. Courage and creativity are likely to be more marked. Express your dramatic instincts in some form that lets you win applause. Let your inner child out to enjoy the world. Generosity, magnetism, and charisma could increase. Self-expressive acts are highlighted.

Sun into 6th House or Virgo: Favorable Functioning

In the years ahead, work or health will be important keys to self-esteem. You may win recognition on the job, coming to be known as a resource, admired for your grasp of information or other skills. You might subconsciously gain attention through illness (especially if your work is unfulfilling). You could find fun in work if it is stimulating, if it lets you be a creative problem-solver. Power and prestige can be attained through efficient functioning, or attention might come from inefficient functioning. If your security needs require keeping an unfulfilling job, look for a hobby that can give you a sense of accomplishment. With reasonable ambition and satisfaction from doing something worth doing and doing it well, these years can be productive and very satisfying.

Sun into 7th House or Libra: Radiant Relationships

In these years ahead, you are likely to experience an increased desire for love and excitement in relationships. You can attract dynamic, magnetic, risk-taking people and/or express your own charisma with others. You might seek power through attractiveness. Romantic instincts are likely to be strong, with value placed on charm, aesthetics and finesse. You could be vulnerable to the opinions of others (either criticism or flattery). An increased need for affection, support and encouragement can be met by being willing to give it as well as to receive it. Guard against letting your sense of personal self-worth depend too much on the responses and attitudes of other people. A comfortable self-acceptance encourages relationships which are mutually pleasurable.

Sun into 8th House or Scorpio: Passionate Power

The years ahead could involve power issues with other people around sex, money, or the control of the material world. Compromise, learning to share for mutual pleasure, is usually the best course, rather than fighting or withdrawal. Your sexual drives may be strong. You might feel torn between being the center of attention and hiding from it. Intense emotions are possible, and could explode occasionally. You may be attracted to challenges. Some kind of competition can be a healthy outlet, letting you test your strength in appropriate ways whether in games or business. Healthy competition involves winning some and losing some while remembering that life is a game. The potential for deep transformations is present, inviting you to grow toward self-knowledge and self-mastery, respecting the rights of others, letting go of the past, and being fully true to yourself.

Sun into 9th House or Sagittarius: Fervent Faith

In these years, confidence will tend to rise along with a desire for expanded horizons (physical, mental and spiritual). Your promotional, persuasive powers may become more marked as you seek and share answers to some of life's most challenging questions. Humor can be a great asset. You may be attracted to larger-than-life ideas, people or actions, and might easily overextend. Optimism tends to be high. Pride/shame may be connected to higher education, travel, interactions with in-laws, grandchildren, religion, or fundamental values. Increased faith can make these years deeply fulfilling. This is a time to formulate your own personal belief system, to gain greater faith in yourself, but also to expand your faith in a Higher Power so you can do your best and then let go and trust the Absolute.

Sun into 10th House or Capricorn: Admirable Ambitions

In the years ahead, you have the potential of gaining prominence in the world through disciplined efforts. Power and responsibility will be important issues which could be faced in your career or in your family, dealing with parents or handling the parental role yourself. You may confront power in the world in the form of natural laws (e.g., time), cultural regulations (e.g., speed limits), authority figures, or your conscience as a form of internalized law and power. You will need to integrate your personal power with its limits as defined by laws and your conscience. When you work **with** the "rules of the game," you can reach the top. Appreciation for your achievements may be important to you. You might seek attention for material attainments, may try to prove self-worth through hard work. There is a danger of defining superiority/inferiority in terms of power. Excessive ambition can lead to attempting more than is humanly possible and consequent failure, or it can lead to giving up rather than risking failing or falling short. Personal courage and will must be blended with realistic efforts to let you reach your full potential.

Sun into 11th House or Aquarius: Noteworthy Networking

The years ahead offer a potential leadership role in groups and associations or in activities involving social causes. You can enjoy increased social involvements, openness to people for casual relating, but you might also be ego-vulnerable to friends. There is likely to be a focus on the future, with creativity and originality highlighted and a willingness to take risks. You may feel some conflict between being special and being equal, or between emotional versus intellectual needs. Recognition may be sought through friends, groups, knowledge including new technology, or an individualistic spirit. On the whole, these years should bring new freedom and a capacity to take things more lightly, with detachment and humor.

Sun into 12th House or Pisces: Riveting Romance

The years ahead could increase your romantic feelings and your search for ideal love. Reasonable expectations for relationships will prevent disappointments, and help to avoid slipping into savior-victim roles. Dramatic skills can be developed, either for personal self-expression, or to use in a career. This is a good time for promotional, advertising, or public relations work, for fields that use creative imagination and persuasive ability. You may want to explore roles, masks, poetics, music, or other aesthetic talents. Escapism might be a danger through drugs, alcohol, illness, etc., if your aspirations are too high. Deep satisfaction and inner peace could come from spiritual quests or from healing-helping roles. Stay open to the potential of personal growth through transcendence of the ego, to experiences of being connected to Life, and to faith in the Infinite.

(See Chapter Nine for Moon through signs and houses.)

MERCURY

Mercury into 1st House or Aries: Impulsive Intellect

This combination highlights quicker, more instinctive verbal expression in thoughts and speech, which can increase the potential for arguments, irony, sarcasm, debate, or just outspokenness. A sharper, quicker mind is the source of the action, along with marked curiosity. You might find yourself speaking without thinking, forgetting in mid-thought, or talking too much. You may feel increased resistance to routine repetition, preferring multiple interests and the challenge of new ideas. There will be a tendency to identify with your mind or to think and/or talk about your identity. Humor could play a larger role in your life. On the physical level, finger and hand dexterity may be improved and faster, along with increasing mechanical skills. Sports, mental games, or a competitive business can offer healthy outlets for this new energy.

Mercury into 2nd House or Taurus: Graceful Gratification

This combination can indicate earning money through the use of mind and tongue and/or the hands. Commercial interchanges may be pleasurable and/or financially rewarding. Pleasure may come through thinking and communicating or from activities with relatives. You may find it easier to relax, to be affable and easygoing. You may be attracted to the verbal or graphic arts. Thinking and talking could focus more on money, pleasure, appearances, comfort, or aesthetics. Interchanges with people could center around beauty, security and feeling good.

Mercury into 3rd House or Gemini: "Curiouser and Curiouser"

It's a time to increase your capacity to be logical and objective and to broaden your perspectives. The mental emphasis could include light and casual discussions, interchanges with many people, visits with relatives, taking classes, and the potential for short trips. The years ahead offer lots of thinking and talking to satisfy a restless curiosity that can focus on learning, sharing knowledge and moving. You may develop more versatility, adaptability, and flexibility. You may find pleasure in mimicry, in flippant humor, or in activity that centers on the immediate environment and people around you.

Mercury into 4th House or Cancer: Building Bridges

This combination calls for sharing ideas with those closest to you. Communication should at least partly be centered around feelings and clarifying emotional needs. You can nurture and be nurtured through words, with increased empathy and nonverbal understanding. Family relationships can be strengthened by intellectual exchanges at home. A new domestic phase is possible. If you feel insecure about expressing feelings, try an inner dialogue with someone who is important to you, but alternate playing yourself and the other person to try to experience where he or she is coming from. This is a good time to listen to your own subconscious guidance, to attend to your own emotional needs, but without cutting yourself off from others. Bring emotional issues into the open with sensitivity as well as objectivity. Psychic awareness may increase as you connect the conscious and subconscious aspects of your mind.

Mercury into 5th House or Leo: Conscious Charisma

This can be a time for increased fun and games! The need for lots of stimulation can lead to changes in your environment or can make recreation important to you. Talk with children, lovers, or anyone willing to be an audience. Your communication style may become more dramatic, witty, and entertaining. Family interactions and interchanges are likely to be important. You may seek knowledge about love, passion, children, creativity, power or fame. Analyze your own needs for self-esteem and look for ways to satisfy them. A healthy ego does not need to put anyone else down. It can give and accept love, and maintain the saving grace of a sense of humor.

Mercury into 6th House or Virgo: Productive Pondering

It is time for a practical and disciplined mind, for thought and speech and conscious action that lead to concrete results. You can develop thinking that is analytical, organizing, categorizing, testing, perfecting. Communication with co-workers will be important, thinking and talking about work or at work. An intellectual/verbal focus on health is also possible. Mental flexibility and adaptability could be applied to daily routines and chores. Avoid excessive criticism of yourself or others. The search for flaws and efforts to correct them are valuable in the job, but harmful when emphasized in human relationships. The years ahead can be a time of real accomplishment—efficient functioning in your work and with your body if you do what you can, keep learning to do more, but also accept your human nature.

Mercury into 7th House or Libra: Intellectual Interchanges

Interchanges with peer relationships are likely to be important in the years ahead. Mutual learning can occur through shared ideas or through imitation. Understanding and communication will be a focus in both cooperative and competitive relationships. You can be very persuasive, tactful, charming, diplomatic if you wish, or direct and argumentative, enjoying the role of devil's advocate, pointing out the "other side" even if you don't believe in it. Concerns involving choices, comparisons, options and the desire for balance might lead to indecision at times. Explanations and fair play will be important. You need to hear and to be heard. Keep your sense of humor, your ability to "watch the show" and to accept the lack of perfection which is part of being human.

Mercury into 8th House or Scorpio: Intense Investigations

This is a time for an in-depth exploration of ideas. You may feel pulled between secrecy and revelation of the knowledge you have grasped. Sex, money, transformation could have attraction as topics for thought and conversation. You may intuit people's weak points and be tempted to use your intellect to gain control. Words can be powerful: sarcasm, satire, irony. The appropriate use of your mind is as a tool for attaining self-knowledge and self-mastery. Even this positive goal could become obsessive, so remember moderation. It is important to know when is enough and how to let go. You could increase your interest in the occult, in death, in history or archaeology or some field of research. Joint resources may be highlighted: investments, debts, taxes, public funds. Medical interests are also possible. Look inside for answers.

Mercury into 9th House or Sagittarius: Expanding Evaluations

The years ahead may be marked by much mental restlessness. You may learn, teach, preach, write or travel. There is often a tendency to try to do more than is possible with the mind and communication. Try to satisfy your desire for new experiences without scattering too widely. A clear value hierarchy is very important. Seek meaning, reasons, understanding; clarify and formulate goals, values and ideals. Humor is highlighted and can be very helpful, though the instinct to be honest and open can lead to excessive bluntness. Alternately, it is possible to exaggerate for a good story. A search for the Absolute in some form can range from intense curiosity about everything to concern with morality, ethics, truth, the nature of reality and a search for a guru. Use your own mental ability to define your belief system and then put your faith in a Higher Power (beyond human limits). Your intellectual explorations may bring many answers, but more questions always exist. Dogmatic beliefs that final truth is known stops our openness to the discovery of new, more inclusive truth.

Mercury into 10th House or Capricorn: Careful Conceptualization

It is time to think in practical terms, to ground your mind in order to produce results in the world and on the job. Organized communication and careful planning can pay dividends in your career. Common sense is a fine potential asset. Critical evaluation can produce tangible rewards or it can result in depression, anxiety, insecurity, and/or defensiveness if overdone. If you have any nagging doubts about your mental abilities, it is important to work with your mind. We learn by practice. You may need to understand authority figures in your life or to make decisions about personal responsibility. You may be getting feedback from the Universe in regard to previous decisions and choices. Pay attention to the consequences of such past actions and use any new understanding to make realistic plans to handle your roles as a member of the human community and any obligations to the other forms of life which share our earth.

Mercury into 11th House or Aquarius: Communal Consciousness

In the years ahead, you should gain an increased ability to talk to anyone. Global issues and humanitarian concerns, as well as any frontier of new knowledge, are potential topics of conversation. Focus on expressing your individuality through the use of language. You may increase the speed of your thinking. You may be inventive with intuitive flashes—but also could jump to overly hasty conclusions or might over-generalize. Objectivity, logic, reason, detachment may be cultivated as useful assets as long as there is also room for warmth in your life. Friends may increase in importance or you may want to broaden your circle of contacts. Personal freedom from limits might be emphasized, leading to possible changes in any area in which you have felt "stuck." It is fine to reach for the future and progress, as long as we build on developed foundations from the past.

Mercury into 12th House or Pisces: Inspired Intellect

This combination indicates thinking intuitively and globally rather than analytically or in discrete chunks. Words can be used to heal, beautify, inspire or victimize. Let them bring love and peace. You will have a visionary potential in the years ahead which may be poetic, evasive, imaginative or deluded. It is important to integrate the head in the clouds with the feet on the ground. Thinking and speech can be symbolic, expressed in metaphors that convey deeper meanings. You might seek perfect words, "magic" understanding. An interest in hidden things may attract you to the subconscious, to dreams, to an interest in the psychic area. You will be dealing with the rational/intuitive polarity, perhaps pulled between the logical, conscious side of the mind and the openness to the subconscious which permits mystical experiences. We need both sides of the mind. Do your own thinking and then trust the Absolute.

VENUS

Venus into 1st House or Aries: Personal Pleasure

The years ahead can offer pleasure through personal action, including such combinations of physical activity with beauty, grace, and rhythm as dancing, gymnastics, swimming, bowling, tennis, etc. You may wish to improve your physical appearance and increased exercise is better than dieting to produce a shapely figure. You can be magnetic, tactful and pleasant when you choose harmony, but you can also stubbornly insist on what you want when you feel you have a right to it. You may feel torn at times between anger when your desires are thwarted and conciliation when pleasure and harmony seem more important. The tendency will be to seek immediate gratification, comfort, pleasure and beauty; to know what you want and to try for it—but preferably in a smooth and easy way.

Venus into 2nd House or Taurus: Satisfied Savoring

This year could mark the beginning of a laid-back time, provided your basic financial needs are being met. You are ready to enjoy life and not push. You have the potential for indulgence of the appetites with a strong appreciation of life's pleasures, whether eating, drinking, sex, possessions, etc. There is a tendency to be easygoing, perhaps even passive, to focus on maintaining, securing, collecting, satisfying and savoring. Comfort, beauty, finances, physical possessions and pleasures can be highlighted. The creation of beauty in some form can be important, or you may just increase your appreciation of the aesthetic side of life. It is essential to be practical in dealing with money, possessions and appetites, but also to relax and enjoy life.

Venus into 3rd House or Gemini: Contented Communication

In the years ahead, pleasure (and income) could come through thinking, talking, and interacting with people close at hand. There may be a tendency to "make nice" in communications, to avoid confrontations, to be diplomatic and tactful. This could increase your ability to be socially adept, considerate and courteous. Comfort, ease, pleasure can be sought with/through siblings or other relatives or through mental activity. Money matters might also concern relatives, transportation or the mind. You also might study in some field of the arts—writing, painting, gardening, music, etc.—or develop skills involving hand dexterity. This combination can help maintain a young attitude, able to watch the world, understand it, talk about is, and accept it.

Venus into 4th House or Cancer: Sustaining Support

This combinations tends to emphasize safety and security urges. Some people need to guard against using food or alcohol for emotional reassurance, or collecting things for security. You could have much pleasure from your home or family, or other ties involving close, deep feelings. One cycle may end and another begin in regard to domestic matters. You may want to spend money on your home or work to make it more beautiful. You may enjoy feeding people or providing other forms of nurturing and help to others. Alternately, you might feel helpless and seek assistance from others. A healthy compromise allows both giving and receiving comfort and reassurance. Life is interdependent.

Venus into 5th House or Leo: Approval and Admiration

In the years ahead you will be combining the quest for pleasure with the urge for emotional expression in new and dramatic forms. You could focus on love and children, enjoying and perhaps overindulging your loved ones or working with young people. Your need for love and/or admiration and attention could attract you to a public role in such fields as sales, public relations, advertising, or the entertainment world. The need for approval can also raise the danger of being susceptible to flattery. The quest for pleasure might lead to extravagance with the appetites or with money and possessions. If the feeling for beauty and the sensuous side of life is directed into artistic creativity, you could both win admiration and build your own self-esteem. It is important that you look to your own actions for your sense of self-worth, rather than to make your self-esteem too dependent on the reactions of others. Gratification comes through expressing yourself.

Venus into 6th House or Virgo: Rewarding Results

In the years ahead, you will want to enjoy your work or to connect it to beauty in some form. It may seem a little easier, perhaps due to pleasant relations with colleagues, or perhaps to monetary or other compensations for your efforts. Unfortunately, if too much pleasure is expected from your work, you could feel let down when the job includes necessary and less enjoyable chores. Generally, this combination encourages practicality, but overindulgence could affect your health, especially if your work is not fulfilling. Monetary or aesthetic satisfactions from the job can help you to stay healthy. Efficiency and productivity should help you to gain both comfort and security.

Venus into 7th House or Libra: Balanced Benefits

This combination invites a focus on harmony, ease and pleasure in peer relationships, though there may be a tendency to be a bit passive, reacting rather than initiating action. Mutual indulgence is possible and enjoyment of people is likely. Love and partnership are generally important. With the instinct for fair play, justice, equality and balance emphasized, you may compare, contrast, compete, cooperate, negotiate or justify with actions and associates. Moderation and harmony are usually preferred, but it is vital that both sides be acknowledged. You could be involved with law and politics, with contracts or counseling, with personnel work, arbitration, etc. Or you might increase your artistic expression. This combination is especially good for the graphic arts such as design, architecture, photography, etc. The ideal blend is to enjoy both people and beauty.

Venus into 8th House or Scorpio: Enough is Enough

This polarity may call for the integration of appetite indulgence and appetite control, whether around sex, food, money, etc. Alternately, the issue may involve learning to give, to receive and to share the physical world of money, possessions or appetites. We have it together when we can share power and really deep emotions with a mate, finding mutual pleasure, understanding ourselves through the mirror of the mate, and attaining self-mastery partly out of respect for the rights of the mate. Pleasure with others is important and only truly realized when love is given without any attempt to possess or control each other. Pleasure may also come from exploring hidden issues, digging up secrets, researching, analyzing, etc. Financial activity could involve inheritance, return on investments, royalties, pensions or other forms of resources coming from others or from the past or owed to others. This is a good combination for work with bookkeeping, accounting, insurance, or some kind of service that is paid by public funds. Remember that moderation brings more pleasure in the end, knowing when is enough and how to let go.

Venus into 9th House or Sagittarius: Delightful Diversions

This can be a delightful combination, though you may be tempted toward overindulgence, with the feeling that "if some is good, more will be better." You might need to hold the line on extravagance if material possessions and pleasures are overvalued. Strong freedom needs may vie with an idealization of relationships or a search for the perfect relationship. Placing a high value on love and sharing ideals and dreams can cement partnerships. Conversely, too high expectations can combine with the desire for more freedom, or with changing values and goals, to lead to broken bonds. Some of your greatest pleasure could come from learning, teaching, exploring for answers, whether this is done through travel, through more education, or through religion or philosophy. Grandchildren can also be a source of great pleasure. With reasonable moderation, the years ahead should offer an enthusiastic optimism which could manifest in anything from the great romantic novel to a joyous faith in Ultimate Good.

Venus into 10th House or Capricorn: Lovely Labor

These years ahead offer the potential for satisfaction through career and achievements. A sense of security is likely to be important, with a desire for a firm foundation. Realism and discipline will pay off on the bottom line. Responsibility will probably be an issue. You could move into a position of power or deal with authority figures. Things may seem more secure or more rewarding than people, yet you can be successful with both. If success needs seem to conflict with love needs, try to compromise, to make room for both in your life. With this combination, you can work at love, work at pleasure, create beauty in your work, or gain pleasure, money or love through your work. In fact, you can do them all if you give yourself time to enjoy the process of climbing to the top of the mountain, and if you are willing to share the effort.

Venus into 11th House or Aquarius: Affectionate Acceptance

In the years ahead, companionship without strings is likely to be a source of enjoyment. You may treat friends as partners and partners as friends. Either you or your partner could want more openness in the relationship or could call for changes. With mutual understanding and acceptance, affection can be shared without "strings," yet with essential commitment. You may also gain pleasure or money through social causes and progress. Both individualism and group endeavors are appropriate with an emphasis on equalitarian groups and voluntary activities. You may enjoy the pursuit of new knowledge, especially with a focus on artistic modalities. Security needs and risk-taking instincts may be in conflict, but it is possible to explore new options without threatening your basic stability, to enjoy both the familiar and the innovative.

Venus into 12th House or Pisces: Pleasure Perfected

This is a great time to tune in to infinite beauty, to develop aesthetic talents in any area of your choice—music, poetry, gardening, etc. Beauty, grace, harmony and ease could all appeal to you. But guard against setting impossible standards for beauty or for the more mundane money and pleasure. If any fragment of life is turned into an idol, made too important, it always lets us down. It is common to be overly idealistic about love, to expect more than is possible from other humans. You might want to be swept away by love, to experience a mystical oneness with another human which is only really possible in a sustained way with the Absolute. If both people can give and receive, with mutual respect, you will be safe from the destructive trap of a savior/victim relationships or "lost loves." If expectations remain reasonable and love is valued enough to make compromises, and goals, beliefs and values are shared, you can build and enjoy a graceful and harmonious life with a mate.

MARS

Mars into 1st House or Aries: Me-Me-Me!

You could experience a high energy level in the years ahead. Involvement in sports or other vigorous physical action would offer a healthy outlet. You also might feel more assertive than usual and find directness more appealing. The tendency is to focus on personal identity and personal action, and to be attracted to new ventures. A pioneering urge is possible; courage may be more marked; challenges or crises may appeal. Excitement, enthusiasm and spontaneity may increase and personal freedom is especially highlighted—the capacity to act on your own wants and desires, to do your "own thing." If other, more cautious, sides of your nature are in conflict with your increasing need for free self-expression, look for constructive ways to try new experiences, to build your self-confidence, to fully be yourself.

Mars into 2nd House or Taurus: Personal Pleasures

The years ahead are likely to encourage indulgence of the appetites. Extravagance is possible and passions may be stronger, more ardent. An active pursuit and/or creation of beauty (dancing, skating, diving, gymnastics, etc.) would offer an appropriate outlet for increased sensuality. You might seek immediate gratification and have trouble waiting. Your sense of personal identity could be tied to possessions or money, equating them with independence and the ability to act. Financial power becomes more of a priority. Or you might actively pursue comfort and pleasure. The feeling of this combination is that we should be able to do what we please and to enjoy whatever we do, but since we always face some duties or limits, including the rights of other people, we might as well learn to enjoy the necessary compromises.

Mars into 3rd House or Gemini: Lively Learning

An increasingly active mind could lead to energetic conversations, debates, new studies, teaching, traveling, etc. Self-expression is likely to be important. Personal rights could become an issue with relatives or you could discover more about yourself in the mirror offered by the people around you. Physical and mental restlessness call for variety, a chance to learn, to satisfy wide-ranging curiosity. Quick wits and a quick tongue could lead to speaking without thinking, to talking too much, or to stumbling in mid-sentence. Increasing physical flexibility and coordination may accompany the increasing mental alertness. A keen sense of humor is also likely to be an asset, providing the direct speech is not so blunt that it alienates others. If you have doubted your mental ability in the past, these years ahead are your time to gain confidence by learning and communicating.

Mars into 4th House or Cancer: Dynamic Domesticity

Your sense of identity and personal action may be increasingly directed into your home, family, or other sources of emotional security. One domestic chapter may close with another opening. You could feel conflict between independence and closeness, or be torn between the expression of intense feelings versus holding them in. The hazards of repressing feelings include the danger of periodic outbursts of frustrated anger (leading to arguments or fights with family) or illness if the frustration is turned against the self. The urge to take action can be channeled constructively into building, moving furniture, gardening or fixing-up tasks. The desire for freedom needs to be integrated with dependency and nurturing urges. You might push others away if you felt trapped in the nurturing role, or if letting others care for you was experienced as threatening to your personal power. Life is a compromise. It is possible to move or to travel or to have other people come and go, and to still maintain warm, caring ties and a sense of roots.

Mars into 5th House or Leo: Fervent and Forceful

This combination suggests confidence, enthusiasm, creativity and a youthful sense of fun. You may want to play more or to enjoy personal expression through creative, dramatic or risk-taking activities that invite applause. Increased courage and energy could lead to adventures, to overextending yourself, to trying to do too much, ultimately leading to burnout or boredom. The combination of great warmth and a strong will can move mountains, but it also can be combative, arrogant and self-centered. Find your own inner child through children and remember that love begets love. You can be a great cheer leader for yourself and others—emphasizing the best, using humor, and focusing on greater possibilities.

Mars into 6th House or Virgo: Confident Capability

The years ahead are a time for accomplishment on the job, for efficient functioning in your work and in your body. You may want to improve habits, and have to guard against too much self-criticism. Appreciate your achievements along with continuing to carry them further. You are likely to increasingly want to do things **your** way on the job and may decide to change jobs or even your whole area of work to attain more independence or just to try something different. If change is desired but not realistically possible, try to find a hobby or avocation that can give you a sense of personal control along with a feeling of achievement. Try not to let your drive be sidetracked into petty arguments or conflicts with colleagues. It is important to find some areas in which you can feel positive about your work since chronic frustration can lead to illness that gets one out of the situation. Try to do something well, but remember that you are more than your job.

Mars into 7th House or Libra: Accommodating Assertion

Peer relationships will be highly important in the years ahead. These can be personal, with fellow workers, involve counseling, etc. It is good to have room for both cooperative and competitive interactions. You will be working on balancing your wants with those of others, avoiding the extremes of over accommodation, excessive competition, or only relating to weaker people in order to feel safe. The polarities to be balanced include acting/reacting, selfish/sharing, independent/committed. In dealing with such polarities, it is common to be conscious of one side and to attract a partner who overdoes the opposite side. Compromise calls for a meeting in the middle, doing some of both—

together. It is normal to feel some ambivalence about doing what one wants versus giving in, to feel pulled between anger and compliance. But lasting, caring, sharing relationships are worth the effort.

Mars into 8th House or Scorpio: Partnership Power

In the years ahead you will be facing the challenge of sharing possessions, pleasure and power with other people. It is possible to struggle over resources, money and sex if assertive energies are not channeled into complete compromises. This combination is one of the most intense and potentially passionate that can be experienced. You can face the depths of your psyche through another person and learn self-mastery partly through respect for the rights of others. Power issues are often central. Fear of power can attract cruel, vindictive, or controlling individuals who abuse power or weak, parasitic people. Successful integration includes cooperative relationships, competition in sports or business or games, and a willingness to help people. Joint efforts can accomplish more than individual ones. Personal willpower can be channeled toward self-control and self-transformation.

Mars into 9th House or Sagittarius: Active Adventuring

This combination has the reputation of being willing to try almost anything, with immense faith and confidence. Risks may be taken for thrills, excitement, or for a sense of vital aliveness and personal power. Freedom and independence can be increasingly important, along with "I should have had it yesterday" impatience. A personal search for truth, understanding, ideals, may lead to changes in personal beliefs, to travel in pursuit of high ambitions, to additional education or teaching or writing, to moral outrage at the world's failure to live up to your standards. Vigorous physical activity should be a regular part of your life, especially some form of a competitive sport. You can be resourceful, enterprising, and quick to take advantage of opportunities, but remember to keep some faith in your own power and some in a Higher Power.

Mars into 10th House or Capricorn: Energetic Enterprise

The years ahead invite an aggressive pursuit of occupational goals. If you are personally motivated and like what you are doing, you will have lots of energy for work. Compromises may be needed to avoid conflicts with authorities since you will tend to believe that your way is the "right" way or that "If you want it done right, do it yourself." If you lack faith in yourself, are overly self-critical or self-doubting, the opposite danger exists. You might give up and not try rather than risk failing or falling short. The overdrive end of the polarity can lead to pushing too much, to compulsive overactivity. The self-blocking end bring fear and/or anger, which, if repressed, can lead to illness. Learning to balance self-will and the limits of the outer world is the big challenge of this combination and it is well worth the effort, with a promise of success and achievement for those who "get it together" by mobilizing personal action within the rules of the game.

Mars into 11th House or Aquarius: Eagerly Exploring

The years ahead can bring exciting new experience, including new freedom, new knowledge, new friends, new causes for which you can fight. There may be increased activity involving groups of all kinds, formal and informal, but mostly voluntary. You are likely to discover or assert your uniqueness, to increase your courage and willingness to take risks, to expand your sense of humor. Don't overdo if you feel tempted to be rash, to take dares, to test your nerves. Changes and excitement, individuality, escape from limits may seem essential, but we still have to live in a material world which we share with our fellow humans. This is a good time to develop mechanical skills, to become more involved with modern technology or to work for humanitarian goals and values.

Mars into 12th House or Pisces: Active Aspirations

These years ahead invite you to enter the world of the artist, the healer, and the mystic. You can develop your unique gifts in any of these areas. You may need to clarify who you really are versus who you "should" be or who you want to be. Aspirations are fine as long as we realize it takes time to "arrive" and we can enjoy the journey. This period is excellent for active expression of grace and harmony through dance, movement, etc. You can also be intuitive, empathic, healing and helping others. If your faith and goals are not clearly formulated or are set too high, there is a danger of being diffuse, discontented, moody, or off chasing rainbows. Try to balance your self-expression as a separate individual meeting your own needs with a partly subconscious desire for absorption by something infinite. Humans cannot do it all. God won't do it all. Together we can create a more ideal world.

OUTER PLANET CHANGES OF HOUSE OR SIGN

When the outer planets change sign or house, it also points to a new chapter. Due to the slow movement in progressions, these shifts are fairly rare. To conserve space, we are not including interpretations for the sign/house changes of Jupiter through Pluto. We are, however, including a "title" for each shift—to provide a bit of the flavor of the issues involved.

Jupiter into 1st House or Aries: Go for God
Jupiter into 2nd House or Taurus: Infinite Indulgence?
Jupiter into 3rd House or Gemini: Limitless Learning
Jupiter into 4th House or Cancer: Finest Families
Jupiter into 5th House or Leo: High Hopes
Jupiter into 6th House or Virgo: Idealizing Improvements
Jupiter into 7th House or Libra: "Perfect" Partners?
Jupiter into 8th House or Scorpio: Growth Goals
Jupiter into 9th House or Sagittarius: Ideal Insights
Jupiter into 10th House or Capricorn: Grounded Goals

Jupiter into 11th House or Aquarius: Beyond the Barriers
Jupiter into 12th House or Pisces: Greatest Good

Saturn into 1st House or Aries: Personal Pragmatism
Saturn into 2nd House or Taurus: Disciplining Desires
Saturn into 3rd House or Gemini: Practical Perceptions
Saturn into 4th House or Cancer: Raising Responsibility
Saturn into 5th House or Leo: Laboring for Love
Saturn into 6th House or Virgo: Disciplined & Dedicated
Saturn into 7th House or Libra: Cautious Cooperation
Saturn into 8th House or Scorpio: Cautious Control
Saturn into 9th House or Sagittarius: Fundamentals of Faith/
        Faith in Fundamentals
Saturn into 10th House or Capricorn: Authoritative Attainments
Saturn into 11th House or Aquarius: Revising Rules
Saturn into 12th House or Pisces: A Cosmic Calling

Uranus into 1st House or Aries: Utterly Unique
Uranus into 2nd House or Taurus: Altered Appetites
Uranus into 3rd House or Gemini: Brainstorming
Uranus into 4th House or Cancer: Family Freedom
Uranus into 5th House or Leo: Playful Progress
Uranus into 6th House or Virgo: Industrious Innovation
Uranus into 7th House or Libra: Revamping Relationships
Uranus into 8th House or Scorpio: Intimate Individuation
Uranus into 9th House or Sagittarius: Challenging Concepts
Uranus into 10th House or Capricorn: Vocational Variations
Uranus into 11th House or Aquarius: Flying Free!
Uranus into 12th House or Pisces: Inspiring Innovations

Neptune into 1st House or Aries: Immediate Insights
Neptune into 2nd House or Taurus: Pleasure Principle
Neptune into 3rd House or Gemini: Idealizing Ideas
Neptune into 4th House or Cancer: Sensitive Succoring
Neptune into 5th House or Leo: Magic Magnetism
Neptune into 6th House or Virgo: Productive Purity
Neptune into 7th House or Libra: Mirrors & Masks
Neptune into 8th House or Scorpio: Dreams of Desire
Neptune into 9th House or Sagittarius: Absolute Awe
Neptune into 10th House or Capricorn: Professional Phantasmagoria
Neptune into 11th House or Aquarius: Visionary Vibrations
Neptune into 12th House or Pisces: Cosmic Consciousness

Pluto into 1st House or Aries: Transmuting/Transforming
Pluto into 2nd House or Taurus: Consuming, Consumption
      & Consummation
Pluto into 3rd House or Gemini: Deepening Dialogues
Pluto into 4th House or Cancer: Submerged Softness
Pluto into 5th House or Leo: The Power of Passion
Pluto into 6th House or Virgo: Functionally Focused
Pluto into 7th House or Libra: Confronting Control
Pluto into 8th House or Scorpio: Doubled Desires
Pluto into 9th House or Sagittarius: Intense Ideals
Pluto into 10th House or Capricorn: Managing Mastery
Pluto into 11th House or Aquarius: Probing People
Pluto into 12th House or Pisces: Mysterious Merging

Chiron into 1st House or Aries: Idealized Identity or Fight for Freedom
Chiron into 2nd House or Taurus: Grandiose Gratification
Chiron into 3rd House or Gemini: Mental Movement
Chiron into 4th House or Cancer: Freer Families
Chiron into 5th House or Leo: Exciting Enhancement
Chiron into 6th House or Virgo: Producing Perfection
Chiron into 7th House or Libra: Tolerant Ties
Chiron into 8th House or Scorpio: Benevolent Bonds
Chiron into 9th House or Sagittarius: Expanding Expectations
Chiron into 10th House or Capricorn: Valuable Vocation
Chiron into 11th House or Aquarius: Restless Reformation
Chiron into 12th House or Pisces: Expecting Ecstasy

CERES

Ceres into 1st House or Aries: Nurturing Nature

You may analyze, make judgments and work more quickly as you tend to identify with your accomplishments. Self-discipline can come naturally; efficient functioning can become spontaneous self-expression. But you may feel some tension between precision and speed. Health matters and/or nurturing and caretaking may be important. For a sense of personal power, you need to be productive, practical and to get the job done.

Ceres into 2nd House or Taurus: Satisfying Sustenance

This combination encourages a relaxed orientation to work and nurturing. Tactile contact is important, with a desire for tangible results from your efforts. Money or possessions may add to your sense of security. You may take up artistic activities or gain pleasure through productive efforts and caretaking activities. Indulgence of your family is possible. Security and comfort are valued.

Ceres into 3rd House or Gemini: Communication & Contact

This combination encourages mental work which might include improving communications, especially with other family members. Increased objectivity and detachment about your caretaking role are possible. You may want to focus on practical achievements through thinking, talking, finger dexterity or general versatility. Juggling multiple interests and tasks is also common with some danger of becoming overextended. You may "mother" siblings or be nurtured by them, or you may encourage an equalitarian relationship with your own mother or your children.

Ceres into 4th House or Cancer: Emotional Efficiency

Home and domestic affairs are likely to be important, with one phase ending and another beginning. You may want to have children, or be involved with their care. You may also want to improve your home, to plant or enlarge a garden, or to develop homemaking skills such as sewing, canning, wood-working or basic repairs. Analysis of your emotional needs could be helpful. Make practical assessment of what you and your loved ones require and work with them to accomplish the desired goals.

Ceres into 5th House or Leo: Parental Power

Parenting instincts often come to the fore with this combination, though children may enter your life in many forms. The desire to care for others is likely to be prominent, or you may seek extra nurturing from those you love. Your inner child may be calling for expression. Creativity could be high if you encourage it. Making things yourself can bring great personal satisfaction, but receiving admiration from others for your accomplishments also is essential.

Ceres into 6th House or Virgo: Realistic Regimes

Work and/or health are likely to increase in importance. Efficient functioning is the name of the game. You need to be practical, sensible and well-grounded on the job. You may take up a new regimen in terms of health, diet or exercise to increase your bodily well-being. Facing facts should come easily with this earth emphasis. You can analyze and sort the possibilities, figure out the best action and then take it.

Ceres into 7th House or Libra: Shared Support

This combination blends parental instincts with partnership. You may become closely involved with a parent, be strong, capable and helpful for your partner, or attract a partner to take care of you. Mutual nurturing works the best. Don't let your equal sharing turn into a one-sided parent/child interaction. The combination is excellent for working with people, for many forms of teamwork or service occupations, including counseling or consulting.

Ceres into 8th House or Scorpio: Involved Intimacy

Your cautious, helpful side is likely to be channeled toward intimacy. Careful analysis of sexual, romantic and intense relationships is likely and can be helpful. You may strive to differentiate between true passion and the need to be needed. Unmet dependency needs could lead to subconscious entanglements with others. Deep emotions call for sensible handling. Appropriate work could include fields involving joint resources such as bookkeeping, accounting, investments or taxes. You may be attracted to research, to history or to depth psychology. This is a good combination for organization and skill with details.

Ceres into 9th House or Sagittarius: Accomplishing Aims

You may find yourself idealizing practical accomplishments, expecting more than is reasonable from yourself as a parent or from others who give you emotional support. Much productive achievement is possible, but there is some danger of wanting more than can be attained. Keep your demands on yourself realistic, pace yourself, and remember to notice what's **been** done as well as what remains to **be** done.

Ceres into 10th House or Capricorn: Capable & Competent

With this combination, tangibles are likely to become more important to you. Measurable results move up on your priority list as you want to see the fruits of your labor. Shifts in responsibility are possible, either in your caretaking of others or with others who help you, with an emphasis on actions that are more physical, practical and sensible. The bottom line may become more valued than emotional nuances, but it is important to keep criticism for the job and to maintain tolerance for people.

Ceres into 11th House or Aquarius: Nurturing Networks

You may be inclined to take care of friends more than usual, or find them nurturing you. The children of humanity could pull at your heartstrings. Your pragmatic approach to tasks can become more unique, more individualistic and inventive. The urge for more freedom in your work is likely to emerge. An unusual approach to health maintenance or to your job is possible, or you may seek more intellectual stimulation in your work. Scientific "tough-mindedness" may come more easily to you now.

Ceres into 12th House or Pisces: Cosmic Coping

With this combination, practicality and idealism must be integrated. Taking care of, rescuing or otherwise saving other people can be done professionally as long as the need to be indispensable is not overdone. If you are the one feeling weak, helpless, or in need of assistance, looking to others to care for you, instead seek ways to increase your sense of personal competence and your faith in a Higher Power. A sense of inspiration, and connection to something higher in life should be combined with confidence in your own ability to cope with life. We gain such personal confidence by doing successfully whatever is within our power and by continuing to do more as we grow in ability.

PALLAS

Pallas into 1st House or Aries: Active Affiliation

This combination encourages acting for justice, equality and fair play. Your competitive side may be more in evidence. Relationship issues could arise, as you strive to balance personal needs and desires with the compromises necessary when we share life with another human being. The law, politics, counseling, arbitration, personnel work, or other involvements stressing one-to-one interaction could gain your attention. Active sharing is indicated.

Pallas into 2nd House or Taurus: Building Beauty

Artistic activities or interests, your feelings for beauty, may become stronger during this period. Visual as well as tactile arts could appeal to you. You may want to create a tangible form for your aesthetic leanings or seek more pleasure in your relationships. Finances could involve others, calling for joint decisions or actions. An old saying suggests that shared pleasure is doubled and shared pain is reduced. Sensual indulgences could be more gratifying or more important than usual.

Pallas into 3rd House or Gemini: Comparisons & Contrasts

Intellectual needs are emphasized with this combination and you may attract information and knowledge like a thirsty sponge. Other people can be sources of intellectual stimulation as relationships stir you up, get you thinking. Batting ideas back and forth is likely to appeal to you. A partnership with a relative is possible, or more social exchanges with others in your vicinity. This is a good combination for sharpening debating skills and might tempt you into playing "devil's advocate" to make sure both sides are represented. The combination also facilitates development of logic, objectivity, detachment and the ability to take things lightly.

Pallas into 4th House or Cancer: Symmetrical Support

A desire for family closeness is highlighted with this combination. One cycle may be ending as another begins in regard to emotional attachments. Some jockeying for positions is possible as a bit of competitiveness may come to light. You may want to deepen your emotional sharing with a partner. Mutual nurturing is likely, but beware of one person giving more than his/her share of support, turning what should be a peer relationship into a parent/child experience. You and a partner can tune into each other's feelings more easily and become conscious of your psychic connections. You might also expand your emotionally supportive interactions beyond family to some kind of helping profession.

Pallas into 5th House or Leo: Creative Caring

Fun and games appeal to this combination. You could play with other people who are emotionally close to you, or you could look for a wider audience for your developing sense of drama and enthusiasm. Artistic creativity would also offer a good outlet for your new fire, and some beautiful objects may be the result, or you might want to take lessons in dancing. Positive feedback in your relationships is essential; you need to give and receive admiration and approval. Let your love light shine, with kids and peers. Balance your increasing need for a sense of personal power with your innate sense of fair play.

Pallas into 6th House or Virgo: Competent Compromising

You are ready to analyze and improve your relationships with others. This period could be a new chapter in working with people in practical ways. Many forms of teamwork are possible, including working as a counselor, a consultant, in personnel or with law or politics. The period could also indicate a focus on improving your intimate associations. Be sure you do not overdo giving or getting criticism. Practicality that is focused on flaws is a useful tool when applied to the job, but when we deal with people, we need to use positive reinforcement—to focus on and encourage assets. A positive attitude can build a solid foundation for sharing.

Pallas into 7th House or Libra: Social Stimulation

Now is the time to share! Partnership is a natural way of life for you during this period, whether the primary emphasis is on an emotional, mate relationship or on teamwork in a job or on systematic activities shared with good friends. You have a need to combine forces with other people, to stimulate one another, to share thoughts and feelings. You need the intellectual challenge of a close peer. Fair play is vital to you, and you may be willing to fight or compete to ensure an even exchange. Or, if you project your power, you may find others challenging you and forcing you to define and/or defend your own needs. An alternate focus could involve your expanding sense of beauty, looking for new forms of artistic expression, or offering your artistic skills to a wider audience.

Pallas into 8th House or Scorpio: Passionate Peers

You are moving into a period of deepening your intimate bonds with others. The intensity can be achieved by taking relationships more seriously, digging beneath the surface to plumb the depths, to really examine the ties that bind you to another human being. Justice and fair play may become central issues in your determination to reach a truly equal exchange with someone. Logic **and** intuition can be harnessed to enhance intimacy. Enjoy the shared pleasure, but also be aware of the need for self-mastery. You may increase your involvement with areas of joint resources: debts, taxes, investments, public funds, etc. Research could attract you, or medical fields. Use your evolving capacity for organization and thoroughness to bring order into your life.

Pallas into 9th House or Sagittarius: Expanding Equality

With this combination, your expectations for relationships (and partners) may increase. You are likely to become more aware of your dreams and visions for the future, and inclined to "think big." Beware of wanting more than is reasonable—from yourself, from your partner, from your relationships. Aspirations are essential to life, but remember to enjoy the process of sharing, as well as the goal of ultimate perfection. You also may experience an increased urge to free yourself to pursue new goals. New studies are possible, or travel, but they will be more rewarding if they are shared with companions. Look for friends who want to journey toward the same promised land.

Pallas into 10th House or Capricorn: Pragmatic Pairing

Pragmatic issues may be increasingly prominent in your relationships during this period. It is a time to be more practical, and to use your common sense about people. A business partnership could become part of the picture, or you might work more closely with other people or meet a partner through your work. A partnership (or more contact) with a parent (or parent figure) is possible. You may wish to create aesthetic objects, beginning or expanding an artistic profession. Pallas professions range from mathematics, design, photography and architecture to personnel work, consulting, law and politics. Behind them all is the search for balance, order and harmony.

Pallas into 11th House or Aquarius: Reforming Relationships

The coming period may signal increasing openness in relationships. If freedom urges override your desire for commitment, you could split from a current association (or someone might leave you). If the desire for openness and free flow is positively channeled, you are likely to make changes in your style of sharing, to allow more intellectual stimulation, more unusual approaches and more individuality for each of you. You might develop new forms of artistic expression, become involved with social causes in new ways, or just widen your social sphere.

Pallas into 12th House or Pisces: Inspired Inclusion

Idealism may increasingly permeate your relationships, driven by a conscious or subconscious hunger for the perfect love. Or you may experience an intense need for beauty, which makes artistic expressions more vital for you now. Relationships could slip into savior/victim roles, with a danger of the savior ending as martyr if the quest for ultimates is directed toward human targets. Shared inspiration, especially shared faith in a Higher Power, works very well—whether through aesthetic interests, involvement with nature, spiritual paths or other uplifting activities which permit a sense of being part of a larger whole that gives meaning to life.

JUNO

Special Note regarding Juno

Juno is a key to one's desire for intimacy and close, committed relationships. It is also a key to marriage and the marriage partner. Because Juno does indicate a partner, as well as one's own needs, the attributes symbolized by Juno can often be projected onto the marriage (or other) partner, and lived out through him or her. It is not uncommon for individuals to deny the traits denoted by their Junos and choose spouses (or lovers/partners) who express those qualities for them.

The problem with projection is: whatever we deny in ourselves, we tend to subconsciously attract **in excess** from other people. So, denied Juno attributes tend to be **overdone** by the close partners in our lives. The following interpretations are written assuming Juno is primarily a key to your own intimacy instincts. Be aware that you may also have a partner who is living out (in an exaggerated fashion) some of the qualities associated with your Juno placement.

Juno into 1st House or Aries: Partnership Power

This combinations shows increasing readiness for more freedom in your relationships. Self-expression is likely to become more important for you; you may be less willing to compromise where your own needs are concerned unless your need for a mate overrides all your other needs. Intimacy is sought in spontaneous, open encounters. A forthright and direct approach to sharing predominates. You may "re-do" the face of your marriage or partnership, changing your interactions to more fully reflect each person's individuality. Alternately, if your nature is heavily weighted toward a desire for committed closeness, the Juno in Aries or in the 1st house may be experienced as an intensification of your identification with partnership and a feeling of loss of personal power and identity if you lack a mate. Such feelings would indicate that this period offers an opportunity to develop more self-reliance, more confidence in your ability to be yourself even while you share a part of your life with others.

Juno into 2nd House or Taurus: Comfortable Contacts

Your aesthetic sensibilities may be heightened. Sensual pleasures may become more of a turn-on. Shared indulgences (food, drink, smoking, sex, sensuality) are likely to be more gratifying than solo pleasures. Trade back-rubs with your partner or enjoy other physical exchanges. Finances could become an issue in your interactions with significant others. Changes are possible in what comes to you from others, or what you give to others. Your taste may be a bit more extravagant than usual: you want the finer things in life. This is a period to develop artistic talents, to create beauty in any of many fields.

Juno into 3rd House or Gemini: Stimulating Surroundings

Communications become a focus in relationships. You want to talk things over with a partner. Shared mental explorations (taking classes or seminars, travel, teaching, bouncing ideas back and forth) are likely. You are drawn toward stimulating each other intellectually. You can be more objective about the process of how you share with one another. Take advantage of new clarity to decide how you want your relationship to proceed in the future. You may also increase your activity with other family members, form closer bonds with brothers or sisters or other relatives. This is a good period to work out warm, sharing projects and plans with the people around you.

Juno into 4th House or Cancer: Committed Caring

Nurturing becomes a focus in your relationships. You may feel called upon to give a lot to a partner, or look to him/her to be extra supportive. Tender, loving care is important. Excessive dependency (by you or by a partner) could create stress, but joint care taking feels very good right now. Home could be more of a focus for sharing. A new chapter is possible in regard to home, family, and dependency. Domestic issues within the marriage or partnership may call for attention and satisfying resolutions. You may deepen or work toward greater mutual understanding in your relationship with a parent or with children. As long as both can give and receive, a partnership across the generations is possible.

Juno into 5th House or Leo: Magnetic Mates

It's party time! You are ready to play with a partner, with kids, or to take center stage for some new viewers. Fun and games with other people have more attraction than usual. Your dynamic, magnetic, exciting side wants an arena of expression. The desire to give and receive love within a committed relationship is strong now. Sexual drives may be highlighted as well. You are ready to leap enthusiastically into partnership activities, eager to enjoy, appreciate, admire and savor the applause of others as well. This is also a good period to expand your artistic creativity. If you have been doing it quietly at home, look for ways to "go public," to share your gift with a wider audience.

Juno into 6th House or Virgo: Competent Compromising

You may be ready to "make over" your marriage or significant relationship. Flaws are more noticeable, somehow, and you want to "make it all better." Guard against being too hard on yourself or on a partner. Remember that everyone is human; don't demand perfection! Everyday tasks could become bones of contention; strive for an equal division of chores. If not involved with someone, you might meet a potential partner through your work, or you might increase the teamwork in your job. This is a good combination for a family business. You also might feel pulled between obligations and time commitments to the work and to your personal relationships. Hopefully, life can be big enough for both. This is also an appropriate time to do handicrafts, to make things that are both attractive and useful.

Juno into 7th House or Libra: Committed Compromises

Equality of exchanges becomes more important to you. You may examine your marriage or partnership in terms of justice and fair play, seeking an evenhandedness between you and a mate. Balance is the key. Score-keeping can be overdone to the point of cutthroat competition, but reasonable trade-offs are highly appropriate. Seek out compromises. Establish win/win situations. If you are not in a committed peer relationship, this combination usually marks a time of increased desire for such a commitment. Your aesthetic sense could also be heightened. Visual beauty, especially in the graphic arts, may have particular appeal. You might want to do more designing or sewing of your own clothes or just be more fashion conscious.

Juno into 8th House or Scorpio: Finishing Feelings

Hidden issues may erupt to the surface of your marriage or partnership. You could find yourself digging up certain information about you, your partner, or the way you relate to each other. Old resentments or anger may come to the light of day. Power issues, financial matters or sexual desires could become an important focus. Intense interactions are likely. It is important to understand the underground processes and feelings in your partnership. Joint resources or the consequences of past actions could also involve business concerns and decisions. You may be finishing old chapters and letting go to make a new start.

Juno into 9th House or Sagittarius: Adventurous Affiliation

You want relating to be an adventure. The sky's the limit as far as your hopes for your marriage or partnership. You are ready to explore the world, seek knowledge, gain illumination, search for enlightenment, and have a plain, old **good time**. Expectations could be an issue, as you or a partner may want more than is possible from each other or the relationship. But shared dreams can lead to truly inspiring exchanges that uplift you both. Since the desire for freedom to pursue ultimate values can sometimes conflict with family commitments, you may need to compromise to make room for both in your life. The romance of the faraway and mysterious can sometimes make the familiar seem dull and uninteresting. A successful compromise enlivens without abandoning loyalty and commitment.

Juno into 10th House or Capricorn: Symmetrical Status

You are entering a period of responsibility toward relating. You are likely to take your partnerships more seriously, to be more grounded and concerned with getting things done within the context of a sharing association. You may feel the urge to make your marriage "work better," but beware of an overly critical eye (from you to a partner or vice versa). Sensible, shared efforts can produce lasting accomplishment and mutual satisfaction. This is a good combination for a family business. It is also good for work which makes life more attractive, more comfortable, more pleasant. Fields involving joint resources such as accounting or investments or taxes are appropriate, as is medical work. A primary issue is likely to be learning to share the power, or you may need to be realistic about standards to be able to handle both marriage and a career.

Juno into 11th House or Aquarius: Exploring Equality

You are moving into a time of increased experimentation in relationships. You may be wanting to explore more options, investigate more possibilities. Willing to make changes, you want to move beyond the past, into the future. New ideas and potentials excite you. You are likely to attract new people into your life and new-age concepts may be applied to your people-exchanges. A spirit of friendliness, openness, tolerance and respect for individuality can enhance your sharing with other people. If your job involves working with people, you are likely to make new contacts or develop new techniques. You may feel pulled between your attraction to increased freedom of action and your loyalty to traditional ways of relating to life.

Juno into 12th House or Pisces: Compassionate Combining

You are entering a period of idealism where relationships are concerned. You may yearn for a beautiful dream in your marriage or committed partnership. Excessive hopes can lead to disappointments or disillusionment. Keep your dreams grounded, and don't demand more than is possible from yourself, your partner, or the relationship. Aesthetic involvements may offer constructive outlets. Let beauty, love and inspiration increase in your life. This is a good time to develop artistic talents or to work with people in a healing-helping profession. When we help professionally, we are less likely to slip into savior-victim roles in our personal life. Personal peer relationships need to include a mutual give and take.

VESTA

Vesta into 1st House or Aries: Identity Improvement

This can be a time to develop sharper and more discriminating analytical powers. Awareness of flaws may come more naturally as you seek to improve your level of efficiency in life. You are likely to work harder than usual, **if** you are personally motivated, doing work you choose to do. Productive effort is a form of self-expression for you now. Health matters may get your attention, or simply the need to be fully competent. To avoid the danger of too much self-criticism, give yourself credit along with the pressure to do even better. If your work has become routine and lacking in challenge, if it does not provide a sense of accomplishment or let you have some control over what, when or how you do what you do, you may want to change jobs or even shift to a totally new field. Or you might decide to work on a new you.

Vesta into 2nd House or Taurus: Earning Ease

Your work orientation may become a bit more relaxed. Changes in income are also possible, in the amount, the source, or how you spend it. Artistic creations could give you great satisfaction as tangible beauty means much to you now. Your discriminating powers can be channeled toward increasing your sense of comfort, pleasure and ease in life. A sense of accomplishment may be gained through work involving money, beauty, security or pleasure. A possible hazard is the feeling that your job ought to be pleasurable and consequent frustration if it isn't. If survival needs prevent you from changing jobs, look for a pleasurable hobby that can provide a sense of accomplishment.

Vesta into 3rd House or Gemini: Capable Communicating

The intellect and communication could become more of a focus in your work, or relatives might become involved. Productive efforts are likely to include a component of speaking, learning, teaching, gathering information, sharing knowledge, traveling, or otherwise stimulating the mind and tongue. Criticism of or by family members is possible, so try to keep the critical attention on the job rather than directed at people. This combination is especially good for the development of skill in logical analysis. Accomplishing many short tasks can bring satisfaction.

Vesta into 4th House or Cancer: Fixing Family

Home improvement is likely to be a focus. The home itself might be done over, rebuilt, refurbished or otherwise made more efficient and workable. One domestic cycle may end, with another beginning. Emotional matters are likely to be faced through a practical lens, with some danger of criticizing or being criticized by mother, children, or other family members. By blending compassion and realism, you can have the best of both sides of this combination. You also might choose to work in your home or in a related field such as real estate, interior design, catering, or some other service for the public. Tradition and security are likely to be important issues in your life.

Vesta into 5th House or Leo: Creative Competence

The urge to improve and "make over" may be channeled into the arena of love, creativity and fun. This combination of work and play can be good for building a better foundation with children and loved ones, but beware of the critical instincts in the family. Focus on shared accomplishments, keeping the judgments for the details of the work and not each other. Don't inhibit your inner child with the need for all action to be "useful" or with too much fear of mistakes. Let your creative and fun-loving side range free and still get things done.

Vesta into 6th House or Virgo: Efficiency Expert

Focused concentration on efficiency is likely with this combination. Both job and health become arenas where you wish to excel, to do everything just right. You can increase your ability to be organized, to handle details, to analyze and discriminate, but too much nit-picking could create problems. A practical, sensible approach could help you to improve your general habits both in terms of health and in work productivity. Tangible results make you feel better. Concentrate on doing things well which give measurable accomplishments, but don't try to do everything well. Part of life is for fun, once we have done one or two things well.

Vesta into 7th House or Libra: Practical Partnership

With this combination, the eye of judgment turns toward your personal relationships. This can be a period of improving your interactions with others: of being truly practical about what is needed, facing facts and building the most solid foundation possible between you. If overdone, criticism (from you toward a partner or vice versa) could drive you apart. Or either partner could become so involved with work that the relationship is neglected. Work and relationship needs must be balanced with care. The combination is appropriate for tasks that involve teamwork, such as counseling or consulting, arbitration and personnel work.

Vesta into 8th House or Scorpio: Organized Overdrive

Focused concentration is highlighted with this combination. You can develop increased stamina, endurance and organizational skills. Your capacity to be dedicated and persevering can increase, permitting rewarding results in many business settings. Your work could involve joint resources in fields such as investment, insurance, taxes, accounting, etc. Research and medical professions are also appropriate, with the capacity to develop spiritual healing power. Be wary of overusing your critical judgments in intimate relationships. Too much concentration on flaws could create barriers within a partnership. As long as you also note the positive, analysis can be helpful, allowing you to probe the depths of your own feelings and to understand others.

Vesta into 9th House or Sagittarius: Attaining Aspirations

Aspirations may increase with this combination or you may feel an increased urge to bring your goals into some kind of outer manifestation. You are likely to expect a lot from yourself, particularly in terms of career or work responsibilities. Beware of overdrive, demanding more than is reasonable. Take time to smell the flowers. Alternately, you could give up too soon, frustrated because you can never do things fast enough or perfectly enough, or haven't found the really big thing that is worthy of your vision: always wanting a little bit more. Keep high standards, but enjoy the process of moving toward the goals! This combination is excellent for involvement in education, writing, traveling and inspiring the world.

Vesta into 10th House or Capricorn: Realistically Responsible

A sense of accomplishment is especially important to you now. Seek out tasks which give measurable results, since you are likely to gain gratification through tangible attainments. Authority figures may be important. Responsibility could be a major factor in your work, whether you take on additional power or reduce your load. Opposite dangers include working too hard or being afraid to try something lest you not "measure up." You could expect too much of yourself in your achievements. With patience, you will be increasing your ability to be disciplined, concentrated and effective, and this can be a highly productive period increasing your ability to cope with the material world.

Vesta into 11th House or Aquarius: Changing Competence

Your work may become more original, unique, inventive or erratic. If freedom needs are ignored, they could lead to rebellious or unconventional outbreaks on the job. If your sense of individuality is used to enlarge and widen your vocational perspective, creative breakthroughs are possible. Scientific, new-age or unusual interests could be strengthened. Work could bring new friends or you could shift to a job involving social causes and humanitarian issues.

Vesta into 12th House or Pisces: Dedicated Dreams

Idealistic instincts may increasingly affect your work efforts. Positively channeled, you could be drawn to tasks involving healing, helping, or artistic fields. If not put into productive use, your pull toward the infinite could lead to escapist (e.g., drugs, alcohol, fantasy, illness, etc.) behavior. Alternately, you might sacrifice too much to "save" other people. Integration of these two sides of life is achieved by bringing our dreams of infinite love and beauty into material form, helping to make a more ideal world. Seek sources of inspiration that help you to feel connected to a Higher Good.

Nodes of the Moon

The nodes always form an opposition, indicating that you are dealing with issues which fall into opposing camps. People have a tendency to polarize with oppositions: overdoing one side or the other. Or they may bounce from one extreme to the other. Sometimes a person will identify with one end of an opposition and attract other people to express the other side. All oppositions point to natural partnerships. The challenge is to find that middle ground which incorporates the best of both sides.

The nodes highlight an area where there tends to be much activity. You may easily seesaw between the issues and drives in focus from the nodes. The challenge is to find satisfying channels for the restlessness and need for activity which the nodes represent.

Nodes into 1st/7th or Aries/Libra: The Self/Other Seesaw

Your close relationships will focus more deeply on the balance between personal and interpersonal needs. You may swing between assertion and accommodation, or overdo one at the expense of the other. You could feel pulled between action and reaction, between forcefulness and diplomacy. Especially in relationships with potential partners, you are learning to balance what you want and need with the desires and needs of another person.

The years ahead are likely to include more back-and-forth and in-and-out tendencies in terms of relationships. Lots of social activity, or work which involves people, or relating to a number of different people can help satisfy the restlessness of this combination. With integration, you can achieve a comfortable balance between yourself and other people. Partnership, negotiation, compromise and taking turns may become easier as intense feelings and resistance to change diminishes.

The over-all movement of the nodes is retrograde, so they will have progressed from houses 2-8 or Taurus-Scorpio, which also deal with the issue of self versus other, but which focus on shared physical possessions and deep emotions. Also, they usually indicate a strong and enduring will and resistance to external pressure.

Nodes into 2nd/8th or Taurus/Scorpio:
Self-Indulgence versus Self-Mastery Seesaw

Your close relationships will focus more deeply on the balance between indulging the physical appetites and attaining mastery over them. You may feel inclined to overdo in terms of eating, drinking, smoking, spending money, collecting possessions, or other forms of sensual pleasures. You might over control to the point of asceticism— denying perfectly natural and reasonable forms of gratification. You and a partner might nag each other about quitting smoking or drinking, about dieting, about who earns the money and who spends it and what it is spent for, or similar issues. The challenge is to be able to give and to be able to receive in terms of money and pleasure, to have a comfortable balance between self and any potential or actual mate in terms of material gratification.

The years ahead are likely to include more back-and-forth and in-and-out tendencies in terms of finances, possessions and pleasures. Your money supply may fluctuate, or you might experience "feast versus famine" in terms of food, drink, possessions, etc. You and a partner might be susceptible to power struggles around money or sex, until the art of compromise is achieved. With integration, this can be a period of intense sensuality, with a stronger focus on shared pleasures in the material world.

Since the over-all motion of the nodes is retrograde, they will have progressed from the mental areas of life (houses 3-9 or signs Gemini-Sagittarius) to face and deal more with the issues of physical security and pleasures and close peer relationships.

Nodes into 3rd/9th or Gemini/Sagittarius:
The Student/Teacher Seesaw

Your close relationships will focus more deeply on the balance between immediate perceptions and dealing with the people in your vicinity and the demands of everyday living versus debating values, philosophizing and seeking life's ultimate meaning. You may feel torn between a long-range versus a short-range focus, between knowledge for its own sake versus knowledge which contributes to a sense of purpose. This polarity emphasizes the mind, so learning, teaching and sharing information tend to be important. Physical restlessness is also possible; you may have a stronger urge to travel.

The years ahead are likely to include more back-and-forth and in-and-out tendencies in terms of thinking, speaking and disseminating knowledge. You may study a variety of topics, have erratic schooling, pick up and drop many interests, travel periodically, etc. You are apt to be more drawn toward variety and mental stimulation in your close associations. You need people who will relate to your intellectual level. This can be a time of great learning, and a time when you share your understanding and inspiration with others as well.

Since the over-all motion of the nodes is retrograde, they will have progressed out of houses 4-10 or signs Cancer-Capricorn, shifting their major focus from family-career roles to more mental activity.

Nodes into 4th/10th or Cancer/Capricorn: The Dependency/Dominance Seesaw

Your close relationships will focus more deeply on the balance between softness, gentleness and leaning on others versus strength, control and taking charge. You may feel torn between the roles of the compassionate "mother" figure versus the disciplinarian "father" figure. You will be working on integrating caring and competence, nurturing and a focus on performance, unconditional versus "tough" love.

The years ahead are likely to include more back-and-forth and in-and-out tendencies in terms of home versus work, or career versus family. You may feel that one takes you away from the other. You could feel torn between the time and energy demands of a domestic life versus professional accomplishments. You may deal more with your own parents, or with your role as a parent. You are likely to face issues of safety, stability and security—and where you seek them in life. With integration, this can be a time when you make a significant contribution both in the outer world (vocationally) and in the "private" world of your home and family. You can blend warmth and capability, emotions and effectiveness.

Since the over-all motion of the nodes is retrograde, the nodes will have progressed out of houses 5-11 or signs Leo-Aquarius, shifting their major emphasis from creativity and outer-directed expressions to more concern with stability, security, and responsibility.

Nodes into 5th/11th or Leo/Aquarius: The Head/Heart Seesaw

Your close relationships will focus more deeply on the balance between passions (intensity, desire for love) and the intellect. You may feel torn between drama and detachment. Your heart might seem at war with your head (and vice versa). You are also striving to integrate freedom needs (desire for independence and space to be your unique self) with closeness needs (desire for attachment, for close, caring commitments with other people). If you overdo either side, your loved ones are apt to overdo the opposite. You clutch; they run (or vice versa). The challenge is to be able to love and care for others, while respecting their individuality and making sure your uniqueness has room to flourish as well.

The years ahead are likely to include more back-and-forth and in-and-out tendencies in terms of love relationships. This might be the question of whether or not to have children, or to commit to a love relationship. It might be tension between time and energy demands of loved ones versus the time and energy demands of friends and groups and causes in the outside world. With integration, this can be a time when the fervor of your feelings backs up your intellectual insights and vice versa. It can be a period of blending freedom and closeness, commitment and individuality.

Since the over-all motion of the nodes is retrograde, the nodes will have progressed out of houses 6-12 or signs Virgo-Pisces, shifting the major focus from trying to make peace between boundless ideals and coping with the physical world to increasing creative activities of heart and mind.

Nodes into 6th/12th or Virgo/Pisces: The Real/Ideal Seesaw

Your close relationships will focus more deeply on the balance between dreams, imagination, fantasy, hopes, wishes, and rose-colored glasses versus pragmatism, details, the nitty-gritty, necessities and duties of daily life. You may feel torn between imagination and "real life." If balance is lacking between your romantic and practical sides, you might fall into "savior/victim" relationships or associations. (One person is trying to create the ideal, "perfect" environment for the other person. The other is running away from reality through drugs, alcohol, fantasy or some form of not facing the facts.) Rescuing and enabling destructive behavior is not a solution in human relationships. Both people have to learn to be practical enough to deal with problems, and idealistic enough to forgive small foibles and shortcomings. Analysis and discrimination may be needed to clarify subconscious ideals and to break them into "bite-sized" goals which can be accomplished.

The years ahead are likely to include more back-and-forth or in-and-out in terms of work, relationships, or any area where you are striving to make dreams real. With integration, this polarity can point to a successful artist or craftsperson, or a skilled healer and helper. The challenge is to share the vision (and the effort/discipline) with close associates—no one expecting another person to give them "heaven on earth." Partners who **both** contribute imagination and seeing the highest potential as well as hard work have a shot at the best of all possible blends.

Since the over-all motion of the nodes is retrograde, the nodes will have progressed out of houses 1-7 or signs Aries-Libra, shifting from the freedom-closeness dilemma with its focus on personal needs versus sustained peer relationships to looking for practical ways to bring transpersonal ideals into the physical world.

Angles Changing House or Sign

The East/West axis and the Antivertex/Vertex axis are similar in meaning to the Ascendant-Descendant axis. The East Point and Antivertex are like auxiliary Ascendants and all are like Mars, signifying what we do naturally when we are just "being ourselves in action." The opposite ends of the axes, the West Point and the Vertex, are like auxiliary Descendants, describing parts of ourselves which we might acknowledge but also might project and discover through interactions with other people.

The progressed MC and East Point move around one degree a year in secondary progressions, but the progressed Ascendant and Antivertex can be much faster or slower, partly depending on their sign and partly on the latitude of birth of the person. Any of the progressing angles can, of course, move into any zodiacal sign, depending on their birth positions. The size of the houses, the speed of the angles, and the longevity of the person will obviously limit how many houses the angles will manage to reach. For advanced astrologers who are using local houses calculated for a residence other than the birth place, the progressing local angles can be in any house. A move east produces angles in later signs than the birth ones, while a move west produces earlier signs on the angles.

Ascendant/Descendant (or East Point/West Point or Antivertex/Vertex) into 1st/7th or Aries/Libra: Assertion versus Accommodation

You are moving into a period of dealing more with the self-other polarity. Issues of assertion versus accommodation will arise between you and other people. You may find yourself pushing too hard sometimes, and other times letting yourself be walked on in relationships. The challenge is to find a middle ground of being true to yourself—neither taking advantage nor being taken advantage of in relationships. You may feel like changing your personal appearance, or making shifts in your partnerships, personal or work-related. Other people may be acting as role models, helping you in the adventure of self-discovery.

Ascendant/Descendant (or East Point/West Point or Antivertex/Vertex) into 2nd/8th or Taurus/Scorpio: Indulgence versus Control

You are moving into a period of confrontation with the self-indulgence versus self-mastery polarity or self-centered versus shared pleasures. This could express as an increased focus on finances, especially self-earned money versus money from others or spending versus saving. Other arenas could include drinking versus abstaining, smoking versus not smoking and overeating versus dieting. You may engage in power struggles with a mate over these issues, until able to reach an inner balance. Changes in income are likely; what you make or how you handle it or what comes to you from others or is shared with others. Sometimes this pattern marks a time for letting go. The key challenge is to appreciate and enjoy the material world without being ruled by it, to be able to give, receive, and share pleasures and possessions.

Ascendant/Descendant (or East Point/West Point or Antivertex/Vertex) into 3rd/9th or Gemini/Sagittarius: Curiosity versus Philosophy

You are moving into a period of trying to integrate short-range goals with long-range dreams and visions. You may swing from immediate needs and demands (especially in terms of relatives and people nearby) to concern over future plans. Much restlessness is likely and travel is quite possible. Your mind will be constantly active, so classes, seminars, teaching, writing, reading and studying are all possible. Try not to scatter too much, while gaining the necessary information for vital decisions. If you have reached the stage in life when the pressure to earn a living is eased, you can fully enjoy the freedom to follow your curiosity wherever it leads.

Ascendant/Descendant (or East Point/West Point or Antivertex/Vertex) into 4th/10th or Cancer/Capricorn: Home versus Career

You are moving into a period of trying to blend pragmatism with compassion. This could be felt as a pull between your contribution to society and your domestic and home demands. It might be felt as the tension between empathy, sympathy and caring warmth versus practicality, common sense and the bottom line. It is possible that you might express one of these polarities more, while a partner lives out the other. The goal is a comfortable blend—a combination which serves both of your best interests. You may be changing your work, status, or residence. If you have completed your major obligations in the world, you may be ready to spend more time curled up in the nest, and letting the world come to you.

Ascendant/Descendant (or East Point/West Point or Antivertex/Vertex) into 5th/11th or Leo/Aquarius: Primacy versus Equality

You are moving into a period of trying to balance the emotions and the intellect. You may feel a push/pull between goals of the head and goals of the heart. Passion may vie with detachment, closeness with freedom, power with equalitarian principles. It is possible that you could express one side of this polarity, while a partner or loved one lives out the other. Learning to compromise and combine the two is essential, for you and for lovers, children and friends. The challenge is to love with an open hand, to use logic with heartfelt sincerity.

Ascendant/Descendant (or East Point/West Point or Antivertex/Vertex) into 6th/12th or Virgo/Pisces: Pragmatism versus Idealism

You are moving into a period of learning to compromise between your ideals or visions of perfection and your sense of material reality and necessity in life. Changes in your job or in health habits are possible. You may swing from over idealism to too much realism and back again—or live out one end while a partner expresses the other. Savior, martyr, or victim roles could suck you in until you learn to balance practicality with vision. You need the yearning for something more, along with the wisdom of knowing that few things in life are perfect, plus the satisfaction of doing what you can to bring your vision into the world.

MC/IC into 1st/7th or Aries/Libra:
Relationships at Home and at Work
You are moving into a period of potential shifts in your life structure. You are likely to examine your sense of identity, your domestic needs and desires for emotional closeness, your partnership and your career. You may feel the desire to alter any or all of these. Your status or place in the world could change. Because life is complicated and you are a multifaceted person, you want some things which seem contradictory. The challenge is to get as much as you can, in a reasonable balance.

MC/IC into 2nd/8th or Taurus/Scorpio:
Finances at Home and at Work
You are moving into a period of potential shifts in your financial structure. You may lose or gain a source of income or change your handling of resources. Money matters involving other people could affect the situation. Your career and home needs may test your balance between self-indulgence and self-control in terms of handling pleasures, possessions and finances. Flipping from one extreme to the other (spending versus saving, earning it yourself versus depending on someone else) is likely to be uncomfortable. Find a way to do a bit of each side. This is a good time to develop artistic skills or just to learn how to relax and be comfortable.

MC/IC into 3rd/9th or Gemini/Sagittarius:
Curiosity about Home and Work
You are moving into a period of thinking and wondering about your place in your nearby world, and in the wider cosmos. You may spend a lot of time talking, discussing, studying, learning or sharing information about the meaning of life. Your goals for your place in society and your relationship to family members may shift. This is a time for opening new doors, for seeing alternate vistas, for investigating other ideas in terms of your sense of purpose in life. Travel is possible, including extended periods in other countries, or you may find your greatest satisfaction in mental excursions.

MC/IC into 4th/10th or Cancer/Capricorn:
Home and Work in Opposition
You are moving into a period of striving to balance outer world vocational drives with inner world emotional needs. Domestic demands may seem at odds with career responsibilities. Cold-hearted realism may fly in the face of warm-hearted compassion. You and a partner may seem on opposite sides of this polarity, or swinging from one to the other. Life is calling for a blend of both practicality and empathy, of dependency and dominance, of control and sensitivity. Responsibility may be a major issue, whether you are taking on more or relinquishing some. There may be changes in your relationship to parents or other authority figures, or changes of residence or of people living there.

Circumstances now are keys to your past handling of the "rules of the game" and can offer guidance for future understanding of what is possible and what is necessary to cope with the material world.

MC/IC into 5th/11th or Leo/Aquarius:
Changes at Home and at Work

You are moving into a period of questioning your standards in terms of work and domestic life. You may seek a sense of greater freedom, flexibility, openness, originality or newness in your job or at home. You need a sense of passionate excitement and aliveness about what you do. Changes are likely. The old ways have less appeal. If carried too far, shocking, rebellious or erratic acts are possible. If expressed moderately, you will enlarge your perspectives and open your life. If you have learned what is possible and what is necessary, and have developed a reasonable internalized conscience, you no longer need outside rules or authority figures to keep you in line.

MC/IC into 6th/12th or Virgo/Pisces:
Perfection at Home and at Work

You are moving into a period of questioning what you are doing with your life and where you want to be going. You are likely to be examining your dreams and feelings and may be disappointed by areas that do not measure up to what you had hoped. Disillusionment with either work or home matters is possible. Beware of demanding more than is reasonable from yourself or from the people you love. This is a time to reaffirm your hopes, to regain a sense of purpose for your life, to refresh your dedication. If you have fulfilled your obligations to society and family, you may be ready to pursue previously neglected artistic talents or to spend more time in contemplation, opening to and experiencing your connection to the Infinite.

Planets Changing Direction

The two Lights (the Sun and Moon) do not have retrograde motion. All the other planets (and asteroids) can be in direct (forward) or retrograde ("backward") motion. (Of course, this is an optical illusion—not physically true. The appearance is caused by a faster planet passing earth or earth passing a slower one.) When planets change apparent direction (from direct to retrograde or from retrograde to direct), they point to a shift in the life. A new chapter is begun in terms of that planet. Sometimes it is very obvious, as with Lyndon Baines Johnson, who had four planets change direction in his life: when he married, when he was first elected to Congress, when he was nominated as Vice President with John F. Kennedy, and, three years later, when Johnson became President following Kennedy's assassination.

Do **not** assume that a planet turning retrograde in progressions will be more inhibited or blocked, nor that a planet turning direct will express more in the outer world. Any change of direction suggests a new direction in the life—but a switch to retrograde motion is not an automatic inhibition. For example, when one woman's Mercury turned direct at age 9 (it had been retrograde at birth), she started doing very poorly in school. She had been a good student previously. The stress came from family pressures. As an adult, she became a professional writer.

The new direction may relate to the basic nature of the planet involved (e.g., Mercury for mental affairs, Venus for love, pleasure, and material resources; Mars for assertion, sports, etc.) or it may follow the rulership of that planet which is changing direction. Some people, for example, have gotten married when the ruler of their 7th house (partnership) or of their 10th house (status) changed direction.

Retrograde planets may mark a potential for increased creativity or uniqueness as the individual looks inside for ways to handle that part of life.

Make note of the years in which progressed planets change direction and consider the possibility of a new chapter in terms of that planet's symbolism and/or the houses that planet rules.

CHAPTER FOUR

PROGRESSED NEW AND FULL MOONS

A progressed New Moon—progressed Moon conjunct progressed Sun—marks the beginning of a new 30 year cycle. An individual's first progressed New Moon can occur at any time up to about age 30, depending on the initial distance between the Sun and Moon in the natal chart. (Someone born just after a New Moon would not have his/her first New Moon until about age 30. Someone born just before a New Moon could have their first New Moon immediately after birth.) After the first New Moon, the progressed Moon moves through the 12 signs in about 28 years while the progressed Sun moves almost one sign. It takes the progressed Moon about two more years to catch up with the progressed Sun to form the progressed New Moon. Each successive New Moon occurs one sign later and close to the same degree as the preceding one.

For most people, the progressed New Moon marks a new beginning, with the areas in the life where the changes occur signaled by the house and sign of the progressed Sun-Moon, often with additional connections to the houses and signs of the natal Sun and Moon, as well as with the houses they rule in the natal chart. Aspects to other natal and progressed planets are also keys to the involvement of other areas of the life. In horoscopes with many concurrent progressed aspects, especially where natal and/or progressed angles are also aspected, the New Moon period may mark a truly major turning point in the life.

Both the last years of the old cycle and the initial years of the new one are often experienced as a time of flux and uncertainty. Old doors are being closed, loose ends tied up, habits shifting, while new ideas, people and activities are explored. Sometimes there is a specific event during the approximately two months period when the progressed Moon is actually conjunct the progressed Sun, and it offers a key to the central issue or activity of the new cycle. Sometimes it is only after the new cycle is well underway that one can look back and recognize the focus of the new cycle. In general, the more aspects involving chart angles, cardinal houses or signs, and fire factors, the more the individual is likely to make outer, visible changes in the life. When the readiness for change is conscious, the person chooses to change and initiates the action. When the readiness for change is largely subconscious, people experience events as outside of personal control, happening to them.

Progressed New Moon
through the Signs and Houses

A progressed New Moon in the sign of Aries or in the 1st house signals new personal action. Aries and the 1st house symbolize personal identity, self-will in action, "doing one's thing." There is often a need for physical activity to express the fire element. Fire wants new experiences, freedom to pursue personal desires, and variety in the life. This is an appropriate year for you to learn a new sport or to take more time for one you have wanted to cultivate further. It is a year in which to focus on the issue of self-confidence and independence, exploring ways in which you can be your unique self. You are likely to be dealing with questions of independence versus dependence. While life is always interdependent, this New Moon usually marks a move toward more self-reliance. We may gain increased courage through almost any kind of action as long as we choose to do it and do it personally. Sports build physical strength and endurance, so they contribute to our self-confidence. A job may achieve the same result. Letting go of a relationship and learning to function independently is sometimes the route we take to finding and being ourselves. For people who have been relatively dependent, the years ahead invite you to discover your own power.

On the other side of the coin are the people who have been excessively independent. These New Moon people may be starting new ventures which call for relinquishing some degree of separateness. They will be entering rather than leaving personal relationships, or learning to work cooperatively without losing their sense of individuality. Astrology shows us the principles underlying our lives, but the details we manifest in our lives depend on how we handle those principles. Life is always a juggling act, trying to make room for all of our basic desires. Whether we are learning how to be more self-reliant or less self-reliant, the Aries or 1st house New Moon tells us that it is time to look at our capacity to be ourselves, to find ways to express our uniqueness without denying the same right to others, and to experience the excitement and power of personal action.

A New Moon in Taurus or in the 2nd house shows a central focus in your new cycle will deal with pleasure in the physical world. Depending on your own definition of pleasure, you may choose to make money, spend money, collect possessions, indulge the appetites, or create beauty. Of course, you may do all of the above. They are not mutually exclusive. And there are many ways to do each of them. For people who are already highly involved in one or more of these activities, the New Moon cycle may mark a shift to a different one of the options or just to different ways of expressing the primary one. It is possible to change the way money is made or the way it is handled, the types of activities chosen for the pursuit of pleasure, or the forms of artistic endeavor. Individuals who have been excessively focused on one channel for their pleasure may widen their options in the New Moon period and discover additional ways to enjoy life. There really are inexpensive or free ways to feel good—smelling the flowers, listening to bird songs, and watching the sunset. Individuals who have been too busy "doing" to enjoy "being" may discover the "laid-back" potential of Taurus and learn how to relax.

On the other side of the coin, individuals who have been "doing their own thing" in less than practical ways may be called by the earth New Moon to focus on earning a living. Learning to handle material resources may be necessary, or learning to diversify one's pleasures to avoid overindulgence in one or a few. The horoscope shows us the issue, but our own past choices determine whether we need to do more or less or something different in our handling of that part of life. If we have been handling that area of life successfully, the New Moon offers us a chance to make a new start on a higher level of the spiral, to carry farther something we have already learned to handle. Remember that Taurus and the 2nd house deal with the tangible, earth world and with personal pleasures, so enjoy the cycle with one foot solidly on the ground.

A New Moon in Gemini or the 3rd house, starts a new cycle focused on the conscious reasoning mind and peer relationships with people in your vicinity (as contrasted with the Aquarian wide ranging tendency). This New Moon connects to insatiable curiosity along with the desire to share the ideas with others. Whether we express the restless mind through learning, teaching, writing, or traveling, your coming years are likely to emphasize communication in some form. Hand dexterity is another Gemini potential, so you may want to develop or expand skills with your hands during this period. Gemini pursuits can range from calligraphy (the art of fine handwriting), to juggling, to slight of hand magic tricks, to debating. Flexibility of mind and body are valuable assets, so yoga lessons or a course of study in a new area might be helpful. Alternately, you might want to begin or expand your activity as a teacher, become involved in sales, or increase your travel.

The "people" side of this New Moon includes brothers and sisters, aunts, uncles, cousins and neighbors; relatives other than parents or grandparents, and people who live nearby. Of course, with modern transportation, a fair-sized city may qualify to be called a neighborhood. Air, the element of Gemini and the 3rd house, symbolizes the conscious aspect of the mind, including the capacity to be a spectator; to look at life objectively in a detached way, to understand it and to accept it. Air marks the gift of "taking things lightly." Sometimes, this New Moon signals a time to develop more of that skill; to learn when to shrug the shoulders, say "so what," and let someone else have a turn. Air can see both the good and the bad, understand, and accept, where fire and earth mark the drive to take physical action. Of course, if we overdo any part of life, we are less effective. Too much emphasis on Gemini or the 3rd house may tempt us to remain in the head and superficial, the jack of all trades and master of none. We can't have too much intelligence, but we do need to leaven it with empathy, warmth and practical action.

A New Moon in Cancer or in the 4th house suggests a focus on home and family for your new cycle. This period calls for attention to domesticity, emotional security needs, roots. Depending on your present stage in life, you may be leaving your original family to form an adult household, or finishing child-rearing and looking for a new nurturing role, or entering a new phase of care taking. Home and relationship changes may be as minor as a deepened interest in tracing your heredity or a role in planning family reunions. Dependency issues may be important. Life is interdependent and we need to be able to both give and receive. The element involved is water, symbolizing the subconscious aspect of the mind. Water cycles are often times for deepening psychic ability, becoming aware of the needs and feelings of others as well as tuning in to our own subconscious hungers. If you have unfinished business with close relationships such as unforgiven parents or siblings or children, it is important to deal with those feelings, to forgive and release. Dreams may offer valuable clues to buried feelings. Imagine yourself "being" the different parts of your dreams, people, animals, plants, buildings, and let the associated feelings tell you the meanings of the dreams. The subconscious is a storehouse of wisdom if we can tap it and make it a partner of the conscious aspect of the mind. But also balance the inner attention with an emotional support system which can include family, close friends, and pets. Emotional ties are a central theme for this New Moon.

A New Moon in Leo or in the 5th house calls for a new cycle that is creative, dramatic and exciting. This cycle marks our drive to do more than we have done before; to pour out our unique, creative energy, and to be recognized for it. We may love and be loved, may procreate children (extensions of ourselves into the world), may be the teacher in front of the class, the actress on stage, or the salesman-promoter. Whichever we choose to do, we need a response from our audience; hopefully, a positive one. However, if we are too vulnerable in our need for attention and approval, an emphasis on Leo or the 5th house may be a call to learn how to feel good about ourselves without that reassurance from others. At least some of our self-esteem should be based on what we do regardless of the response of others.

A fire focus, which is present here, is usually experienced as an urge to start something really new, which reinforces the natural tendency of a New Moon. Look for ways to enlarge your life. Find outlets for emotional expression. A course in public speaking or drama or dancing lessons might be helpful. The full flowering of Leo and the 5th house involves passion and joy, but we each find our own forms to manifest that intensity. Mixing in earth will call for creativity that produces tangible results. Mixing in air sharpens the sense of humor and love of fun. Mixing in water increases the emotional intensity and demands an outlet so the water is not allowed to inhibit the fire. It is time for you to shine.

A New Moon in Virgo or the 6th house describes a new cycle that highlights efficient functioning, whether in your job or your health or both. The keynote of Virgo and the 6th house is the ability to do something worth doing and to do it well. Like the other drives associated with the earth element, Virgo is basically practical, wanting tangible results. Both the 6th and 10th houses are inclined toward the puritan virtues of hard work, being responsible, conscientious, thorough, organized, and finishing tasks. Individuals with an emphasis on Virgo or the 6th house who like their work are usually very effective and very successful. They do run the risk of becoming so involved in the work that they neglect other parts of life such as play and personal relationships. Individuals who do not like their work may be less effective, may change jobs often looking for more fulfillment, or may get sick as a way out of the frustration. Illness is produced at the subconscious level and is less likely if people remain conscious of their feelings, do what they can to change the situation, and then release the problem for the moment until they are able to take further action.

During this new cycle, it is important for you to do something that gives you a sense of accomplishment. The action need not involve money. It could be a hobby that develops your skill and produces useful results. It could be humanitarian service for social causes. Additional studies or apprentice training might be helpful to increase your competence. Where survival demands that one stay with unfulfilling work, look for a side interest to bring the needed sense of accomplishment. Gaining information or learning techniques that enhance health can be rewarding, e.g., physiotherapy, nutrition, acupressure, exercise. Normally, there is a strong drive toward some type of healing and helping service when Virgo or the 6th house is emphasized in the horoscope, and finding one's niche can be deeply satisfying.

A New Moon in Libra or in the 7th house signifies the importance of close, peer relationships in your new cycle. Libra and the 7th house cover a variety of ongoing, systematic equalitarian relationships, including marriage, counseling associations, fellow workers who really work together, not just side by side, and even good friendships where there is regular interaction like a weekly game of bridge or bowling. Also, the relationships may be either cooperative or competitive, but in keeping with a Venus-ruled, air side of life, they should be open and reasonably pleasant. Air symbolizes the ability to look at both sides of a situation, to understand it, talk about it and accept it. Air is basically a spectator and commentator. But Venus wants pleasure, so Libra is not as impersonal as Gemini and Aquarius, and Libra relationships are more systematic, less intermittent or casual.

Your new cycle points to changes in your attitudes or actions in this area of peer relationships. It is important for you to have people in your life with whom you can share. You may want to work to improve already existing relationships or you may need to form new ones. If you have a strong Venus, Libra, seventh house and/or Pluto, Scorpio, eighth house in your natal chart, the new cycle may mark your opportunity to re-evaluate the importance of other people in your life. Sometimes our need for other people can lead to too much dependency on the approval of others for a sense of self-worth, and we have to increase our emotional independence. For other people, the challenge involves learning to compromise, learning to put themselves in the place of others, learning to maintain true fair play. The horoscope shows the issue, a focus on balance through cooperation and competition. The personal choices determine the details in the life.

Since Venus and its signs and houses are also keys to aesthetic pleasure, another potential outlet for this New Moon cycle would be through some kind of artistic expression. Libra and the 7th house are especially associated with the visual arts such as photography, graphic design, architecture, etc. If you have wanted to try your hand in one of the arts, by all means go ahead. Or if you are already involved, you may want to try new media, or you may be ready to go professional or teach. A Venus-ruled cycle should bring pleasure to you and to others.

A New Moon in Scorpio or in the 8th house symbolizes a new cycle that is likely to involve some form of joint resources and pleasures or a concern with self-knowledge and self-mastery. Scorpio and the 8th house are the polar partners of Taurus and the 2nd house, so this cycle calls us to move from self-indulgence to self-mastery, or from personal possessions and pleasures to shared possessions and pleasures. Like all water sides of life, Scorpio and the 8th house symbolize the subconscious aspect of mind. When emphasized in the chart, we are drawn to probe inside ourselves and others, to search below the surface, whether we do this through psychotherapy, through self-analysis, or through the mirror of a mate. It is also partly respect for the rights of others that helps us learn to control only ourselves, not others. This side of life can be a real challenge, for the feelings run deep, the will is strong, the urge is to go to the end, wherever that takes us, and we have to learn when to stop, when is enough, how to let go. Learning how to give, how to receive, and how to share the physical world, really deep emotions, and power with a mate is often the theme of a Scorpio cycle.

Alternately, depending on your own past interests and actions, your new cycle could attract you into a study of the mind, or of the past (history, genealogy, archaeology), or into research. Or you might become more involved in the area of joint resources (banking, investment, bookkeeping, accounting, taxes, etc.). Other related areas would include inheritance and royalties; anything coming from others or from past efforts rather than current ones, and anything owed to or shared with others. Increased psychic ability often develops during periods with a water emphasis. At the subconscious level, we are all connected; there are no barriers. Such openness can also mean feelings of increased vulnerability. It is important to find ways to express the deep emotions and to reassure ourselves of our own power. We should have a place to cooperate (to share power), a place to compete (winning some and losing some), and a place to help others. The ultimate goal of this New Moon is to become the adept.

A New Moon in Sagittarius or in the 9th house brings a new cycle which involves a search for something higher. Depending on your present stage in life, you may want to pursue higher education, you may deepen or widen your faith, or you may re-evaluate your value hierarchy and goals. You may be drawn to other countries in the search for answers to the ancient questions about the meaning of life. If you feel you have already found helpful answers, you may want to share them with others through teaching or writing. As with all of the fire sides of life, there is apt to be an inner restlessness that demands new action. Though Sagittarius and the 9th house are highly mental in contrast to the other fire signs (Aries and Leo), they still need physical action for full expression, so sports, outdoor activity, involvement with animals, etc. are healthy outlets.

A desire for freedom is also normal with an emphasis on Sagittarius or the 9th house. We need the freedom to pursue our search for the Absolute, but it is important to also keep some time and energy for personal relationships and for the practical demands of survival in a physical world. All twelve of the basic drives of astrology are part of our nature, and to ignore any of them is to invite trouble. Sometimes, an emphasis on Sagittarius or the 9th house can lead to overconfidence which produces impulsive and/or excessive action. But it is important to do something to move toward our personal vision of a better world even if we can't expect to make it in one flying leap. It is also important to enjoy the journey toward the ideal rather than waiting until we get there to be happy. Fortunately, a Sagittarian cycle is normally accompanied by increased faith, optimism, and a sense of humor. If we do the best we can, day by day, a Higher Power will handle the rest.

A New Moon in Capricorn or in the 10th house initiates a new cycle centered on one's role in society, whether in a career, as a partner in marriage, as a parent, etc. This cycle deals with the "rules of the game" and the consequences of our previous handling of the rules; natural law, cultural regulations, authority figures who enforce the law, and the conscience, our inner law. A Capricorn (or 10th house) New Moon often signals a move into a position of power and responsibility. The opposite is possible, though less common. If we have already fulfilled our duties, the New Moon may mark the time we relinquish the Atlas role, the attempt to carry the world. However, since this earthy focus calls for productive action, if you are retiring from a previous role, it will be important for you to find a new outlet to provide a sense of accomplishment and power.

Capricorn and the 10th house are normally keys to a father-figure as well as to our capacity to be a father, that is, to play the role of a conditional love parent who reminds the child that actions bring consequences. If you hold ambivalent feelings about your early father-figure, this cycle is the time to work out those feelings, to accept the humanness and limitations of authority figures and to forgive and release any hurts. The 10th house and Capricorn teach us by consequences. We learn what we can do, what we can't do, and what we have to do to survive in this world. Once we have internalized the conscience and voluntarily accepted the necessary limits, we can handle personal power and the power of others. As we learn to work productively and to handle legitimate responsibility (our share of the power), we are less likely to be caught in power struggles. When we use power wisely, we avoid projecting our power into others, which attracts people who abuse power. And by voluntarily doing our share, the universe is not obliged to coerce us into making a contribution to life. But always remember that we are not asked to be Atlas, to carry the world. We are required to do our share, not too much or too little. A balanced approach to duty, responsibility, authority and accomplishment allows others to also do their share.

A New Moon in Aquarius or in the 11th house begins a new cycle which could involve a dramatic breaking of new ground in your life. The primary urge of this cycle is to get out of the rut and to resist any kind of limitations. The years ahead may bring new knowledge, new friends, new humanitarian causes, new experiences. But since all twelve of astrology's basic drives are part of life, it is important to balance the desire for freedom and change with some attention to the need for stability and security. Life should be big enough for both family and friends; for some tradition and some innovation.

For most people, an emphasis on Aquarius or the 11th house is associated with deliberate, consciously chosen and produced changes in the life. But even though the eleventh house and Aquarius are air, which symbolizes the conscious aspect of the mind, in charts with little additional air, the earth and water need for security may block the Aquarian daring. In such cases, the individual may remain unaware of the inner desire for change and the subconscious may lead the person into the change situations. When we stay conscious of the urge to escape the mundane, we are less likely to have such experiences in which things "happen to us" to jolt us out of our ruts. Such experiences can range from natural disasters like earthquakes to getting fired from a job, to having a spouse walk out. Moderate, voluntary, practical changes may forestall major life disruptions. Compromise is usually the wisest course. We can make new friends and gain new knowledge or take up new hobbies without pulling up our roots (the water side of our nature) or abandoning the skills which enable us to cope with the material world (the earth side of our nature). This is a time to increase your options, to look at wider possibilities.

A New Moon in Pisces or in the 12th house invites a new cycle featuring increased artistic or spiritual expression. Pisces and the 12th house mark the completion of our journey through life, with the mystic's realization of oneness with the whole. Faith in a Higher Power is vitally important, and a focus on Pisces or the 12th house is often manifested through some form of healing, helping service in the world. But the great, inspirational artists also tend to have a strong Neptune or twelfth house or Pisces. It is our personal choice whether we try to bring our ideals into the world through the creation of beauty in any of many forms, or whether we offer loving service to heal others. Unfortunately, traditional astrology tends to emphasize the victim potential of this sign and house; the individuals who have a beautiful dream (like the artists and saviors) but who are failing to take effective action to bring the dream into the world. The victims may be running away from the world through drugs or alcohol or illness or emotional shut-down, or through milder escapism such as excessive sleep, daydreams, romantic fiction and TV. But we have the option of shifting from victim to artist or savior, hopefully remembering to stop the savior role short of being a martyr.

The years ahead can be deeply rewarding if you develop your artistic skills in any field of your choice, and at the same time, you work to deepen your faith in a Higher Power. We have to do our share toward making a more ideal world and then let go and trust that God will do the rest. We can't do it all and God won't do it all. We can increase our faith by reading inspirational literature, by associating with others who have faith, by meditation and prayer. Music helps some people open to the mystical experience of oneness. Being close to nature (water, trees, mountains etc.) helps others. Some people find the profound meaningful order of the cosmos through astrology and are helped to achieve inner peace and trust. If you have already found that faith, this cycle can be used to share it with the world.

Current Progressed Full Moons by Sign and House and Related to Preceding New Moons

A progressed Full Moon occurs when the progressed Moon forms an opposition to the progressed Sun. The aspect occurs about midway through the 30-year progressed lunar cycle, about 15 years after the previous New Moon. When the

New Moon has marked a successful beginning, the period following the Full Moon is often a peak time for the activities of the cycle. Of course, the nature of the activities are connected to the signs and houses involved, including both the progressed and the natal positions of the Sun and Moon. If the major focus of the New Moon has not worked out, the Full Moon may mark an end to the effort and a decision to move in a different direction.

Oppositions always highlight the sign and house polarities of the progressed planets or angles. The personality system of astrology is composed of six polarities: Aries/Libra (first house/seventh house), Taurus/Scorpio (second house/eighth house), etc. Each of these polarities can be thought of as a natural partnership. The ends represent opposing extremes in a continuum. Humans experience increasing problems if one end of a polarity is carried to excess and not balanced by some attention to the other end. It is important to have ways to express all twelve sides of ourselves. Progressed aspects indicate the parts of life which call for extra attention during the period they are in effect. Normally, the progressed aspects of the Moon only last about two months. But since the aspects of progressed Moon to progressed Sun are like turning points in a long cycle, they carry more significance than most progressed Moon aspects.

The following paragraphs discuss each Full Moon combination—including the themes and issues highlighted based on the previous New Moon.

Individuals with a progressed Full Moon in Aries/Libra or in the 1st house/ 7th house will be dealing with the issue of personal will in action (just doing what you please) versus the need to compromise to maintain lasting personal relationships. Try to analyze your life to make sure that you are meeting your own needs to be self-reliant, self-confident, self-expressive without denying the rights of your close associates to also be themselves. Unless we are prepared to be hermits, life requires compromise, but excessive self-denial in order to please or appease others can be very self-destructive.

At this time, you may change your personal actions, try out new ventures, test your personal power or courage or independence in new ways. Or you may change your handling of partners, clients, or the public. Depending on your stage of life, you may want to widen your contacts and look for new opportunities with other people. Or you may be looking for more time for neglected hobbies and personal interests.

If your previous New Moon was in Aries or the 1st house, there is a little extra emphasis on learning to "be yourself in action" without overdoing the self-will.

If your previous New Moon was in Libra or the 7th house, there is a little extra emphasis on learning to live cooperatively without losing yourself in the partnership.

Your present opportunities and challenges are somewhat more complex if **your previous New Moon was in Pisces or the 12th house**, bringing in a strong focus on faith and ideals. The present effort to balance personal desires and shared action should include an awareness of the role of beliefs, values, and expectations in your life. It is important to direct one's faith to a Higher Power and not to expect too much of oneself or of mates. Since your progressed Sun has moved out of Pisces into Aries (or out of the 12th and into the 1st house), personal growth can come through personal action but it is important to stay conscious of one's humanness.

Your present opportunities and challenges are also somewhat more complex if **your previous New Moon was in Virgo or in the 6th house**, bringing in a strong focus on competence in your job and/or your health. Since your progressed Sun has moved out of Virgo into Libra (or out of the 6th and into the 7th house), you can enhance your personal growth though interactions with others, including fellow-workers. As you seek to balance personal desires with the rights of others, try to stay practical and productive, keeping an analytical eye on your work but avoiding excessive criticism of yourself or of other people in your life.

When your Full Moon is in Taurus/Scorpio or in the 2nd house/8th house, you are called to integrate your personal money, possessions and pleasures with the pleasures, possessions and power of others. Alternately, your issue might involve the need for moderation in handling the physical appetites, to avoid the extremes of excessive self-indulgence or self-denial. Life is here for our pleasure, but Scorpio (and the 8th house) also call for self-mastery and for sharing the physical world and power with others.

Financial changes could involve the area of earning or spending or saving, and they could include individual action or may require discussions with partners and joint decisions. You may expand or change your sources of personal pleasure, focus more on artistic hobbies, or become more involved with collecting for fun or for profit. Or shared pleasures and possessions may become more important and may require decisions. The eighth side of life can involve anything coming to us from others or from past efforts, and/or anything we owe to or share with others. So current issues could include an inheritance, return on investments, pensions, debts, taxes, etc. Cooperation usually works better, but conflict and litigation are possible. It is important to be clear about your own rights but also to be fair about the rights of others.

If your previous New Moon was in Taurus or in the 2nd house, there is a little extra emphasis on your ability to earn a living, handle personal finances and possessions, and/or appetites, but it important to do this without cutting yourself off from shared pleasures.

If your previous New Moon was in Scorpio or in the 8th house, you may need to pay extra attention to shared possessions, pleasures and power or to expanding your self-awareness and self-mastery. Frequently, an important Scorpio (or 8th house) lesson involves learning when is enough, when to stop, when to let go, forgive, and forget. You need to be confident about your own strength but also able to compromise.

If your previous New Moon was in Aries or in the 1st house, your overall cycle involves issues of independence and personal action. You are developing your capacity to be your unique self with spontaneity and confidence while still keeping space for the other parts of life, including other people. Since your progressed Sun has moved out of Aries into Taurus (or out of the 1st into the 2nd house), you can increase your personal growth through activities involving money, possessions and/or artistic skills.

If your previous New Moon was in Libra or in the 7th house, your overall cycle emphasizes the focus on shared activities. Since your progressed Sun has moved out of Libra into Scorpio (or out of the 7th into the 8th house), you can continue your personal growth through awareness of the rights and needs of others, seeking fair play and social justice without denying your own rights, paying increased attention to the handling of joint resources and pleasures.

With your Full Moon in Gemini/Sagittarius or in the 3rd house/9th house, this period puts a high focus on mental activity. Whether you are learning, teaching, writing or traveling, you need to stay conscious of the world right around you and also of your long-range values and goals. A successful integration of these two parts of life provides clear priorities (Sagittarius) so we are not too scattered but are able to bring our ideals into our everyday life (Gemini). Simultaneously, the Gemini capacity for acceptance helps us avoid being too frustrated when our Sagittarian ideals remain hard to reach.

This period is a time to use your intellect and perhaps to enlarge your mental skills through studies or practice. Relatives and neighbors may also be important in your life. Understanding and communication are important talents to be cultivated. You may be searching for a more secure faith, for a deeper sense of meaning in your life. Remember that the Truth, like all Absolutes, is a long-range goal. Enjoy the journey of life.

If your previous New Moon was in Gemini or in the 3rd house, the stronger focus may be on increasing or maintaining detachment and objectivity, on the ability to "take things lightly," and on communication with people around you.

If your previous New Moon was in Sagittarius or in the 9th house, you may need to pay extra attention to your spiritual faith, making sure that it is clear and reasonable and that you are doing what you can to manifest it in your daily life.

If your previous New Moon was in Taurus or in the 2nd house, your over-all cycle reminds you to use your mind to help you handle your own resources and enjoy the physical world. Since your progressed Sun has moved out of Taurus into Gemini (or out of the 2nd into the 3rd house), mental activities can promote personal growth as well as offering a source of pleasure and/or material rewards.

If your previous New Moon was in Scorpio or in the 8th house, your over-all cycle points to an emphasis on self-knowledge and self-mastery which is usually achieved partly through interaction with close relationships. Since your progressed Sun has moved out of Scorpio into Sagittarius (or out of the 8th into the 9th house), increasing clarity in your beliefs and conscious faith in a Higher Power should contribute to your personal growth.

A Full Moon in Cancer/Capricorn or in the 4th house/10th house marks an extra emphasis on security issues around home, family and career, including dealing with authority figures or your own exercise of responsible power. Often, the challenge involves trying to do justice to both family and career, and struggling with a sense of never enough time to do it all. We have to realize that no one can provide total security for themselves or anyone else. We need to accept help from others while giving help to the extent that we can.

If other aspects support a major change at this time, the approximately two months period of the full Moon could mark a change of residence or of job. Alternately, other people may come or go in your home or work situation, including authority figures or dependents. If your life is basically stable at this point, the Moon aspect may mark a more temporary change in the home or job situation such as a trip or a visit, your own or by personal associates or by an authority figure.

If your previous New Moon was in Cancer or in the 4th house, emotional security is very important for you in this cycle. Life is interdependent, so let others help you and try to be aware of their needs and sensitivities. The "nesting urge" may be very strong but it has to be integrated with all the other drives that are part of you. If you do not have your own home or family to provide an emotional support system, a pet, a kitchen herb garden, and/or close friends may offer substitute emotional warmth. Be conscious of your need for connections, for roots.

If your previous New Moon was in Capricorn or in the 10th house, your larger role in society or place in the world is very important in this cycle. Part of your personal growth is coming through dealing with power, whether through authority figures (father, boss, teacher, police etc.) or through your own position of responsible power. Capricorn (and the 10th house) represent the "rules of the game" and the consequences of how we have handled the rules in the past. A Capricorn/10th house cycle calls for Puritan virtues, being practical and productive without neglecting the other parts of life.

If your previous New Moon was in Gemini or in the 3rd house, the current focus on home and career occurs within a cycle that emphasizes the conscious mind whether through learning, communicating, or traveling. With your progressed Sun moved from Gemini into Cancer (or from the 3rd to the 4th house), you are likely to achieve some of your mental development through home and family or through dealing with the public in some way. Some of the

Gemini objectivity can help you to handle the sensitivity and security needs of the current Cancer focus and the emotional warmth of Cancer can modify the sometimes overly rational Gemini (3rd house).

If your previous New Moon was in Sagittarius or in the 9th house, your current focus on career or other public roles is part of a cycle that emphasizes beliefs, values, and long range goals. Part of your personal growth can come through bringing your ideals into the material world in your career. If your search for Truth and your capacity to share what you find is properly grounded and realistic, you can leave the world a better place than when you entered it.

A Full Moon in Leo/Aquarius or in the 5th house/11th house calls us to make peace between the desire to love, be loved, and to express creative power versus the desire to detach, live in the intellect, and accept the equality of everyone. We need all twelve sides of life to be a whole person, so there should be room for both passion and intellect, for self-esteem and for tolerance of others, for personal power and for democracy, for intimate relationships and for casual friends.

During this period, loved ones may be important, whether you are seeking to deepen relationships or to "let go" the ones that are outgrown. It is a time to expand creative outlets which could provide personal enjoyment or could lead to professional confidence and success. New ideas and new acquaintances may play a role in a wider, more stimulating life. Social issues may increase in importance. You may want to contribute to a favored "cause."

If your previous New Moon was in Leo or in the 5th house, the focus on close emotional attachments and personal creativity may seem more important than the desire for space, but integration allows a place in the life for both. Both sides of this polarity can be creative, but the fifth sign and house tend to be more ego-involved and emotional while the eleventh sign and house tend to be more rational and objective.

If your previous New Moon was in Aquarius or in the 11th house, this cycle points to growth coming through new knowledge and/or transpersonal activity involving society in general or groups of people. Social causes could be important, but the Full Moon is a reminder that personal relationships and self-esteem are also needed in a full life.

If your previous New Moon was in Cancer or in the 4th house, emotional security remains important through the cycle. Personal growth can come through home and family or other love relationships, including activities which put you in front of the public in some way. The Full Moon reminds you of the need for both private and public roles in life.

If your previous New Moon was in Capricorn or in the 10th house, your over-all cycle calls for some kind of productive contribution to society. Now that your progressed Sun has moved into Aquarius (or into the 11th house), you may have (or may just wish you had) more freedom to explore new ideas or just be sociable. Personal growth may be helped by new knowledge or new people or new experiences, but it remains important to feel a sense of achievement in your life.

With your Full Moon in Virgo/Pisces or in the 6th house/12th house, you will need to bring your ideals into some kind of tangible form in your work. The Virgo-Pisces polarity can manifest as an artist-craftsperson or as a healing-helping person. In its painful variant, it can be expressed as a victim, whether the problems are psychological, physical, or involve life events. Obviously, it is more satisfying to produce things which are both beautiful and useful or to offer service that helps to make a more ideal world. Astrology shows the principles underlying our lives and the details can be changed with faith and personal effort to manifest more comfortable forms of the astrological principles.

During this period, there may be changes in the details of your work or involving the people who work with you. Moon aspects sometimes mark changes like vacations, which are only temporary. You may also re-think some of your deepest values, searching for a clearer or more practical faith and looking for ways to ground your faith. You may help others to find a deeper faith or you may find inspiration and encouragement through the assistance of others. If health issues exist, look for practical steps which can nourish and strengthen your body and also try to strengthen your faith in a Higher Power. A positive attitude has healing power.

If your previous New Moon was in Virgo or in the 6th house, your underlying cycle calls for some kind of work that produces helpful tangible results. Personal growth can come through learning to function more effectively, doing something that you feel is worth doing and doing it well. Your Full Moon reminds you that though work is sometimes done simply for its own sake, or for a sense of accomplishment, mostly it needs to be directed by a vision so that it finds its place in the larger scene.

It is also possible for a Virgo cycle to call for attention to personal health. This Full Moon period may mark a new stage in your achievement of optimal body functioning, helped by sound nutrition, exercise, and positive attitudes.

If your previous New Moon was in Pisces or in the 12th house, your underlying cycle involves issues of faith, often at least partly subconscious. You may be growing in your faith, or in your artistic talents, or in your psychic openness. You may develop healing skills or learn to inspire others with your vision of a better world. Your Full Moon reminds you to stay in touch with the material world of ordinary work, always seeking ways to bring your dreams into tangible form in the world around you.

If your previous New Moon was in Leo or in the 5th house, your underlying cycle calls for growth through some type of personal creativity. As your progressed Sun has moved from Leo into Virgo (or from the 5th into the 6th house), your growth could come from creative work, or from work with young people. Your Full Moon reminds you to leave room for friends and larger social issues.

If your previous New Moon was in Aquarius or in the 11th house, your underlying cycle calls for growth through new knowledge or through some type of transpersonal activities. As your progressed Sun has moved from Aquarius into Pisces (or from the 11th into the 12th house), your growth may come partly through humanitarian service that expands human knowledge in some way. Your Full Moon reminds you to stay grounded and realistic as you follow your vision toward a more ideal world.

CHAPTER FIVE
CONJUNCTIONS: RULERSHIPS

Conjunctions are the most important aspect in progressions. Long-term conjunctions among the outer planets are discussed in Chapter 2. Conjunctions made by the progressed Moon are discussed in Chapter 10. Here, interpretations are provided for planetary conjunctions from the Sun, Mercury, Venus, Mars, and the "big four" asteroids (Ceres, Pallas, Juno, and Vesta) to all the other planets and major asteroids.

We find that similar themes and issues prevail when the outer planet conjuncts the inner planet, but the time frame is much longer. In such cases, those conjunctions would fall into the category of the long-term trends and enduring characteristics covered in Chapter 2. Where the designation "long-term" is applied to a planetary pair, consider the potentials given here as existing over a period of years (sometimes a lifetime).

In most cases (except when indicated otherwise), these conjunctions can be between a progressed planet and a natal planet or a progressed planet and a progressed planet. The only difference is that in the latter case, the issues and potentials will sometimes last for a longer period of time. (For example, progressed Venus will conjunct natal Sun for only about two years, but progressed Sun and Venus could travel together, maintaining a one-degree orb for seven to nine years.)

In addition to the nature of the planets involved in a conjunction, one must include rulerships. Thus, when two planets conjunct in progressions, consider that matters pertaining to the two (or more) houses ruled by those planets are likely to be combined or blended in some fashion. For more advanced students, remember to include all signs in a house when looking at rulers, not just the sign on the cusp. At higher latitudes, a house can contain a whole intercepted sign plus part of two other signs, so the house will have three rulers of the three signs. Always look for the theme, the repeated emphasis, in a complex mixture of planets, signs, and houses.   The use of traditional rulers is an additional complication. These are now called "co-rulers," and include Mars for Scorpio, Jupiter for Pisces, and Saturn for Aquarius.

Houses Linked by Rulers

Ruler of the 1st and ruler of the 1st

You'll want to be more independent, to live on your own terms. Impatience may arise, along with brash or impulsive behavior. Spontaneity and expressiveness are likely to increase. Courage, risk-taking, and a pioneering spirit are highlighted. You'll want to be first and may take chances. Restlessness rises, especially if you feel confined. You may do things **once** and then want to move on. Often, the need to be physically active becomes more important. Being yourself and acting on your own desires energizes you now.

Ruler of the 1st and ruler of the 2nd

You'll want to assert yourself more in regard to pleasure, money, sensuality, and beauty, but can move with a steady, measured pace. You might become more self-indulgent or get more pleasure from being who you are (liking yourself better). Financial independence matters. You may start your own business or exercise entrepreneurial skills. Impulsive spending or spur-of-the-moment gratification may appeal. You can make (or spend) money for anything active, physical, self-directed, personal, or pioneering. Beauty could become a focus of personal expression (skating, dancing, etc.). You'll instinctively seek comfort, aesthetics, material resources, and to feel good. You will want to call the shots regarding what you earn, own, and enjoy, and you can become quite energetic and pioneering in your pursuit of material gain or sensual gratification.

Ruler of the 1st and ruler of the 3rd

You will become more identified with your mind. You may see yourself more as a thinker and communicator: naturally curious, naturally interested in many different things. You may assert yourself linguistically—perhaps to the point of biting wit or arguments. You will learn voraciously and can teach others. Siblings (or other relatives) could trigger issues around anger, personal will, and independence. Your mind (and potentially, tongue) will be quicker and more self-assertive now. You may do well at crisis intervention, debate, or comedy. Dexterity could increase along with humor. Variety is important; you need the stimulation of new and different experiences. You can become a pioneer in acquiring and dispersing information.

Ruler of the 1st and ruler of the 4th

Two very different styles could develop. With one, warmth and caring could increase. You may care more for others, or lean on them. You may revisit the impact of a nurturing parent on your sense of self and handling of anger. You will learn about yourself through getting close to others. With the other style, you can be quite independent and assertive in regard to home, family, and emotional matters. You could change your home or center lots of activity there, or not be at home much. You may want to do things once domestically—and then move on. Your nurturing style could be immediate; you do best when caretaking in spurts rather than for long periods of time. You will want your abode to be run on your terms and may attend to family matters alone to ensure that your personal desires are met. Generally, your first impulse will be to feel, to go within. You are likely to feel pulled between expressing emotions and holding them inside.

Ruler of the 1st and ruler of the 5th

Charisma rises. You need to be a star now, to shine, to gain love, attention, or admiration from others. You could become a better entertainer, salesperson, promoter, speculator, actor, etc. (Or, you could become more pompous and arrogant.) You will want to pour out into the world (physically, emotionally, financially), hoping for a bigger return—for positive feedback. Talent for charades, sales, public relations, the theater could develop. You are apt to prefer creative projects which you can do quickly. You will want to be noticed, to stand out, for people to see how special you are. You may seek attention and applause in a pioneering fashion ("I did it **my** way.") You want to be proud of who you are and all that you do. You especially need to be proud of your assertion, courage, or ability to be independent. You can provide your own approval much of the time, but loving and being loved are probably also important. Let yourself sparkle, excite, and motivate others. If you deny your own dynamism, you are apt to get involved with arrogant, self-centered lovers or children. You may want children, but also want independence, so if you have children, you are apt to encourage their freedom to ensure your own. Sometimes impatience or feeling trapped is an issue. Risky businesses or pleasures may appeal, as the need for excitement is high. Or, thrills may be sought through torrid love affairs. You need to expand, to do more than you've done before.

Ruler of the 1st and ruler of the 6th

You need to work now. You will define yourself partially through productive efforts, through getting tangible results. Competence matters to you. A personal focus on health or craftsmanship is possible, along with increased appreciation for purity. Self-criticism is a danger as you tend to seek the flaw in yourself. (Count assets too!) You can do well at repairing things or enhancing projects. You may become more oriented toward efficiency. All the puritan virtues (thrift, craftsmanship, service, etc.) become more natural.

You can put a lot of energy into getting things done and asserting yourself on the job. You may start your own business or become more of a solo operator. You will want to work for yourself, on your own. You won't want anyone telling you what to do. If you trust yourself, you can deal well with crises and you probably have a sharp competitive edge on the job. Movement, self-direction, and doing things once can keep you eager for the next vocational challenge. You might like to work quickly and do best in bursts and starts. Becoming more of an initiator now, you may pioneer and break new ground vocationally. Physical activity could become necessary on the job. You may want movement or changes of scene. Relationships with coworkers could involve assertion (or aggression), anger, immediacy, crisis, or directness. You may become more skilled mechanically, medically, in sports, or with a competitive instinct. You can be quite energetic on the job as long as you are doing **what** you want **when** you want to!

Ruler of the 1st and ruler of the 7th

You could define yourself through relationships with others. This may express as pleasing and appeasing ("I need you to like me"), as competing or even attacking ("I'll protect myself by getting you before you can hurt me"), as withdrawing ("I'm too vulnerable to let you close") or by learning to balance assertion and accommodation, personal desires and those of partners, your needs and other people's. The dance between self and other becomes central. Diplomatic potentials increase and you are apt to be more sensitive to appearances. Polarities become more emphasized; you easily compare and contrast in life. Aesthetic interests may become more important. You may be attracted to a partner who is active, direct, courageous, assertive, independent. You are learning about autonomy through relationships. You could share a sense of freedom with a partner, or attract individuals who are unwilling to commit or are too self-centered. Your interpersonal exchanges offer opportunities for you to know yourself better, assert yourself and become more forthright, direct and courageous. People who share your life now may become more self-centered or content to be alone. You need relationships which foster your freedom, affirm your sense of self, and encourage you to be open, direct, and energetic.

Ruler of the 1st and ruler of the 8th

Emotional intensity is accented now. Your feelings may run deep, but you will tend not to reveal them. You may instinctively dig deeper—trying to understand fundamentals and underlying causes. You could go into therapy. You may constantly question your own motives, trying to figure out what is driving you. You need to grasp your basic motivations and needs. Psychological courage—and willingness to face the dark side—could increase. Self-knowledge, self-insight, and self-control matter more. Issues around addiction or appetites may emerge. Learning to share power, possessions, and pleasures with another person is a focus. Provided you are not projecting your power into others, you will have tremendous inner resources and great stamina. You will want (or learn) to be direct, open, and quick in handling shared resources. Intimate interactions strongly affect how you see yourself. Your mate could be freedom-loving, rash, impulsive—or you could strengthen each other's courage, integrity and willingness to break new ground. Rash or impulsive behavior is possible in regard to sexuality, shared resources, and intense encounters. The best of this combination is heightened passions and personal transformation on a deep level.

Ruler of the 1st and ruler of the 9th

The seeking of truth is highlighted now. Quests will draw you onward to define and reach for your personal goals and values. You may travel, pursue a spiritual path, a dream, an education, or anything involving ideas, ideals, and ethics. Self-righteous beliefs or fights about principles are possible. Optimism rises; you are likely to develop a core of faith and self-confidence. Your sense of humor could increase—along with the ability to wheel and deal, taking on large projects. Exposure to the wider world energizes you and you may increasingly thrive on freedom. The urge to inspire and uplift others is accented. Your standards for your own behavior may become higher. This can vary from: "I should be perfect (and if I'm not, I'm terrible)" to "I am perfect. I'm wonderful and the world owes me whatever I want" to "I should know all the right answers." Your world view must be personal. Freedom needs and restlessness are apt to increase.

Ruler of the 1st and ruler of the 10th

Career, authority, power and the rules of the game become more central to your life. One extreme is pushing the limits and constantly fighting reality. Another extreme is feeling blocked, inhibited, frustrated by authorities and "the way things are." (This could include depression, anxiety, or just or too much serious-ness.) A compromise calls for putting lots of energy into working within the rules of life, with a strong focus on achievement and making a personal contribution to society. You might confront rules head-on and either fight authority figures, feel constricted by them, or learn to put a lot of energy into working within a structure. In the latter case, you are energized by tangible accomplishments. A "salt of the earth" period is likely. Ambition rises. You will want your career to be more self-directed, on your own terms. It could include physical action and independence in regard to your contribution to society.

Ruler of the 1st and ruler of the 11th

Personal independence is highlighted now. You will be drawn toward the new, different, unusual. You may become more assertive as a champion for humani-tarian principles, for friends, or for progress. You will seek variety, intellectual stimulation, and the unconventional. (You might even enjoy shocking people now.) You're apt to be different—ranging from strange and eccentric to brilliant and innovative. You can be the rebel or the creative, inventive individualist. You are more likely to question authorities and dogmas. Friends are more important to your sense of self and you may model your behavior on theirs. Your perspective is likely to enlarge; transpersonal issues become more personally important.

Ruler of the 1st and ruler of the 12th

You may become a victim or a saint! You could sacrifice yourself for the larger Whole, absorbing the troubles of the Universe. Or, you might act in an inspired manner and devote yourself to a holy cause. You may start to live in a state of grace. Questions about the Cosmos and life's Whole are apt to draw you in. You could become a natural mystic, sensing the underlying Oneness of life. You may be drawn to personally help, heal, save, rescue, or create beauty to make the world more ideal If carried to an extreme, you can be a martyr—personal energy drained away by hurt, dashed dreams, or overwhelming feelings picked up from others. Sensitivity—physical and emotional—could increase. Imagination (and fantasy) are accented now; you can enter nonmaterial realms and be a visionary. Positively, you tune in to the Universe and your faith refreshes you. You might also strengthen your faith in yourself by achieving deeply held aspirations. You could develop personal artistic talents, a more attractive appearance, increased graceful movements, etc. Remember that you are a unique and valuable, individual part of the Whole of Life.

Ruler of the 2nd and ruler of the 1st

(See Ruler of the 1st and Ruler of the 2nd above.)

Ruler of the 2nd and ruler of the 2nd

The focus on pleasure, finances, and beauty is doubled now. This can be a artistic/aesthetic combination. It can also indicate self-indulgence—an increase in hedonism, gratification, or collecting money and possessions. Sensuality is apt to become stronger. Feeling good is more important. Money will be sought in easy, comfortable, regular, steady ways. Predictability probably appeals. You can make money through (and spend it on) gratifying the senses or creating beauty. You can also use money to make money (financial fields and investment). Tactile experiences appeal (e.g., sculpture, fabrics, pottery, massage, etc.). You seek greater dependability in regard to material matters.

Ruler of the 2nd and ruler of the 3rd

The world of the mind and the tongue becomes more pleasing. You love to learn. You may enjoy and feel increased affection for your relatives. You could use beauty and grace with your fingers or with your language. Your voice may become more melodic. You gravitate toward comfortable communications but can be stubborn in your thinking. You may gain income through your mind, your communication or verbal skills (e.g., sales, teaching, etc.), or through your dexterity or hands (e.g., hairdresser, surgeon). You could develop more than one source of income. Relatives could influence the financial picture. You are likely to be curious about money and enjoy discussing financial matters. Your pursuit of pleasure and material gain is likely to be directed toward the mental world. You can spend money on intellectual goods (such as seminars, trips, books, software, etc.). You can be objective about money matters (but also a good rationalizer in regard to purchases).

Ruler of the 2nd and ruler of the 4th

You may really enjoy your home, family, hearth, and emotional commitments or attachments now. You could develop a more affectionate relationship with your nurturing parent. You might make money through the home, land, real estate, food, shelter, clothing, family businesses, women, the public or anything which involves care-taking. Your money could get mixed with your Mom's. You will tend to hang on to money and possessions and could become a collector. You may open more than one bank account—to add to a sense of safety. Emotional moods and subconscious childhood scripts will have more impact on how you handle money and possessions now. Strive to remain aware. You want your home to be comfortable, stable, and secure. Material possessions probably seem important; you will tend to hang on to things. You want the domestic arena to be smooth, flowing, and easy now. Indulgence (in food, drink, etc.) could become a focus within the household. You can nurture people by helping them relax. A beautiful abode appeals and you may spend money in order to create an attractive environment.

Ruler of the 2nd and ruler of the 5th

You are likely to enjoy being on stage or noticed now. You can get more pleasure from being a star, from being in the limelight. This could include roles as a creative artist, or the person who enjoys gambling and speculating for greater return, or someone who is very fond of children and loved ones. You can be extremely creative about making money or enjoying the material world. You want your earning power, income, possessions, or pleasures to be noteworthy. Your self-esteem is on the line in regard to resources now. You want to be proud of your possessions, financial status, beauty, artistic talent, or easygoing nature. Your enthusiasm is directed toward creating comfort, stability, and gratifying sensual experiences. You might make money through the entertainment world, sales, promotion, youth groups, creativity, recreation, love, romance, teaching, investment (including Stock Market) or anything expressive. You can have more fun with money and are capable of grand and generous financial gestures. You could become more indulgent of children or lovers, or attract loved ones who are stubborn, stodgy, or materialistic.

Ruler of the 2nd and ruler of the 6th

You are likely to enjoy doing things well, but might be pulled between the "easy" way and the "right" way. You may take more pleasure in crafts or precision work. You could focus on health and get real gratification from healing or repairing the physical body. You want to work comfortably. You want your job to be smooth, solid and predictable. You'd prefer it pay well, and may want your tasks to involve beauty, sensuality, money, or creature comforts. Slow and steady will get the job done because you endure and follow through. You could make money through any business or health-related fields, especially those requiring attention to detail, organization, and thoroughness. You can deal better with budgeting and careful analysis of finances and resources and could work within a monetary field (e.g., accounting, taxes, etc.). Artistic activities are possible, such as singing, sculpting, make-up, design, etc., but so are fields involving basic material goods or sensuality (massage, physiotherapy, etc.). You are likely to work best in an environment which is physically comfortable: aesthetically pleasing, with a good chair, appropriate temperature, kind colleagues, etc. Relations with coworkers tend to be relaxed. If carried too far, colleagues may be lazy, indulgent, or stuck in ruts. Being thrifty and comparison shopping could have more appeal. You are apt to spend money on anything which advances your career or improves your health or efficiency. A practical, businesslike approach to resources is probable.

Ruler of the 2nd and ruler of the 7th

You might have an artistic focus. Pleasure comes through grace, line, form, balance and harmony. You are apt to prefer to earn a living in a way that is comfortable and attractive (forget dirt and unpleasantness!). If this drive is overdone, you might want your work to be unrealistically easy. Earning money through your own physical appearance or through artistic talents may be possible now. Visual arts (design, photography, fashion, etc.) are possible options. You are also likely to buy pretty things. Good taste and attractive possessions are accented. You could enjoy people and be very affectionate with partners. Your money is apt to be involved with other people. This can include personnel work, counseling, consulting, being supported by or supporting a spouse, etc. Negotiating activities could bring in revenue as well. You are inclined to bounce financial decisions off other people rather than going it alone. Feedback helps you make up your mind. You may give more priority to your partner being a good provider or able to handle money and material possessions. You could attract people who are comfortable, easygoing, stable—or stolid, stubborn and hedonistic. You are drawn to relationships which feed your sensual nature, help you to feel at ease, and help you further develop your resources and financial base.

Ruler of the 2nd and ruler of the 8th

You may increasingly enjoy depth work, digging beneath the surface, probing, ferreting out secrets, and discovering underlying causes and motivations. You may get pleasure from intensity, sexuality, shared resources. Your money is likely to become involved with other people's—giving or getting much from partners. This can include the politician who handles public funds, inheritance, therapy, or spousal support (given or received). You are likely to have intense reactions in regard to financial matters and could be obsessive or too concerned with control. You might use money as a weapon or to manipulate others—or suspect that others are doing that to you. Power struggles usually call for compromise. You may experience feast versus famine swings around food, drinking, making money, spending money, sex/celibacy until you reach an inner balance: moderation. You can make money with money (e.g., banking, investment) and also through physical manipulation (e.g., body work of all kinds, massage, acupuncture, etc.). Your income may come from fields with intense emotions or life-and-death circumstances (e.g., hospice work, emergency rooms, past life regression) or with a focus on power (corporate world, politics). You are apt to examine possessions and finances more carefully (and might expect complications). You may obsess over what you own, what you have, trying to figure it all out and gain full control. You can be seduced (and attract others) by sensual pleasures, loyalty, dependability, practicality, and beauty.

Ruler of the 2nd and ruler of the 9th

You may seek infinite resources—or spend your resources in seeking Infinite answers. You could place a high value on pleasure, beauty, possessions, or finances. Your world view now may center on comfort, feeling good, and enjoying the physical world. If so, you will more easily spot financial opportunities and tend to be optimistic in regard to the material world. Extravagance and falling for "get rich quick" schemes are potential dangers. This combination can turn money into an ultimate value—and seek more and more of it, risking disillusionment that forces one to find a bigger God. You might look to the material world to provide a sense of meaning, and then expect more than is humanly possible in regard to monetary matters, pleasures, or what you own. Alternately, money can be used to fuel the quest for Truth—buying books, classes, etc. Dreams are likely to be big. With this choice, you will get more pleasure from learning, from expanding your mind and your horizons, travel, philosophy, religion—or anything which provides a sense of higher meaning and truth. You could make or spend money now through travel, higher education, more training, inspiration, the law, science, publishing, or anything which gives people a sense of meaning in life.

Ruler of the 2nd and ruler of the 10th

You are likely to enjoy responsibility, power, and authority now. You may get pleasure from the role of expert or executive. You have more appreciation for stability, safety, knowing the rules and the bottom line. Father images could influence your current financial prospects and attitudes. You might make money through business, or anything that requires a strong sense of responsibility, organization, thoroughness and plain old hard work. You need to keep a balance between the urge for pleasure (2nd house) and workaholic tendencies (10th house).

You want your career to be comfortable, easygoing, and to provide well materially. You may work more with money, beauty, sensuality, or comfort. You can confront rules with patience and endurance, working steadily and well.. You may become more laid-back with authority figures, and work best in a stable, secure setting.

You are apt to be more conservative in regard to resources and preservation of capital could become a priority. Purchases are apt to be "classic" or "timeless" and may be done during sales. Getting value for your money is important and permanence appeals.

Ruler of the 2nd and ruler of the 11th

This is a time to get out of the rut, to enjoy progress, the new, the individualistic, the different, but not at the cost of risking basic security and stability. You may get increased pleasure from humanitarian causes: equality, justice, fair play. You could enjoy groups and organizations, astrology, anything on the cutting edge of change. You could make money through those channels, as well as technology, or anything that is new, unusual, or innovative. You may begin working on your own, on a commission basis or with unusual or irregular hours or circumstances. Your investments could become progressive (or strange). Your income could fluctuate as financial independence increases in importance. Friends may become involved in your financial picture (income or outgo) and you can be more objective than most people about resources and money. Enjoying the material world is more of a focus with friends and groups. Either you are apt to be sensual and savoring yourself, or you may attract people who go to the extremes of stolidity, stubbornness, and materialism. You thrive in groups and friendships which are comfortable and easygoing, with massage, money, collections, business contacts, or anything which indulges the senses as a focus. Your casual connections to others and expanding knowledge give you an arena to build your financial means, comfort level, stability, and sensual indulgences.

Ruler of the 2nd and ruler of the 12th

You may enjoy mysticism or nature worship. You could find meditation gratifying—or anything which helps you to tune into your Higher Self, to feel a connection to the Cosmos. You could make money through art, through helping and healing activities, or through being a victim (e.g., welfare, public assistance). You could also spend money in pursuit of beauty or a dream. Financial fantasies or confusion could result if passivity and dreaming are overdone. Your quest for the Source, for life's ultimate meaning, may become tied to pleasure and ease. Constructively, your creative imagination and visualizing skills could be commercial assets. Idealism and imagery (e.g., movies, advertising) can bring in revenue. This 2-12 combination can denote both infinite resources (great wealth) and periods of helplessness in regard to money. You may over idealize money, possessions, comfort, or physical pleasures now, or you could become disillusioned with "having" and "getting" in life.

One path is to become artistic or involved with nature on a very tactile level, seeking inspiration in patience, loyalty, pleasantness, sensuality and life's goodies. Enlightenment may come through the physical senses, being with nature, and enjoying the material realm. Activities in which you can be placid, sensual, comfortable, stable, artistic, and relaxed can help you to tap into your Higher Self. Alternately, you may find your ultimate security and personal pleasure through your contributions to the realization of infinite love and beauty by the Whole in which you participate and grow.

Ruler of the 3rd and ruler of the 1st
(See Ruler of the 1st and ruler of the 3rd above.)

Ruler of the 3rd and ruler of the 2nd
(See Ruler of the 2nd and ruler of the 3rd above.)

Ruler of the 3rd and ruler of the 3rd
The focus on mental activity, stimulation, curiosity, speaking, and learning is doubled. An urge to share information with others is strong; you may become more articulate. You might become a trivia collector. You probably want to know a bit about everything and could get scattered in your studies. Surface skimming is apt to win over depth investigation. You might become active with siblings, relatives, or neighbors. Your mind is more flexible, witty, and multi-faceted. Curiosity is rampant. You could become more physically as well as mentally restless. The desire for new experiences is intense now. Increasing detachment and logic can make you an excellent observer. You may thrive on stimulation and may enjoy moving about physically as well as traveling everywhere within your head.

Ruler of the 3rd and ruler of the 4th
If there is any threat to your security, your communication style in this period is apt to become more reticent, more silent, more concerned with emotional needs. There's a protective element here, not wanting to hurt anyone (or yourself) by what you say. Curiosity may surface about mother issues, home and family concerns or caretaking needs. This combination can indicate a period of nurturing with language, of being supportive and gentle in handling information OR

of seeking emotional security through the mind. In the latter case, rationality will be equated with safety. The intellect could become the bedrock of your life. You will want your home to be mentally stimulating. You will probably fill your home with ideas and information. You'll want people there to be talkative, to bring up ideas, or to involve you in the world of the mind and learning. Changes of residence are possible, as you are more likely to get easily bored with the domestic environment. You might even get two homes or a travel trailer!

Ruler of the 3rd and ruler of the 5th

You will want to be on stage through your mind now. You may garner applause through your communication skills (verbal or written) or thinking. You could become a natural entertainer, or storyteller, or salesperson, or someone who cracks jokes and puns. Your communication style is apt to become more dramatic (and possibly exaggerative). You're ready to make a splash with the words you choose, gestures, and the whole presentation. You need people to admire your intellectual or verbal prowess. You will want to be proud of your mind, tongue, dexterity, or flexibility. Excitement comes through concepts and information exchange. Mental activity revitalizes you now. A fun-loving, youthful attitude is likely, along with a love of learning. Children and lovers are apt to be verbal, versatile or bright now. You may get involved with people who are too flighty, curious, scattered or superficial. Endlessly curious about love, you may have a hard time settling down now as you easily get distracted by someone new. Communication and learning are vital in your love relationships and a major outlet for creativity.

Ruler of the 3rd and ruler of the 6th

You will want to put your mind to work in the world. Language and thinking are tools now. You want communication to be efficient and serve a purpose. Your speech may become directed mainly toward work or accomplishing tasks. (Sociability for its own sake is not a priority.) Your skills at research could improve. You might become more nit-picking or judgmental of your own phrasing vocabulary—and/or other people's. A flaw-finding lens is directed toward the mental world. Analytical abilities could increase. Writing could improve. You are apt to seek tangible results from your mind.

You also might use your hands in your work in addition to information, knowledge, facts and figures. Ideas and people offer a forum for your talents. You might begin working with relatives. Multiple talents could develop. You could have trouble settling down vocationally. Boredom could lead to job changes unless your field has lots of variety. Indeed, this is one indicator for the potential of two jobs simultaneously. You work best with people who are bright, adaptable and mentally stimulating, but may end up with the occasional colleague who is flighty, too talkative, superficial or scattered. Sociability and information exchange should be built into your job. You might be torn between being casual about routines and lighthearted about job responsibilities versus being serious and thorough. You need **interesting** work.

Ruler of the 3rd and ruler of the 7th

You are probably being drawn toward graceful, flowing language. You may take up poetry, song writing, singing, playing a musical instrument or other activities which combine beauty with your hands or communication skills. You may be quite diplomatic, knowing what people want to hear and giving it to them. Polite lies are possible (to avoid unpleasantness or discord). Or if you enjoy competition, you could be a good debater or "devil's advocate." Sociability is apt to rise; you prefer a dialogue to a monologue.

You will want more communication and intellectual stimulation from your partner. Versatility will become a plus in relationships—or you could play the field or have trouble settling with just one person. You may draw in people who are too cool, scattered, verbose, or hard to pin down. You need relationships which keep you learning, encourage you to discuss matters, and bring lots of information and new experiences into your life. Giving and receiving data is apt to be an important form of sharing. You learn much through relationships. Your curiosity is largely directed toward people now.

Ruler of the 3rd and ruler of the 8th

You are probably becoming more curious about depth matters. You may decide to study the occult, taboos, research, or people's deeper motives. Detective instincts could develop. Skill with nonverbal cues, hints, innuendoes, and indirect references is likely to increase. Your mind can be more incisive and probing as you understand the power of information and ideas. Your thoughts are apt to be better organized (even obsessive). Complications and layers of meaning become clearer to you. You can be objective when discussing sex, shared resources, power, death, and emotionally intense subjects. (A bit of voyeurism or off-color jokes and stories might occur.) You seek to bring touchy subjects to the light of day and open up discussion. With increasing intuition, you can tune in to what others are thinking, even without words. Learning seems fascinating and seductive now. You can use both words and silence very potently.

Intimate interactions stimulate your thinking and urge to communicate. You may get easily bored in intimate exchanges and need variety (in partners, circumstances, or surroundings, etc.).You are apt to be seduced by quick wits, alertness, facility, versatility, and multiple interests.

Ruler of the 3rd and ruler of the 9th

Gregariousness is on the rise, along with the desire to learn about anything and everything. This can be a time when you are the professional student. Interests broaden and travel usually appeals. You may learn lots through other cultures, education, science, religion. The quest for ultimate understanding is important to you now. You are looking for meaning, for absolutes, for the purpose of existence. You're likely to be more expressive, talkative, and honest (sometimes too blunt). Humor comes easily and practical jokes are possible. Truth is apt to become an issue—being or dealing with others who are either too forthright or are "con artists" using "truth" for personal aims.

You will tend to place a high value on the mind and communication now. You may think that objectivity and looking at things logically will solve any problem. You could over idealize words, concepts, learning, and information in your current world view. You might add lightness, variety and constant new input to your list of imperatives. Or relatives could become more important

Ruler of the 3rd and ruler of the 10th

You may start using your mind, tongue, or hands in a professional manner, and/or prefer task-oriented conversations to casual chit-chat. Your mind will tend to become more serious, down-to-earth, practical and organized. You may prefer to focus on tangible concerns. Business skills are likely. You can move up in the world through logic and planning. You might become too judgmental of your own (or other people's) intellect or communication skills. If overdone, inhibition could be a problem. Seek out ideas which are useful. A career in communication could begin. You might work with relatives, with eye-mind-hand coordination and dexterity, with paperwork, or ideas and information in any form. Versatility increases and you may have more than one career now. You will prefer variety on the job and could get bored easily, so you may work best with multiple duties. You also might be more casual with authority figures, looking for a more equalitarian relationship.

Ruler of the 3rd and ruler of the 11th

Your mind edges toward the unconventional, perhaps rebellious or even erratic. This can be a period of genius—or of flakiness. Interests tend toward the new, unusual, humanitarian. Talkative, but detached, you can relate to anyone, but as an objective observer. Flashes of brilliance are likely. Your communication style may become abrupt or independent and original. You can be quite a brainstormer, willing to break the rules to gain more knowledge. Friends may stimulate much of your thinking. Original thinking is accented. You are not going to toe the party line. Shocking statements are possible. Logic and rationality come more easily.

You can thrive in groups and friendships which stimulate your mind. Activities could include classes, games, trivia, information exchange or dissemination, neighborhood activities, literary (or book) club or group, or anything involving hand-eye coordination. You may be attracted to people who are articulate, multi-talented, and curious about everything—or draw in people who are too chatty, superficial and scattered. Unbonded relationships which support your inquisitiveness, quick wits, and flexibility are best. Your casual connections to others are encouraging you to learn, laugh and take life lightly. Involvement with humanity on a large scale is like a school for you—a place to exercise your mind, hone your verbal and writing skills, increase your fund of knowledge, and be alert to the many interesting people from whom you can learn.

Ruler of the 3rd and ruler of the 12th

Your creative imagination is gaining strength. You can blend the conscious and subconscious mind, the rational and the intuitive. You may be drawn to many artistic fields: films, poetry, painting, writing fiction, music, song writing, etc. Beautiful words and imagery are likely to increase. Facility with accents and languages is possible. You can bring intuitive insights into consciousness and express them. You may create beauty with your hands or mind. You are inspired by versatility, multiple interests and talents, verbal skills, and quick wits. Your fantasy skills are strong now. Good ideas may come in the waking/dreaming twilight zone. Be sure you can distinguish achievable aims from impossible wishful thinking. Evasive or escapist thinking or speech is a hazard. Healing, compassionate communication is a positive option. You could become more psychic—or more confused as you absorb too much input to sort it out logically. Keeping clear priorities and mental categories is vital.

You may idealize thinking, communicating, learning or logic. Or, you could become disillusioned with intellectual understanding or superficial answers. Your quest for the Source, for life's ultimate meaning, must make sense to you. One path to enlightenment lies in pursuing your curiosity, exercising your wits, discussing ideas, comparing and contrasting concepts, collecting and disseminating information and being alert to your environment. Mental stimulation helps you to tap into your Higher Self, as well as contribute your understanding to the evolving Whole.

Ruler of the 4th and ruler of the 1st

(See Ruler of the 1st and ruler of the 4th above.)

Ruler of the 4th and ruler of the 2nd

(See Ruler of the 2nd and ruler of the 4th above.)

Ruler of the 4th and ruler of the 3rd

(See Ruler of the 3rd and ruler of the 4th above.)

Ruler of the 4th and ruler of the 4th

An increasing emphasis is likely on your home as a key to your emotional security and safety. You want to feel that you have a real nest. Protection is essential now. Family feelings may strengthen—or the quest for people who will always be on your side. Patriotism or a connection to the land may increase. Ancestry could become a focus. Caretaking needs to be gentle, supportive, reassuring. Your home environment might become more traditional: warm or nurturing. You want security within your domestic routine and may enjoy caring for others (people, pets, plants) as well as being cared for. Privacy in your abode could matter much to you. A strong nurturing period is likely—or a great deal of dependency. Your challenge is to have a balance between looking after others and leaning on others. You can truly make a house a home now, bringing in emotional attachments and cherishing roots.

Ruler of the 4th and ruler of the 5th

You probably want your home to be more majestic, impressive, or noteworthy. You may want applause and admiration for your residence—or center the household around children or creative acts. Your pride is on the line. A grand abode, or important ancestry or family members, could feel essential at this time, with self-esteem connected to your household. You may nurture others by paying attention, praising, and urging others on. You can become a great coach or supporter of loved ones. Your need to love and be loved is likely to increase. Family attachments may become central—or whatever you nurture (plants, animals, etc.). You want to be proud of your home and loved ones or have a starring role within the household. Your creative projects may involve family members, be done at home, have a domestic connection, or involve water or emotions. You are energized by nurturing, nesting, and nestling.

Ruler of the 4th and ruler of the 6th

You will want your home (and probably family) to be more practical, healthy, and well organized. Mind-centered activities may become more important. You want your domestic arena to be productive. Working from the home is possible, or family businesses, or simply a very orderly, thorough approach to the domestic realm. Fix-it projects may abound. You will be ever ready to repair, enhance, or improve your base of operations. Nurturing may center around pragmatic matters. Housekeeping could be very precise and exacting or a different kind of work and efficiency will take priority (e.g., keeping files in order).

Security is more important in your work—emotional and perhaps physical as well. You might provide the basic needs (food, shelter, clothing, real estate) of the public, work in a nurturing role, or share a job with family members. You might care for animals, plants, or people. You could work out of your home, get into a patriotic ("homeland") career, or become a homemaker. You tend to get closer to your coworkers now. You can create a family feeling on the job (or work with family members). If carried too far, colleagues could become smothering, dependent, needy or too emotional. Or you could become emotionally attached to your current duties, being a care-taker on many levels. Being productive will help you to feel safe and you are likely to feel happier in a job which is safe and secure.

Ruler of the 4th and ruler of the 7th

You will want your home to be more lovely, graceful and attractive. You may use artistic talents within your nest. A home which is pleasant is important and you may try to "cover over" disagreements in order to "keep things nice." Appearances could be over valued. Home or family could become an important connection with a partner—ranging from family influences, to ancestral ties, to creating a partnership that revolves around the nest or children. Emotional connections are central, hopefully an abode filled with kind, sociable people. You will want your partner to be warm, compassionate, able to care for you (or willing to let you care for him/her). You need relationships which are secure now and help you feel safe, which strengthen and affirm emotional ties, and help you to create a nest. Old parental messages may affect your current partnerships. Make sure you have a good balance between nurturing and being nurtured.

Ruler of the 4th and ruler of the 8th

You may want more privacy in your abode. Preserving secrets gains priority. Intense emotional experiences may take place in your home, perhaps even life-and-death crises or confrontations. You may become involved in transformational or regenerative activities in your domicile. You nurture through encouraging depth, investigation, research, and an inward searching, and you may deal with cathartic experiences in regard to a parent. Issues around control, elimination, emotional blackmail, and/or joint resources may come up with family members, especially parent figures. Loyalty and betrayal could become central issues with those in your home. You will tend to dig at your roots, at your emotional foundation. You might figure out the family tree, bring up skeletons from the closet, or confront family members with intense emotional issues. You might seek security in regard to shared resources. You might feel safest when in control. Intimate interactions are apt to trigger any unresolved questions involving issues of nurturing, protection, and/or dependency. A mate may trigger feelings which relate to a parent or your early childhood experiences. Old emotional scripts are likely to come up in intimate, sharing situations.

Ruler of the 4th and ruler of the 9th

You might be tempted to make your home on the road now. You could live in a foreign country, or in a trailer as a traveling home. An urge for the "ideal" abode may make settling down a challenge, or much energy might be devoted to improving your residence. Your household might emphasize philosophy, religion, questions and intellectual exchange (especially about the meaning of life and important goals and values). People are likely to come and go and lots of travel and/or changes of residence are also possible. Good humor and good times are likely within your nest. You could feel "at home" in the world or get a bigger than average place to live. You may bring people from all over the world into your home. Your values could become tied to the family, emotional connections, and the home. You might idealize your roots, ancestry, nurturing parent, or physical abode. You might want more than is humanly possible in regard to family warmth, connections, and unity. Your world view is apt to emphasize caring, protection, and a strong parental streak. You may become attracted toward maternal religions or the revival of the Goddess if your seeking and searching side gets directed toward safety for yourself and others.

Ruler of the 4th and ruler of the 10th

You will want a home which provides stability, security, and known rules now, with domestic matters structured, organized, and well-defined. You might work out of your residence, with family members (family business), in a nurturing or in a caretaking profession, or with the public, women, resources, land/real estate, or anything that meets human needs, from commodities to emotional warmth. You may feel obligated to carry more than your fair share of the domestic load and could be overly responsible—especially in regard to family matters. You will be working on the blend between compassion and bottom line, dominance and dependency. You can deal with rules through empathy and caring. You may soften the bottom line. Applying structure to the home may help promote safety, security and protection.

Ruler of the 4th and ruler of the 11th

You can turn your friends into family now—becoming warmer, more closely involved with them, more emotionally attached. You may also turn your family into friends—more casual than most about domestic matters. You may nurture freedom and individuality and support people in a manner that feeds their uniqueness. You probably would like to change your abode by moving or by filling your home with unusual people, new technology, astrology, or anything innovative. Domestic surprises are possible. You will want your base of operations to be unusual or unconventional, and that means sometimes it might be a bit unstable or unpredictable as you look for a way to keep your core security while avoiding boredom.

Ruler of the 4th and ruler of the 12th

You will want your home to be a sanctuary now: a place where you can meditate or tune in to your Higher Self, merge with the Cosmos, feel a sense of infinite grace, beauty and compassion. You may create a lovely domicile. Savior/victim relationships with family or people in your abode could develop. Alcohol or other escapist activity could become a problem in the home. A family member might become confused, escapist, or just inclined toward wishful thinking. You need beauty, mysticism, transcendence, idealism, and inspiration in your nest. You may be more compassionate, loving, and close. Nurturing could be seen as a holy path. Emotional connections are apt to be idealized now.

Ruler of the 5th and ruler of the 1st

(See Ruler of the 1st and ruler of the 5th above.)

Ruler of the 5th and ruler of the 2nd

(See Ruler of the 2nd and ruler of the 5th above.)

Ruler of the 5th and ruler of the 3rd
(See Ruler of the 3rd and ruler of the 5th above.)

Ruler of the 5th and ruler of the 4th
(See Ruler of the 4th and ruler of the 5th above.)

Ruler of the 5th and ruler of the 5th
The need to be on stage in some fashion grows stronger. You may gain admiration and applause through children, play, drama, teaching, sales, or any activities which allow you to shine and be noticed. Eager to express now, you will seek a greater return on what you pour out into the world (love, money, zest, etc.). You are energized and excited by pouring out from your own center and receiving recognition. Your quest for adrenaline could play out with lovers and/ or children and you may egg each other on for more excitement, or attract loved ones who take risks or believe they have a regal right to what they want. Love is thrilling, but many forms of creativity and/or ways to feel powerful are possible, including gambling and speculation in hopes of an increased return from the world. It is time to shine.

Ruler of the 5th and ruler of the 6th
Your creativity will now be channeled toward productive work. Outlets might involve precision and an eye for detail. Skill with handicrafts may manifest. Models, miniatures, carpentry, writing and many other painstaking hobbies are possible. You could ground your creativity into tangible output. Your self-esteem is connected to being effective in your job and healthy in your body. You could take center stage for good health (or ill) or for competence and the ability to consistently improve. Your personal vitality will be fed by efficiency. In love relationships, a pragmatic streak is likely to surface. You might be critical toward (or be criticized by) children or lovers. You might work hard at creativity and at love. This is a good combination for working with loved ones (e.g., a family business) or constantly trying to improve your loving associations.

You need to shine in your work! You could take risks for greater gain. Children, recreation, or creativity could become central to your job. Or, you might work with loved ones. You may want a role as a leader, or excitement on the job. You need an adrenaline rush. You may use drama, magnetism, excitement, speculation, or persuasion on the job. The world of entertainment, recreation, sales, and advertising are all possible. Sometimes, colleagues become prima donnas or self-centered egotists. Try to encourage everyone to share a sense of zest, fun, and sparkle on the job. You can develop skills for revving people up, but more effort might be needed on follow-through. Your magnetism and drive can be vocational assets now. You can light a fire under other people, persuade them to join your momentum.

Ruler of the 5th and ruler of the 7th

Your creativity is stimulated by other people and vice versa. A partner may spur you to greater heights. Feedback from others encourages you to risk more, express more. You may be too ego-vulnerable in relationships, needing the other person's approval—or you might attract someone magnetic, exciting, expressive to shine for you. Artistic and aesthetic skills are likely. You can use a feeling for balance, space and form in your creative output. Persuasive talents are also accented now. You could begin treating children more like partners—as peers and equals, or a partner could seem more childlike—enthusiastic and exciting or ego-centered and arrogant. You want your partner to be scintillating, dynamic, sexy, magnetic, and dramatic. You might attract individuals who are arrogant, egotistical and expect everything to be their way if you deny your own sense of self-worth. You need relationships which offer thrills, provide opportunities for everyone to shine and be applauded, and which affirm your self-esteem. Mutual admiration is essential. Love relationships which feature equality will work the best now.

Ruler of the 5th and ruler of the 8th

Your creativity is stimulated by going into your inner depths. Privacy energizes you. Your self-esteem is connected to inner discipline, mastery, and the handling of shared resources. You may be proud of your sexuality, intensity, or capacity to deal with hidden matters. The better your intimate associations go, the better you feel about yourself. You could seek drama, excitement, and an adrenaline rush in a new or deeper relationship with a mate now. You may try to analyze your need for love, attention, and the limelight. You might obsess over issues of applause and positive regard. A passionate streak is likely. Relationships with children and lovers are likely to become quite intense. All-or-nothing associations are quite possible. Love (and hate) may become very strong. Power issues are probable. A focus on sharing the power (neither overpowering others nor being intimidated) is essential. You may have to deal with very private, strong-willed loved ones, although resourcefulness is also likely. Loyalty will be a major issue in love affairs. When you commit, you want total, complete immersion and absorption.

Ruler of the 5th and ruler of the 9th

Your creativity is oriented toward large-scale projects. You may be proud of your philosophy, religion, education, or inspirational side, though any part of life can be turned into an ultimate value and goal and be connected to self-esteem. Ambitious dreams and eagerness to hit the big-time could lead you to take major risks. You may trust your magnetism or persuasive power to carry you through difficulties. You could thrive on rising to the challenges, expanding on opportunities and enlarging your creative scope. You could idealize creativity. You believe in and value zest, enthusiasm, being on stage in some fashion. You might expect too much from activities involving gambling, speculation, or risking for greater gain. Faith and confidence could go overboard since the world view of this combination emphasizes excitement and fun. Issues of faith, beliefs, and values may involve children and loved ones. You may expect more than is humanly possible (or they might have unreasonably high expectations for you). Sharing a spiritual, religious, or ethical focus can strengthen your love bonds. Travel, sports, education or humor can become sources of joy in your life.

Ruler of the 5th and ruler of the 10th

Career ambitions are likely to increase. You want to wield power and to be noticed and noteworthy within your profession. Choose a focus which allows you to shine or puts your creativity, charisma, or magnetism to work. You may gravitate toward creative professions or something with an element of risk. You could work with loved ones, or anything whereby you are the center of attention. You might confront rules with drama, persuasion, and exaggeration. With leadership instincts, you can reach a pinnacle in your ambitions—and you want it fast. You can impress authorities if you avoid over-confidence and stay productive. Your contribution to the world should excite you and turn you on now. You need to be seen as a mover, shaker, and doer in the world. Your vocation will be more satisfying if it lets you express zest, drama, and enthusiasm. Your creativity may manifest in the business realm—or anything involving structure. You need tangible output. Because you will take this area seriously, you could inhibit your talents—being overly judgmental. Don't hide your light under a bushel for fear of not measuring up. Work, duty, and responsibility are apt to become issues with loved ones. You may do too much for your children or carry too much of the load with loved ones. You might be judgmental toward them—or they toward you. This combination is excellent for working together (family businesses) and for encouraging one another's strength, power, and competence.

Ruler of the 5th and ruler of the 11th

Your creativity may be on call for humanity. You could bring sparkle to groups, organizations, or gatherings of friends. You might to be proud of your humanitarian instincts, of your friends, or of your cutting-edge intellect. You can liven things up, get people motivated, and brainstorm well. Your magnetism and personal appeal are increased in unusual settings. Doing things differently feeds your personal vitality now. Your creative efforts may be unique and individualistic. Your taste is your very own. You may garner applause through your efforts with new technology or anything unconventional. Issues of independence are apt to emerge with lovers and children. Your children may jockey for more freedom—or be erratic and unpredictable. Encourage them to become more autonomous, but not irresponsible. Lovers could become erratic, cool, aloof, unavailable—or exciting, unique, and stimulating. People may trade roles between lover and friend (both ways). You're learning to find freedom in love, to balance head and heart.

Ruler of the 5th and ruler of the 12th

You could get a touch of magic in your soul. Romance is accented and you may fall in love with love. You might become quite dramatic, persuasive and skilled at "casting a spell" on your audience. You could be extremely artistic now. You may discover life and excitement in dreams and visions and carry others along with your enthusiasms. Your self-esteem can be fed through idealism, through spiritual pursuits, through your mystical, imaginative, visionary side, or your artistic creativity could flower. You might don rose-colored glasses where lovers and children are concerned. You may attract children or lovers who are illusive, overly sensitive, escapist—or wonderful artists, very compassionate, and instinctively mystical. Seeking a fantasy can lead to disillusionment. You will want to be uplifted in love relationships. Share beauty, ideals, or a vision with those you love. Look for life's meaning and zest in the spirit—not in human love affairs.

Ruler of the 6th and ruler of the 1st

(See Ruler of the 1st and ruler of the 6th above.)

Ruler of the 6th and ruler of the 2nd

(See Ruler of the 2nd and ruler of the 6th above.)

Ruler of the 6th and ruler of the 3rd

(See Ruler of the 3rd and ruler of the 6th above.)

Ruler of the 6th and ruler of the 4th

(See Ruler of the 4th and ruler of the 6th above.)

Ruler of the 6th and ruler of the 5th

(See Ruler of the 5th and ruler of the 6th above.)

Ruler of the 6th and ruler of the 6th

You need to work with precision, with details, with thoroughness, with efficiency now. You could repair, fix, or improve things—on the physical, mental, or emotional level. Health fields may appeal, or anything involving technical analysis, facts, figures, or tangible output. You may need to be quite analytical on the job. You may work too hard trying to get things "just right." An "indispensability syndrome" could develop—believing, "If you want it done right, do it yourself." At least relax after your have done your job! You are likely to function best in a working environment which is orderly, organized, and on-time. If you focus too exclusively on flaws, you may be hard on coworkers (or on yourself)—noting imperfections. Efficiency is important, but no one can do **everything** well. Health is a likely focus now—either very good health or possibly the reverse. If you stay practical, you can take excellent care of your body.

Ruler of the 6th and ruler of the 7th

People work is a natural now. You may gravitate toward counseling, the law, personnel administration or highly competitive fields. You might start working with a spouse, or decide to make marriage your career. You could take up aesthetic or artistic work (e.g., music, modeling, design, photography, etc.). Satisfaction could come through working with beauty or through teamwork. Grace, harmony, balance, design or form could be central in your vocation. Charm, negotiating skills, cooperation, or passivity could permeate your job routines. You are likely to prefer an attractive environment on the job. Coworkers might be very kind or vacillating. Other people might also help you focus and achieve. You are apt to work on your romantic relationships. This can include making a better and better partnership, or feeling like your partner has become a "chore" or a burden. You might end up rather critical and judgmental of your spouse—or feel your spouse is all too ready to identify your flaws. You are apt to attract people who are precise, organized, practical, hardworking, dedicated, or able to figure out what's wrong and fix it, or you could draw in people who are critical, judgmental, or workaholics. You will excel and find greater satisfaction in relationships in which efforts are shared so each of you contributes both vocationally and by improving your interactions with one another.

Ruler of the 6th and ruler of the 8th

You can bring great willpower to your work in this period. You may be drawn to financial fields (accounting, tax law, investment counseling, loan officer, etc.). Your investigative nose could lead you into insurance investigation, detective work or research or science of any kind. Or, you may be drawn toward psychotherapy, archaeology, occult studies, or looking into taboo areas. Business skills are also highlighted now. You could get involved with politics, sex therapy, budgeting or similar fields. Vocations where power, crises, or life-and-death situations are featured tend to draw you attention. You may need to handle intensity carefully. Power struggles with coworkers are possible, even to the point of dominance games, intimidation, threats, etc. Strong emotions are apt to be present within your work arena. You could use your intuition professionally now. Your job might begin to probe beneath the surface, be intense, or transform you, other people, or the material world. Joint resources could become a focus—government grants, insurance, return on investment, inheritance, spousal support, etc. Sexuality, power, or secrecy may become significant.

You can work doggedly, relentlessly, tenaciously. An effort to understand and control every detail of your work could lead to obsessive-compulsive behavior. Total control is obviously impossible when money and resources involve others. You can be and need to be practical, grounded, and sensible in shared efforts. Intimate interactions may stimulate your drive for competence and productivity. Sexual inhibition (by you or a partner) is possible if nit-picking tendencies or critical judgments are allowed to get out of hand, making intimacy feel more like a job than a joy. But with common sense about shared resources, you can enjoy deep bonds with other people.

Ruler of the 6th and ruler of the 9th

You may become interested in work with ideas, travel, religion, or anything educational or inspirational. Big, expansive projects could attract you, especially those which provide a sense of meaning, truth, justice, or knowledge to the world—e.g., through broadcasting, publishing, education, libraries, law courts, etc. You will tend to expect a lot of your job now—or of yourself as a worker. This could lead to job-hopping (in search of the "ideal" job) or lots of discontent (wanting everything to be better). Working to improve the world is a more constructive approach. Coworkers could become adventurous, generous, lively, and on the go—or overextended, intellectually arrogant, and prone to jumping to conclusions. You may have high expectations of your health, or try to do a good job in everything, or apply more common sense to your beliefs. A practical religion or world view could help you bring dreams down to earth. Matters of philosophy, metaphysics, and morality can be tested and measured against the physical demands of our earth world.

Ruler of the 6th and ruler of the 10th

You will seek ways to take charge on the job. An executive role comes more naturally now. Your sense of responsibility is apt to increase, and you can become the authority, the expert within your vocation. You also might slip into a workaholic role if you don't set limits. Be willing to delegate. A business field or anything offering solid accomplishments could attract you. If you overdo your focus on limits and what is possible, you could feel very blocked and inhibited vocationally. The best results come with a very disciplined, dedicated, achievement-oriented approach. Your career now needs to include precision, thoroughness, organization, and doing something really well. You may be drawn to fields involving health, nutrition, repairs, technical analysis or careful attention to detail. Success comes from working sensibly within the rules and being willing to pay your dues in terms of effort in order to succeed.

Ruler of the 6th and ruler of the 11th

You may change your job, voluntarily or involuntarily, during this period. You'll find yourself getting bored more easily on the job, needing a lot of variety in your day-to-day efforts. You might opt for irregular hours, unusual routines, self-employment, an unconventional vocation, or a unique twist to help keep yourself interested and effective on the job. New technology, groups, networking, or the future could become part of your work. Coworkers may become more objective and original—or erratic, flaky, and unpredictable. You are more apt to thrive in a working environment which is casual, unusual, and democratic. Being friends with your colleagues has more appeal now. Work routines can be unusual, unique, variety-oriented. You might quit, be fired, or have unpredictable experiences if you don't have enough freedom on the job. Flashes of insight may increase your competence. You may develop more working associations or friendships which are job-related. You could start working hard to improve your friendships—or find yourself becoming judgmental toward your buddies—or getting involved with comrades who pick at your perceived flaws. Bring common sense to humanitarian causes and find practical ways to promote equal opportunity and justice for all.

Ruler of the 6th and ruler of the 12th

You are apt to want your work to be ideal now. Bear in mind that you cannot find the "perfect" job nor do it flawlessly. Trying for either of those will just bring disillusionment and dissatisfaction. Gravitating toward a vocation which makes the world more beautiful, or a little closer to a utopian ideal is more helpful. You may exhibit more healing skills—on an emotional or spiritual level. You could become more involved with the aesthetic components of your job. Compassion, visualizing skills, dealing with the very small or infinitely large, or with intuition, can become assets within your profession. Colleagues may act in a more sensitive, caring fashion—or become rather confused and unclear. Beautifying the office might lift your spirits, or the quest for perfection may be directed to health matters. Remember that no one can do everything right and permit yourself to be human and fallible. Activities which allow you to bring a bit of your dream down into your earth world will be most satisfying now.

Ruler of the 7th and ruler of the 1st

(See Ruler of the 1st and ruler of the 7th above.)

Ruler of the 7th and ruler of the 2nd

(See Ruler of the 2nd and ruler of the 7th above.)

Ruler of the 7th and ruler of the 3rd

(See Ruler of the 3rd and ruler of the 7th above.)

Ruler of the 7th and ruler of the 4th

(See Ruler of the 4th and ruler of the 7th above.)

Ruler of the 7th and ruler of the 5th

(See Ruler of the 4th and ruler of the 7th above.)

Ruler of the 7th and ruler of the 6th

(See Ruler of the 6th and ruler of the 7th above.)

Ruler of the 7th and ruler of the 7th

Partnership, balance, and harmony are apt to become more important in your life. You yearn for a partner who is attractive, graceful, diplomatic, able to see both sides, well balanced, or cooperative. Unfortunately, if your subconscious is at odds with your conscious desires, you might attract individuals who are competitive, wishy-washy, passive, or too concerned with appearances. You need relationships which are equal, which support your aesthetic instincts and encourage togetherness—being a couple. This is a time when any sharing activities are accented—as well as the pursuit of beauty. You could become more involved with people exchanges of all sorts or with pursuing an artistic hobby or vocation. Wherever you have been out of balance in your life, you will want to return to the middle. Compromises and win/win solutions are important goals. Let your diplomatic skills and personal grace flower.

Ruler of the 7th and ruler of the 8th

You will learn about subterranean drives in your relationships in this period. You may share an intense urge for self-knowledge and self-mastery with a partner—or attract someone who is intimidating and powerful, or emotionally iced-out and withdrawn. Your interpersonal exchanges permit or push you to build your sense of power, resourcefulness and enduring will. You are apt to seek a partner who is intense, probing, involved in the search for underlying answers. You could draw in passionate, sexual, confrontational, manipulative, or resourceful people. You need relationships which are very deep, which encourage physical and emotional intimacy, and which offer opportunities to share power over money, possessions, and pleasures. You will tend to analyze your relationships more now—trying to figure out your partner, seeking hidden messages behind what is said. You might get involved with compulsive partners, but greater satisfaction lies in being graceful, diplomatic and equalitarian when dealing with shared finances and resources. Intimate and sexual exchanges will tend to stimulate your desire for ease and harmony, and you are learning much about compromising and sharing power.

Ruler of the 7th and ruler of the 9th

You will want a partner who is fun-loving, witty, inspirational, bright, or confident now. If these aspirations are carried to the point of excess, you could get involved with someone who is rash, overextended, or self-righteous. High expectations are likely—for your partner, for the relationship, and for yourself within the relationship. If idealism is carried too far, cosmic discontent is possible. Or, you may try multiple relationships—each time thinking, "This could be the one." Your best course is to pursue shared ideals and goals with your beloved, but not to expect perfection from each other. Your relationships now will influence your faith, beliefs, values, religious and spiritual principles. You may meet someone who plays a "guru" role (positively or negatively). Your relationships could become a forum for discussion and pursuit of higher knowledge and ultimate meaning. You probably will place more value on equality, justice and fair play. Your world view is apt to incorporate increased balance, harmony, beauty, and sharing. You can inspire and be inspired by close partners as long as both accept each other's humanness.

Ruler of the 7th and ruler of the 10th

If you are dealing with self-doubt, you may delay or hold back somewhat in the area of relationships while facing fear, anxiety, or inadequacy feelings. Or, you could be attracted to people who are strong, stable, responsible, hardworking, or oriented toward "making it" in the real world, people to "cope" with the world for you. Or, you might get involved with someone who pushes the same buttons as your authority parent did. Or you might marry someone who lets you play "parent." Work and responsibility need to be shared equally, lest one of you carry most of the burden of the relationship. You are learning about power, responsibility, authority and control in your relationships. You can work together to achieve with a partner and need to avoid choosing someone who is dominating and dictatorial or who expects you to do all the work. With a mutual commitment to teamwork, your interpersonal exchanges can enhance your strength, expertise, and dedication to doing well.

When teamwork has been achieved, you can work well with people, relationships, beauty, balance, and grace. A career may involve marriage, counseling, consulting, art, mathematics or other forms of balance. Business partnerships are also very possible. By confronting the rules with diplomacy and good taste, you can charm authorities and find win/win outcomes.

Ruler of the 7th and ruler of the 11th

In this period, you are apt to attract people who are independent, unusual, intellectual—or unconventional. You could get involved with unavailable partners (married, long-distance, etc.). Sharing new-age knowledge, technology, change, innovation, and encouraging each other's independence works well. Your relationships should feed your freedom now. You are learning about innovation and individuality in your relationships. You may share a sense of uniqueness with a partner who is quite different—or attract people who are strange, flaky, or unwilling to get involved. Your interpersonal exchanges can strengthen your willingness to break the rules, to go in new directions. You can have sudden attractions (and fall out of love suddenly as well). Tolerance and appreciation of each other's individuality strengthens your bonds. You, or those you attract, will want relationships that are open and equalitarian, that emphasize both people's uniqueness. You and your partner may become best friends—or one person may overdo the free soul and rebel role, carrying it to an extreme and disrupting the relationship. Love each other's differences. Friends may become partners and partners may stay friends (even after relationships end). Sociability reigns while knowledge expands exponentially.

Ruler of the 7th and ruler of the 12th

You are learning about compassion, sacrifice and idealism in your relationships. You may share an artistic vision or a utopian dream with a partner—or fall into savior/victim (rescuer/enabler) roles. Your interpersonal exchanges will give you a chance to visualize the best while avoiding extremes of escapism and martyrdom. You will want a partner who is idealistic, beautiful or compassionate, a relationship which affirms your imagination, sensitivity, and quest for transcendence. You will be drawn toward relationships which are flowing, serene, and lovely. You may be attracted to a person who is sweet, a healer, artistic (or a victim, escapist). You could fall into a love which is based on sacrifice or rose-colored glasses. Putting a partner on a pedestal guarantees s/he will fall off (or be lost). Your urge for transcendent experiences can be shared with a partner, but neither of you will provide Heaven on Earth for the other. Sharing spiritual, philanthropic, aesthetic, or visionary activities can help strengthen your connections with a partner. Pursuing a vision and working together to make the world better or more beautiful works best. Or functioning as a "professional savior" in a healing/helping role may provide profound satisfaction.

Ruler of the 8th and ruler of the 1st

(See Ruler of the 1st and ruler of the 8th above.)

Ruler of the 8th and ruler of the 2nd

(See Ruler of the 2nd and ruler of the 8th above.)

Ruler of the 8th and ruler of the 3rd

(See Ruler of the 3rd and ruler of the 8th above.)

Ruler of the 8th and ruler of the 4th

(See Ruler of the 4th and ruler of the 8th above.)

Ruler of the 8th and ruler of the 5th

(See Ruler of the 5th and ruler of the 8th above.)

Ruler of the 8th and ruler of the 6th

(See Ruler of the 6th and ruler of the 8th above.)

Ruler of the 8th and ruler of the 7th

(See Ruler of the 7th and ruler of the 8th above.)

Ruler of the 8th and ruler of the 8th

You are being drawn to probe and question in regard to sexuality, shared resources, money, taboos, or hidden matters. You can be quite an investigator now, getting to the bottom of things. Intimate interactions may trigger your urge to look beneath the surface of life. You can see complications and many layers of life. You may be drawn to occult studies, forbidden territory, sex, money, psychology, horror, or anything which has a profound emotional impact. Sensitive to clues, cues, and innuendoes, you often tune in to underlying messages and nonverbal hints. Power issues are likely to be highlighted and you may have to work to achieve comfortable giving, receiving, and sharing with a mate in regard to financial, sensual, and material arenas. Endurance, resourcefulness, strength of will, concentration, and depth of insight are accented, providing the capacity to go to the end. Knowing when is enough and when to let go is sometimes the final challenge.

Ruler of the 8th and ruler of the 9th

You may probe more into values and belief systems in this period. Where people put their faith and what they trust may seem more important. You may obsess about truth, justice, or moral and ethical principles, or revel in unending complexity when exploring world views and philosophy. The principles and ethics which you follow must resonate to the core of your being. You could even become a bit fanatic about values, truth and trust, wanting to be swept away spiritually as you seek a full understanding of your obsessions, compulsions, and emotional drives.. Power issues could arise within the religion or philosophy to which you adhere. Religions or spiritual paths which emphasize balancing (or combining) the spiritual and carnal may appeal to you (e.g., tantric yoga). You can pursue understanding on a wide scale as well as with a single-minded, intense focus. The analysis of discrepancies may be important as you decide what to keep and what to throw away while you clarify your values and goals.

Intimate interactions might affect your quest for meaning and ultimate answers. You might idealize self-knowledge and self-mastery—or put great value (perhaps too much) on shared resources, sensuality, or sexuality. You may look to intimate relationships to supply a sense of meaning, purpose and inspiration in life. You could be seduced by guru types or by the lure of inspired knowledge. Or you could give your devotion to the spirit of optimism, adventure, idealism, and honesty which transcends human nature.

Ruler of the 8th and ruler of the 10th

You are concerned with the issue of power and power drives now. You may analyze the establishment, authority figures, or your own need for mastery. When the desire for self-control joins the belief in one's obligation to manage the world, the urge to control can become a compulsion which needs to be directed into a professional career. Organizational skills and the capacity to handle details are likely to increase and to be helpful in such a career. Power struggles can be constructive competition, provided we are not fighting our own "team," or jousting against limits which are necessary for survival. The latter can include adequate rest, food, exercise, etc. Fighting a team member can mean struggles with a spouse over finances, or sensuality, or sexuality. Compromise is the name of the game for any kind of teamwork. Over-doing responsibility may produce an Atlas trying to carry the world, while a projection of one's power into the world can lead to self-doubt, self-blocking, and the potential for illness. Intimate interactions can become the site of power issues if either member of a peer relationship is trying to be parent or dictator over the other. With your potential for reliability and practicality added to your ambition for achievement, you have the capacity for major success in this period. You might work for the government at some level, as a manager for a big business or as an entrepreneur running your own business, or in a family business. Alternately, a career in a professions such as the law, politics, or consulting would be appropriate. Work with joint resources could include accounting, investment, insurance, etc. An interest in the past or what lies under the surface can lead to archaeology, work as a detective, or as a psychotherapist. Both security and power are important goals. Just stay alert to the rights of others, to your own human limits, and keep looking for the hidden answers.

Ruler of the 8th and ruler of the 11th

You may analyze and probe and seek to peel away the layers of friends, organizations, progress, or social causes. A muckraking (reforming) role may seem natural. With increasing concern about freedom and individuality, you might man the barricades or join the protest marches for social causes. You are likely to probe deeply into the future and technology, combining the ability to handle details with a broad overview. You could become friends with former mates or turn a friend into a mate as you seek to resolve the "freedom-closeness" dilemma. You want intimate interactions but also want tolerance, openness, and the freedom to pursue new interests. In fact, you cannot imagine intimacy without freedom. The inner conflict could produce a commitment which leaves the door open, an emotional bond which you will be free to leave. Or, you may attract mates unwilling to settle down.

You might decide to pursue a depth investigation into unconventional, unusual, or futuristic matters. You could be fascinated and enthralled by the new and different. In regard to taboo areas—including death, shared resources, money and sexuality—you can be more detached than most people during this period, tending to be attracted to the unique or avant garde. Research in astrology, parapsychology, near-death experiences, or the underworld of hackers could fascinate you. The pursuit of deeper and wider knowledge is endless.

Ruler of the 8th and ruler of the 12th

This is a period in which to plumb your own subconscious, to get to the depths of your psyche. If you have unresolved inner conflicts, it is an appropriate time to consider psychotherapy. If you have or could get the education or training, you might select a healing field as a vocation. Alternately, a search for spiritual answers might help resolve inner tensions. Running away from the world through escapist, including addictive, behavior only intensifies the anguish the morning after. Meditation, ritual, music, nature, may open up mystical experiences for you.

This period is combining a desire for a human mate with the mystic's desire for union with the Absolute. One possible reaction is a compulsive quest for a "happily ever after" marriage. Looking for a soul mate who will be God and give us heaven on earth is a futile quest. You may have incredible, romantic, ecstatic sensual/sexual experiences, but don't value human connections as if they were cosmic. Do utilize your depth insights and ability to tune into your partner's psyche. We can either settle for a human being who shares our values and goals, or devote our lives to helping humanity in a service profession.

Another alternative is a deep commitment to the aesthetic side of life. We can create (or promote and sell) beauty as a way of sharing with the world. Inspired writing or music can draw on the psychic potential of this period, which connects two water houses. Since excessive sensitivity can be a two-edged sword, it is important to know how to control it. We manage this by fire action focused on personal desire, or by practical earth action, or by air detachment and analysis.

Ruler of the 9th and ruler of the 1st
(See Ruler of the 1st and ruler of the 9th above.)

Ruler of the 9th and ruler of the 2nd
(See Ruler of the 2nd and ruler of the 9th above.)

Ruler of the 9th and ruler of the 3rd
(See Ruler of the 3rd and ruler of the 9th above.)

Ruler of the 9th and ruler of the 4th
(See Ruler of the 4th and ruler of the 9th above.)

Ruler of the 9th and ruler of the 5th
(See Ruler of the 5th and ruler of the 9th above.)

Ruler of the 9th and ruler of the 6th
(See Ruler of the 6th and ruler of the 9th above.)

Ruler of the 9th and ruler of the 7th
(See Ruler of the 7th and ruler of the 9th above.)

Ruler of the 9th and ruler of the 8th
(See Ruler of the 8th and ruler of the 9th above.)

Ruler of the 9th and ruler of the 9th
You tend to value beliefs, education, travel, spirituality—or anything which broadens your horizons. You might put teachers or gurus on pedestals now (and be disillusioned if they fall off). This is a time to deepen your faith and

confidence. Your world view may expand to emphasize trust, outreach, and exposure to the wider world. Your quest for the truth could take you to any by-way or highway of the world or of the mind. Alternately, you may feel that you have found at least some answers which you want to give to others through teaching or writing. You will tend to increase your idealism, so make sure your goals are clear and try to enjoy the journey toward them. Excessive expectations can lead to over-enthusiasm, overly blunt speech, and later disillusionment. On the positive side, benevolent tendencies may emerge, urges to help the world. Enjoy discussions of philosophy, religion, beliefs, put your faith in the future, and try to do your share to improve the world.

Ruler of the 9th and ruler of the 10th

You may idolize responsibility now—whether in terms of doing it right, taking care of business, fitting in, or "making it" (success) in society's terms. Traditions and rules could be over valued. You could idealize authority figures or power in general, or you may just believe in hard work and doing what's necessary. You may tend to expect a lot of authorities, but also see their highest potential. Too high expectations do lead to disillusionment. Find ways to offer your ideas, ideals and principles to authorities.

Tangibles could play a large role in your world view, and your quest for the truth could become formal, cautious, conventional, or economical. You can seek answers conscientiously, thoroughly, and responsibly. However, limiting trust to the material world with an inability to conceive of a reality beyond the material world can lead to insecurity and sometimes to an increased need for personal control to gain a sense of security. Career ambitions and status may become priorities, and dictatorial tendencies and/or depression could follow. If there is much self-doubt, inhibition could lead to serious self-blocking.

An effective synthesis of these principles can produce work which is inspirational or broadening. This could attract you to fields involving travel, religion, education, broadcasting, journalism, publishing, promotion, or anything which widely disseminates knowledge or gives people a sense of meaning. Enthusiasm and confidence can spur others on. You will work best when your ideals are involved and you are pursuing a vision. You can change reality by altering belief systems, values, and world views.

Ruler of the 9th and ruler of the 11th

During this period, you may increasingly idealize friends or humanity—the "common man or common woman." You might place too much faith in progress, technology, or anything on the cutting edge. Organizations and networking for humanitarian causes could be important. A belief in the future might lead you deeper into astrology. Your world view must emphasize tolerance and freedom, and you could break the rules to make it unique. You are likely to question and go beyond traditional boundaries in the quest for life's meaning, possibly even becoming a rebel in your beliefs, leaving your childhood faith to find your own truth, your own path. Philosophy, religion, learning, ideals, ethics, principles could be explored with friends and groups. Your own wit and wisdom may grow, or you might fall in with rash, self-righteous, or overly blunt individuals. When you interact with humanity, your enthusiastic, adventurous, seeking and searching side is activated and a broad-minded approach to meaning will help to create opportunities for dreaming, inspiring, and uplifting. Enjoy an unconventional, inventive, and progressive quest for the truth as you seek answers in your own unique way. Freedom of thought is a priority. Rebelliousness, eccentricity, and flashes of insight could emerge from discussions of philosophy, religion, beliefs or the pursuit of any area of new knowledge with increased trust in the unusual and the new.

Ruler of the 9th and ruler of the 12th

You might idealize the quest for infinite love and beauty now, tending to believe in the artistic, spiritual, or mystical. You might worship nature, or be inspired by the infinitely large (the Galactic view of astronomy), or the infinitesimally small (the search for theorized quarks). You need to believe in something Higher, whether a personal God or an impersonal Truth.

Intuitive forms of knowing may become more appealing, with a world view which includes compassion. Your quest for answers may be sensitive, intuitive, and gentle, pursued with imagination, mystical feelings, or an artistic eye. You need to stay grounded to avoid escapism which ends in confusion, or excessive idealism which leads to overdoing philanthropy to the point of sacrifice. Discussions of philosophy, religion, beliefs with compatible friends could be helpful. Your tendency may be to trust nature, beauty, God. One path to enlightenment lies in being benevolent, optimistic, enthusiastic, idealistic, philosophical, and freedom-loving. Activities which allow you to travel, educate, inspire, seek the truth, move, or be with nature can help you to tap into your Higher Self. Another path seeks inspiration in religion and spirituality, though it carries the danger of being deluded or confused by dogmatic preachers or gurus, each convinced that his way is **the** way. No one has all your answers, but the quest for meaning and faith can help energize you. Beauty, nature, and mystical activities may all offer support.

Ruler of the 10th and ruler of the 1st
(See Ruler of the 1st and ruler of the 10th above.)

Ruler of the 10th and ruler of the 2nd
(See Ruler of the 2nd and ruler of the 10th above.)

Ruler of the 10th and ruler of the 3rd
(See Ruler of the 3rd and ruler of the 10th above.)

Ruler of the 10th and ruler of the 4th
(See Ruler of the 4th and ruler of the 10th above.)

Ruler of the 10th and ruler of the 5th
(See Ruler of the 5th and ruler of the 10th above.)

Ruler of the 10th and ruler of the 6th
(See Ruler of the 6th and ruler of the 10th above.)

Ruler of the 10th and ruler of the 7th
(See Ruler of the 7th and ruler of the 10th above.)

Ruler of the 10th and ruler of the 8th
(See Ruler of the 8th and ruler of the 10th above.)

Ruler of the 10th and ruler of the 9th
(See Ruler of the 9th and ruler of the 10th above.)

Ruler of the 10th and ruler of the 10th
You need power and authority in your career now. A role as executive or expert is likely to come more naturally. You will want to make the rules, but might first have to struggle with current authorities. Clear demarcation of responsibilities and limits is essential. The better you understand the structure, the more effectively you can take control and increase your status. You want your work to be grounded and effective. You are likely to have a strong sense of responsibility and may carry more than your fair share of the load. You are probably ambitious, but very willing to pay your dues (work your way up). You work best when you are achieving tangible results and can measure your progress. You are likely to work quite hard—perhaps too much on occasion. Be clear about the limits to your authority as well as time limits. Learn to delegate! Organizational and executive ability, common sense, an understanding of rules, a willingness to expend effort, and precision with details are needed for a job at the top, and are likely to increase. Unless you have projected your power into others, you will do best and be most fulfilled in fields where you can—over time—reach the top.

Ruler of the 10th and ruler of the 11th
Your inclinations in this period will pull you toward a career full of variety, mental stimulation, or anything new and different. You may change careers, change the way you work, or pick a field with built-in diversity or on the cutting edge. You might confront the rules by breaking them, or making them over. Your urge will be to treat authorities as friends and equals, refusing to recognize a hierarchical set-up. An innovative, inventive approach to your career is likely. Society may see you as a rebel, or at least an individualist. A desire for individuality on the job may draw you to a field which is unusual, or to nonstandard hours and styles of work. You can be quite innovative or inventive on the job, especially one where you work with your mind, with independence, and with many choices and alternatives.

This is a time to apply real world demands in an unconventional or unusual framework. You may be torn between changing the current structure and building a new, revolutionary structure. It is time to balance the old and new, change and established form. When we recognize and voluntarily work within the necessary limits, we are able to transcend many formerly accepted limits.

Ruler of the 10th and ruler of the 12th

Part of you is now calling for a career that will give people a glimpse of infinite love and beauty. You could be drawn to art, to healing, or feel the need to be healed. You could confront the rules of life in a material body and world by mentally dissolving them, or viewing them from such a cosmic perspective that they become meaningless. But, you need to structure your inspiration to succeed in bringing a touch of magic to the real world. Solutions include choosing work that tries to save, heal, rescue, or beautify the world. You may expect a lot of yourself as a worker, of authorities, and of your job, but you do have a dream to pursue. You will work best when you are inspired by faith, seeking to bring dreams down to earth and to make them real.

Combining pragmatism and idealism is part of your professional challenge. Don't give up on your visions, but don't live frustrated because the material world is never as perfect as what you can imagine! You can handle power with compassion and sensitivity. Your career could make the world better, more beautiful, or touch people's imaginations in fields such as the entertainment world or advertising or PR. Even a would-be transcendent career must recognize practical limits. What you do won't ever be as perfect as what your imagination can conceive, and soul can dream, but you can contribute your part to uplifting the world.

Ruler of the 11th and ruler of the 1st
(See Ruler of the 1st and ruler of the 11th above.)

Ruler of the 11th and ruler of the 2nd
(See Ruler of the 2nd and ruler of the 11th above.)

Ruler of the 11th and ruler of the 3rd
(See Ruler of the 3rd and ruler of the 11th above.)

Ruler of the 11th and ruler of the 4th
(See Ruler of the 4th and ruler of the 11th above.)

Ruler of the 11th and ruler of the 5th
(See Ruler of the 5th and ruler of the 11th above.)

Ruler of the 11th and ruler of the 6th
(See Ruler of the 6th and ruler of the 11th above.)

Ruler of the 11th and ruler of the 7th
(See Ruler of the 7th and ruler of the 11th above.)

Ruler of the 11th and ruler of the 8th
(See Ruler of the 8th and ruler of the 11th above.)

Ruler of the 11th and ruler of the 9th
(See Ruler of the 9th and ruler of the 11th above.)

Ruler of the 11th and ruler of the 10th
(See Ruler of the 10th and ruler of the 11th above.)

Ruler of the 11th and ruler of the 11th
It's doubly important now for you to be an individual, to be involved with the future, the cutting edge. You need a sense of movement, variety, independence, and involvement with free-wheeling activities. Find some rules you can break without disastrous consequences to express your increasing individuality, inventiveness, and innovation. Freedom can be pursued with friends and groups. Associations need to be looser, more open-ended and full of mutual tolerance. They can provide intellectual stimulation and contribute to progress with a shared interest in the future. If you are not the person on the cutting edge, projection could jolt your life out of a rut through others, abrupt, unpredictable, aloof, cold, or strange people, or by changing circumstances outside of your control.

When involved with the widest reach of humanity, you are likely to become more broad-minded, adroit, and creative. Problem-solving abilities and the capacity to see many options are highlighted. You may thrive in groups and friendships which are unusual, futuristic, or intellectual. New age knowledge, technology, astrology, social causes, revolution, surprises, or anything offbeat and eccentric could be a focus. You may be attracted to people who are unconventional, rebellious, or inventive. Unbonded relationships which reaffirm your innovation, tolerance, and broad perspective are best. Even super-individualists need others to fortify their progressive, insightful uniqueness.

Ruler of the 11th and ruler of the 12th
You may be unconventional now in your approach to aesthetic experiences, to inspiration, to meditation, to your view of the psychic or subconscious realms. Your urge will be to go beyond tradition in seeking a connection to the Source. You may experiment with friendships which are imaginative, illusory, or idealistic. Magic, film, art, mysticism, nature, philanthropy, healing, fantasy, symbols, or anything otherworldly could be a focus. You may be attracted to buddies who are sweet, helpless, or visionary. Unbonded relationships which build up your intuition, artistic inclinations and/or visualizing skills could be helpful by strengthening your spiritual, compassionate, transcendent side. And

you may bring them a unique perspective where matters of intuition, spirituality, and beauty are concerned. An avant garde or technological connection to art is possible, such as computer-aided design. Or biofeedback to develop the capacity to sustain theta brain waves could break new ground in terms of transcendent tools.

Romantic, idealistic urges are in focus with friends and groups. Too much sensitivity to the pain of others could trap you in savior/victim games or psychic/emotional overwhelm. Your challenge is to blend absorption and detachment, the urge to merge and the urge to separate. You could be inspired in terms of individuality and involvement with social causes—or be used, abused, and taken advantage of by friends, groups, or organizations. You may want to heal humanity; don't over idealize the downtrodden. Others can assist your quest for faith. Inspiration may come from being unconventional, futuristic, independent, inventive, detached, progressive, and open-minded. Activities which allow you to break outgrown rules, to look ahead, and to consider humanity and progress will help you to tap into your Higher Self.

Ruler of the 12th and ruler of the 1st
(See Ruler of the 1st and ruler of the 12th above.)

Ruler of the 12th and ruler of the 2nd
(See Ruler of the 2nd and ruler of the 12th above.)

Ruler of the 12th and ruler of the 3rd
(See Ruler of the 3rd and ruler of the 12th above.)

Ruler of the 12th and ruler of the 4th
(See Ruler of the 4th and ruler of the 12th above.)

Ruler of the 12th and ruler of the 5th
(See Ruler of the 5th and ruler of the 12th above.)

Ruler of the 12th and ruler of the 6th
(See Ruler of the 6th and ruler of the 12th above.)

Ruler of the 12th and ruler of the 7th
(See Ruler of the 7th and ruler of the 12th above.)

Ruler of the 12th and ruler of the 8th
(See Ruler of the 8th and ruler of the 12th above.)

Ruler of the 12th and ruler of the 9th
(See Ruler of the 9th and ruler of the 12th above.)

Ruler of the 12th and ruler of the 10th
(See Ruler of the 10th and ruler of the 12th above.)

Ruler of the 12th and ruler of the 11th
(See Ruler of the 11th and ruler of the 12th above.)

Ruler of the 12th and ruler of the 12th
In this period, you could feel confused, romantic, escapist—or incredibly inspired, spiritual, able to connect with your Higher Self and bring its vision into the world. Privacy and a sanctuary (sheltered, serene) are important to let you commune with your Higher Self. You could be uplifted by art, beauty, nature, cosmic images, meditation, or ritual. You may idealize the mystical, sensitive, intuitive, otherworldly, and non rational sides of life, or become disillusioned with lack of clarity, gullibility, passivity, and impractical escapism. You could want to help less fortunate, vulnerable life forms, whether humans, endangered animals, or rain forests. You want your quest for the Source, for life's ultimate meaning, to uplift you, sweep you away. With a strong connection to transcendence, you can see beauty in many forms. You can be inspired by art, nature, healing, and compassion.

CHAPTER SIX
CONJUNCTIONS: PLANET/ PLANET (AND ASTEROIDS)

Sun Conjunct (Natal) Moon

(Progressed Sun Conjunct Progressed Moon is New Moon—see Chapter 4.)
Domestic and maternal matters are dear to the heart. Home and family are likely to be a central focus. Pregnancy, childbirth, and other important nurturing activities could be highlighted. Self-esteem is connected to emotional ties. You may take pride in your ability to nurture or your capacity to be emotionally open to others. You may decide to enlarge your home or make it more impressive. Positive attention could be sought through the physical home, the ancestry, family members or anything that is a part of the nest. Caring is accented.

Mundane Options: having a child (or gaining one through adoption, marriage, etc.), making an emotional commitment, promotional or sales activities, acting, expanding your home (physically or emotionally), nurturing people or animals, protecting creative efforts.

Sun Conjunct Mercury or Mercury Conjunct Sun

You are likely to experience your self-esteem as directly connected to your mental capacities. You may feel a lot of pride (or shame) based on how you think, theorize, communicate or write. You could be ego-vulnerable in this area and may take people's opinions of your intellectual capacity too much to heart. Or, if overconfident, you could be too self-assured in your opinions and come across as bombastic, arrogant or pompous. You need to shine through your mind, and may enjoy word play or other mental games.

Your creative thrust is intimately connected with your mental capacities. Your perceptions may be influenced by your drive for zest, for fun, for joy in life. Pure, objective thought is less likely during this period, as your thinking is tinged by passion. At the same time, your passions and heartfelt drives have a component of detachment and objectivity. You can compare and contrast speculative or risk-taking options. You may observe children or other creative outlets with a lighthearted eye. Humor and a youthful outlook probably come more easily.

If these themes are denied in you, children or lovers may express the mental focus for you and be talkative, casual, flippant, quick-witted, detached or adaptable. Siblings or other relatives may manifest the drive toward extroversion, confidence, creativity and doing more than has been done before.

Mundane Options: thinking about a love affair; flirtation; many social activities; sales; promotions; investments (or gambling); involvements with relatives, lovers, children; excitement from classes, books or teaching; love of learning; learning (studying) love.

Sun Conjunct Venus or Venus Conjunct Sun

This period highlights a zestful pursuit of pleasure. Sensuality is usually more marked, and overindulgence is possible. All the physical sense pleasures (eating, drinking, smoking, lovemaking) could have increased appeal. Extravagance is more likely, as you are drawn to the finer things in life. Romantic urges are strengthened. You could "fall in love" or commit (marriage, living together) seriously to a partner.

Artistic and aesthetic feelings may abound. Beauty could be exciting, and becoming active in the creative and/or performing arts is quite possible. You might also achieve recognition through a larger salary or other physical demonstrations of your worth. Taking pleasure through being the center of attention, enjoying children, thrills or risk-taking are all potentials. Increased self-esteem is possible as you learn to like yourself better and solidify any creative accomplishments.

If these potentials are not actualized by you, you might subconsciously encourage indulgence in your children or loved ones. You might attract a partner who is charismatic, exciting and magnetic who can express the dynamic solar qualities for you. The focus of this aspect is on your ability to enjoy life and love.

Mundane Options: money earned (or spent) through children, recreation, speculation, lovers, risks; love deepened and intensified; strong sensual/sexual satisfaction; artistic creativity; hedonism; enjoying sales, promotion, entertainment, "starring" role; new love interest or marriage; exciting partner; recreation with partner; artistic/aesthetic creations; team sports; sales group; partnership with a child; courtship; child custody issue; vacation.

Sun Conjunct Mars or Mars Conjunct Sun

Personal will is a core issue for this period. With two fire planets backing each other up, the impetus is forward and outward. This is all about getting what **you** want. You could take an assertiveness training class, start working out, take up a sport or adopt another form of physical activity. You may get more in touch with your anger. You might begin to make your desires more of a priority in life. The challenge is to be yourself and meet your personal needs while still maintaining love relationships with others.

If the "I'm number one" side of this combination is denied in you, it is likely to be lived out by those near and dear to you—especially lovers and children. Those individuals could seem selfish, self-centered, aggressive or pushy. In such cases, they are overdoing the energy you need to explore more in yourself and to express yourself (in moderation).

Self-consciousness may rise; you are more aware of yourself, and perhaps more aware of how others see you—and whether or not they approve of your actions. You probably want love and admiration, but would prefer to get them your own way. Some healthy self-centeredness is constructive during this period. You are really defining yourself and learning to take more joy and pride in your strengths.

Mundane Options: having a child, new recreational involvements, sports, new creative venture, sales, promotional work, speculation, socializing, entertaining, humor, fame or recognition. If your fire urge to express yourself is blocked, physical problems are possible—ranging from low energy to heart or head or other disabilities.

Sun Conjunct Jupiter or Jupiter Conjunct Sun (long-term)

The theme of this aspect involves expansion of world views. You may feel the urge to travel, take classes, discuss or otherwise explore the question of life's meaning. Ethical or moral issues could be expanded and expounded upon. Faith and confidence are likely to grow during this period. Restlessness is probable; you need action—possibly physically, as well as with ideas.

High expectations for love may predominate. Hearts and flowers could appeal, and you may want more than is possible from children and other loved ones. Remember that people are only human. You may find yourself dreaming big dreams and excited by expansive projects. Excess enthusiasm could lead you to overreach—stay grounded. Humor is highlighted; this is a good-time combination! You are likely to be more generous than usual—with money, with time, with promises. Remember that life has limits as well! (If you are feeling insecure, you may deny the outgoing potential of this combination and subconsciously attract people—most likely loved ones—who manifest it for you. They are then likely to be **too** fun-loving, playful, overconfident, rash or self-righteous.) Positive expression means constant growth and expansion, but not to the point where you leave behind other valuable talents and accomplishments.

Mundane Options: wheeling and dealing; vacation; selling imports, education, travel, sports, speculation/gambling; investing in the future; onstage in a religious context; leadership role in college; extravagance; playing the field (in relationships), creative writing, publishing, dealing with the law, increased faith.

Sun Conjunct Saturn or Saturn Conjunct Sun (long-term)

"If it is worth doing, it is worth doing well" is the motto for this era. How you react to that depends on your inner security and sense of strength. If you are in touch with most of your power, you are likely to work very hard, gain recognition, accomplish much and earn personal satisfaction as well as approval from others. If you doubt your abilities, you may feel inhibited and frustrated, afraid to try what you would like to attempt, timid about reaching for the heights lest you fall flat on your face. Self-doubts could cripple your confidence. This is an ambitious combination, but you choose how to handle that ambition and power drive.

Mundane Options: promotion at work; working in sales, recreation, with children, speculation or entertainment; lacking self-esteem if your career falls short of your ambitions; rejecting a parent role because of the career being more important or from subconscious feelings of inadequacy, executive role; busman's holiday; controlling/structuring love; responsible parent or parenting.

Sun Conjunct Uranus or Uranus Conjunct Sun (long-term)

Innovation, creativity and change are in the air. You are working with a theme of risk-taking, pioneering and moving toward the future. You may make changes in any area of your life—especially where love, children and friends are concerned. You could be creative in a very unique and individualistic fashion. You are likely to thrive on challenges and excitement. If you are not aware of this desire, you could subconsciously create negative excitement—just so life keeps hopping. If this electric, disruptive and unpredictable theme is denied in you, it could be lived out in excess by those near and dear to you.

A part of the focus is the polarity of passion versus detachment or of emotional intensity, commitment and love versus friendship, separation and logic. You could swing from one extreme to the other, or you might live out one side, while someone close to you expresses the other. Relationships might have a stop/go quality, or abrupt shifts as you move from wanting them, back to not wanting them. Ambivalence might be felt about committing to a love relationship, or having children. Part of you is unsure you are ready to be "tied down." You need to make room in your life for freedom as well as closeness.

Mundane Options: involvement with children, step-children, foster children; love affair; children leaving the nest or you wanting to get away from them; leadership role in groups/ associations; emotional investment in social causes; unusual or unique creative projects; selling technology; teaching astrology (or teaching in general), new studies or hobbies, public service.

Sun Conjunct Neptune or Neptune Conjunct Sun (long-term)

This period centers on romance and magic. On the positive side, you could find the love of your life, someone you admire, someone who touches your soul, someone who shares that "special something" with you. Less positively, you might fall "in love with love" and end up misled, deceived, disillusioned and disappointed (since it was your own dream that you loved rather than the real person). Savior/victim relationships are also a danger if your idealism does not have a constructive outlet. One extreme is just fantasizing about one's "perfect love" and not doing anything. A likely talent is the ability to see the best in those you love. As long as this is balanced with some facing-of-facts, it can help ameliorate stress, add the oil of forgiveness and help strengthen relationships.

Charisma is highlighted. Drama comes more naturally to you now. You are likely to seem a little bit romantic, idealistic, mysterious or alluring to people around you. There is a touch of magic here. This can be a useful quality when promoting, selling, or persuading people. You can touch people emotionally.

Inspired beauty is another possible theme. Artistic and creative activities are quite possible. Film-making or editing, little theater, magic shows or other "illusory" fields could appeal, as could anything in the performing (and other) arts. The urge is to lift people out of their ordinary lives, onto a higher plane, through the use of beauty.

Mundane Options: creating something beautiful; secret love affair; savior/victim relationships with lovers or children; the "perfect" vacation; fund-raising for charity; gambling; finding or becoming a guru; inspired love/lovemaking.

Sun Conjunct Pluto or Pluto Conjunct Sun (long-term)

Intensity and passion are the theme and it can last for many years if progressed Pluto is on the Sun. Your emotional life may have an "all or nothing" quality about it. Commitments, when made, are deeply felt—"to the death." Because the level of involvement can be so total, it can also be threatening, and withdrawal may be preferred. This combination could show the deepest of love bonds as well as a retreat from the prospect of mating and sharing souls.

Your sensual nature is highlighted, yet you may be torn between indulgence and self-mastery. Zest, joy and passion are possible, but so are inhibition, holding back and over control. Feast or famine seesaws may come in the areas of sexuality, finances and love relationships.

Power is probably an issue. You may be confronting the question of where to direct your power drive—inward toward self-mastery, or outward toward other people. If power is not directly faced and appropriately used, manipulative emotional games may occur. It is essential to learn to share the power, especially with lovers and children. Learning how to give as well as to receive (or how to receive as well as give) could be part of the challenge. Knowing how to let go—when something is truly over—is apt to be a challenge. When you give your heart, you give your soul. Is it any wonder you may be cautious about sharing with another?

Mundane Options: increased passion (or sexual withdrawal); the temptation to speculate or gamble or invest or concern with the return on investments; financial issues (may involve debts, taxes, inheritance); extravagance versus penny-pinching; surgery; end of a creative project; family teamwork; expenses (or income) through children or close peer relationships; owning power which is yours and recognizing what you have no control over.

Sun Conjunct Ceres or Ceres Conjunct Sun

A nurturing, parenting theme is paramount in this period. Options are varied and might include having (or adopting) a child, becoming a grandparent, becoming a parent by marriage, gaining a parent by marriage, significant interactions with a parent figure, nurturing people in a job such as teaching or nursing, or working in some creative fashion.

If the desire for significance and recognized accomplishments is not being satisfied through your work or what you see as your "job" in life, health problems are a possibility. Illness can be a source of attention if other sources are blocked. You might find more attention through illness than other avenues. Whether you look to be parented and protected by others, or seek to nurture, support, love and look after them, the issue revolves around care-taking, creativity, and achieving an effective love.

Mundane Options: having, adopting or nurturing a child, becoming a grandparent or parent through marriage, more contact with a parental figure, increased parenting duties, creative work, recognition for your care-taking skills.

Sun Conjunct Pallas or Pallas Conjunct Sun

Beauty and justice are highlighted during this time. You may be extra-creative, especially in the visual arts (photography, fashion, design, architecture, painting, etc.). With more warmth and vivaciousness, you might find it easier to influence others. Diplomacy, negotiations and contracting could help develop your skills. Love relationships may be more important than usual.

Zest and enthusiasm are tied to other people. This can include finding exciting, dynamic relationships. It can include attracting a thrill-seeker as a partner, someone always wanting the adrenaline rush who lives out that side of life for you. If you deny your own magnetism, you may subconsciously feel your partner is more important, more noteworthy, etc. Another possibility is to find drama in sharing and in truly loving, equal exchanges.

Mundane Options: new love interest; exciting partner; recreation with partner; artistic/aesthetic creations; team sports; sales group; partnership with a child; courtship; child custody concerns, fun vacation.

Sun Conjunct Juno or Juno Conjunct Sun

Marriage or an emotional commitment is likely to be in high focus. Issues revolve around sharing love, possessions and pleasures. You may create a deep, lasting bond of love during this period. You could deepen and strengthen an already existing relationship (or make the commitment to one). You could find ways to add excitement to a relationship—or expect a partner to be the exciting, vibrant one. An artistic emphasis is also likely, so a focus on beauty is quite possible as well.

Establishing a mutual admiration society is your best bet. If either partner tries to "supervise" the other, power struggles could follow. Admiration and love work wonders. Power struggles breed more strife. Sexual and/or financial confrontations or issues are possible, but love **can** find a way! Focusing on a shared depth of feeling can enable you and a mate to work through challenges and enjoy the inner gold.

You might also be involved in joint resources including investments, taxes, debts, inheritances, insurance, pensions, looking for new creative solutions.

Mundane Options: marriage, new love interest; exciting partner; recreation with partner; artistic/aesthetic creations; team sports; increased sales; partnership with a child; courtship; child custody concerns; fun vacations, decisions involving joint resources, dealing with debts or income from others or from past actions.

Sun Conjunct Vesta or Vesta Conjunct Sun

This period highlights a drive to accomplish and to achieve positive feedback for your practical efforts. You are likely to seek more recognition through your work, make your work more exciting, explore new creative outlets or in some way expand your scope. This can be a highly productive period, where you channel lots of zest, enthusiasm, confidence and joy into doing things well, a time for personal success if you like your work. Unfortunately, there is also a danger of feeling inhibited, self-critical, blocked or even ill if you want to do more than you can, or if you are frustrated by your current career focus, feeling it is not sufficiently exciting or challenging or worthy of your ability.

You may undertake a new creative project. Possible work could involve children, recreation, speculation, promotion, sales or the limelight. You may solidify growth gains, consolidating your position and getting ready for the next thrust into the future.

Mundane Options: a job involving creative flair; work in sales, promotion, entertainment, recreation, speculation or with children; a job promotion; health problems (if your need to shine, to be admired, is denied); handicrafts; toymaking; sports as a health measure.

Sun Conjunct Chiron or Chiron Conjunct Sun (long-term)

An emphasis on fire marks this period, encouraging creativity, zest for life, enthusiasm, and confidence which can lead to impulsive action. Over-confidence might be a danger at times. Keep one foot on the ground but do look for ways to enlarge your world, whether through new studies, teaching, writing, travel, or a search for personal meaning that will strengthen your sense of self-worth.

Mundane Options: increased education, writing, traveling, speculation, gambling, wheeling and dealing, quest for excitement, drama found in inspirational activities.

Sun Conjunct/Opposite Nodes
or Nodes Conjunct/Opposite Sun (long-term)

A conjunction/opposition between the Sun and the nodes of the Moon suggest a need to make room in your life for both your expansive, creative, power-seeking side and your ability to be empathic and sensitive to the needs of others. Fire (Sun) is instinctively independent in the sense of wanting to be in control. Water (the Moon and its nodes) is instinctively dependent or nurturing. Life should be big enough for both. Successful integration involves finding an appropriate way to shine, be admired and express your power while also allowing softness and vulnerability, your own and that of others.

Sun Conjunct North Node

The focus is on emotional needs, and parental instincts. You may be inclined to enlarge your family, or extend your nurturing focus. You need to give and receive love with the people closest to you; the reach is outward and expressive in terms of love relationships. Emotions are apt to be intense, but you may feel pulled between expressing versus holding back. Now is the time to build your sense of security and attachment. Concentrate on close, sharing exchanges with family or other loved ones, which can include pets.

Sun Conjunct South Node

Your feelings are apt to be more intense than usual, and volatility is also possible. You may feel torn between spontaneously pouring out into the world and holding in to protect yourself or others. Self-esteem is likely to be an issue. The challenge is to express yourself in ways which will bring positive feedback—love, admiration, applause, attention—without excessive ego. You may experience too much pride (or shame). Build on what you know is good within yourself and be willing to share with those closest to you.

Sun Conjunct Ascendant

A high focus on self-esteem issues is likely. Personal action may center on creativity, children, or risk-taking. Personal pride (for good or ill) takes center stage. The possibilities include a strong desire to give and receive love, admiration and recognition, plus more willfulness, with confidence higher than usual. This is your time to shine and show your specialness to the world.

Sun Conjunct MC

This period usually brings an intense desire for recognition from the world. Yearnings for success and high-level achievement are very strong. Ambition is highlighted. You may channel your creative, speculative or confident spirit into a career. You are willing to risk to move up in the world. A change of status is possible.

Sun Conjunct Descendant

Self-esteem is tied to relationships during this period. You are looking for love, admiration and applause from others, especially partner(s). You may attract dynamic, exciting, sparkling peers, or personally play a "starring" role. Your risk-taking, creative side is channeled toward relationships and aesthetics. Romance, charm, beauty, and grace come more easily. Extravagance is possible. You are eager to celebrate love.

Sun Conjunct IC

Focus on building an inner sense of pride and personal adequacy with a stable, secure base. Desire for emotional attachments is highlighted. Involvement with children, parents, or creative acts is quite likely. Self-esteem is connected to domestic issues. You strive to gain recognition through your home and family, through your parenting, preserving, protecting or securing instincts.
(Progressed Moon aspects are covered in Chapter 10.)

Mercury Conjunct Sun (See Sun Conjunct Mercury.)

Mercury Conjunct Moon

This period suggests a time when the line between thoughts and feelings becomes very fine indeed. Your emotions are likely to influence your thinking and your logic can affect your emotional reactions. This air/water combination can point to potential psychic insights, or to the blending of rationality and intuition. Much flux is likely in both interests and emotions.

This period might involve more contact than usual with relatives and family matters. Travel in the immediate vicinity could be more common. Mental matters may become more of a focus in the home, e.g., taking classes, writing, more discussions, etc. Nurturing could be shared by other relatives (e.g., a brother, sister, aunt or uncle might play a parental role, you might look after a relative, etc.). The mind could be seen as a source of security and support or emotions could fluctuate greatly and change from moment to moment.

Mundane Options: talking about home, children, nurturing, land, commodities, food; discussions with relatives; visits to or from relatives; contacts by mail or phone; safety sought through logic; security concerns shared with neighbors; comparing/ contrasting roots and family backgrounds; a moveable home (e.g., trailer); child-care; home changes such as leaving home to travel or visitors in the home.

Mercury Conjunct (Natal) Mercury

The emphasis is on all Mercury functions—mind, communication, transportation, commerce, curiosity, flexibility, versatility, tendency to scatter, etc. Note houses ruled by Mercury. There may be more action than usual pertaining to matters of those houses.

Mundane Options: more discussion, classes, teaching, reading, short trips, involvement with relatives, transportation or commerce, increased diversity and multi-tasking, greater objectivity, a lighthearted perspective, more focus on the mind, the tongue, or the hands.

Mercury Conjunct Venus (and vice versa)

The themes of this aspect include pleasure from the mind, and thinking or communicating about tangibles, finances, sensual gratifications, or relationships. This might include your attention, conversation, thinking or talking centering around money, possessions, pleasures or tangible forms of beauty. You may also enjoy relatives, classes, discussions, learning, variety and being on the go.

Mercury-ruled items (hands, finger dexterity, thinking, learning, networking, paperwork, communication) might contribute to your source of income. Venus-ruled areas (ease, comfort, stability, money, sensuality, indulgences, beauty) are likely to interest you, sparking thinking, talking and exchanges with people around you.

Mundane Options: money earned through voice, communication, or dexterity; money matters come up with relatives; family pleasures; buying a car, enjoying short trips, pleasure from learning, communications about finances; discussing relationships; partnership with a relative; competition with a relative; joint learning; teamwork; talking about marriage; negotiations; counseling or consulting; teaching/learning to relate.

Mercury Conjunct Mars (and vice versa)

This aspect suggests an increased quickness of mind for the period involved. Both thinking and speaking may come more rapidly. Impulsive speech is possible, as are arguments, debates, sarcasm, irony and anything which uses words as a weapon. Mental aggression is possible. Using the mind competitively can be an asset in business or in games.

Sometimes reflexes are more keen, and dexterity may be better than usual, so consider involvement in sports, playing a musical instrument or other tasks calling on flexibility or the use of the hands. (One could also literally use the hands as weapons in terms of martial arts.) Speed might appeal; pay attention, stay focused when involved in transportation or working with tools. Aggression could become an issue with relatives and sibling rivalry is possible. Team sports may help to channel the competitive instincts of brothers and sisters into constructive channels—and business can be a positive outlet for adult siblings.

Directness and honesty may matter more to you now than ever. You probably want to be straightforward and forthright in your communications, and prefer it from others as well. Diplomacy may take a bit of work. You will tend to say what you mean and mean what you say unless you are attracting others who "do it for you.".

Interests could be picked up and dropped quickly. Your mind may grasp concepts (and words) more rapidly, but is eager to keep moving on as well. Try to find constructive outlets for the quick-wittedness.

Mundane Options: short trips, arguments, accidents, aggression with neighbors, sibling rivalry, quick thinking, debates, skillful sports, rapid speech, capacity to be more articulate, more objective understanding of yourself, quick wits, gaining confidence through new studies, writing articles or short stories.

Mercury Conjunct Jupiter
or Jupiter Conjunct Mercury (long-term)

Mental restlessness is suggested by this aspect. You are probably eager to learn, to teach, to travel for knowledge. Your quest for information and understanding may range widely over the world (mentally and/or physically). Each answer can bring new questions. An insatiable curiosity is quite likely.

Travel (both short and long-range) is possible at any time during this period. You could go back to school, change your major subject or courses of instruction, study "on your own," teach, write, publish and do anything and everything in the world of the mind and education. You are likely to think about life's meaning and explore different world views, philosophies and religions. Mental activities rate to have a high priority.

Mundane Options: travel (short trips or long ones), additional education, writing, publishing, legal involvements, teaching, sharing/ gaining knowledge about religion/ philosophy/ beliefs, discussing ideals/ goals/ dreams, formulating religious/ philosophical beliefs, involvement with siblings or grandchildren.

Mercury Conjunct Saturn
or Saturn Conjunct Mercury (long-term)

This can be a period of solid intellectual accomplishments, or one of inhibition, depression and blocked communication. The theme revolves around a grounded use of the intellectual capacities. One option is applying your mind to your career, or using your mind to further other productive ambitions. This can indicate speaking, writing, communicating, researching or otherwise applying the use of information and knowledge to your professional life. It can mean working hard at your studies, being dedicated and disciplined in your approach to the intellect. Interests are likely to be "proper" or professional—those which "fit in" or help you to rise in the world.

Guard against overdoing the control and critical side of the intellect and being too judgmental. There is a danger of finding fault with your thinking, feeling inhibited and insecure and spiraling downward in a cycle of more and more restriction and constriction of your communicative/intellectual capabilities.

If the horoscope is that of a child, the father (or father figure) is having a very strong impact (positive or negative) upon the child's intellectual development and communication skills. Even if you are grown now, it could be helpful to see how your perceptions of power, authority and the laws and rules of society may affect your thinking and communication skills.

Mundane Options: professional communication (or blocked/inhibited/criticized communication); working with or for relatives; involvement with transportation or communication industries; limited/ limiting or productive, realistic siblings; traveling for your work.

Mercury Conjunct Uranus
or Uranus Conjunct Mercury (long-term)

This can be a period of great inventiveness, innovation and original thinking—or of chaotic thinking, anarchistic ideas and defiant communications. The focus is on unconventionality of mind.

It is possible to rebel against all of the old ideas, against anything traditional, formal or conventional. Such action will come across as erratic, unpredictable, upsetting and difficult to deal with. Tearing down should lead to building up something better. In extreme cases, unusual thinking may be judged abnormal by traditionalists.

A more moderate approach permits one to maintain a fresh perspective, to see alternatives, options and other possibilities. Detachment—avoiding being attached to either defending or attacking the status quo—can help one discover innovative solutions and helpful changes, producing the inventors and sometimes the geniuses of our world.

Intuitive flashes may occur and should be checked against other sources of information rather than blindly followed. The stimulation of other people is important, but the orientation is casual and friendly. Unless other chart factors point to the reverse, the focus is likely to be detached and intellectual (not warm and emotional). "Everyone's my friend, but don't get too close."

Mundane Options: changes in speaking or writing style; new studies; new friendships; different neighborhood; sudden trips; impulsive speech; original thinking; inventive communications; activity in social, political or humanitarian causes; group mind (networking).

Mercury Conjunct Neptune
or Neptune Conjunct Mercury (long-term)

The creative imagination is highlighted. One option is the poetic visionary, the inspired idealist. Other possibilities are the confused victim and the con artist. The theme centers on a combination of intuition with logic and rationality. In question is the degree of balance between the two.

Poets use inspired images to bring beauty into language. Effective visionaries see transcendent potentials and uplift us through their images to envision a better, more ideal world. They share a pipeline to the Infinite, but can also keep one foot solidly on the ground.

The confused victim cannot separate dreams from reality, and foggily floats from one to the other. Victims may be deceived by others as well as by themselves, wanting so much to believe in "happily ever after" that they fool themselves into thinking it already exists. Con artists use their creative imaginations to "cast a spell" upon the "mark" (victim). To succumb to a con, however, one may be greedy or naively idealistic to buy into the "beautiful dream" image.

The mind can be used to help heal, to succor others. Counseling and similar activities come naturally with this air/water blend, which can bring subconscious feelings to the surface and can discuss them rationally. In addition to beauty in language, it is possible to make beautiful objects with the hands. The goal is to tune in to the "cosmic flow" in a constructive manner and somehow share the experience with others in our world.

Mundane Options: poetry; song writing; composing; lies; confusion; flowing language; talent for fantasy; grace and beauty in your gestures; making beautiful things with your hands; running away from unpleasant thoughts; visualization and affirmation skills, psychic or mystical experiences and insights.

Mercury Conjunct Pluto or Pluto Conjunct Mercury (long-term)

Mind control is a central issue during this period. Will you master your thinking, discipline your intellect, and control your mentation, or will you succumb to obsessive thoughts and compulsive rituals which control you? The mind is likely to turn to deep issues: psychological complexes, the nature of hidden motives, occult questions, etc. Matters traditionally kept "secret" (e.g., death, salaries, abuse, etc.) may be probed and investigated.

Talent is likely for any sort of research. Mental focus, organization, concentration and thoroughness are more marked. You can hone in on essentials, screening out the rest. A relentless perseverance can be applied to thinking, questioning, uncovering, discussing and investigating.

If this extreme focus is overdone, the individual may become obsessed with a topic, seeming unable to shift gears with the mind. Compulsive behaviors or rituals could become a habit. Over concern with details is possible. The need to control every bit of information could lead to dictatorial or manipulative exchanges.

Interest may center on any Plutonian areas: resources, shared finances, sexuality, hidden matters, the occult, death, transformation, self-control, pollution and power. Much thinking and discussing on these matters (or manipulation and power plays) is possible. The mate relationship may also be a source of curiosity or topic for discussion. If a new relationship begins, it is likely to be an initial meeting of minds. Old, buried feelings about early relatives may be unearthed and worked through as well.

Mundane Options: research; discussions of sex, occult, hidden matters or the economy; learning/ teaching hypnosis or other forms of mind-control; studying investments; power struggles with neighbors; sibling partnerships or jealousy/ rivalry; mechanical skills; incisive/ invasive questions; deeply personal gossip; transformation in thinking/ speaking.

Mercury Conjunct Ceres (and vice versa)

Putting the mind to work in the world is one of the ways to express this aspect. There is a mental focus, and a need for useful results. Theory is not enough; you also want applications. During this period, you may be involved in work that features the mind: writing, speaking, teaching, training, editing, etc. Your job could also highlight communication, transportation, the hands or information retrieval/ dissemination. You may enjoy nurturing your mind now.

Another option is comparing, contrasting, analyzing and discussing your work and/or health. The curious eye of Mercury might be turned on your personal health habits or work routines. There is an urge to learn more about work or health, in ways that can be applied toward immediate improvement. A "repairing" orientation is likely.

A relative may play a mothering/nurturing role (brother/sister acting as a mother/father, for example, or aunt doing some of the parenting, etc.) or you might do some caretaking of a relative, especially one who is ill. If the chart belongs to a child, the mother figure is having a very significant impact (positive or negative) on that child's intellectual development. Overall, the general trend is to seek ideas that will contribute to useful improvements in the "job in life."

Mundane Options: Family discussions, work centers around communication, negotiations with relatives; quantity versus quality concerns; learning about nurturing; tracing family history; analyzing and improving health habits.

Mercury Conjunct Pallas (and vice versa)

The mental world is important during this period. People and ideas are central. Objectivity, logic and some degree of detachment need to blend with social interactions.

Beautiful language can be cultivated with flowing words, music and poetry. The eye-mind-hand coordination associated with Mercury might also be channeled toward playing a musical instrument or making pretty things. Graphic arts such as design and photography could bring satisfaction. Counseling or consulting are other options.

Unfinished business with an early relative (brother, sister, aunt, uncle, etc.) may surface in a partnership. The themes revolve around the mind and communication. A current spouse or partner may be triggering old feelings about your mental capacity or communication skills. Bring things out into the open and talk about them in order to resolve the issues. You might also consider a partnership with a relative or get involved with a partner whose focus is strongly mental/ intellectual. You need to share ideas with those around you.

Mundane Options: discussing relationships; partnership with a relative; competition with a relative; joint learning; teamwork; talking about marriage; negotiations; counseling or consulting; teaching/ learning to relate.

Mercury Conjunct Juno (and vice versa)

Communications with others, especially partners, are highlighted. Are you in touch with your own intellectual capacities, or have you picked a bright spouse to "think" for you? Do you believe in your own communication skills, or depend on your partner's ability to be articulate? Are you able to easily share the mental world with other people?

Old issues (dating back to an early family member such as brother, sister, aunt, uncle, cousin) about thinking and communicating may be influencing a current relationship. If so, it is time to dig them up, discuss them, and work them out. Were you always compared to a "brighter" sibling? Did you have a "chatterbox" relative who taught you that "Silence is golden"? Issues of detachment and objectivity may be important to examine.

You may be inclined to make some lovely things, creating beauty with your mind, hands or tongue (language). You might consider a partnership endeavor with a relative, or share more mental interactions with a current partner.

Mundane Options: marriage; discussing relationships; partnership with a relative; competition with a relative; joint learning; teamwork; talking about marriage; negotiating joint finances; counseling or consulting; teaching/ learning to relate; analyzing family history, researching investments, debts, taxes, reading/writing detective stories, or investigating almost anything.

Mercury Conjunct Vesta (and vice versa)

This is a time to learn by doing. Pure theory is not likely to be enough for you: you want to apply what you know to "real life" or to learn useful facts and techniques. The school of experience is apt to be valued most. An apprenticeship period is one of the potentials.

You could become involved in a job that highlights Mercury functions: thinking, speaking, writing, training, teaching, editing, transporting, using the hands, collecting/disseminating information. You might also be extra-analytical, critical, nit-picking and exacting in your mental approach. Precision is likely to be extra-important.

A flaw-finding attitude could create difficulties with relatives (whether they judge you or you judge them). If the tunnel vision (or absorption with work) is carried too far, alienation from family relationships is even possible. Sometimes duties include an extra burden in the form of an ill family member who requires more care.

Getting the details just right, being organized, being thorough and meticulously accurate in your thinking and speech are basic goals. This can be a great strength, when used wisely and with compassion.

Mundane Options: working in a field involving communication, speaking, writing, such as teaching, sales, receptionist, for the phone company or postal service, etc. Alternately, you might work with your hands or with relatives. Criticizing (or being criticized by) relatives or other associates; blocked communication (due to inhibition or criticism) OR efficient communication (due to careful analysis and realism); tangible output from ideas; putting the mind to use, personal or professional attention directed to health, your own or others.

Mercury Conjunct Chiron
or Chiron Conjunct Mercury (long-term)

This patterns shows a compelling drive for knowledge, whether we satisfy it by studying, teaching, writing, or traveling. There is a major focus on the mind, with a need to expand horizons in some way. Creativity is encouraged, and humor can be highlighted. If air and fire are emphasized, it might be well to remember that there are times for tact. There is a possibility of too many interests and talents, which can lead to the scattering of energy. Stay clearly focused on primary goals but make room for mental exploration. Health or healing could be a focus for attention.

Mundane Options: idealization of knowledge (or siblings, relatives, neighbors); travel; communication issues (good and/or bad) crop up, media connections, multiple mind activities; teaching; disseminating information, concern with health or healing.

Mercury Conjunct/Opposite Nodes
or Nodes Conjunct/Opposite Mercury (long-term)

This combination shows a connection between mental attitudes and close relationships. Possible issues include ambivalence over being dependent or nurturing versus being an equal, or feeling pulled between rational objectivity versus emotional sensitivity. An opposition is often experienced as a conflict, though it symbolizes a natural partnership. Conflict aspects usually call for compromise. We need to make room for both thinking and feeling, for both helping and being helped and for operating as an equal. Usually, Mercury-Node conflicts involve close relationships; parents, siblings, children, mates, but any "nearby" associates may be part of the issue. By developing both the capacity for objective logic (Mercury) and for empathy for the feelings of others (nodes), we can work out compromises which are fair to all concerned. Increased psychic ability is also possible during this period, and can be cultivated by paying attention to feelings and hunches. Sometimes dreams can be revealing. Ask questions of your subconscious and then listen.

Mercury Conjunct North Node

Your mental focus is apt to revolve around emotional attachments. Communication issues may arise with those nearest and dearest to you. You may think and talk about feelings more than usual. Family concerns permeate your consciousness. You can make more sense of the emotional needs of yourself and others at this time.

Mercury Conjunct South Node

Emotional security issues may arise concerning communication and logic. You may feel torn between thinking versus feeling. You may doubt your observations, your intellect, or your communicative abilities. You may work harder than usual in relating to others, in learning, and processing information. Tension with relatives is possible until clarity and compassion are balanced in your life.

Mercury Conjunct Ascendant

Learning and gathering information take center stage. With this aspect, your mind will tend to work more quickly than usual—and your tongue may as well! Communication could be an important focus. Relatives may be more important in your life right now. More travel, especially short trips, is likely. Curiosity is more marked. Restlessness is likely. Seek self-understanding.

Mercury Conjunct MC

Much "busy-ness" and business is likely. Paperwork, phone contact, writing, memos or meetings could increase at work. Short trips could become a part of your career—or anything requiring variety, the gathering or dissemination of information. You may think or communicate more about your vocational role, ambitions, authorities or the handling of power.

Mercury Conjunct Descendant

This is a time for more openness and communication in your relationships. You need to bat ideas back and forth with a partner. Discussions help you reach more balance and equality in your interactions with others. A relative may offer you a partnership or affect your current partnership. Correspondence, paperwork and business contacts may increase, or new people come into your life. A wider public role is possible.

Mercury Conjunct IC

Communication regarding home or security issues is likely. You may feel a need to discuss things more with relatives, bringing issues into the open to be clarified. Thinking about and discussing children, home routines, protection or other issues related to emotional attachments and safety is important. A short trip away from home, visitors to the home, or a move are possible.

Venus Conjunct Sun (See Sun Conjunct Venus above.)

Venus Conjunct Moon

This period suggests a physical, sensual focus of some kind. Food may have greater appeal, so remember to exercise and eat sensibly if you wish to avoid weight gain. Back rubs, hot tubs, smoking, drinking, collecting possessions, and other sensual gratifications could become sources of support and nourishment, but try to emphasize healthy pleasures.

Ease, comfort, pleasure and nurturing are likely to be preferred. You may gain pleasure through children, through your home, through your family, through protective activities, or through being taken care of by others. Possessions, money, sensuality, tangible beauty, partners, or comfort may be looked to for security (perhaps too much so). Stability and safety are likely to be sought. You may look to love for security; be careful who you depend upon. Feel-good activities are likely to be pursued.

Mundane Options: saving money, buying a home, starting or enlarging a collection (stamps, books, coins, etc.), enjoying motherhood, nurturing partnerships (or seeking security through a beloved), gaining weight, earning money through women, a family business, real estate, interior design, food, clothing, or anything which meets the needs of the public, committing to a relationship, finances involved with mother (figure), beautifying the home.

Venus Conjunct Mercury (See Mercury Conjunct Venus above.)

Venus Conjunct Natal Venus

The focus here is on pleasure, which could be primarily personal or could involve pleasure shared with others. Consider also the houses ruled by Venus. Activities pertaining to those areas may increase.

Mundane Options: involvement with finances, artistic endeavors, earning, saving, sharing, and/or spending money, especially for beauty or comfort. When pleasure needs are denied, throat or skin problems or faulty sugar metabolism are possible. Attention and action directed to partners, charm, appearance, grace, affection, and a variety of gratifications.

Venus Conjunct Mars (and vice versa)

The focus revolves around pleasure, doing what you enjoy. Increased sensuality is a possibility, whether gratification is sought through eating, drinking, smoking, making love, making money and/or spending money. Relationships may be more exciting with magnetism between the sexes highlighted. Active creation of beauty may appeal: dancing, skating, diving, gymnastics, Tai Chi, etc. Sports could be a source of pleasure.

Overindulgence is possible, but with moderation, you may just enjoy yourself and appreciate yourself more. This could be a time when you come to like who you are as you are or you may decide to beautify your own appearance—to make your physical body more attractive. Extravagance is possible; spending money may be easier than usual. Another option is beginning a new source of income—perhaps from some form of self-employment.

Relationships are likely to be attractive. Flirtation or a new romance is possible. The balance between assertion and accommodation is highlighted. The challenge is to find pleasure and excitement with other people without having it all on your terms—or everything their way. Your sexual charisma could rise.

Mundane Options: new source of income or ways of handling resources, self-earned money, active creation of beauty (dancing, gymnastics, skating, skiing, playing a musical instrument, etc.), pioneering in business, hedonism, extravagance, self-satisfaction, feeling good about who you are; new relationships or separations, enhancing your personal appearance (especially physical body), forming a partnership, fighting with other people (until compromise is achieved), competition, litigation, shared perspectives, changing public roles.

Venus Conjunct Jupiter or Jupiter Conjunct Venus (long-term)

Depending on your basic values, this aspect could point to a period where you: (1) focus on making lots of money, (2) are very hedonistic and indulge in numerous physical pleasures or in acquiring possessions, and/or (3) enjoy philosophy, travel, religion, spiritual quests or broadened intellectual horizons.

If pleasure is an ultimate value, overindulgence is a hazard, whether in eating, drinking, smoking, making money, spending money, making love, collecting possessions, etc. Materialism could be overvalued and physical gratification pursued as "what matters" in life. In such cases, "excess is not nearly enough" and overdoing is quite likely. Alternately, a mate could be idealized and overvalued, made too important.

If the ideals incline toward a quest for truth or meaning, pleasure is gained through books, study, travel, or other philosophical, religious, educational or scientific pursuits. Finances can go toward buying books, attending seminars, etc. This option could also be carried too far if the idealistic quest for answers causes one to spend beyond the means or overlook the practicalities of life. An insatiable quest for **more** (of whatever you value) can bring perpetual discontent if we make a small part of life into an absolute so we cannot be happy until we have enough, but we never have "enough."

Mundane Options: money earned (or spent) through travel, education, writing, publishing, spiritual quests, ideas, ideals; hedonism; enjoying adventures; overvaluing money or possessions or material pleasures; stolid/stable world view; conservative beliefs; idealizing love; putting partner on pedestal or playing God to partner; a relationship which broadens your horizons.

Venus Conjunct Saturn or Saturn Conjunct Venus (long-term)

This period holds the potential of increased gratification and satisfaction in your career, or alternately, it may call for belt-tightening and caution in the financial and sensual realm.

Look for ways to enjoy your work, to find satisfaction in necessary responsibilities and duties. You could become involved with an artistic project—or with financial work. There is the potential of comfort, ease, stability and security in your career if past actions have been realistic and productive.

If past actions have been less realistic, this could be a period of financial caution, perhaps calling for budgeting due to decreased funds. It could be voluntary saving for an expected large purchase in the future. It might be that you are into a "poverty consciousness," subconsciously believing that unless you work hard, you haven't "earned" it. In such a case, affirmations and visualizations of your right to be well-recompensed might be helpful. Saturn periods are feedback times when we see the consequences of our past attitudes and actions.

In relationships, reality is emphasized. If you are practical and grounded, this could be a time to take on the responsibility of marriage or a serious emotional commitment. If you are still dealing with issues of abandonment or judgment and criticism, you may feel deprived, lacking in love or limited in regard to pleasure and affection. Now is a time for responsible relationships!

Mundane Options: money earned through hard work, responsibility, executive roles; career includes beauty, sensuality or financial matters; business investments; belt-tightening (e.g., re-budgeting or saving for a big purchase); enjoying father(ing); limited indulgences (e.g., dieting, self-discipline), serious commitment to a relationship or limited love; practical about people.

Venus Conjunct Uranus or Uranus Conjunct Venus (long-term)

This aspect suggests a period for confronting the issue of security versus risk or stability versus change. Both your desire for comfort, ease, predictability and your drive for innovation, the new and risk-taking are in high focus. If they are not integrated, you might swing from one to the other. Or, you could risk too much in one area of life and be too stuck-in-the-mud in another area. You might express one side of the seesaw, and have confrontations with someone near and dear who is living out the opposite potential. The challenge is to create some of both in your life.

Relationships may tend toward the erratic, the freedom-loving, the unusual, or involving people who are quite individualistic or aloof. You could look for stimulation, excitement, and variety in your relationships or be attracted to someone who is quite unique (or downright weird). Relationships involving different races, backgrounds, and interests are possible. The tendency is to "break the rules" in some way in terms of love.

If you are not in touch with your desire for alterations, you may experience sudden, unexpected changes in finances, possessions, sensual gratification or associates. If you are not conscious of your yearnings for safety and continuity, your attempts to change may keep on turning out as the same old thing. Pleasure can be found in new hobbies, in technology, in new age activities, astrology, the media or other Uranian outlets. Friends or groups could affect your finances or your attitudes about possessions and pleasures.

Mundane Options: sudden changes in income or in the handling of possessions or pleasures, self-employment, financial upsets, unusual sources of income (or outgo), friends or groups involved in the financial picture, innovative artistic endeavors; marriage encounter (or divorce); friends become lovers; lovers become friends; unusual relationships; more social activity; involvement in social causes; changing associations; sudden love ("falling in love"); expanded knowledge or new ways of enjoying technology and progress.

Venus Conjunct Neptune or Neptune Conjunct Venus (long-term)

Romance is in the air! Art, beauty, love and ideals are suggested as important foci with this aspect.

Artistic talents could be further developed. A feeling for inspired beauty is highlighted, and you could contribute to aesthetic creations in the world. If sensuality is over idealized, indulgence is possible—with food, drugs, financial extravagance, or other sensual outlets. The yearning for a sense of total union (oneness) works best with nature, God or beauty. Human pleasures are limited and cannot provide infinite satisfaction.

Another option is falling in love—with a person, with an ideal, with the idea of love, or with a fantasy. Fairy-tale images are quite possible, and looking for Prince/Princess Charming could keep you busy (and disillusioned). The quest for the perfect partner or perfect relationship leads to disappointment. One can search forever (never satisfied), go into the Church (marry God literally), believe you've found a soul mate and be disappointed when s/he turns out to be human and fallible. Savior/victim relationships are traps for the unwary who try to be everything to a partner, or expect a partner to provide their heaven on earth.

The handling of pleasures and sensuality may be idealistic. Don't expect God to balance your checkbook; high ideals must learn to live with awareness of physical reality and its rules. This combination can be quite passive/receptive, so overindulgence in physical forms of gratification is possible. "Getting high" on nature or through spiritual activities or meditation will work better than overeating, drinking, spending or turning to drugs. You can contribute to a more attractive and better world if you choose.

Mundane Options: money earned (or spent) through art, beauty, rescuing people, escapist activities, spiritual ideals; great wealth (or just dreams of it); philanthropy; artistic activities of any kind (including but not limited to music, photography, painting, decorating, film making, writing, dancing, acting, fashion design, sewing, make-up, hairdressing, composing, etc.); idealized love or idealizing love and romance; "amazing grace"; savior/victim relationships and sacred marriages; hidden partners; public service; spiritual teamwork to help make a more ideal world.

Venus Conjunct Pluto or Pluto Conjunct Venus (long-term)

A polarity is in high focus for this period. In the inner form of this polarity we learn to integrate self-indulgence with self-control. The battleground might center around food (dieting versus overeating), alcohol (drinking versus going on the wagon), continuing to smoke versus stopping it, or spending money versus saving it. The outer form of this polarity involves learning to share the material world with close associates. The issue may involve earning one's own way versus depending on others, learning to give, receive and share for mutual pleasure. There is the potential of "feast or famine" swings in your life. An "all or nothing" approach is common.

Facing the issue with a partner can include a mixture of the inner and outer versions. One might nag the other about weight; the second might nag the first about money, etc. By externalizing the conflict, we may be able to see the issues more clearly. Power plays, manipulation or emotional blackmail may be exercised until balance is learned (on both sides).

Financial changes are possible, with involvement with money from others as well as self-earned income. The resources of others can include inheritance, taxes, return on investment, debts, partner's income, etc. Sensuality and sexuality are in high focus, but only you can decide when, how much, and how to indulge (and control) your various appetites. Enjoying a variety of pleasures, including artistic creativity, helps to avoid excesses in one.

Mundane Options: money earned through investments, physical manipulation (e.g., massage, acupressure, chiropractic), sexuality or psychotherapy; much pleasure/gratification from sensual/sexual channels **or** sensual/sexual withdrawal; intense reactions to monetary situation; swings in appetite control and spending versus saving; enjoying self-mastery, work in fields such as investment, insurance, taxes, or fields supported by public funds, including grants.

Venus Conjunct Ceres (and vice versa)

This period could point to more pleasure from work or nurturing, but it also might indicate more caution and restraint where sensuality or money is concerned. A significant artistic hobby (especially handicrafts or something you build/sew/make) is possible. You may beautify your work area, or become involved with aesthetics on the job. A change in salary is also possible.

An alternate theme could be enjoying parenting. A child might come into the family (through birth, adoption, marriage, etc.). Money could be spent on family or nurturing/assisting activities could be a source of funds. Common sense might be applied to the area of possessions, pleasures and finances, with more budgeting or reserve in the area of sensuality.

Parenting and partnership could be mixed. You may reach a more equal level with a parent, or get involved with a partner who pushes old parental buttons. Care taking could become a focus within your close relationships.

Mundane Options: financial caution; pleasure through family and/or work; budgeting and common sense with money; food which is delicious and nutritious; increase in pay.

Venus Conjunct Pallas (and vice versa)

Relationships are highlighted by this aspect. The drive is likely to be toward wanting more pleasure, grace, balance and comfort in your associations with other people. Making a marital commitment (or engagement) is quite possible. If you are already in a relationship, you are likely to look for ways to make it even more enjoyable. As long as both partners contribute to the increased satisfaction, all is well. If one expects the other to provide "feeling good" on a silver platter, problems could ensue.

Money may also be involved with artistic endeavors (making or spending money through beautiful things). Issues of fairness or justice might arise over financial matters (in the partnership, in terms of salary, in terms of social justice).

Generally, social activity is likely to be a source of pleasure. You will tend to seek out others, to enjoy time spent sharing and to appreciate and savor more fully all forms of beauty.

Mundane Options: money earned through art, beauty, appearance, grace, charm or partners; pleasure from aesthetics; joint finances; consulting or other teamwork earns money; affection in partnership.

Venus Conjunct Juno (and vice versa)

Emotional commitments and/or financial matters are likely areas for attention during this period. If other chart factors support, you may get engaged or married. It is likely that you will be more drawn toward emotional attachments since there is a desire for pleasure from relationships. If you are already married, you may be moved to look for ways to increase mutual enjoyment.

Money might also be a focus. Financial matters could occupy your attention. You might deal with issues of spending versus saving, how much you earn yourself versus depending on someone else's income, and how to comfortably share finances and pleasures with a mate—neither ruling the other. Income from counseling or consulting is possible.

Mundane Options: money earned through art, beauty, appearance, grace, charm or a partner; supporting another financially; pleasure from aesthetics; joint finances; teamwork earns money; affection in partnership.

Venus Conjunct Vesta (and vice versa)

The theme of this period could be "disciplined pleasures" or "enjoyable work." One option is to restrain, contain, deny certain sensual indulgences (whether pleasure from food, drink, sex, money, etc.). A puritan attitude is possible. Or, work and productivity may simply be given priority over physical gratification or over relationships. It may seem hard to do justice to both work and human pleasures. The work attitude (nit-picking and flaw-finding) could affect your love relationships (whether directed from you toward a partner or from a partner toward you). Or, you might meet a partner through work, or labor with a loved one, combining romance and effort.

Another potential is to gain more satisfaction from work. This could range from a salary increase, to beautifying the work area, to routines which are more enjoyable, to a significant artistic outlet, to a job which involves sensuality (e.g., massage, acupressure, chiropractic, etc.), or finances (e.g. investments, insurance, taxes etc.). It is important to avoid excessive criticism of close associates—too much focus on "flaws" and not enough on "assets."

Mundane Options: making beautiful objects (handicrafts); earning money through service, health careers, dealing with facts or figures; analyzing your finances or those of others in your work; improving your monetary assets; enjoying work and coworkers or employees; meeting partner on job or working with spouse; critical (or practical) about people.

Venus Conjunct Chiron or Chiron Conjunct Venus (long-term)

In its purest form, this pattern can mean pleasure from knowledge, whether we enjoy our studies or earn our living by teaching, writing, or traveling. We may also over-value money, material possessions, appetites, or love relationships, expecting too much of them and never feeling satisfied. A basic optimism is usually present, but it is important not to turn a fragment of life (love or money) into an Absolute that is expected to provide all of our heart's desires. A compromise position blends idealism and realism and lets us enjoy our quest for something more.

Mundane Options: idealization of love, pleasure, or money; increased pleasure through learning; income tied to writing, education, healing, the law, travel, etc.; widened horizons sought through partnership.

Venus Conjunct/Opposite Nodes
or Nodes Conjunct/Opposite Venus (long-term)

This combination suggests a connection between your security needs and your potential for pleasure, whether from the material world or from people in your life. Challenges usually involve close relationships. Personal needs and power may conflict with the power and desires of others. Issues may involve finances, or the handling of possessions and appetites, or the handling of dependency. Oppositions are natural partnerships with each end needing the other, but compromise is usually needed to make room in the life for both.

Venus Conjunct North Node

Love and security needs are in focus. You may get involved in a new love relationship or closer family ties. An addition to the family is possible, or a deepening of attachments which already exist. Finances or resources could be highlighted, with a desire to achieve a sense of safety and protection. Build on what provides material and emotional security in your life.

Venus Conjunct South Node

Love relationships and material resources are highlighted. Security issues are likely around questions of finances or emotional closeness. You may have to deal with doubts, tensions or stresses concerning finances, possessions or affection. You may question your ability or the ability of others to love, to commit or to handle the physical world successfully. You can put much energy into being there for others, and the possibility of support from others also exists. Value yourself in order that others will appreciate your worth as well.

Venus Conjunct Ascendant

Beauty, comfort and sensuality move into high focus. Your appetite for pleasure is stronger. You instinctively direct your actions toward enjoyment. Any of the physical pleasures (eating, drinking, smoking, sex, etc.) might be overdone and financial extravagance is possible. Focus on a variety of healthy pleasures. You could marry or get involved in an important relationship. You may decide on a personal beautification scheme or become more active artistically. If the desire for comfort and ease is overdone, you could be a bit passive, complacent or lazy. Gratification is highlighted.

Venus Conjunct MC

You want more gratification from your professional role. This could range from looking for a raise, to changing your job so that it is more enjoyable, to beautifying your office environment. Women or art may become more important in your career. You have more grace, charm, tact, diplomacy at your professional fingertips and might develop a better relationship with authority figures. You may want things to come a bit more easily than is practical, but can make this a period of increased pleasure from work. You might change your status, especially in regard to marriage, or find your status is affected due to a partner.

Venus Conjunct Descendant

"Love is in the air." The urge is for more pleasure from peer relationships. You may meet a new partner or deepen a current commitment (including a possible marriage). Shared sensuality and/or beauty and art become more important. Money matters may be affected by your involvements with other people. Gratification appeals. You prefer harmony, ease, balance, and sensual indulgences.

Venus Conjunct IC

You feel the need for a solidly secure, comfortable grounding in life. You may take steps to make your home more attractive. Your emotions are soothed by grace and harmony, especially in the domestic realm. You may play a peacemaking role in the family or seek to smooth out parental hassles. Food could be used as an emotional reassurance; beware of overindulging. Money may be spent on the home or come through land or immovable assets.

Mars Conjunct Sun (See Sun Conjunct Mars above.)

Mars Conjunct Moon

During this time, you are trying to combine somewhat contradictory drives. On the one hand is a desire for nurturing, dependency, emotional closeness, security and safety. On the other hand is a drive to take risks, pioneer, be alone, be active and pursue independence. You are challenged to make space for both in your life.

Until the conflicting desires are integrated, you might blow hot and cold in relationships. Or, other people could manifest the "come closer/go away" policy. You might consciously identify with the need for freedom and attract clinging vines, or consciously want commitment and be drawn to "free souls" or loners who shun attachments. The more you can integrate both sides, the more you are likely to attract other people who are balanced as well.

Some ambivalence about mother(ing) and the home is likely as well. If you are still interacting with your own mother, you could live out the freedom side while she expresses the closeness or vice versa. If you are now a parent yourself, be aware that, as much as you care for your children, you still need space to be yourself and do your own thing. Otherwise, a push/pull situation could arise. If you are a would-be mother, be aware that some strong ambivalence is present; a part of you is opposed to being "tied down" by a child. You might also find yourself wanting your home, yet being away from it a lot. Variations abound. The solutions lie in maintaining the ability to be yourself and to meet your own needs while still supporting significant relationships and the ability to make a domestic commitment to others.

Mundane Options: hot/cold seesaws in relationships, temper outbursts, change of residence, altering the home environment, including changes of people living in the home or visiting, having a child, a new or intensified emotional commitment, stress with mother(ing), stomach problems, headaches or cuts, burns, or accidents if emotions are repressed, self-nurturing, mood swings, identification with a family member or other source of emotional security.

Mars Conjunct Mercury (See Mercury Conjunct Mars above.)

Mars Conjunct Venus (See Venus Conjunct Mars above.)

Mars Conjunct (Natal) Mars

All Martian themes of personal action, power, movement, and freedom are accented. Consider also the house(s) ruled by Mars as pursuits pertaining to those areas may increase.

Mundane Options: sports or other kinds of vigorous physical movement, surgery if ability to do what you want is seriously blocked (or cuts, burns, accidents), temper, increased personal self-expression, living life more on your own terms, more time on your own, more activities which are self-directed, asserting yourself, giving priority to what you want, working with metal tools, weapons, aggression or men, pursuits which involve speed, dealing with anger, impulsiveness, exercising your independence.

Mars Conjunct Jupiter or Jupiter Conjunct Mars (long-term)

With two fire planets backing each other up, much potential energy, enthusiasm and confidence is available within your nature. A key issue is how much you are willing to let your inner fire out and the need to find constructive outlets for it. Sports are often a good outlet.

An excess of fire could lead to rashness, pomposity, foolhardiness, leaping before you look, overextending and trying to do too much, too fast. An extreme form is the "guru" position ("I am God") which tends to feel: "I can do anything." A lack of trust in this inner fire could lead to an approach of: "I'll wait until I can do it perfectly." Impossibly high demands are a good way to halt any action.

If the fire burns too hotly, arguments, assertion or aggression could be carried too far in terms of religion, philosophy, beliefs, values, ethics, and goals. This can be the "true believer" syndrome—or a key to "religious war." One extreme is the "missionary" who feels: "I have the truth, the whole truth, and no one else's truth has any validity." This is an appropriate time for putting personal beliefs and values into action, but be wary of pushing them onto other people. Remember that one can turn anything into a supreme value (God)— from personal will to money to relationships to a job to knowledge to ??? Blocking an expression of the fire can lead to accidents or illness from an impaired immune system.

A constructive use of this high-energy combination produces lots of confidence, energy and enthusiasm for moving toward long-range goals. You can act on your dreams!

Mundane Options: travel (especially to foreign countries), leaping before you look, new studies, new ideas, new goals, new interests, higher standards for your personal behavior, increased optimism, wheeling and dealing in life, contacts with churches, universities, libraries, law courts.

Mars Conjunct Saturn or Saturn Conjunct Mars (long-term)

The fire/earth themes of these two planets can be lived out as scorched earth, buried fire or bricks (productive accomplishment). The issue is coming to terms with self-will or personal desires and the limits to self (the rules of reality in the game of life in a physical world).

The "overdrive" personality carries Martian themes too far, trying too much, too fast. Societal laws may be ignored (criminals) or physical laws may be ignored (not getting enough rest, right diet, proper exercise) resulting in eventual health consequences. (The workaholic is one form of this variation.) One can fight or argue with authority figures, battle "the system" or otherwise butt heads with reality.

The "self-blocking" personality carries Saturnian themes too far, afraid to try, fearing failure, convinced more limits exist than are actually the case or doubting personal skills. These individuals stop themselves, give up before even starting, sure they will be criticized, judged, put down, sat upon or otherwise blocked by the world. Depression, illness, insecurity, inadequacy or poverty could become a way of life.

The middle ground involves active, assertive steps within the realistic limits of society and natural law. These integrated people do as much as they can, within the structures and rules of the game. They put their full power out into career accomplishments, into tangible achievements that work **with** the laws of the society and of life, rather than against them. For such individuals, this can be a period of high productivity, more control over their career, and much achievement.

Mundane Options: new business, leadership role in your career, arguments with authorities, back, teeth, or bone problems, headaches, cuts or colds (if personal desires are totally blocked and not allowed some kind of constructive expression), positive, reasonable self-discipline, energetic accomplishments, working out issues with authority figures (parents, bosses, police, etc.).

Mars Conjunct Uranus or Uranus Conjunct Mars (long-term)

Independence and risk-taking are the major themes of this aspect. How well you integrate those needs into the rest of your personality will tell the tale of the results.

People who overdo the rebelliousness and individualism of this combination may be rash, foolhardy, impulsive. They could take unnecessary chances. They might be cantankerous and recalcitrant, unwilling to play by any rules. They could go to the extreme of the runaway: "If it can't be **my** way, I won't play."

People who are not comfortable with the freedom side of this combination may subconsciously attract other people into their lives who live it out—usually to excess. These others may be hard to handle, impossible to pin down, chaotic or just downright strange. Sometimes individuals who have thoroughly repressed their breaking-loose and breaking-free instincts subconsciously do it on a physical level, and accidents become a possibility.

If you use this period to take reasonable risks (for rewards which you personally desire), to make some needed changes, to assert yourself in healthy ways and to maintain independence where it matters and is constructive, this can be a refreshing, enlivening and creative period.

Mundane Options: inventions, rebellion, revolutions, new friends, new associations, accidents (if an accident would "get you out of" an intolerable situation, or if you are overly impulsive, rash or headstrong), new hobbies, changes in your personal appearance and body, dealing with unusual males, being an eccentric, breaking loose from confinements.

Mars Conjunct Neptune or Neptune Conjunct Mars (long-term)

This can be a period of great inspiration and transcendence, or of self-denial, self-sacrifice and (in extremes) self-wipeout. Part of the issue is how you handle the drive to merge with something higher in life.

One option is being swept up in, or swept away by, artistic or aesthetic yearnings. Great art can become a channel to the Infinite. You might find inspiration in aesthetic activities, especially if your own body can become a channel for grace and beauty (e.g., dancing, skiing, akido, gymnastics, etc.). You may be active in creating beauty in the world.

Another option is finding transcendence through spiritual, religious, or healing activities. Merging with the universe (or a Higher Power) can be an uplifting experience. Your own sense of personal power is heightened by being a channel for infinite love and beauty. You can help to bring the utopian dream down to earth and share it with others.

Ultimately painful alternatives involve trying to merge and find inner peace through drugs, alcohol, fantasy, psychosis, sleeping a lot, or other escapist activities. These are ineffective ways to seek infinite love, beauty and oneness. Unnecessarily high personal expectations are also common, leading to per-petual discontent with oneself and life. It is important to have some faith in yourself, but also to accept your humanness and to put some of your faith in a Higher Power. No human can save the world single-handed, but we can do our share. You have the opportunity to open the channel to your Higher Self, to add grace, beauty and love to the world.

Mundane Options: self-sacrifice (e.g., hospitalization, victimization), merg-ing self/identity with something larger (through spiritual paths, drugs, inspira-tion, etc.), active creation of beauty (dancing, gymnastics, synchronized swimming, etc.), fighting for a cause (directly, financially, etc.), high standards for personal behavior (beware perfectionism), drive to help/rescue.

Mars Conjunct Pluto or Pluto Conjunct Mars (long-term)

Power issues are highlighted by this aspect. A part of the picture calls for balancing the inner power of self-mastery with the power of outward action and assertion. You may face choices about your use of power and when one option is more appropriate than another. Impulses and immediate action may vie with cautious planning in finances, possessions, or pleasures and you may confront that polarity with someone close to you. This fire-water blend is usually a key to strong passions.

Financial and sexual issues could easily be battlegrounds for facing the power issue with a mate, partner or spouse. You may be learning to give, receive and share equally where money, possessions and pleasures are concerned. Until balance is achieved, power struggles, intimidation, jealousy, control tactics, emotional blackmail (tears, suicide threats, guilt-tripping) and force are all possible within the self-other confrontation. Resolution calls for mutual com-promise and comfortable inter-dependency.

Mundane Options: new sexual relationship, activity involving investments, debts, inheritance, insurance, etc., temper outbursts, surgery (if anger/power are blocked and turned inward against the self), medical interests or involvement, psychotherapy, sarcasm, irony, debates, sports building endurance, self-discipline and mastery.

Mars Conjunct Ceres (and vice versa)

This aspect emphasizes fire/earth: the drive to make an impact in the world, to be effective. One option is working hard, being dedicated and accomplishing a lot on the job. Another option is focusing on nurturing activities, doing a lot of assisting and support. If your job is frustrating or unfulfilling, there is the danger of illness or excessive self-criticism. You could focus too much on flaws, neglecting assets.

More activity on the job would be appropriate, or you might start working for yourself. The need to work in your own way is highlighted. Personal projects provide the most satisfaction.

You might also choose to focus on health. A positive option would be a new health regime, being disciplined in your physical expression. This could be an exercise program, a new look at nutrition, etc.

Mother(ing) may be a part of the focus. Interactions with your own mother might include anger, assertion, vitality or spontaneity. You are likely to want to be helpful and assisting to others, but only on your own terms. If parenting is in the picture, be aware that you might be ambivalent. Keep room for your own activities and interests as well as for care-taking.

Mundane Options: taking on parental role; repairs of any kind, refurbishing, improvement or "make-over" projects, handicrafts, working with mechanical things, self-employment, stress with coworkers or people who tell you how to do something, illness (if work is frustrating), self-criticism, active nurturing or much verve put into the home; energetic dedication to accomplishments, job changes.

Mars Conjunct Pallas (and vice versa)

The theme of this period is the polarity of self-other interactions. You are seeking to balance personal needs with interpersonal drives and desires. Your own preferences and wishes must be weighed against those of other people (especially partners and competitors). Assertion and accommodation may vie with each other in your psyche.

A new relationship tie is quite possible, but ambivalence is also likely. A part of you is drawn toward an emotional attachment; another part wants to hold on to independence and separateness. If you deny one side, your partner is likely to overdo that side, while you overdo the opposite. Or, you could swing from hot to cold, from attraction to repulsion in relationships.

Competitive instincts may surface during this period, and are a constructive outlet for the dance between your power and the power of other people when they are expressed with a "game-playing" attitude. Whether in games, sports, or business, a healthy attitude includes the ability to win some and to lose some and to take it lightly. You may feel an urge to fight for justice, for equality, or for fair play. Lawsuits are possible, as is counseling or any one-to-one encounters which feature face-to-face confrontations. An energetic pursuit of beauty is also an option.

Mundane Options: new relationships, separations, active beauty (e.g., aerobic dancing, skiing, skating, diving), enhancing your personal appearance (especially physical body), forming a partnership, fighting with other people (until balance is achieved), competition, litigation, shared perspectives, changing public roles.

Mars Conjunct Juno (and vice versa)

The issue highlighted by this period has to do with owning personal power. Several variant expressions are possible, three more painful and three more satisfying, but all related to the interpersonal dance between personal needs and the desire for significant relationships.

One variation is feeling vulnerable to other people, seeing them as having the power (to approve or disapprove, to like or dislike). This can lead to trying to placate and to please others. If carried to the extreme of constant appeasement, one can be used or abused by others.

An alternative response to feeling vulnerable assumes that "the best defense is a good offense" and attacks others as a form of self-defense. Aggression against others might be an attempt to protect inner feelings of insecurity.

A third variation is withdrawal from relationships. If other people are seen as having the power, hiding out can be an option. Retreat may feel safer than risking rejection or other hurts. Retreat may be seen as the road to self-protection.

A fourth variation involves cooperation. Both individuals in the relationship learn to negotiate and share. Each person gives up **some** (but not all) of the power and they meet in a middle ground. Compromise is learned. This aspect can point to a significant new relationship (up to and including marriage), or improving an existing one—once power issues are faced and handled.

A fifth variation involves competition. This can be healthy—in sports, games or business where rules and regulations ensure that no one gets hurt too much. In proper competition, we win some and lose some and learn to take it lightly. The competitive urge also could be channeled into fighting for a cause. If it is cutthroat, however, too much aggression may be addressed toward others, with destructive results.

A sixth variation is becoming involved with helping and healing situations. Healers own their own power, but use it to assist others—to lift them up, not to put them down. When there is some insecurity and vulnerability to other people, assisting weaker individuals (who are not a threat) can be reassuring.

All the above variations are possible during this period, and it is sometimes helpful to express all three of the more positive variations: to have a place to cooperate, a place to compete and a place to help. The key questions revolve around learning to share power (and possessions and pleasures) with other people for **mutual** benefit. Freedom needs must also be balanced with desires for attachment. Much activity between the self and other people is likely with intense emotion. It is important to have appropriate ways to express the emotions.

Mundane Options: new relationships, separations, active beauty (e.g., aerobic dancing, skiing, skating, diving), enhancing your personal appearance (especially physical body), forming a partnership, fighting with other people (until balance is achieved), dealing with joint resources, endings or elimination, competition, litigation, shared perspectives, intense emotional exchanges, learning to own your personal power, changing public roles.

Mars Conjunct Vesta (and vice versa)

You need results which are tangible and measurable during this period. One potential is directing a lot of energy and assertion into your work. This could be a time of high productivity and efficiency. You can get a lot accomplished, having both enthusiasm and follow-through. Mechanical and technical skills could be emphasized. Physical projects (where you can see a result) are likely to be most satisfying. Your sense of personal identity and personal power is connected to your accomplishments.

If work is not a source of gratification, you may succumb to self-criticism (or even illness). There is the danger of focusing on flaws, looking for what is wrong in order to fix it and make it better. This, however, could be self-directed, and overdone. Remember to count your strengths—and not just weaknesses. Illness is often connected to frustrations on the job. You may need more measurable attainments, or to gain more control over what you do, or to have more variety. Self-employment or doing things your own way is preferred. Realistic step-by-step planning at work and in terms of your health can lead to improvement.

Mundane Options: repairs of any kind, refurbishing, improvement or "makeover" projects, handicrafts, working with mechanical things, self-employment, stress with coworkers or people who tell you how to do something, illness (if work is frustrating), self-criticism, energetic dedication to accomplishments, a new job or changes in the work details or associates.

Mars Conjunct Chiron or Chiron Conjunct Mars (long-term)

This combination is a strong fire statement which calls for spontaneous action. You may be drawn to competitive sports or to a competitive business or to exploring new parts of the world. Creativity is encouraged. This is a time for inventions. Confidence is usually high, sometimes leading to over-confidence and overdoing or to overly blunt speech. There is usually a strong sense of having a right to what one wants, but it is important to keep one foot solidly on the ground. If the high energy and confidence and clear sense of what you want are effectively channeled into action, this period can be exciting and successful.

Mundane Options: travel, adventures; risk-taking; religious wars; assertive philosophizing; search for personal Truth; high standards for self; desire to be and seek the best.

Mars Conjunct/Opposite Nodes
or Nodes Conjunct/Opposite Mars (long-term)

These aspects indicate a possible freedom-closeness or independence-dependence issue. It is normal to want the freedom to do what we please, but also to need some sort of emotional support system. For most people, the latter is provided by close human relationships, though it is possible to substitute pets, a home, food, etc. for people connections. Normally, a compromise offers the best solution, emotional ties which allow some space. Individuals who have been overly dependent may need to learn to function more on their own. Individuals who have been reluctant to accept any limits on personal freedom may need to discover that emotional sharing can be rewarding even though it requires compromises.

Mars Conjunct North Node

You are likely to confront issues of assertion, anger and self-expression in your close, emotional attachments. Arguments and strife with family members are possible. You may want to pull away from your nearest and dearest, or feel that they are seeking space and detachment. The challenge is to balance personal needs and relationship desires without overdoing either one. You can be true to yourself, while still staying involved in caring exchanges with others. You are capable of much emotional warmth.

Mars Conjunct South Node

Your sense of self and inner security (or lack thereof) are highlighted. You may be more susceptible to self-doubts or self-criticism during this period. You could swing from expecting everything to be **your** way to inhibition and refusal to pursue your rights. The challenge is to express yourself, especially in regard to personal freedom and individuality, without stepping on the rights of others. You need warm, emotional connections with others, but not at the expense of your own identity. Seek emotional ties that encourage you to be true to yourself.

Mars Conjunct Ascendant

Your energy and vitality are higher than usual, but so is impulsiveness. Restless, you need the freedom to go your own way. Penning up your impatience might lead to accidents or headaches. Rather seek to channel your assertiveness into physical activity, competitive business, or healthy confrontations. Anger may come up and is best dealt with directly and immediately. Be true to who you are and what you want. Stifling yourself right now is not advisable, but also stay conscious of other parts of your nature.

Mars Conjunct MC

This can be a high-energy time for you in your work. Much drive and ambition lies at your fingertips. The urge is strong, however, to do your work in your own way, on your own terms. A job change is possible. If you carry the willfulness too far, arguments with authority figures (possibly including the boss) could occur. Personal will and power have to express within the limits of the economic system, cultural regulations, and other "rules of the game." With realism, you can accomplish much during this period, as you have the potential to channel lots of enterprise and enthusiasm into pioneering projects. You're ready to really get things moving along!

Mars Conjunct Descendant

Assertiveness, action, and change are highlighted in your relationships. If comfortably shared, you and your peers enjoy lively exchanges, with everyone willing to express his/her opinions and needs. If out of balance, fights or arguments are possible in relationships where cooperation would be more effective.. One person could be **too** self-centered, even to the point of aggression. The key in teamwork relationships is a joint sense of freedom, energy and willingness to be wholly yourselves within a committed partnership. Life can also include healthy, game-playing, competitive interactions.

Mars Conjunct IC

You're ready to stir the emotional waters a bit. Restless and perhaps discontented, you may feel the urge for more freedom at home. This could be expressed in a move, domestic changes, or fights and arguments with family if not positively directed. You have more energy for domestic issues and are eager to arrange your home base the way **you** want it. Attachment urges vie with separative impulses. Don't burn all your bridges by fleeing emotional commitments, but do balance your independence needs with your desire for emotional support. Constructive action could include painting or remodeling your home, planting a garden, family games, or other shared activities which achieve mutual goals.

Ceres Conjunct Sun (See Sun Conjunct Ceres above.)

Ceres Conjunct Moon (See Chapter Eleven.)

Ceres Conjunct Mercury (See Mercury Conjunct Ceres above.)

Ceres Conjunct Venus (See Venus Conjunct Ceres above.)

Ceres Conjunct Mars (See Mars Conjunct Ceres above.)

Ceres Conjunct Jupiter or Jupiter Conjunct Ceres (long-term)

This aspect blends work and nurturing with ideals, goals, values and ultimate beliefs. One possibility is involvement with Jupiterian fields of work: travel, philosophy, education, law, religion, publishing, writing, teaching, promoting, import/export, etc. Another option is expecting the best from your job (wanting perfect hours, perfect pay, etc.) or from yourself as a worker (demanding perfection, unwilling to allow mistakes). The urge to illuminate, inspire, heal, or uplift through your work (to "save the world") may be present.

Ambivalence in regard to nurturing is possible. You would like to mother (or be mothered) in the perfect, ultimate fashion, yet freedom needs may pull you away from commitments. How you handled interactions with your mother figure will affect your ability to integrate your own nurturing and idealistic sides. During this period you may find it easy to give much through your work, but more challenging to handle close connections. Yet the blend of fire (Jupiter) and earth (Ceres) can be highly effective and helpful when intelligence and inspiration are tied to practical accomplishments.

Mundane Options: more schooling to enhance vocation; a new career dream; revising philosophies, religions or ideas; travel for your job; dissatisfaction because life does not measure up to your standards; writing and publishing; work connected to other countries, education, law, etc.; taking home on the road; living in foreign country; seeking ideal nurturing experiences.

Ceres Conjunct Saturn or Saturn Conjunct Ceres (long-term)

This combination suggests a blending of the mother and father archetypes in your psyche. It usually indicates a strong need to work, to achieve, to be practical and to get the job done. Personal responsibility is likely to be marked. Care taking may come very naturally to you.

When carried too far, this can point to the workaholic, or the overly serious individual who is taking care of everyone else and feels the weight of the world upon his/her shoulders. If the "heaviness" gets to be too much, the individual may even give up, stop trying, feel that they just "cannot manage." Illness could become a subconscious escape from feeling guilty (about not accomplishing enough). A sense of pressure, limitation and demands could be excessive.

If this aspect was present at birth, parental roles may have been mixed in some way in your early life. Perhaps mother worked or was a power figure in the home. Perhaps father did some of the nurturing or was more present in the home. Perhaps one parent had to play both roles. You also might play "super-parent"—doing it all yourself because no one else will do it up to your standards. Alternately, you might give up, afraid of failure, or you might be sensible and constructive, learning from past mistakes and constantly improving your parental interactions.

With a double earth focus, tangible accomplishments are more important than usual. During the years of this aspect, you need to be productive, to see results and to feel satisfaction from achieving them. You may be conscious of this achievement drive or you may feel that life is forcing you to work harder than you would choose to do. When we have to work, it is important to focus on the positive parts of the experience—on increasing skills and confidence in our ability to cope with the world.

Mundane Options: becoming a parent or more contact with parental figures; career advancement (or limitation); mentoring (or being mentored) at work; health regime; efficiency project at work; criticism of or by colleagues; parent(ing) affects job or vice versa; responsibilities mount; accomplishments increase.

Ceres Conjunct Uranus or Uranus Conjunct Ceres (long-term)

Freedom is connected to work and/or nurturing. This period can be a time of innovation, change, openness and intellectual stimulation in terms of your work, or it could point to upsets, surprises and chaotic alterations. You may be drawn to Uranian fields: technology, astrology, science, social causes, humanitarian pursuits, intellectual interests or working with groups and organizations. You could change your job, your hours, or your usual tasks. If the desire for variety is subconscious, change could be "forced" upon you by outside events (company being sold, being fired or laid off, change in management, etc.). By focusing on ways to innovate and alter your tasks constructively, you can help create positive alternatives.

Independence could be an ongoing issue in terms of care taking. This might be with your own mother (figure) or in terms of your nurturing potential. You want to be friends and equals, with lots of room to breathe. A detached, equalitarian relationship can be achieved if both people are open to it. If one individual denies mutual needs for freedom, the other is likely to pull away, detach, or be unpredictable. Respecting each other's individuality is vital. Stimulating each other mentally is a very constructive move. By appreciating your differences, you can each grow, learn and expand your vision of possibilities.

Mundane Options: interrupted or erratic nurturing; home full of changes; different job; self-employment; an unusual profession; innovative and inventive worker; more independence on the job (or being fired, downsized, quitting); unusual tenant; astrological or media or computer work; friendships with colleagues; altered routines on the job.

Ceres Conjunct Neptune or Neptune Conjunct Ceres (long-term)

The challenge of this aspect is to bring dreams down to earth and make them tangible in some fashion. Constructively, it can point to inspired art, healing or helping activities or applied idealism.

Working with any form of beauty would be appropriate, as would tasks involving magic, glamour, illusions (e.g., film), dreams, institutions, mysteries, the infinite, religious service, or intuition. The work could also involve fields such as chemicals, fluids, oil, shipping, or creative imagination used in sales, public relations, advertising, the media, etc.

The urge to assist, to heal, to care for others is often strong with this aspect, so service, medicine, healing and protective activities are common. If inner security is lacking, the individual may be the one looking for healing or protection.

With the long-term aspect, a mother (figure) is often an important influence in terms of one's basic faith and trust in the universe, one's ideals and quest for infinite love and beauty. Savior/victim relationships with a mother figure are possible, but so is idealization. Mother may have lived out the best (or the most escapist) potentials through her example. Hopefully, you learned from her what **to** do and what **not** to do in terms of rescuing, care taking and dreaming.

Fulfillment can come through helping to create the best and most beautiful of worlds through one's tangible achievements and assisting service. A blend of inspiration and practicality can produce wonderful artists, healers and builders of a better world.

Mundane Options: handicrafts; objects that are beautiful and useful; health or healing activities; illness (mental/emotional/physical, if you subconsciously feel helpless to improve your life); that "dream job" (with the risk of expecting too much from the job or yourself as a worker); rescue work; spiritual discipline; idealized nurturing (could overdo need to assist); inspired accomplishments.

Ceres Conjunct Pluto or Pluto Conjunct Ceres (long-term)

Emotional intensity is linked with work and nurturing. This can be played out mainly through one's job and/or through interactions with a mother (figure) or one's own nurturing potential.

You may be drawn toward work which is deep, probing, looking beneath the surface or into the past, work that is investigative or involves much thoroughness, organization and perseverance (e.g., research). Fields which highlight hidden matters—the occult, psychotherapy, detecting—are possible. Joint resources and finances could be involved in your work (pollution control, ecology, insurance, investments, business partnerships, etc.). Endings (and beginnings) could also be part of the picture (e.g., death, inheritances, medical work).

Your mother (figure) may be playing a role in your current life with a strong emotional impact on you and you might subconsciously absorb a lot of her emotional "baggage." It would be helpful to you to clear up and clean up any leftover obsessions, compulsions, phobias, power issues or resentments you have connected to your mother. Forgiveness (of yourself as well as her) may be necessary to hasten healing. Unfinished business with Mom could be lived out with a mate. You or your mate might end up playing "parent" rather than partner. Focus on shared nurturing and interdependency.

This combination sometimes indicates special healing skills, so it is worth checking to see if you have talent in that area.

Mundane Options: start a diet; quit smoking or drinking; clean closets literally and metaphorically; business partnership; rebudgeting; work with taxes, insurance, debts, inheritance or investments; sexual withdrawal or sex therapy; end of a project (or job); transformation of work duties; depth analysis of yourself and/or others; steps to improve your health; healing or psychokinetic ability; finishing up issues with mother figure; letting go or eliminating as needed with family or nest.

Ceres Conjunct (Natal) Ceres

This aspect highlights all natal Ceres potentials.

Mundane Options: more involvement with mother (or mother figure), increased nurturing role (with own children, other people's kids, pets, plants, our planet, etc.), health becomes a focus, nutrition concerns accented, craftsmanship emphasized, doing a good job for the sake of the people involved, working on, from, or in the home (or with family members).

Ceres Conjunct Pallas (and vice versa)

This aspect blends the themes of people and work. You may be drawn to work with people (personnel, counseling, consulting, etc.). Artistic or aesthetic work is also a possibility, especially in the visual or graphic arts—or fields involving balance and harmony (including mathematics and music). You might also meet a partner through work, or share a career or project with a partner.

You might need to examine the influence of a mother figure on your capacity to form relationships. Early or current messages and imprints may be affecting your concepts of equality, sharing and interchanges with partners and competitors. Try to keep a balance between nurturing and being nurtured in close relationships.

You could choose to pursue more equality, justice or fairness in terms of the working world—either in your own tasks or in the larger sphere such as union action, political organization or consumer protection. An alternative is working on relationships, seeking pragmatic steps to enhance your peer relationships, to improve your sharing with others.

Mundane Options: new artistic work; increased training in aesthetics, counseling, personnel work, law, arbitration and negotiation work; handicrafts; emotional relationship with coworker; criticism in relationships; beautifying the office; business partnership; shared nurturing; teamwork in the family.

Ceres Conjunct Juno (and vice versa)

Mother, work and spouse are mixed together in this aspect. Possibilities include: (1) mother as a partner (or competitor), (2) mothering or being mothered by a partner, (3) a family business, (4) a practical focus in relationships, (5) working with people or aesthetics. There are many variations within each of these possibilities.

Your mother's original or current influence (positive and/or negative) is likely to affect your potential to be a partner; it may be worth investigating your feelings and reactions here. If competence is not shared by both partners, one could fall into the role of "earth mother," taking care of and looking after the other one. Potentials include meeting a spouse through your job, working with a partner or family businesses in general, practicality mixed with emotional attachments.

The urge for efficiency may be channeled into relationships or the partner. Beware of turning another person into a "job." Flaw-finding is effective when directed at the physical world; it is less helpful directed at people. Practical results may also be sought through artistic endeavors. You might make constructive improvement in your people associations, or bring more beauty or equality into your working routine.

Mundane Options: combining love and work; meeting partner on the job or working with romantic partner; new artistic work; increased training in aesthetics, counseling, personnel work, law, work with finances; handicrafts; emotional relationship with coworker; criticism in relationships; beautifying the office; mother issues affect marriage; business partnership.

Ceres Conjunct Vesta (and vice versa)

The focus of this period is likely to center on work or health. Efficient functioning is important. You may be extremely dedicated, disciplined, productive and practical, wanting to get the job done **well**. Tangible results are likely to be pursued and you could further develop analysis, discrimination, organizational skills and a talent for handling details.

If these themes are carried too far, a workaholic life is possible. You might get too caught up in "taking care of business"—tending to feel that you are the only one who can "fix" things and inclined to put out effort whenever you see something that needs to be done. The influence of a mother figure is important in terms of work—what is seen as work, what entails doing a "good" job, how one "ought" to work, etc. Alternately, your work may center on nurturing others.

If the focus on flaws is overdone and you are feeling frustrated by your work, or unable to accomplish as you wish, illness could be a subconscious escape hatch. Your "job" might become the improving of your own physical functioning, or you could be involved in assisting and taking care of other people. Practical support or pragmatic nurturing are constructive expressions of this aspect. For greatest satisfaction, take practical steps to improve either work routines, your job, or your health.

Mundane Options: nurturing coworkers (or dependent colleagues); a job involving women, the public, the land, food, shelter, clothing or emotional assistance; turning homemaking into a career for a time; criticism of/ toward/ in the home; practical mothering; nutritional improvements; healthy food.

Ceres Conjunct Chiron or Chiron Conjunct Ceres (long-term)

This combination can range from idealizing home and children (or grandchildren) to avoiding family commitments in order to travel, pursue knowledge or seek the Absolute in almost any area of life. Of course, we might integrate the principles by traveling with the family, or by making a home in distant areas. With successful integration, this pattern shows the confidence and clarity about goals to initiate action, and the willingness to work in practical ways to actually reach the goals. It is an excellent combination for any type of service which contributes to the well-being of life and the planet, especially to any kind of healing work.

Mundane Options: working in a knowledge field; putting ideas and ideals into form; a job which involves travel, philosophy, religion, healing, or inspiration; mother issues affect one's faith; seeing and encouraging the best in family.

Ceres Conjunct/Opposite Nodes
or Nodes Conjunct/Opposite Ceres (long-term)

This pattern suggests an emphasis on material and/or emotional security. Pressures may stem from the need to integrate work demands with family obligations. There may be questions about dependency versus nurturing and a need to work out an equitable sharing of the load. With mutual sensitivity to the feelings of all concerned, it should be possible to build a support system that offers joint protection.

Ceres Conjunct North Node

Family feelings are in strong focus. You may add to your family, or share more with family members. Emotional closeness is more important during this period, and nurturing is highlighted. Now is the time to work on your support system—both what you give to and receive from others in terms of emotional assistance. You may also make some changes in your work in order to gain more security or to help others. Labor and love are intertwined, with a desire to extend emotional bonds, to deepen commitments and to care for others.

Ceres Conjunct South Node

Mothering and nurturing urges are emphasized. Tension is possible over issues of emotional and physical support. You may feel that you have to give more than usual, or be wanting more assistance than has been the norm. Anxiety over issues of protection, sustenance or parenting is possible. You may experience some discomfort with your mother (or mother figure), with a nurturing/parenting role, or with your own need to be taken care of. The challenge is to work productively, to be caring and helpful—without doing more than your share. You may wish to expand your family at this time, or simply strive to extend the circle of warmth and support wider than it has been in the past.

Ceres Conjunct Ascendant

Mothering and efficiency are in high focus. You may examine your role as a parent or children (or grandchildren) may enter your life. You are likely to critically examine where you get results in life and seek increased competence. You could focus on your health and undertake regimens to increase your physical well-being. You could become a parent or leave a parental role. Your "earth mother" instincts are in the foreground.

Ceres Conjunct MC

Parenting instincts affect your professional role. You may accept more responsibility at work, adopting an "I'll take care of it" attitude. You could decide being a parent is your most important job, or find your career course being affected by a parent or mentor. Efficiency is likely to matter more than usual to you as you strive for tangible, measurable achievements.

Ceres Conjunct Descendant

There is an increased focus on care taking in your peer relationships. This could be a business involvement with a partner. It could be one partner leaning increasingly on the other. A parent could influence the status of your partnership, or become a partner in a family business. Health issues could affect relationships. The goal is sharing tasks and emotional support easily and comfortably and encouraging each other to be more aware of health needs and to conscientiously support your bodies' efficient functioning.

Ceres Conjunct IC

Issues around nurturing and dependency influence your emotional state. Old feelings about how you were mothered may have to be faced and worked out. You may have additional dealings with a mother figure or take on a nurturing role in your home. Children, grandchildren, a parent, or a pet may enter the domestic scene and look to you for care taking. You may also feel an urge to improve your diet and focus on increased nutritional efficiency. You might conduct your career in your home, or through service to the public (e.g. real estate). Compassionate competence is your motto.

Pallas Conjunct Sun (See Sun Conjunct Pallas above.)

Pallas Conjunct Moon (See Chapter Eleven.)

Pallas Conjunct Mercury (See Mercury Conjunct Pallas above.)

Pallas Conjunct Venus (See Venus Conjunct Pallas above.)

Pallas Conjunct Mars (See Mars Conjunct Pallas above.)

Pallas Conjunct Jupiter or Jupiter Conjunct Pallas (long-term)

Justice and fair play are highlighted with this combination. Politics may attract you, or social causes could offer an outlet for the drive to "even things up." Involvement with the legal system is possible as you may seek to further the cause of righteousness. Or a combination of teaching and counseling could be practical.

Ideals are likely to be high in regard to relationships and you might expect more than is possible—of yourself, a partner, or relationships in general. Looking for the best is okay as long as it is not used as an excuse to never settle down (since no one measures up to an impossible standard). Shared ideals and goals are essential to success in relationships; make sure you and a partner are moving in the same direction for the long-term.

This combination often points to liveliness and a spirit of fun. You may enjoy expansive activities, especially with a partner—shared trips, sports, classes, discussions or anything which lifts the spirits and brings a sense of optimism.

Mundane Options: ideal relationship (or too high expectations, your own or your partner's); social activity for a religious ideal; travel with a partner; flirtations; artistic grandchild; education or training in art, competitive sports or business, work as a consultant, involvement with the law or litigation; cooperative writing.

Pallas Conjunct Saturn or Saturn Conjunct Pallas (long-term)

Professional beauty or professional relationships are two of the options with this combination. Your career drives may be connected to aesthetic outlets or to one-on-one interactions. You may pursue beauty, grace or charm in your work in the world. Success might come through increasing skill in seeing or creating patterns. Appropriate fields would include the graphic arts such as architecture, photography, beautician, design, etc. You might also be involved in any variety of "people professions"—ranging from lawyers and politicians to counselors and astrologers.

Power issues in personal relationships may be important in this period. A competitive business or a career in a highly competitive field can help to direct the "need to win" or to be "on top" into constructive channels. If not applied in appropriate areas, the competition might spill into peer relationships which should be cooperative, possibly leading to control struggles with team members. Equal relationships could become more like parent/child interactions with one party the dominant, controlling, strong responsible one. Or, if that outcome is feared, relationships may be avoided and inhibited due to anxiety about power, criticism or responsibility. Once relationship commitments are made, however, the sense of commitment is usually strong and the tendency is to hang in—determined to "make things work."

Objectivity may be easier to achieve during this period, using the logic of Pallas and the practicality of Saturn. You can be sensible about areas needing improvement, while maintaining empathy toward the viewpoints of others.

Successful integration of the two principles involved can make your career more pleasurable or appealing and can build a stronger, more stable foundation in your relationships.

Mundane Options: business partnership; attraction to politics; work involving "causes" or as a consultant, tangible project with a partner; issues with in-laws or with parents/grandparents; aesthetic involvement on the job; personnel work; improved marriage; criticism in relationships; power through cooperation/teamwork.

Pallas Conjunct Uranus or Uranus Conjunct Pallas (long-term)

Social interactions are highlighted by this aspect, and you may relate to more people. New friendships as well as new partnerships are possible. A sense of openness is likely and a desire for intellectual stimulation which keeps attracting you to new ideas and perspectives. Your relationships require room for the individuality and freedom needs of both people. The accent is on tolerance of differences and **long** leashes. If either person feels tied down, breaks or splits are possible. New relationships may enter your life at any time with this aspect, but expect friendship first. This is not an aspect of heavy commitment.

New artistic endeavors are also possible at any time. You may utilize your creativity and inventiveness in different aesthetic forms. You could take up a new hobby, a new group, a club or some other activity involving lots of contact with other people.

Passion for justice may be marked, so involvement in politics is possible (up to and including running for legislative office). You may also be drawn to the law, to social causes or to humanitarian endeavors. You are likely to be more aware of contexts and how issues fit into the larger overview of society.

Through the period of this aspect you can be drawn to stimulating your mind, expanding your networking capabilities, experimenting with ideas and practicing tolerance, acceptance and openness in your relationships.

Mundane Options: marriage encounter (or divorce); friends become lovers; lovers become friends; unusual relationships; more social activity; involvement in social causes; changing associations; sudden love ("falling in love"); progressive or unusual art; unconventional beauty; expanded knowledge or new ways of sharing information with others.

Pallas Conjunct Neptune or Neptune Conjunct Pallas (long-term)

Beauty and grace are usually very appealing with this aspect. The urge is likely to be toward sweetness and succor. This combination may highlight an inspired pursuit of beauty or an idealistic desire to assist and rescue others. Any of the healing or helping pursuits may provide satisfaction—as well as a variety of artistic endeavors.

This blend tends to be somewhat passive and receptive, so you may be more inclined toward enjoying beauty, grace and ease than toward doing a lot of creating yourself. If the rose-colored glasses are overdone, victim scripts are possible due to wanting things to be easier or more perfect than is realistic. You could look to partnership for inspiration. Shared dreams and visions work well; mutual illusions are not so wise.

Faith may be sought through a partner, in art, or in harmony and balance. Turning another person into an idol does not work, but you need to share your sense of inspiration in some way. Appearances and "looking good" could be overvalued, or you may utilize talents for diplomacy, charm and grace to make your interactions more loving, smooth, and pleasant.

Mundane Options: anything artistic (including but not limited to music, photography, painting, decorating, film making, fashion design, sewing, make-up, hairdressing, composing, etc.); idealized love or idealizing love and romance; "amazing grace"; equality as a mystical goal; savior/victim relationships and sacred marriages; hidden partners; public service; spiritual teamwork to help the world.

Pallas Conjunct Pluto or Pluto Conjunct Pallas (long-term)

Relationship issues are focused by this aspect. When integrated so they work together, the air/ water blend shows potential insight and understanding. You have the capacity for empathy and intuitive understanding as well as objectivity and intellectual understanding. You and a partner may see more deeply into one another and may communicate more clearly.

A possible issue could revolve around depth and intensity versus lightness associated with a broad perspective. You may feel torn between a thorough, deep probing versus dealing with what is immediately and obviously on the surface. You and your partner may have to decide how much each should really know about the life of the other. How much secrecy is appropriate? Sexual matters or issues of joint resources and finances may also require compromise. Finding a truly equalitarian balance of power with another individual can be a considerable challenge.

Generally, this aspect suggests an openness to and desire for relationships. If not currently involved, you may meet someone during this period. If already involved, you may deepen your ties. The tendency is toward increasing closeness and commitment.

Mundane Options: marriage; living together; business partnership; going into counseling; lawsuits; financial or sexual issues with partners; intense relationships; competition; learning to compromise, learning when is enough and how to let go.

Pallas Conjunct Ceres, (See Ceres Conjunct Pallas above.)

Pallas Conjunct (Natal) Pallas

The emphasis is upon relationships, aesthetics, harmony and balance (whether cooperative or competitive.

Mundane Options: beginning or ending a partnership (business or personal), litigation, aesthetic activities, counseling, consulting, peer review, teamwork, increased sense of justice or concern with fair play, greater wisdom and perspective.

Pallas Conjunct Juno (and vice versa)

Beauty and relationships are central themes with this aspect. People involvements remain very important or become more so. A significant relationship (marriage, living together, therapy) could be initiated, or a current one deepened. Competitive interactions are possible; one-on-one exchanges are the focus. Equality, sharing, balance and harmony could all be emphasized.

Aesthetic pursuits might cover a wide range, although the visual arts are most likely, e.g., photography, design, decorating, fashion, modeling, painting, etc. Appearances may increase in importance and "looking good" might be a goal.

Questions of justice and equality could arise. Lawsuits are possible, or political or social activism. Fairness and balance are highlighted. The drive for fair play will need to be integrated with the desire for harmony and sweetness. Diplomacy may vie with confrontation, face-to-face encounters with more subtle maneuvering. The general theme, however, is sharing one's life with others and seeking to bring more beauty and more balance into the world.

Mundane Options: marriage; starting therapy; litigation; manipulative or passive-aggressive relationships; competition; focus on joint resources, sexuality highlighted, visual arts (or any arts); focus on appearance; drive for justice.

Pallas Conjunct Vesta (and vice versa)

Efficiency is connected to your drive for fairness, balance, beauty and sharing. You might choose artistic/ aesthetic work or people-work, including a dedication to justice. Alternately, you might desire to improve/ repair personal relationships.

Possible fields of work which involve relationships with others include personnel work,˙ psychotherapy, consulting, etc. You might develop a significant relationship at or through your job, work as a member of a team, or establish a business partnership.

Your capacity for critical analysis could be directed toward interpersonal interactions. You might criticize or be criticized by a partner, or end up with an excessively practical or nit-picking attitude about others. Criticism should mostly be applied to one's job rather than to people. Managers who must evaluate subordinates should remember to notice assets as well as flaws, to praise what is done well in addition to correcting mistakes. You can also put your competency drives into a quest for more equality, fairness, balance or beauty in the world.

It is possible to improve your relationships (without turning the other person into a "job" or arduous task). You can beautify your work, or make your job routines more appealing and gratifying.

Mundane Options: working with people or beauty; business partnership; critical in (or criticized within) relationships; working hard for balance and fair play.

Pallas Conjunct Chiron or Chiron Conjunct Pallas (long-term)

This combination can indicate a high value placed on peer relationships. For one person with this pattern, sharing life might be so important that living alone is unthinkable, while another person might prefer to stay alone rather than settle for an imperfect partner. One can also attract other people who are looking for perfection or choose a profession which involves working with people as a counselor or consultant, using the Chiron ideals and love of knowledge to help others. Interest in and talent for the graphic arts is possible. Usually, there is an increased emphasis on fair play and social justice, which may draw you into activity with social causes. The essential principles of the combination call for a blending of activities with peer relationships and high values and ideals.

Mundane Options: High standards for relationships; legal developments; shared quest for knowledge and justice.

Pallas Conjunct/Opposite Nodes
or Nodes Conjunct/Opposite Pallas (long-term)

This combination suggests an emphasis on relationships and security issues. Compromises may be necessary to achieve equality while still satisfying the need to nurture or to be nurtured. It may seem difficult to satisfy both children and a mate. Or family obligations may interfere with artistic expressions, with pleasure with friends, or with the desire to play a role in the transpersonal realm working for social causes. You have the capacity to be both sensitive and empathic to the feelings of others but also intellectually logical and objective. The best compromise usually leads to interdependence where everyone can both give and receive.

Pallas Conjunct North Node

Justice within relationships is apt to be important during this period. You may be concerned with issues of cooperation, competition, fair play or equality. If an imbalance of power is evident, you may seek to right it. Taking turns could become an issue. You may measure yourself in relationship to other people. You are likely to seek more emotional connections, particularly on a partnership level. You need to share with others, to have the give-and-take of interpersonal exchanges.

Pallas Conjunct South Node

Your emotional security may be sought through promoting justice and fair play. Your sense of righteousness could be aroused on behalf of the downtrodden, or you may seek more evenhandedness in your personal associations with others. If inequality exists, you are probably motivated to alter it. You could look for ways for people to take turns, to share, to achieve a balance of power. Cooperation may vie with competition in your life. You may experience some tension in relationships until a comfortable exchange can be achieved.

Pallas Conjunct Ascendant

Equality issues become more personal. You seek to act in ways which are truly balanced, and you are willing to fight for your rights—or to ensure that fair play occurs. Artistic expression could be channeled through physical activity (dance, skiing, skating, etc.) or through your personal appearance. Competitive instincts are stimulated. Your perceptions of justice (or injustice) affect what you do. Compromise is usually required to satisfy both the need to be one's self and the need to share life with others.

Pallas Conjunct MC

A partnership may affect your career. This could include a business contact or a personal, romantic involvement. Beauty issues may become more prominent in your work, or face-to-face interactions with others. The focus is on sharing aesthetic, cooperative or competitive activities with other people through your work in the world. "Making it" in conventional terms may have greater appeal than usual, or working in a career which promotes a "cause."

Pallas Conjunct Descendant

Equality over all is your motto. You strive for fair play in all your dealings with others. Cooperation is possible, but so is competition. Face to face dealings with others are a major focus. New partnerships are possible, but you might also revamp established ties. A sense of give-and-take and share-and-share-alike is very strong. You are looking for ways to truly be peers with those around you.

Pallas Conjunct IC

You are likely to experience the urge to balance your home life. Relationships with people sharing your domestic environment may be reworked. You could decide to beautify your residence, or support Gaia, the earth. Competition for nurturing is possible. You may find a partner leaning on you more than usual—or vice versa. Emotional commitments call for care and attention. Cherish and support your relationships.

Juno Conjunct Sun (See Sun Conjunct Juno above.)

Juno Conjunct Moon (See Chapter Eleven.)

Juno Conjunct Mercury (See Mercury Conjunct Juno above.)

Juno Conjunct Venus (See Venus Conjunct Juno above.)

Juno Conjunct Mars (See Mars Conjunct Juno above.)

Juno Conjunct Jupiter or Jupiter Conjunct Juno (long-term)

Relationships or aesthetics are likely candidates for idealization with this aspect. Marriage may be seen as an ultimate value in life, and a marriage partner might be put upon a pedestal. Also possible, however, is the quest for the nonexistent perfect partner. Some people will handle the restlessness of Jupiter by keeping relationship standards too high to ever be reached. Multiple relationships are possible if you believe that "perhaps the next one will be more ideal." Partners who share a spiritual outlook (or other Jupiterian activities, such as travel, education, love of nature, etc.) gain their inspiration through shared activities—and neither need nor expect the other to "be everything" for them.

Beauty may also provide a sense of inspiration to the life. Faith can be bulwarked through artistic creation, enjoyment of nature or aesthetic involvement. Harmony and fair play may hold prominent roles in your ethics and moral principles.

Mundane Options: ideal relationship (or too high expectations, your own or your partner's); social activity for a religious ideal; travel with a partner; flirtations; education or training in art, law, as a consultant, etc.; involvement with the law or litigation; cooperative writing; beliefs and values as a significant issue in relationships; faith in cooperation.

Juno Conjunct Saturn or Saturn Conjunct Juno (long-term)

Responsibility issues may surface in relationships and art may take a tangible form or professional place in your life. One option is a career that involves aesthetics. The visual arts, particularly, may be pursued in your work. Besides the fine arts, this can include fields such as color analysis, architecture, modeling, decorating, fashion, cosmetology, etc.

Alternately, your profession may involve work with people. This can range from law, psychology, management, etc., to business partnerships, office affairs or meeting a spouse/partner through your work. (You may even marry the boss literally!) You also might stay emotionally attached to your father or a father figure.

Power drives, or the need to control, may spill over into your partnerships. You might end up having to be strong, responsible, hardworking and competent for a weaker partner—or seek out a "father figure" sort of partner who is older, more dominant, capable, responsible, etc., for you. If you want a more equalitarian partnership, look for ways to share the power, share the responsibilities and take turns being strong for one another. With this aspect, you are likely to be more realistic and pragmatic about relationships, so will tend to take them seriously and to be cautious about commitments. One possibility is literally "making marriage real"—taking that final step to get legally tied to another person. Once you take the step of getting involved, you are likely to hang in, to try everything to "make it work."

Mundane Options: business partnership or marriage; attraction to politics; tangible project with a partner; issues with in-laws or with parents/ grandparents; aesthetic involvement on the job; personnel work; improved marriage; criticism in relationships; power through cooperation/ teamwork.

Juno Conjunct Uranus or Uranus Conjunct Juno (long-term)

This combination suggests a possible confrontation between freedom needs and the desire for attachment and emotional commitment. If handled consciously, one option is creating more openness, tolerance, flexibility and individuality within an already-existing marriage or relationship. Relationships might also tend to be unusual, highly intellectual, political, long-distance, open or futuristic. Other options include sudden marriages (or commitments) or breaks in relationships. The issue calls for making room in one's life for both freedom and closeness. If we stay out of touch with our emotional yearning for commitment, we may "fall in love" suddenly—and fall hard! If we ignore or repress the need for more independence or space in relationships, we may periodically feel a need to break loose and break free—or our partner may express that need for freedom for us. If we completely suppress our freedom needs, we are likely to attract people unwilling to commit or fall for married men or women—people not really available. When we want both independence and emotional involvement, a long-distance relationship is one way to have both!

This combination suggests a general friendliness. Friends can turn into spouses or partners, and partners may stay friends even after a separation. The Uranus principle encourages being tolerant and appreciating differences between people, acknowledging everyone's uniqueness. Relationships may also take on a transpersonal overtone—more counseling-oriented (rather than marriage), or involved with politics, causes, social action or groups. Networking is a natural focus for you.

Another option is innovation in terms of the arts. You may become more original, avant garde or unusual in your aesthetic involvement. You could use or present beauty in a very unique fashion. Your perceptions may be quite individualistic.

Mundane Options: marriage encounter (or divorce); friends become lovers; lovers become friends; unusual relationships; more social activity; involvement in social causes; changing associations; sudden love ("falling in love"); expanded knowledge or new ways of sharing information with others.

Juno Conjunct Neptune or Neptune Conjunct Juno (long-term)

The theme revolves around a quest for infinite love and beauty. This may be directed toward artistic endeavors or toward relationships—or both. The challenge is to seek ecstasy and perfection in parts of life that are truly infinite (art, nature, God), but allow people to be human.

This is an appropriate time for any kind of creation or appreciation of beauty. Whether the focus is on music, visual arts, grace in motion, the performing or other arts, there is a strong feeling for balance, harmony and aesthetics.

Ideals for relationships are apt to be high. This could indicate the search for Prince or Princess Charming. If the need find a "perfect love" overwhelms the practical side, repeated involvements can occur—each time thinking that **this** one will be the ideal soul mate. Or, people may subconsciously attract saviors to help them in their victim (escapist) role or victims that they try to rescue, assist and lift out of their unhappy lives. "Playing God" to a partner does not work when equality is the name of the game. Sharing a vision with a partner can build love and beauty together. You could be fellow artists, two mystics, or share an idealistic or healing quest in the world. Your artistic talent, inspirational faith or empathic compassion can help to bring more beauty, more hope, and more joy into the world.

Mundane Options: anything artistic (including, but not limited to, photography, music, design, hairdressing, film making, etc.); idealized love or idealizing love and romance; "amazing grace"; savior/ victim relationships and sacred marriages; hidden partners; public service; spiritual teamwork to help "heal the planet."

Juno Conjunct Pluto or Pluto Conjunct Juno (long-term)

The likely focus for this period revolves around intimacy, psychological depths and the issue of sharing, including the sharing of power. This is most commonly a time when relationships are important, especially commitments such as marriage. You are likely to learn about yourself through the mirror of a mate. You may also come to master and control yourself for the sake of a sharing relationship. Sex, money and shared possessions are likely subjects to come up when the two of you are learning to give freely, receive easily, and share comfortably.

Because there is also a theme of privacy and withdrawal, there may be times when you or your mate feels the need to be alone. Self-analysis may necessitate intervals of separation. Some inner processing may be essential before you can return to the one-to-one confrontations. Communication and compromise may be needed to agree on where one person's rights end and the other person's rights begin.

Making a commitment to marriage is possible during this period. A strong focus on finances may be present, especially those involving others—debts, taxes, investments, inheritance. Sexuality may be especially intense or controlled and withheld. Issues are likely to be intense and emotional for you (and your mate). With insight, discipline and perseverance, you can transform yourself and your relationships. The highest side of this combination is "turning lead into gold" (negatives into positives).

Mundane Options: marriage; living together; business partnership; going into counseling; lawsuits; financial or sexual issues with partners; intense relationships; competition; learning to compromise, when is enough and how to let go.

Juno Conjunct Ceres (See Ceres Conjunct Juno above.)

Juno Conjunct Pallas (See Pallas Conjunct Juno above.)

Juno Conjunct (Natal) Juno

All the basic potentials of Juno are accentuated.

Mundane Options: increased intimacy, sexual awakening, focus on joint resources, owning your personal power (or unequal relationships—perhaps to the point of abuse), issues of elimination and letting go, greater emotional intensity, marriage (or other partnership).

Juno Conjunct Vesta (and vice versa)

Personal, intimate encounters are mixed with the need to be competent and effective. One option is working in fields of personnel, consulting, psychotherapy or in any job involving relating to others. Investment work or financial areas which involve the resources of others are also possible. You might meet a partner through your job, work with a partner, or form a business partnership. Aesthetic or artistic interests could also be important on the job.

The desire to improve may be channeled toward your relationships. This can be constructive in terms of facing facts and being willing to work to make things better. If overdone, however, criticism could become a problem (from you to a partner or vice versa). Too much focus on what needs to be fixed can lead to negative interactions. Shared tasks or joint projects help to constructively channel any nit-picking energies. It is also possible to feel pulled between work and partnership obligations. It may seem hard to do justice to both. Life is a juggling act. You can both strengthen relationships and make your work more attractive and appealing during this period. But no one can do everything perfectly, so keep your priorities clear.

Mundane Options: a working relationship; meeting spouse on the job; business partnership; critical of (or receiving criticism from) spouse; dedication to teamwork; job involves people or aesthetics, in-depth analysis or research to improve efficiency in either work or health.

Juno Conjunct Chiron or Chiron Conjunct Juno (long-term)

This combination suggests idealization of marriage or a desire for an ideal mate, though it is also possible that you are attracting others who are searching for an ideal. Human relationships are never perfect, but it is possible to share beliefs, values and goals with a mate, to create a mutually fulfilling bond. Shared knowledge can play an important role in your interpersonal life, exploring together both the depths and the heights of human consciousness. You may want to work for social justice or develop artistic talents or investigate new horizons to broaden your world, but achieving a satisfying relationship with a mate is likely to remain a central and important focus of attention.

Mundane Options: ideal marriage; seeking too much in relationships; shared pursuit of ideas and ultimate answers or any major goal.

Juno Conjunct/Opposite Nodes
or Nodes Conjunct/Opposite Juno (long-term)

This combination emphasizes security issues and relationships. There may be friction between family and a mate. Issues of dependency and power are possible. Seek interdependency so each individual can both give and receive. Strong emotions and sensitivity are likely with this pattern. If security is too tied to one or more relationships, it may be hard to let go when it is time to focus more on personal self-reliance. Try to enjoy emotional ties and closeness, but do not make your happiness depend on them.

Juno Conjunct North Node

Emotional connections are highlighted. You may want to form a committed partnership, or seek ways in which to strengthen and deepen an already existing commitment. Your security is on the line in relationships—particularly marital or partnership ones. With a strong yearning for intimacy and close bonds, you are more open to sharing intensely with a special someone. This could also be a period when you are deeply moved by beauty or aesthetic creativity. Now is the time to delve into your psyche, exploring feelings about intimacy, shared resources, possessions and pleasures—and learning to handle the sensual world jointly with another person.

Juno Conjunct South Node

This is a learning period in relationships. Emotional attachments are in high focus. If you are married, there may be some tension in the relationship, while intense issues are confronted and resolved. If you are not married, close inter-personal associations may be a temporary battleground or a point of anxiety and insecurity. Power struggles over sex or money are possible. Withdrawing from relationships because you feel threatened is also possible. Or you may be dealing with issues of inequality and injustice, striving for an equitable division of labor and pleasures with those who share a close, intimate bond in your life. Stay conscious of your emotional needs and seek their fulfillment fairly through reasonable compromises. Remembering moderation, a wider perspective, and a little humor may help.

Juno Conjunct Ascendant

Intimacy needs take center stage in terms of personal action. You may meet a partner, make a commitment to marry or otherwise focus on sharing the world with someone else. If married, your relationship could deepen, or conversely, it may require more independence and your partner may make a move for more space. Be willing to compromise to make sure everyone's needs are met in an equitable fashion.

Juno Conjunct MC

A partner or partnership relationship could affect your career. Beauty issues may be incorporated more into your work. Financial questions could come up and power issues with the people at work are also possible. The challenge is to blend your equalitarian, sharing side with your executive, "take charge" side. You need both love and work; let them supplement, **not** compete with one another.

Juno Conjunct Descendant

Pairing comes naturally now. If not married, this is an appropriate time for meeting someone, or making the commitment of a legal bond. If married, you may find yourselves strengthening and deepening the connections between you. Less constructively, issues of shared power (its use and abuse) may require attention. Areas of sensuality, sexuality or shared resources may come up for discussion. A goal is to find a truly equalitarian exchange while still being there for each another.

Juno Conjunct IC

You are ready for a deep, emotional commitment. Marriage is a possibility, or strengthening and intensifying a partnership bond which already exists. Knowing when is enough, how to let go and move on may be an issue. The handling of power, possessions, and pleasures is highlighted. You could share your home environment with a partner, explore your interdependence, or beautify the sharing between you or the physical surroundings of your residence. You need someone to care about, and who cares about you. Security could be increasingly connected to financial or sensual sharing. Exploring the past, family, roots, etc., could occur.

Vesta Conjunct Sun (See Sun Conjunct Vesta above.)

Vesta Conjunct Moon (See Chapter Eleven.)

Vesta Conjunct Mercury (See Mercury Conjunct Vesta above.)

Vesta Conjunct Venus (See Venus Conjunct Vesta above.)

Vesta Conjunct Mars (See Mars Conjunct Vesta above.)

Vesta Conjunct Jupiter or Jupiter Conjunct Vesta (long-term)

This can potentially be a period of high accomplishment. You may be building dreams, making cherished visions into a reality, using idealistic fervor and enthusiasm to fuel dedicated effort and productivity.

   You could be drawn toward Jupiterian work—involving travel, writing, publishing, teaching, education, philosophy, religion, the law, media work, promotion or sales, or anything which broadens horizons or offers hope of something more and something better. You may wish to inspire and uplift people through your work. There is a danger of looking for the "perfect" job, idealizing the work ethic, or trying to do everything perfectly. "Inspired achievement" is the constructive keynote for this time.

Your beliefs and values remain important both in terms of work and health. Your concepts and world view tend to manifest in your state of health (or illness) as well as in your productivity (or lack of it). Part of the challenge of this aspect is to develop (or increase) a secure sense of faith and confidence that is grounded and effective in the real world.

Mundane Options: more schooling to enhance vocation; a new career dream; revising philosophies, religions or ideas; travel for your job; dissatisfaction because life does not measure up to your standards; writing and publishing; work connected to other countries, education, law, etc.

Vesta Conjunct Saturn or Saturn Conjunct Vesta (long-term)

Hard work, effort, dedication and discipline are key themes for this period. Constructively applied, this can be a period where you get a lot done. Tangible accomplishments are very possible. Measurable results are apt to be most satisfying, and the most sought-after. You want to do something **real,** which most people define as having results in the world.

If this theme is carried too far, you could be overly responsible, becoming a workaholic. You may be overly serious, dedicated and effective, feeling "If you want it done right, do it yourself." You could carry too much of the load. There are limits to everyone's authority and responsibility. If you have been playing "Atlas" by carrying the world, you may need to learn to delegate.

The opposite reaction, which is sometimes found with this aspect, includes feeling blocked, inhibited, limited and frustrated. In extreme cases, illness is possible. Everything may just seem too hard and a serious outlook could slide into depression. You could feel that an ordinary job is worthless, that you are only OK if you do something to re-make the world. Practice focusing on what **has been** accomplished as well as what remains to be done. Break tasks into "bite-sized" pieces so that no part seems overwhelming. Look for projects with physical, measurable results; they will feed your sense of accomplishment and encourage you to do more.

Mundane Options: career advancement (or limitation); mentoring (or being mentored) at work; health regimen; efficiency project at work; criticism of or by colleagues; parent(ing) affects job; responsibilities mount; accomplishments increase.

Vesta Conjunct Uranus or Uranus Conjunct Vesta (long-term)

This period highlights a theme of innovation connected to work and/or health. Options might include a new career, new duties, or new ways of accomplishing your tasks. Another possibility is a new health routine or way of dealing with your physical maintenance. If your drive for change is out of conscious awareness, shifts might be "forced" by outside circumstances.

You may be more inclined to work for yourself now, or to alter established routines with more variety. You could be drawn toward Uranian fields: astrology, computers, new technology such as electronic media, science, organizations, clubs, social causes, politics, or anything unusual, different or futuristic.

You might focus on repairs or improvements in Uranian areas such as friendships, groups, or social causes. The "fix-it" mentality can be helpful, if not carried to the extreme of excessive criticism or nit-picking. You may be able to strengthen your individuality, your networking prospects and your friendships.

Mundane Options: more independence at work (or quitting or being fired); repair work; criticism of or by friends; unusual employee or tenant; working association; working at astrology, media work, group action or new-age activities; altering work routines; friendship with a colleague.

Vesta Conjunct Neptune or Neptune Conjunct Vesta (long-term)

This aspect highlights the polarity of material reality versus fantasy. A constructive integration might involve professional artwork, healing, rescuing or service endeavors or manifesting any dreams for a better or more beautiful world. Utopian images need to be brought to earth.

A less constructive alternative would involve looking for the ideal job, and job-hopping in hopes that the next will have more perfect hours, pay, tasks, etc. Another potential danger is illness or escapist behavior (e.g., fantasy, alcoholism, drugs, etc.) to avoid facing a less-than-perfect world and to evade acknowledging one's failure to do anything about it.

Depending on one's faith and efforts, this aspect can point to the victim or the savior/healer who is helping others. Developing a firm sense of faith and trust in the goodness of life is important, but confidence in your own ability to act, to do, to accomplish is equally vital.

Mundane Options: handicrafts; objects that are beautiful and useful; health or healing activities; illness (mental/ emotional/ physical, if you subconsciously feel helpless to improve your life); that "dream job" (with the risk of expecting too much from the job or yourself as a worker); rescue work; spiritual discipline.

Vesta Conjunct Pluto or Pluto Conjunct Vesta (long-term)

Focus, concentration, follow-through, endurance and tunnel vision are among the potentials of this aspect. Talent may be strong for business endeavors, research, or anything requiring thoroughness and the capacity to organize lots of details and to be disciplined. There is usually a desire to get to the end of things.

Work might bring a mate into your life, be accomplished with a partner (business or romantic), or involve joint resources and finances. Medical or healing interests are quite possible, and this combination can point to healing talent. You could feel the urge to analyze and improve any hidden matters, to dig things up, rework them and make them better in the end. Learning when and how to let go and release may be an issue some of the time.

Intimate exchanges may be overlaid with a desire for "efficiency." Self-control and an attraction to asceticism could be overdone to the point of interfering with sexuality or sensuality. It is possible to have overcontrol in some areas and overindulgence in other areas, or to swing between the two. Inhibition or caution might also affect financial matters. Practicality is necessary, but do not allow it to block the natural pleasures of life. Analysis and flaw-finding can contribute to success in work efforts; keep spontaneity and a free flow for your loving, sharing exchanges.

Mundane Options: start a diet; quit smoking or drinking; clean closets literally and metaphorically; business partnership; budgeting; work with taxes, insurance, debts, inheritance or investments; sexual withdrawal or sex therapy; end of a project (or job); transformation of work duties; depth analysis of yourself and/or others; steps to improve your health; good organizational skills and the ability to focus.

Vesta Conjunct Ceres (See Ceres Conjunct Vesta above.)

Vesta Conjunct Pallas (See Pallas Conjunct Vesta above.)

Vesta Conjunct Juno (See Juno Conjunct Vesta above.)

Vesta Conjunct (Natal) Vesta
All general Vesta themes are highlighted.

Mundane Options: increased focus on work or health (good or bad health), more productivity, skill with details and craftsmanship, good analytical abilities, flaw-finding tendencies rise (could lead to alienation in relationships), improvement instincts are accented, efficient functioning on the job and in the body is the goal.

Vesta Conjunct Chiron or Chiron Conjunct Vesta (long-term)
This combination can be experienced as a total commitment to one's work, and can lead to outstanding success. Alternately, if you are in a job which is unfulfilling, which fails to use your talents, you are likely to be very frustrated and run the risk of personal illness, as the subconscious mind will often produce illness to escape such jobs. Appropriate work should be mentally stimulating, offer variety, and satisfy your ideals. Some field of healing is especially appropriate. But guard against searching for the "perfect" job or being too perfectionistic in any area. Life always demands some compromise. This combination blends your vision of perfection with the reality of needing to function effectively within the limits of the material world. Do what you can, living one day at a time.

Mundane Options: work which involves ideas or ideals; frustration because work is not perfect; healing or educational work; dedication to the quest for knowledge; practical philosophizing.

Vesta Conjunct/Opposite Nodes
or Nodes Conjunct/Opposite Vesta (long-term)

This combination connects work and security issues. Available jobs may fail to satisfy your physical or emotional needs. Or they may conflict with your family obligations. Illness is a hazard when we become too frustrated with our work, as the subconscious enables us to escape the job. Sometimes an earth-water emphasis is a sign that we are taking ourselves and life too seriously and we need to lighten up. Practical realism and emotional sensitivity are both emphasized in this pattern, so you have the capacity to cope with the situation by combining your ability to work and your ability to be aware of the feelings of others. An effective integration of the principles calls for balance between handling your share of the responsibility and allowing others to do their share.

Vesta Conjunct North Node

Relationships with colleagues are highlighted. You may strive to improve or enhance your working associations. You are likely to examine the interrelationships at your job, and seek ways to be more productive. Your "repairing instincts" might also become directed toward emotional relationships or toward your physical body and general health. Be wary of overdoing the critical eye (from you toward others or from others toward you). Shared tasks help direct flaw-finding toward the physical world rather than nit-picking one another's personalities. You may seek more security and safety within your working environment.

Vesta Conjunct South Node

Your analytical, discriminating side is apt to be highlighted. This could be expressed through seeking more safety or security in your job, through striving to improve your health or physical functioning, or through a desire to enhance your emotional relationships. Your drive to repair and "make better" can be extremely useful, if you do not succumb to the extremes of excessive criticism and judgmentalism. You may work on improving your interpersonal associations, your work in the world, or your body. You can direct both emotional warmth and practical dedication toward whatever tasks you choose.

Vesta Conjunct Ascendant

Work and health become more central, personal concerns with this aspect. You may decide to put a new bodily regimen into action, or adopt new habits to improve your physical well-being. If you like what you are doing, you will have more self-discipline than usual, and find concentrating easier. The need to "do a good job" at whatever you accomplish is strong, so you might incline toward excessive self-criticism. Measurable results matter much to you. Don't work too hard, but do something that you feel is worth doing and that you can do well. Then relax!

Vesta Conjunct MC

Doing what needs to be done and making sure it gets done right is a prominent theme. The workaholic trap looms if you fall into the feeling of indispensability ("If you want it done right, do it yourself."). You could end up overworked, underpaid and very burdened. If your flaw-finding lens is too strong, you might give up before you start, figuring you'll never do things well enough anyway. With reasonable ambitions and expectations, you have the potential of much productive accomplishment and fine self-discipline.

Vesta Conjunct Descendant

Your analytical eye is apt to focus on one-to-one relationships. This could enhance your working relationships, with an increased focus on shared accomplishments and taking care of business. The flaw-finding lens, however, might result in you criticizing partners—or being criticized by them. The urge to "make over" relationships or partners could be carried too far. Be practical, and remember everybody's human!

Vesta Conjunct IC

Your flaw-finding side is directed toward your home environment and deeper emotional needs. You may find yourself criticizing your home or family members—or being criticized by them. "Fix it" projects for the home may provide a constructive outlet. Feelings of alienation are a danger unless assets are acknowledged along with flaws. You may feel burdened or overworked by domestic demands unless duties are shared. Efficiency appeals and you may try to streamline your dependent and nurturing relationships. You might work in a field such as real estate, home construction, agriculture or ranching, or develop a business in your own home.

Chiron Conjunct Sun (See Sun Conjunct Chiron above.)

Chiron Conjunct Moon (See Chapter Eleven.)

Chiron Conjunct Mercury (See Mercury Conjunct Chiron above.)

Chiron Conjunct Venus (See Venus Conjunct Chiron above.)

Chiron Conjunct Mars (See Mars Conjunct Chiron above.)

Chiron Conjunct Jupiter through Pluto (See Chapter Two (long-term).)

Chiron Conjunct Nodes (See Chapter Two (long-term).)

Chiron Conjunct Ascendant

Personal idealistic action is emphasized. This may be expressed in terms of teaching, taking classes, going on spiritual quests, discussing philosophy and religion, engaging in healing activities, or seeking the best in many different parts of life. Beware of demanding more of yourself than is humanly possible. Ethical and moral standards may be highlighted.

Chiron Conjunct MC

High ideals are connected to your career and status. This can indicate reaching a long-desired goal. It could point to seeking the ideal job, trying to do your work perfectly, or working to make the world better in some fashion—such as through teaching, healing, inspiring activities.

Chiron Conjunct Descendant

A quest for the best is tied to relationships. You may feel you have found a truly special someone or share spiritual, idealistic, healing or inspirational activities with a mate. Less constructively, you may yearn for an ideal partner (who does not exist), try to play "guru" to a partner, or attract people who look to you to provide "heaven on Earth" in the relationship. Finding ways to share the quest for Infinite Understanding is your best bet.

Chiron Conjunct IC

Home and family matters are connected with seeking and searching motifs. You may find the ideal home, or spend time focusing on creating your "dream" domicile. Your may idealize family members (and expect too much) or easily accent the positive among loved ones. The restless quest for answers (including travel to find meaning) could compete with emotional security needs. Find a way to combine roots and restlessness, to share healing and inspired visions with the people you nurture and who nurture you.

For any conjunctions involving the angles (Ascendant/Descendant and Midheaven/IC), also see Chapter Seven.

CHAPTER SEVEN

HARD ASPECTS
TO THE ANGLES

Traditionally, the "hard" aspects in astrology (conjunction, square [and also octile or semi-square plus trioctile or sesqui-quadrate], and opposition) are most associated with events. The quincunx is also often an indicator that something will change—perhaps through a separation. (That can include separating from a part of the body, through surgery, as well as separations from people, positions, places, and states of being.) "Hard" aspects can indicate challenges, since they symbolize inner conflict between different drives. Often they are keys to "action" or "manifestation" because we try to resolve the conflict by "doing" something, or we subconsciously attract events to try to resolve the inner conflict. Certainly, as we project ahead, it is most effective to visualize what action we can take to best express the symbolism in our unfolding progressions. We integrate the conflicts which are an inherent part of life by making a place in our lives for all of our (sometimes competing) primary desires. They can be satisfied alternately or by compromising and having a little of several. The emphasis in this chapter is a shorthand summary of some of the potentials of hard aspects (and quincunxes) to the angles. Possible events are mentioned.

Table of Aspects

ASPECT NAME	SYMBOL	DEGREE	ORB (in progressions)
Conjunction	☌	0	1 degree
Semi-Sextile	⚺	30	1 degree
Octile (Semi-Square)	∠	45	1 degree
Sextile	✶	60	1 degree
Square	□	90	1 degree
Trine	△	120	1 degree
Trioctile (Sesqui-quadrate)	⚎	135	1 degree
Quincunx	⚻	150	1 degree
Opposition	☍	180	1 degree

Hard aspects are in **boldface**.
Separative aspects are in *italics*.
Soft aspects are in regular type.

The angles of the horoscope (Midheaven, IC, Ascendant and Descendant) are sensitive points. When events occur, there are usually aspects to the angles. The reverse is **not** necessarily true. **Just because there are aspects to the angles is no guarantee that events will happen.** The general rule of thumb does apply: the more angle aspects which exist, the more likely that something will happen.

When dealing with "hard" aspects, the angles must be viewed as an axis. If a planet squares the Ascendant, it—perforce—squares the Descendant. If a planet is conjunct the Midheaven, it is opposite the IC, etc. Even with quincunxes, the paired angle will have a semi-sextile. This interconnectedness reflects life. Changes in our identity, body, and personal action (Ascendant) often affect— and are affected by—our close relationships and partners (Descendant). Events which affect our status and profession (Midheaven) are also likely to affect our home and family life (IC)—and vice versa.

The aspects can include a progressed planet reaching a natal angle (although aspects from the outer planets would usually qualify as long-term, enduring character issues rather than being timers for temporary events), a progressed angle aspecting a natal planet or a progressed angle aspecting a progressed planet.

Remember that the **conjunction** is the strongest aspect, so when a planet conjuncts an angle or an angle conjuncts a planet, it is likely to be a more significant time than when the other hard aspects are created. (See Chapter 6 for general descriptions of conjunctions to the angles of the horoscope.) Conjunctions with the angles often highlight cycle changes—the ending of one chapter and beginning of a new one.

Conjunctions with the Ascendant are most likely to involve a new phase in regard to personal action, appearance, health, or sense of identity. You may begin to see yourself differently. **Conjunctions with the IC** can indicate a new direction in regard to home, family (especially parents) and domestic matters (including the literal physical home). Dependency and nurturing relationships may shift. (A common shift is changing residence—moving—or home occupants may come or go.) Since the 4th house is a house of endings, any planet entering the 4th house (conjuncting the IC) can point to letting go, releasing and moving on—whether from a home, a person, a job, etc. Strong feelings are likely and our emotional foundation will probably be affected.

Conjunctions to the Descendant point to a new cycle in regard to relationships—whether cooperative or competitive, personal or business. Shifts in face-to-face interactions are probable. Planets traditionally associated with closeness (Moon, Venus, Juno and Sun) can be one of the indicators of marriage or living together, but many other cycle changes can occur, including a more public life.

Conjunctions to the Midheaven point to a new chapter in terms of status, reputation, career, power or authority figures (including boss, parents, police, etc.). Our contribution to society, relationship to the powers-that-be, or identifying (public) "label" in the eyes of others may shift.

Squares (and octiles and trioctiles) can indicate challenges and conflicts to be resolved or taking action and making something manifest.

Oppositions and quincunxes are most often associated with a fork in the road, letting go or moving on from something or someone (voluntarily or involuntarily). Because of their separative associations, they will be discussed in a later section.

Again, just because there are aspects does not guarantee there will be events.

Because the progressed Moon moves so quickly, its aspects to the angles are likely to be more ephemeral. They can indicate changes, but are more likely to be minor ones—unless a network of other aspects is also in the picture. Thus, the progressed Ascendant conjunct the natal Moon is usually more significant than the progressed Moon conjunct the natal Ascendant—unless a number of other aspects are tied into the picture.

Rulerships

These delineations are based on the nature of the planet which is making a "hard" aspect. (Quincunxes are included in "hard" aspects.) As always, consider also the house which that planet rules. For example, the ruler of the 2nd house (money, possessions, and pleasures) making a hard aspect (especially a conjunction) to the Ascendant could indicate: self-employment, more financial independence, impulsive spending, purchases for one's body, arguments about money, active pursuit of beauty, identification with what one owns, or assertive pursuit of "feel-good" activities, etc. A square involving the 2nd house ruler and Ascendant can indicate tension in regard to these issues (e.g., conflicts over extravagance or indulgence, or a struggle to attain financial independence, etc.) or it can indicate taking action to achieve monetary autonomy, grace in movement, etc. The quincunx and opposition carry the potential of similar actions, but can also point to separations. This might indicate polarizing with a partner over financial issues, or losing money—or voluntarily spending it—in order to pursue self-sufficiency. And so on. (Be creative in your combinations!)

The ruler of the 2nd house making a hard aspect (especially a conjunction) to the IC could symbolize: spending money to buy a home, selling one's home, beautifying the home, making the home more comfortable, enjoying the home (or family), pleasure through nurturing and care taking activities, gaining through a parent (or assisting a parent financially), etc.

The ruler of the 2nd house making a hard aspect (especially a conjunction) to the Descendant can represent: indulging a partner, attracting an indulgent partner, spending money on a partner, receiving goodies from a partner, financial disagreements which might be carried to the point of litigation, artistic activities, pleasure in relationships, treating a partner like one owns him/her (or receiving such behavior from one's partner), etc.

The ruler of the 2nd house making a hard aspect (especially a conjunction) to the Midheaven could point to: a raise (or drop) in pay or other changes in financial standing, purchasing high-status items, "buying" respect in the world, enjoying one's career, pleasure found through power, gaining through a parent (or assisting a parent financially), professional artistry, getting involved with monetary fields or those involving sensuality, beauty, or indulgence, and so on.

The rulership material presented in Chapter Five can also be applied here. Thus, links between the 2nd house and the 10th house could occur through: aspects between the two rulers (whether progressed to progressed or progressed to natal ; the progressed 2nd house ruler aspecting the Midheaven; or the progressed Midheaven aspecting the 2nd house ruler. (We have not found the intermediate house cusps timing events as often as the angles, but aspects such as the progressed ruler of the Midheaven aspecting the 2nd house cusp and the progressed 2nd house cusp aspecting the Midheaven or its ruler can add their significance to a theme that is already present in a chart in a variety of other ways.)

An additional complication for advanced students who are deepening their understanding of astrology is the use of "local houses." When they are aspected, the angles of a chart calculated for a residence other than one's birthplace can be just as meaningful as the birthplace angles. You calculate the local chart for the new latitude and longitude, but use the original data and UT (Universal or Greenwich birth time). For a comprehensive reference on astrology and relocation, see *Planets on the Move*.

Hard Aspects between the Planets and the Angles
Conjunctions, Squares, Octiles (Semi-squares).
Trioctiles (Sesqui-Quadrates)

Sun/Ascendant

Increased vitality; opportunity for personal recognition; enhanced creativity; procreation; promotional or marketing activities; leadership or owning personal power; joy and generosity; confidence and charisma, love relationship may flower; too much pride or shame is possible; self-esteem (and ego) are emphasized; childlike enthusiasm accented; a willingness to risk for greater gain is likely.

Sun/IC

Turning home into showplace, pride in ancestors, enlarging home or family (can range from pregnancy to marriage of a family member, or a child or grandchild having or adopting children), ego clashes in the home, more contact with a parent or parent figure, family focus; purchase of a home; reevaluating career/status; creative home-making activities.

Sun/Descendant

Marriage; desire for exciting relationship, attraction to fiery individuals, generosity toward partners (or partners being magnanimous), separation from a loved one; intense love bonds; leadership opportunities; power/control issues with peer relationships and issues of who shines (you or others) in relationships; artistic creativity.

Sun/Midheaven

Ambition, professional recognition, sales or marketing pursuits, more contact with a parent or parent figure, a boss who demands center stage, a mentor who affects your worth; leadership; career change; seeking more fun, creativity, excitement, recognition, or risk-taking within your career.

Moon/Ascendant

Feeling "at home"—through family, nest, community, etc.; nurturing self, becoming a parent (or grandparent)—through birth, adoption, marriage of your child, etc., changing residence, increased dependency, a deepening urge for emotional attachments, a time of vivid dreams and increased psychic openness, more contact with a mother figure; more physical sensitivity; seeking more personal safety; emotional expressiveness.

Moon/IC

Becoming a parent (or grandparent)—through birth, adoption, marriage of your child, etc., changing residence or people in home, new direction in career or status, increased dependency, nesting urges stronger, emotional foundation affected by a parent; intuition, weight, or food issues could increase; desire for safety stronger; home-centered activities (involvement with pets, plants, family) accented; reworking feelings about mother figure and early childhood, investigating roots, family history.

Moon/Descendant

Marriage; becoming a parent (or grandparent)—through birth, adoption, marriage of your child, etc., changing residence, parent/partner tendencies (you might mother a partner or a partner nurture—or smother—you; a relationship with a much older or much younger person); in-law issues, issues of empathy and support central to one-on-one interactions; a focus on emotional balance, seeking emotional security through artistic outlets.

Moon/Midheaven

Becoming a parent (or grandparent)—through birth, adoption, marriage, etc., changing residence, new direction in career or status, emotional impact from a parent or boss; relocation for career reasons; power and status sought to feel safe; career may involve women, real estate, protection, patriotism, emotions, the public, or commodities.

Mercury/Ascendant

You find your personal "voice," increased desire to communicate, a sibling or neighbor becomes more important to you, dexterity, "quick hands," curiosity and the desire for variety increase, more desire to be out and about, multitasking (and scattering) easier; important contracts or other paperwork, perceptions and wits sharpen; increasing alertness; learning to reason well under pressure.

Mercury/IC

Change of residence or home occupants, lots of family conversations, home full of talk or movement, increased perspective on family members and emotional needs; restlessness at home; negotiating for or in the home; many quick, short trips or errands; safety sought through the mind; parenting or being parented by another relative (e.g., sibling, aunt, etc.); variety in living situation.

Mercury/Descendant

More people contact and communication, a talkative partner or you speaking more with partner(s), an urge for more variety or stimulation in relationships, learning through other people, important contracts or legal decisions, more objectivity about others, a job change; light-hearted relationships; two significant partners; working with hands to create beauty.

Mercury/Midheaven

Significant career paperwork or contracts; professional communication; achievement through the eyes, mind, hands, or tongue; detachment as a vocational asset; masses of data (overload?), easily bored by routine work, education aids achievement, fast-paced career; vocation could involve commerce, media, business or anything with mental stimulation, variety, lots of paperwork, relatives, or dexterity; two careers at once.

Venus/Ascendant

Marriage; self-employment, more financial independence, impulsive spending, purchases for one's body, arguments about money, active pursuit of beauty, identification with what one owns, or assertive pursuit of "feel-good" activities, appealing persona (and physical appearance), beautifying one's self; too other-directed or challenges balancing personal needs and the desires of others; increased personal grace and charm.

Venus/IC

Spending money to buy a home, selling one's home, beautiful home or beautifying the home, making the home more comfortable, collecting more; enjoying the home (or family), pleasure through nurturing and care taking activities or connecting with the past, gaining through a parent (or assisting a parent financially); comfort equated with safety.

Venus/Descendant

Marriage; indulging a partner or attracting an indulgent partner, spending money on a partner, receiving goodies from a partner, financial focus; litigation, artistic activities, pleasure in relationships, treating a partner like one owns him/her (or receiving such behavior from one's partner); beautification efforts; drawn to attractive people; too concerned with being liked; choosing style over substance; increased charm and diplomatic skills.

Venus/Midheaven

Marriage; working with a spouse or meeting a spouse through work or having a business partner; task-oriented relationships; a raise (or drop) in pay or other changes in financial standing, purchasing high-status items, "buying" respect in the world, enjoying one's career (or seeking an easy job), pleasure found through power, gaining through a parent (or assisting a parent financially), professional artistry, getting involved with monetary fields or those involving sensuality, beauty, or indulgence; financial security becoming more important.

Mars/Ascendant

Self-assertion in focus; may do physical workouts or play more sports; independence of action more vital; handling of anger highlighted; new courage; surgery; pioneering actions; conflict and competition; increased sexual drive; impatience; defining your identity important.

Mars/IC

Change of residence which could be a move, remodeling it or changing occupants; much anger or action in the home; expressing one's self through nurturing; reevaluating or separating from job; fights with family or learning to balance self-expression and emotional attachments; assertion regarding domestic concerns; fire (literally) or excitement and zest in the home.

Mars/Descendant
Personal will in focus in relationships; potential for entering and/or leaving relationships; you or partner may overdo the "me" principle; desire for excitement; sexual attractions significant; conflict and competition; surgery; adventure; violence; learning to own your personal power; balancing assertion and accommodation.

Mars/Midheaven
Urge for vocational independence; self-employment; anger or assertion with authorities or feeling blocked and frustrated; exercising one's power; energetic accomplishment; can take charge or butt heads with authority figures; impatience, freedom, rashness, and courage on the rise vocationally; career may involve more physical action, self-reliance, loner instincts, men, metal tools and weapons, or nerve, etc.

Jupiter/Ascendant
Confidence which can be overdone; good fortune; active pursuit of knowledge; expressing personal beliefs; assertive (perhaps aggressive) about religion and philosophy; can be "righteous" in regard to values and principles; weight gain; humor and travel may increase; more personal involvement with beliefs and values, faith, other cultures, or wider horizons; optimism; questing urges strengthen.

Jupiter/IC
Taking home into world (going on road; trailer, etc.) or world into home (filling with books, philosophical discussions, etc.); home in foreign country or with people from other cultures; expanding or enlarging the nest; leaving home often to travel; change of residence; wanting more than is possible from your home or the people in it; creating your ideal home.

Jupiter/Descendant
Ideals emphasized in relationships (may be too high—seeking perfection); restlessness in association; could get involved with someone from another country or culture; educational or inspiring individuals are attractive; separating from an ideal or goal; pompous, self-righteous individuals may enter your life; sharing a search for ultimate answers (through books, travel, spiritual quests, etc.) with others; exciting opportunity or adventure through a relationship.

Jupiter/Midheaven
Opportunity knocks vocationally; expanded achievement; reaching a dream; venture capitalism; speculating for greater gain; career that involves travel, education, the law, religion, writing, publishing, or anything which expands

horizons; balancing optimism and pessimism, expansion and contraction; putting faith into authority (or authority figures), power, status or seeking to express ideals and beliefs through your contribution to the world.

Saturn/Ascendant

Self-employment; health challenges if unrealistic or frustrated with work; confrontations with authority figures or owning your own power; physical discipline; rigid body or outlook (if control needs overdone); increased dedication; workaholic period; practical self-assessment; working hard at self-improvement.

Saturn/IC

Family obligations increase (e.g., new child, grown child moves home, taking care of aged parent, etc.); facing facts about family members; working hard around the house; starting a business from your home or with family members; reevaluating or separating from career; confronting authority figures and your handling of power; balancing pragmatism and emotional support.

Saturn/Descendant

Making love real—including marriage; limited love (if critical judgments or inhibitions are allowed to interfere); becoming partner with a parent or playing parent to a partner or spouse trying to parent (including control and dominate) you; people work (counseling, consulting, etc.); an aesthetic career; separating from a job; working hard as team member; business partnership; solidifying a relationship.

Saturn/Midheaven

Increased achievement and professional recognition OR feeling blocked and/or inhibited in vocation; more duties and responsibilities or contact with a parent figure; change of status (including marriage, move, job shift, becoming a parent, etc.); change of career; consequences are clear; reliability, responsibility, and realism needed along with dedication and discipline.

Uranus/Ascendant

Inventing a new self; changing your appearance; declaring your independence; erratic impulses; progressive or humanitarian urges; sudden moves; accident-prone if freedom needs are ignored; new excitement in self-expression; risk-taking; personal action for humanitarian causes, new age principles or progress.

Uranus/IC

Change of residence; upsets in the domestic routine; family members behave erratically; ambivalence about nurturing (do not want to be trapped); new technology in the home; communal living; new approaches to care taking; chaos or community within the nest; can nurture inventiveness; lack of safety/protection; distant relations (cool, aloof) with family members; need to balance freedom and nurturing urges.

Uranus/Descendant

New excitement in relationships; divorce (if your individuality or partner's has been denied); unusual relationships; open associations; partnerships with built-in space (e.g., long-distance); erratic or irresponsible partners (if your needs are repressed); refreshing ways of sharing; falling in love; sudden attraction.

Uranus/Midheaven

Change in status, especially in career; sudden break in vocational matters; self-employment; unexpected vocational opportunity; quitting or being fired (if freedom needs are frustrated); inventive work; more new technology in your profession; working with friends, astrology, or social causes; authorities are unpredictable and odd or you rebel against convention; you may be objective and detached (or erratic and careless) about traditions, control, responsibilities, and laws.

Neptune/Ascendant

Increased sensitivity (physical, emotional, spiritual); personal (and often active) expression of beauty; graceful motion; beautifying physical body; wearing many masks; idealizing assertion or identifying with self-sacrifice; personal mystical experiences; increased devotion, faith, psychic ability; involvement with scandals, secrets, fantasies.

Neptune/IC

Finding ideal home; communal living; beautifying the home; putting family members on pedestals or co-dependent, rescuing relationships; spiritual home; dealing with illusions about mother and mothering; increased sensitivity (could be psychic); idealistic and caring behavior or escapism and victim behavior; picking up moods of others; exercising cosmic compassion.

Neptune/Descendant

In love with love; idealizing partner or seeking perfect "soul mate" partner or unconsciously drawn to people you can "save" (alcoholics, addicts, etc.); beautiful relationships or appearance a priority; artistic focus; healing and being healed through one-on-one exchanges; deception or illusion an issue in relationships; dissolving a partnership; illuminating, inspiring associations.

Neptune/Midheaven

Finding ideal career; contribution to society through art, compassion, or inspiration; bringing the mystical into form; dissolving career; confusion, deception or illusion in vocation; professional rescuer or victim (if idealism gets out of hand); authority figures may be idealistic, unclear, compassionate or aesthetic; reaching highest potential in profession.

Pluto/Ascendant

Intense emotions prevail; going into therapy; eliminating bad habits; self-mastery through diet, control of spending, etc.; intimate encounters with a mate and with your own psyche; fascination with hidden matters; more focus on death, the occult, power, and taboos; surgery; major reconstruction of self—whether physically, mentally, emotionally, spiritually; tremendous focus; facing the Shadow; learning to forgive, forget, and let go.

Pluto/IC

Remodeling or renovation; plumbing (or pipefitting, or anything beneath surface of home) may be a focus; skeletons in family closet come to light; digging at your roots and childhood scripts; facing the shadow in terms of parents and ancestral history; changing residence; having to let go of family members; learning to forgive and forget in close, emotional relationships; control and addiction issues within the home.

Pluto/Descendant

Relationships which are intensely emotional; powerful partner (or partner you control); joint finances and resources an issue in relationship (who earns it; who owns it; who spends it and for what); sexual matters emphasized (could be swings between sex and celibacy); letting go of partners and close relationships; practicing forgiveness with/of a spouse; loyalty and betrayal central issues; increased depth and psychological courage and awareness through relationships.

Pluto/Midheaven

Change of profession; major reorganization of career; elimination of particular status or societal contribution; learning to forgive and forget hurts by authority figures; focus on handling power; self-discipline and concentration may increase; work could center on joint resources, power, hidden matters, or intense emotions; potential for obsessive-compulsive behavior; power struggles; tremendous willpower.

Ceres/Ascendant

May have, adopt, or gain a child through marriage; nurturing self (and others); focus on health (good or bad); personal involvement with the Earth (e.g., gardening, ecology, etc.); working on mother issues; self-employment; working more quickly or in pioneering ways; change of residence or changes within the home (including who is living there, who is taking care of whom).

Ceres/IC

Change of residence; making a house a home; may have, adopt or gain a child through marriage; may be too much of a caretaker; extra family responsibilities (e.g., aged parent, sick pets, new child, etc.) possible; working out of home or with family members; increased connection to the Earth.

Ceres/Descendant

Learning to share nurturing; may mother partner or expect partner to nurture you or reach equality with mother figure; beautiful handicrafts; separation from a nurturing figure; practical associations; may be servant to partner, expect partner to serve you, or share a dedication to the world.

Ceres/Midheaven

Nurturing work; working with family members; parenthood or more involvement with parents; might take too much responsibility; family business; efficiency and productivity highlighted (could become workaholic); service and nurturing become a route to power; health matters become a vocational focus or career; power issues with family members or gaining clout through blood ties.

Pallas/Ascendant

Competitive instincts highlighted; concern for justice increases; perceptive abilities strong; objectivity accented; defining self through others; instinct for comparisons, contrasts, and polarities; new relationship; balancing personal desires and those of other people.

Pallas/IC

Teamwork in the home; spouse parents you or you parent a spouse; decorating a home; achieving equality with a parent; more intellectual stimulation or beauty in the home.

Pallas/Descendant

New relationship or commitment to a partnership; legal matters (could include litigation); aesthetic pursuits; competitive encounter; may seek more equality or attract partners who are obsessed with taking turns or with appearances; concern for fairness increases.

Pallas/Midheaven

Drive for justice at work; career involving people (e.g., consulting, counseling, personnel, etc.) or beauty (such as design, fashion, etc.); working with a spouse; negotiations, arbitration or politics possible; status affected by a spouse; cooperative project(s) with a parent; business partnership or working with a spouse.

Juno/Ascendant

Marriage or committed relationship; intense focus on joint resources and possessions; issues around shared power; may gain (or lose) through marriage; attracted to a powerful partner or a weak one who lets you keep all the power; possibility of major self-analysis and increased self-understanding and self-mastery; facing issue of independence versus need for others.

Juno/IC

Parenting a spouse or being parented by a spouse; beautifying the home; reaching equality with a parent; in-law issues (balance between parents and partners); shared resources (money, possessions, pleasures, and power) are highlighted in the home; questions of who is taking care of whom may arise; might be necessary to let go of a partner or parent, jealousy and possessiveness could be issues; intimacy urges strong.

Juno/Descendant

Marriage; negotiations and interpersonal exchanges highlighted; aesthetic pursuits; litigation and competition; questions of sharing (resources, possessions, money, power) important; intense need for togetherness.

Juno/Midheaven

Marriage; business partnership; working with a spouse; meeting a partner through the job; vocation involving people or beauty; "perks" and issues of equality emerge on the job; sharing projects with a parent.

Vesta/Ascendant

Self-employment; workaholic phase; increased attention to nutrition and good health OR health problems (possibly related to work frustration); could increase organizational skills, focus, concentration, self-criticism, tunnel vision and craftsmanship; need to accomplish personal, tangible results.

Vesta/IC

Working on or in or from the home; family business; change in career; critical judgments toward (or from) family members; health concerns in the home or with a parent; obsessive behavior; alienation if critical judgment is overdone; care taking could be carried too far, home improvements or concern for the earth.

Vesta/Descendant

Working relationships (including business partnerships); partner who works hard or you labor long on your associations; critical judgment an issue with other people; desire to improve relationships but danger of alienation from people; work may compete with relationships; mutual acceptance and shared projects can build a solid relationship; job that involves more beauty or people contact.

Vesta/Midheaven

Dedication to craftsmanship; workaholic phase; health issues (due to excessive work or job frustrations); vocation which involves flaw-finding, analysis, attention to detail, health (and healing) or common sense; criticism an issue with (toward or from) authorities (including parents); responsibility and skill with details accented; efficiency instincts highlighted.

Chiron/Ascendant
High expectations for self; increased travel, study, idealism, seeking of ultimate Truth; restlessness; more optimism or faith possible; drive for adventure; seeking your personal dream, concern with healing.

Chiron/IC
Quest for ideal home; may see best in family members, want more than is humanly possible or deal with perfectionistic demands from loved ones; much intellectual stimulation, discussion, optimism, faith, or quest for answers within the nest; restlessness; possible change of residence (including living abroad) or travel.

Chiron/Descendant
May idealize "the other" or want more than is possible in relationships or share the quest for ultimate knowledge with a partner—through travel, reading, discussions, spiritual studies, etc.; mental stimulation accented; partner may be restless (or you have trouble settling down); optimism is possible or a search for healing.

Chiron/Midheaven
Quest for the perfect job (which may not exist) or working to make a more ideal world—through education, enlightenment, inspiration, etc.; may over value power; authority figures may be visionary or want more than is possible; professional seeker; high value placed on work and success; career could involve intellect, healing, travel, variety; bringing long-range goals into manifestation.

Ascendant-Descendant/Nodes
or Nodes/Ascendant-Descendant (long-term)
The self-other polarity is activated in terms of close relationships. Individuals who push your emotional buttons will bring up issues of assertion versus accommodation and being alone versus being together. The sign and house polarities involved will require additional balancing (e.g., Virgo/Pisces polarity emphasizes balancing ideal versus real; bits versus whole; spiritual versus material; the 2nd house/8th house polarity emphasizes a middle ground in terms of who earns the money, who spends it; who enjoys what; and how to share power and possessions for mutual pleasure). The challenge is to have much interaction with other people without going to extremes of self-will or appeasement. Changes in relationships, your identity, appearance, or home/family circumstances are possible.

MC-IC/Nodes or Nodes/MC-IC (long-term)
The balancing act between home/family and career/outer world demands is being triggered. Individuals who push your emotional buttons will bring up issues of dominance versus dependency and hard-nosed pragmatism versus

compassionate caring. The sign and house polarities will require additional integration (e.g., the Leo/Aquarius polarity emphasizes finding a balance between head and heart, between passions and intellect, between loved ones and friends; the 3rd house/9th house polarity emphasizes the integration of knowledge and wisdom; information and enlightenment; the near at hand and far away). Your challenge is to bring caring and compassion into your workplace and/or work into your home—and to divide your time and energy between the public and private spheres without succumbing to burnout or excessive guilt.

Oppositions/Quincunxes between Planets and the Angles (and Vice Versa)

Oppositions point primarily to polarities needing to be balanced. This is often accomplished through relationships. We may identify with one end of an opposition and attract people into our lives who express the opposite extreme. The challenge is to find the golden mean which combines the best of both sides. Any opposition (regardless of the planet or asteroid involved) to the Ascendant or Descendant (or East Point/West Point or Anitvertex/Vertex) is highlighting the issue of self versus other, assertion versus accommodation, being alone versus being together. Any opposition (regardless of planet or asteroid involved) to the Midheaven or IC is emphasizing the balancing act between public and private, home/family versus work in the world, dominance versus dependency, and compassion versus the bottom line.

In addition, oppositions do carry the potential of separations—ending chapters—just as quincunxes do. Finally, an opposition to one angle automatically involves a conjunction to the opposing angle. So, interpret oppositions on three levels:

 • the polarity being highlighted (self/other or home/career).
 • the possibility of separation in terms of what is being opposed
   (see interpretations below).
 • the conjunction which is occurring (see text above).

With any opposition involving the Nodes of the Moon—which are an opposition themselves—the primary focus is the urge to balance polarities—the sign polarity of the Nodes, the polarity of the angles involved, and the polarity of the houses the Nodes are occupying.

Quincunxes, especially if a repeated theme in the progressions, can indicate separations—voluntary or involuntary (although subconscious drives may play a part in what appears to be an involuntary result). Sometimes the patterns are very literal, e.g., a quincunx or opposition—

  —to the Midheaven: can involve changes in work or separation from a
     parental or authority figure.
  —to the IC: can indicate changes of residence or separation from a family
     member.
  —to the Descendant: can symbolize separations from partners (temporary
     or permanent).

—to the Ascendant: can indicate you separating from just about anything (including—sometimes—a part of yourself through surgery or major psychological shifts).

The planet involved also may work literally (but not always!). For example, Juno or Pallas or Venus can represent a partner. Saturn, Moon, Sun, or Ceres can represent a parent or authority figure. Moon and Ceres can also represent your actual home or family members or your own nurturing potential. Ceres (and Vesta) are also keys to work and health. Remember that multiple options do exist! The literal possibilities are more likely when that theme is repeated with several different aspects. Being creative and thinking up many alternatives will be helpful in your forecasting. Be willing to brainstorm a bit!

Sun/Ascendant Quincunxes/Oppositions
Changing leadership role; moving away from or ambivalent about limelight; separation from a parent; working on personal creativity or self-esteem; if health issues develop, probably related to need to shine.

Sun/IC Quincunxes/Oppositions
Separation from a parent; change of residence or of occupants of home; shifts in reward system at home; domestic warmth a concern.

Sun/Descendant Quincunxes/Oppositions
Separations in relationships, challenge to share the attention, limelight and positive feedback (with self as well as others) in one-on-one encounters.

Sun/Midheaven Quincunxes/Oppositions
Changes in work or career; separating from an authority figure or from a power role; challenges present opportunity to shine more vocationally (or lead to less prominence, retreat from public life).

Moon/Ascendant Quincunxes/Oppositions
Change of residence or occupants within the home; alterations in your nurturing activities; separation from mother (figure); working on balance between personal desires and family needs or freedom versus roots or pioneering versus security; if health issues, probably related to safety urges.

Moon/IC Quincunxes/Oppositions
Change of residence or occupants within the home; alterations in your nurturing activities; separation from mother (figure); shifts in balance between dependency and nurturing—doing for self versus doing for others.

Moon/Descendant Quincunxes/Oppositions
Changes in dependency and nurturing relationships; challenge to balance equality and care taking; parental duties (as a parent or to your parents) may vie with partnership; working to both nurture and be nurtured within your relationships.

Moon/Midheaven Quincunxes/Oppositions

Changes in your work or career; shifts within the home or its occupants; a move; separation from an authority figure; time and energy constraints between home and family versus career and work in the world.

Mercury/Ascendant Quincunxes/Oppositions

Changes in studies, job, or health; may alter communication style; may separate from a sibling or collateral relative; might leave school or change transportation modes; may clarify thoughts about self; may gain objectivity in regard to personal desires

Mercury/IC Quincunxes/Oppositions

Change of residence or occupants of home; differing ideas than family members; communication issues may arise with loved ones; working on balance between emotions and intellect, between compassion and objectivity.

Mercury/Descendant Quincunxes/Oppositions

Communication challenges in relationships; learning to be more objective; keeping a give-and-take with partners in regard to listening and speaking; owning your own mental ability.

Mercury/Midheaven Quincunxes/Oppositions

Changes in career or status or in relationship to authority figures; challenges can lead to new mental skills and communication abilities being used on the job or blocked channels of understanding with authority figures and the powers-that-be; balancing serious and light-hearted attitudes.

Venus/Ascendant Quincunxes/Oppositions

Ending—or beginning—love relationships; shifts in finances or resources; becoming less hedonistic; changes in pleasures and possessions; if health issues, probably related to relationships or resources; getting enough beauty in life may prove challenging; urge to balance self/other polarity, being alone versus being together.

Venus/IC Quincunxes/Oppositions

Financial issues may arise with family members; challenge to balance equality and nurturing or parents and partners; family may compete with spouse; finding paths to promote both safety and pleasure.

Venus/Descendant Quincunxes/Oppositions

Ending—or beginning—love relationships; developing a different artistic style; shifting your quest for pleasure—whether from possessions, senses, or people; revising your personal grace and charm.

Venus/Midheaven Quincunxes/Oppositions

Changes in career or finances; challenge to balance love and work or ease and effort; confrontations can lead to more grace, people skills, charm and pleasure on the job—or to evasive action and looking for "Easy Street" professionally; a partner may compete with a vocation.

Mars/Ascendant Quincunxes/Oppositions

Changes in physical body, vitality, if health issues, probably related to independence and self-expressive urges; surgery; highlights issues around personal freedom, anger, assertion, courage, and pioneering spirit; learning how to healthily "do your own thing" in life.

Mars/IC Quincunxes/Oppositions

Change of residence or occupants of home; separation from a parent (figure); leaving home; balancing freedom urges with the desire for a nest; personal desires may compete with parental duties or cautions; a pioneering spirit may be at odds with safety needs.

Mars/Descendant Quincunxes/Oppositions

Assertion, anger and personal power likely issues in relationships; learning to balance self and other or freedom and closeness; hot/cold interactions are possible with other people; if you want freedom, others may overdo closeness needs and vice versa.

Mars/Midheaven Quincunxes/Oppositions

Change of career or status; separation from authority or authority figure; challenge to balance personal will with the rules of the game (and natural limits); learning to work constructively with anger, assertion, independence, and urgency.

Jupiter/Ascendant Quincunxes/Oppositions

Changes in religion, philosophy, beliefs, faith, long-range goals; may change educational activity or take significant trip; may separate from a guru figure or alter values; if health issues, probably related to expectations (and perfectionism).

Jupiter/IC Quincunxes/Oppositions

Excessively high standards may present challenges with family members (from them to you or you to them); leaving home to travel; home in a foreign country; taking home on the road; questing side must be balanced with urge for safety and a nest.

Jupiter/Descendant Quincunxes/Oppositions

Values and moral/ethical principles become a focus in relationships; excessively high expectations are probable in relationships (from you toward partner and/or partner toward you); travel or quest for ultimate answers competes with partnership.

Jupiter/Midheaven Quincunxes/Oppositions

The polarity of idealism and realism is emphasized; moral or ethical concerns, or excessive expectations, could lead to separating from a job; conflicts with an authority figure are possible in regard to beliefs and values.

Saturn/Ascendant Quincunxes/Oppositions

Separating from a job, authority figure, or leaving behind old limits; balancing personal will within the limits of the world; compromising between spontaneity and caution; if health issues, probably related to frustration, blockages or feelings of inadequacy.

Saturn/IC Quincunxes/Oppositions

Separation from a parent (figure); changes (oriented toward facing reality) within the home itself or the occupants; learning to balance between home/family and work in the world or between compassion and the bottom line.

Saturn/Descendant Quincunxes/Oppositions

Need to balance love and work, equality and control; possible competition between parents (or parent figures) and spouse; beauty or ease may compete with effort or necessity; practical matters or the demands of the physical world require adjustments in relationships.

Saturn/Midheaven Quincunxes/Oppositions

Changes in work, career, status, or power position; separating from an authority figure; clarifying the "rules of the game" and what is truly most practical; a challenge/opportunity to own your own authority is likely; time to "grow up" and demonstrate maturity.

Uranus/Ascendant Quincunxes/Oppositions

Changes (could be surprising or sudden) in your own actions, appearance, or health (probably related to carelessness or frustrated urges for independence); freedom urges are accented; originality could increase; learning to express your individuality constructively.

Uranus/IC Quincunxes/Oppositions

Changes within the home or in regard to its occupants; could be abrupt domestic shifts; challenge to balance freedom needs with nesting urges; friends may compete with family for your time and energy; learning to integrate objectivity and emotional warmth.

Uranus/Descendant Quincunxes/Oppositions

Separations in relationships (could be sudden); the need for independence may compete with the urge for partnership; working on the balance between friendship and intimacy; unconventional urges may require adjustments in relationships.

Uranus/Midheaven Quincunxes/Oppositions

Possible separations from work, career, authority roles, parental figures; challenge to balance the old and new, conventional and unconventional; societal pressures may compete with personal independence or originality; a challenge allows you to contribute originality to your career (or leads to vocational disruption).

Neptune/Ascendant Quincunxes/Oppositions

May dissolve old identity; self-assertion is apt to vie with self-sacrifice; if health issues, probably related to excessive idealism or sensitivity; intuitive potentials are accented; finding constructive expressions for your compassion, idealism, artistic urges and spiritual yearnings.

Neptune/IC Quincunxes/Oppositions

High ideals or rose-colored glasses may prove challenging within the domestic sphere or with family members (from you to them or them to you); having trouble putting down roots due to seeking the "perfect" home; personal home and family may compete with compassion for the wider world.

Neptune/Descendant Quincunxes/Oppositions

Romantic, idealistic urges may challenge equalitarian exchanges; artistic abilities are highlighted; a personal love relationship may compete with more universal compassion, philanthropic urges; rescuing tendencies could present challenges for your partnership(s).

Neptune/Midheaven Quincunxes/Oppositions

Career or status dissolves (possibly due to scandal, lack of clarity, or excessive idealism); compassion vies with realism and the bottom line; artistic urges may compete with the "real world"; charitable or artistic impulses may be integrated into (or compete with) your career.

Pluto/Ascendant Quincunxes/Oppositions

Claiming personal power is an issue; challenges are possible regarding shared resources, finances, sexuality, and intimacy; self-mastery concerns are highlighted; the urge to transform self may lead to psychotherapy, occult studies, surgery, research, etc.

Pluto/IC Quincunxes/Oppositions

Separating from a home or family members; eliminating old emotional habit patterns, roots, or traditional ways; questions regarding shared resources and joint pleasures require adjustments on the domestic front; manipulation and indirect emotional ploys are possible; an intimate partner may compete with a parent or child.

Pluto/Descendant Quincunxes/Oppositions

Balance is needed between personal power and shared power; could be challenges in reaching equality in regard to money, pleasures, and possessions; sexuality can become a path for learning how to be fair; intense emotional reactions are likely in partnership.

Pluto/Midheaven Quincunxes/Oppositions

Career or status could be eliminated (downsizing, fired; renovation and redoing a vocational field); separation from power or from an authority figure; issues of control/power (its wise use or abuse) are apt to arise; perseverance and dogged determination will become either a liability or asset for your career..

Ceres/Ascendant Quincunxes/Oppositions

Separation from a job, mother (figure), home, family member, or nurturing responsibilities; health matters or nutrition could be in focus.

Ceres/IC Quincunxes/Oppositions

Separation from a parental figure, home, family member, or work is possible.

Ceres/Descendant Quincunxes/Oppositions

Working on balance between love and work; between children and spouse; between parental figures and partner(s).

Ceres/Midheaven Quincunxes/Oppositions

Separating from a career, status, power role, authority figure; balancing compassion and the bottom line or public and private needs; time and energy constraints between family and outer world success.

Pallas/Ascendant Quincunxes/Oppositions

Entering—or leaving—a relationship; seeking more equality; aesthetic urges highlighted.

Pallas/IC Quincunxes/Oppositions

Working on balance between children and partner; parent(s) and spouse, nurturing/dependency and equality.

Pallas/Descendant Quincunxes/Oppositions

Entering—or leaving—a relationship; emphasis on balance, harmony, and equality; increased passion for justice and fair play.

Pallas/Midheaven Quincunxes/Oppositions

Working on balance between love and work, between equality and control; between parent(s) and partner(s).

Juno/Ascendant Quincunxes/Oppositions

Beginning—or separating from—a relationship; issues around intimacy, joint resources, control and power with other people are probably emphasized.

Juno/IC Quincunxes/Oppositions

Balancing love and work; children and partners or parent(s) and spouse; intense emotional encounters are likely.

Juno/Descendant Quincunxes/Oppositions

Challenges in sharing power, possessions, pleasures in relationships; intense emotions featured.

Juno/Midheaven Quincunxes/Oppositions

Working on balance between love and work or equality and control; needs of a partner may compete with needs of a parent or of a child; ending a chapter in regard to family matters.

Vesta/Ascendant Quincunxes/Oppositions

Health matters may be highlighted; changing jobs is possible; self-criticism could be an issue.

Vesta/IC Quincunxes/Oppositions

Balancing work and home is challenging; critical judgments could alienate you from family members; family issues affect health.

Vesta/Descendant Quincunxes/Oppositions

Making room for both love and work is challenging; ease may vie with effort; judgmental attitudes could affect relationships; physical well-being is influenced by partnership.

Vesta/Midheaven Quincunxes/Oppositions

Changes in health due to career are possible; shifts in work may occur; separating from former ideas about reality and structure.

Chiron/Ascendant Quincunxes/Oppositions

Personal idealism could lead to excessive pressure on yourself; more restlessness, quest for answers, and freedom urges are likely.

Chiron/IC Quincunxes/Oppositions

Unclear or overly idealistic goals and values could affect family life; the lure of the faraway competes with nesting urges.

Chiron/Descendant Quincunxes/Oppositions

Relationships are affected by a quest for the best; religious, philosophical, moral or ethical concerns become significant within your partnership.

Chiron/Midheaven Quincunxes/Oppositions

Changes in career or status due to shifting goals or excessively high expectations; urge for travel or more answers competes with ambition to make a mark in the world; polarity of idealism versus realism is activated.

For Nodal oppositions to the Ascendant/Descendant axis and the Midheaven/ IC axis, see the material earlier in this chapter. (A Nodal opposition is automatically a conjunction as well.)

Nodes/Ascendant Quincunxes

Possible separations from close, emotional ties, especially with family members or people who "push your buttons"; you personally do more work to integrate the house and sign polarity of your Nodes.

Nodes/IC Quincunxes

Changes, including possible separations, from home or family members; shifts in your emotional foundation; altering what provides security to you.

Nodes/Descendant Quincunxes

Separations in relationships may occur; working on the balance between children and spouse or partner and parent(s).

Nodes/Midheaven Quincunxes

Highlighting the polarity of public versus private, home and family versus career; compassion versus the bottom line; could be changes in work or home (or both).

CHAPTER EIGHT
ASPECT CONFIGURATIONS

Aspect configurations involve three or more planets aspecting each other. The more planets involved in a network with one another, the more likely that the individual will be dealing with intense emotions or actual events in the life. Aspect configurations can be formed by progressed factors aspecting each other, and progressed factors can trigger natal configurations. Those do "count," and are sometimes even more important since they describe basic habits.

SIGN	RULER	HOUSE	QUALITY	ELEMENT	MAJOR THIRD
Aries (♈)	Mars (♂)	1	Cardinal	Fire	Personal
Taurus (♉)	Venus (♀)	2	Fixed	Earth	Personal
Gemini (♊)	Mercury (☿)	3	Mutable	Air	Personal
Cancer (♋)	Moon (☽)	4	Cardinal	Water	Personal/Interpersonal
Leo (♌)	Sun (☉)	5	Fixed	Fire	Interpersonal
Virgo (♍)	Mercury (☿)	6	Mutable	Earth	Interpersonal
Libra (♎)	Venus (♀)	7	Cardinal	Air	Interpersonal
Scorpio (♏)	Pluto (♇)	8	Fixed	Water	Interpersonal
Sagittarius (♐)	Jupiter (♃)	9	Mutable	Fire	Transpersonal
Capricorn (♑)	Saturn (♄)	10	Cardinal	Earth	Transpersonal
Aquarius (♒)	Uranus (♅)	11	Fixed	Air	Transpersonal
Pisces (♓)	Neptune (♆)	12	Mutable	Water	Transpersonal

Grand Trines

Grand trines are formed when three planets are all 120 degrees from one another. In the following interpretations, grand trines are "typed" by predominant element(s). That classification is based on the nature of the planets involved (e.g., Mars in a fire planet; Saturn is an earth planet), the houses involved, and the signs involved. Obviously, most configurations will include a mixture of elements, so look for a repeated emphasis. You could have water planets in fire signs in earth houses as a complex example. The planets are the most important, the houses are next most important, and the signs are last, though every factor is part of the picture.

Grand Trine in Fire

This pattern suggests inner harmony and potential talent at your fingertips in terms of confidence, extroversion, energy and the ability to go after what you want in the world. Zest and enthusiasm are likely to be more marked than usual. You may pioneer and be a ground-breaker for a new project. If the enthusiasm is carried too far, you might fall into self-centeredness, with a feeling that you have a right to whatever you want from the world. Impulsiveness, impatience or accidents are possible if you are too rushed. You will have more creativity, more liveliness, more spontaneity and the ability to live life to the hilt, but may need to hang on to common sense.

Grand Trine in Earth

This pattern suggests inner harmony and potential talent available to you in terms of working and making a living. You can be effective in dealing with the material world at this time and can take great satisfaction in achieving, particularly when the results are tangible and can be measured. If carried too far, you could overdo the pragmatic focus to the point of excessive materialism or could succumb to a dry, boring focus on the mundane aspects of life. If you use the indicated abilities sensibly, you are likely to be highly productive and to build the foundation for even more accomplishments in your life. You can truly get the job done now.

Grand Trine in Air

This pattern suggests inner harmony and highlights your mental and communicative talents. You can be more objective than usual. Logic and rationality come more easily and you are willing to consider the overview of any situation. "Perspective" is a good air word. Dealings with people and ideas can flow more smoothly, as your equalitarian instincts are easily tapped. If carried too far, you could overdo to the point of rationalization, intellectualization and a cold, detached viewpoint. You could turn observation into a retreat rather than a tool. Moderation means you can relate easily and naturally, communicate well, and use your head in appropriate, helpful ways.

Grand Trine in Water

This pattern suggests inner harmony in terms of sensitivity and psychic openness. Your intuitive side is more available, so be aware of "vibes" and impressions. You could find it easier to empathize with others and are likely to be more aware of your own emotions and feelings. If these qualities are carried to an excess, you could be too sensitive, easily hurt, absorb the ills and problems of others, or feel overwhelmed by the world of emotions. If positively channeled, you find it easier to tap into your Higher Self (inner wisdom). Some alone time helps you to process and to sort things out. You can understand the underlying patterns in life, especially your own subconscious. Reach for self-knowledge. Your strong protective instincts could attract help from others when needed, and also give help to others.

Grand Trine in Fire and Earth

This pattern suggests inner harmony and talent in terms of your capacity to accomplish. Both initiative and follow-through are highlighted, so you can both start and finish projects. There is a strong need to affect the outer world; this is a "doing" time. If carried too far, you could "steamroller" yourself and other people into things you later regret. If expressed in a moderate manner, you will find this a time of attainment and making your mark in some way. Your confidence is likely to be a bit higher than usual, but your practicality is also highlighted. "Go for the gold" as this is your time to achieve.

Grand Trine in Fire and Air

This pattern suggests inner harmony and talent is likely in terms of a light touch, sense of humor and capacity to enjoy life. You have more sparkle than usual and selling, promoting or persuading abilities are more prominent in your nature. You know how to laugh and can share a sense of fun with others. If overdone, this could be a time of just partying, avoiding responsibility, and flitting restlessly from one possibility to the next. If channeled wisely, you can lighten the load for yourself and others, bringing a twinkle to everyone's eye and generally enlivening the world. Laugh, love and live, but also remember to keep paying the bills!

Grand Trine in Fire and Water

This pattern suggests inner harmony and highlights your emotional nature. You are likely to be dealing a lot with strong feelings. This can be a period where intense emotions are a focus for much attention. You are capable of incredible warmth and caring now. You may have to strive to balance between your fire need to express outwardly what you are feeling and your water instinct to hold back and hold in for safety (so you are not hurt or do not hurt the feelings of others). You could experience some mood swings (up with elation, down with caution), but are generally likely to relate with depth and intensity to those around you.

Grand Trine in Earth and Air

This pattern suggests inner harmony and puts your logical and rational faculties in high focus. This could be an excellent time for problem-solving—figuring out what is wrong and fixing it. You can be sensible, detached and practical.

Both analytical and pragmatic thinking are at your fingertips. If overdone, you could be too concerned with the bottom line, and ignore important emotional issues. Intellect might take too much precedence over feelings. If you are balanced in using your abilities, this can be a time to truly make your life better. You can identify areas needing improvement and take steps to enhance life sensibly.

Grand Trine in Earth and Water

This pattern implies inner harmony and focuses on your compassion as well as practicality. You could easily become involved in care-taking projects: assisting people in very practical ways. If this is carried too far, you could end up "needing to be needed" and give too much to others, perhaps draining yourself, trying to be father-mother-savior of the world. The other extreme is leaning on other people too much if you lack faith in your own abilities. Whether helping or being helped, it is possible to take yourself and life too seriously. Security concerns could lead to being overly cautious and clinging to the status quo. Generally, however, the harmony suggests an excellent capacity to meld practicality and emotions. You can tune in to needs, your own and those of others, and take the sensible steps to achieve whatever is required.

Grand Trine in Air and Water

This pattern denotes inner harmony and indicates a marked talent for creative imagination at this time. Your inner life is likely to be rich and full. You can visualize possibilities and may invent products, stories, or just about anything. Fantasy could be carried too far and you might be tempted to live inside your head most of the time, ignoring much of the outside world. The air-water ability to blend the conscious and subconscious aspects of the mind, or logic and intuition, is an excellent combination for therapy. You can help others verbalize dimly felt feelings. Theorizing and imagining and psychic openness are talents you can use well now and develop further.

Grand Trine with Fire/Earth and Air/Water

This pattern mirrors inner harmony in your nature and talents which lie at your fingertips currently. There is a focus on two very different sides. One is extroverted, oriented toward accomplishment and acting on the outer world. The other is inward, imaginative, and oriented toward thinking and feeling about life. If you are able to blend the two, you can have the best of both worlds. If you set it up as a contest, you may feel torn (or flip between) introversion versus extroversion or doing versus visualizing. A reasonable blend allows you to imagine and plan out the pattern and then act forcefully and practically to make it real.

Grand Trine with Fire/Air and Earth/Water

This pattern indicates inner harmony in your nature and points to issues currently in your life which require balance. Two very different sides are highlighted. One is fun-loving, restless, variety-oriented and "up." The other is serious, stable, security-oriented and "down." If you can make a comfortable marriage between the two, you have appropriate reactions available at any time. Otherwise, you may fight (or flip) between work versus recreation, security versus risk, elation versus depression, or commitments versus fun. A reasonable blend allows you to be dedicated as well as playful, helpful **and** humorous, stable and able to handle changes.

Grand Trine with Fire/Water and Earth/Air

This pattern represents inner harmony in your nature as well as the need for balance. Two very different sides occupy center stage. One is intensely warm, caring and emotional. The other is cool, logical, practical and detached. If you can do some of each side, you can create a balanced, satisfying time. If you set the scene as a war, you are likely to feel torn between your head and your heart, and perhaps go from one extreme to the other. A moderate combination means that you can use both rationality and empathy, compassion and pragmatism, feelings and logic. Your life will be richer and fuller for the blend.

Grand Trine with Mixed Elements

This pattern indicates inner harmony in your nature, but cannot be "typed" as to theme. You may experience more confidence, more practicality, more objectivity, and/or more sensitivity. Your talents for accomplishment, imagination, communication or initiation may be more marked than usual. If these mixed themes are not integrated, you could feel torn between your different paths and abilities. If you are able to use some of each, you are likely to be multi-talented, with a number of different options to pursue. A little bit of everything can contribute to a satisfying wholeness. The number one challenge of life is often just knowing when and where to do which. Everyone really has all the potentials, though some are less developed.

T-Squares and Grand Crosses

A T-square is formed when two planets make an opposition and both are square a third planet. Drawing lines on the horoscope between the planets would produce a "T." A grand cross (or grand square) is formed when one pair of opposing planets is square another pair of opposing planets. (Lines drawn between them would form a cross. Lines drawn outside the circle, connecting the four planets, would form a square.)

These conflict patterns are "typed" in terms of quality—cardinal, fixed, mutable, or mixtures. This classification is based on the nature of the planet involved (Mars is a cardinal planet), the houses, and the signs. A complex example could be cardinal planets in fixed signs in mutable houses.

Cardinal

This pattern indicates possible changes in your life structure. You may decide to alter how you act, your domestic environment, your peer relationships, or your career. It is also possible that outer events may trigger changes in any of these areas. Crises may seem to demand action or reaction. (Usually current crises are the result of choices made earlier in terms of your work, relationships, home, or personal self-expression.) You are likely to be very conscious of time and energy demands, feeling as if there is not room in your life for everything. The challenge is to find a way to express all your different needs: freedom, dependency, nurturing, equality and competent control. You may feel as if you have to choose between concentrating on yourself, your home life, your partnership or your career. The goal is to be able to do some of each, without sacrificing any of the others.

Fixed

This pattern indicates a strong focus on issues of power, sensuality, money and resources. Major shifts are not likely, but when they occur, it may be with explosive force. Power struggles are common if balance (usually through compromise) is not found. You may find yourself torn between security and safety versus risk and taking chances (in terms of money, relationships, career, etc.). You could feel a tug of war between self-indulgence versus self-control in terms of physical pleasures. Your own internal ambivalence is likely to be mirrored by the people closest to you. Intimacy could become a battleground if you end up trying to control a mate, child or other loved one—or if they try to control you. Self-determination is essential. Game-playing, guilt-tripping, manipulation or intimidation are counter-productive. The challenge is to find a way to share pleasures, resources, finances, and power comfortably and easily with those nearest and dearest—without anyone succumbing to a "take charge" urge, or nagging or trying to change the other. Accept both sides within yourself (hedonistic and self-disciplined; speculative and cautious) and you will be able to accept both in those around you. Deny either side in yourself and others will live it out in a magnified fashion, usually with unpleasant exchanges as you each try to "make over" the other. Acceptance and tolerance work wonders.

Mutable

Mental restlessness is highlighted in this pattern. There is a need to move—at least mentally and often physically as well. Travel is possible, although it may only be through the mind with books, seminars, classes, etc. You are likely to be intensely curious about more things than usual, and eager to expand your base of knowledge. Information gathering becomes more important. Philosophical issues and questions abound as you spend more time contemplating the meaning of your life, your long-range goals and values, what you really trust and where you want to be going. If you do not establish firm priorities, then you could end up scattering your forces and being over-extended. The lack of a sense of direction, the tendency to get lost, is often a sign of a problem with faith. Our belief system determines what we trust, where we look for meaning, our ultimate goals and the ways to reach them. Perfectionism is another potential mutable trap. Wanting more than is possible is a strong temptation—particularly in terms of your work, your relationships, your self-image, or your gathering of knowledge and understanding. Remember that you are human. Keep your aspirations and goals, but give yourself time to work toward them. Explore many mental by-ways, but remember that you cannot learn everything in one lifetime and that no one is perfect.

Cardinal/Fixed

This configuration emphasizes possible life structure changes with the danger of succumbing to power struggles. Just as you would rather not be told what to do by others, so may others resist your input. Don't fall into trying to change someone (or fighting with someone who is trying to change you). Find mutually satisfactory activities. Changes are possible in your career, home, relationships and self-expression, but you will want to be sure they are on your terms. Matters involving finances, pleasures or resources could become an important focus. A competitive outlet in your life (games, sports, business, politics) is advisable; it will help you sidestep power struggles in areas where cooperation is more effective. You need to push the world around in some arena, but compete with the "other" team, not members of your "own" team. Feeling that you have made your mark is important, and that you can protect yourself and be yourself while still relating to other people.

Cardinal/Mutable

Many shifts are probable. A restless spirit is highlighted. Although some changes in the structure of your life are possible, you could equally just **think about** alterations and choose not to make them. You are likely to review your goals and values, perhaps modifying some. If your priorities change sufficiently, you may indeed make major shifts in terms of career, relationships, home life and/or personal activities. High expectations enter the picture and any changes are likely to be based on a desire to improve, to move closer to an ideal. Just be sure you do not yearn for more than is possible, or make alterations only to feel afterward "is that all there is?" New studies would be an excellent outlet for the need to do, to learn and to move. A flexible, adaptable attitude can be one of your best assets at this time.

Fixed/Mutable

During this period, you may feel a strong need to follow values and ideals more truly yours. You could winnow out and eliminate ideas and concepts which come from parents, the culture or other sources. You are likely to work toward firming your own sense of moral principles and life ethics. Your perspectives on life become more truly your own. This may entail some shifting and adapting of your perspectives. Areas which are candidates for examination include sensuality, sexuality, financial habits. You could get involved with power struggles, especially where concepts of intimacy, money and right and wrong are concerned. You might experience difficulty in letting go in some areas. The challenge is to explore moral principles and life directions with openness and tolerance, while developing a point of view which is more truly a reflection of your own nature and needs, but also respecting the views of others who are close to you.

Mixed Qualities

This configuration cannot really be typed as to one central theme. It reflects potential inner conflict and the need for balance, but the areas involved could be myriad. You may confront issues of sensuality, sexuality, money and intimacy, especially with a partner. You may deal with unreasonably high expectations (your own or other people's). You may consider (or be forced to face the issue of) changes in your career, partnership, home environment or life structure and style in general. You may examine your values, change your goals, take up new studies, alter your spiritual path or rededicate yourself to a search for life's meaning. The message is a need to balance the many sides of yourself, to avoid denying any important part of life, to remain open, flexible, and willing to make a place for everything that is necessary for a full and happy life.

Yods and Boomerangs

A yod is formed when two planets sextile each other and both are quincunx a third planet. If lines were drawn on the chart, a yod would look like a "Y." A boomerang is formed when the planet which is the "focal point" of the yod (the "stem" of the "Y" which makes the two quincunxes) forms an opposition to a fourth planet.

   These conflict patterns point to inner struggles which are likely to lead to important choices and changes in your life. You may feel as if you have reached a fork in the road of life, or as if you have a "forced choice" situation. Two or more parts of your nature are probably at odds. The challenge is to find a reasonable blend (a bit of each) or a satisfying way to take turns between the various needs. If peace is not achieved in the inner war, several unpleasant outcomes are possible. You could subconsciously repress one side, and develop physical problems or an illness symptomatic of the issues not being faced (e.g., repressed anger and assertion can lead to headaches, cuts, burns, accidents, etc.). You might identify with one part of your nature, and subconsciously choose other people who live out another part (such as a partner or a coworker). Unfortunately, these people are likely to **overdo** (express to an extreme) what you are denying within yourself. Or you could swing between extremes yourself, until you learn to integrate the basic conflict, to create room for all sides of your nature, all the drives in your psyche.

   Quincunxes and oppositions are both associated with separations in the life. Often, when lots of quincunxes or oppositions are present by progressions, you are separated—from a job (quitting, being fired or downsized, etc.), a relationship (through death, divorce, moves), a home (change of residence), or emotional habit patterns. When a number of separative aspects are present, it is a good idea to get rid of what is no longer useful in your life—to make voluntary separations which will improve your life. We may change some of the details to resolve the frustrations without "throwing out the baby with the bath water." Compromise can work wonders.

In the following paragraphs, yods and boomerangs are classified as primarily personal, interpersonal, or transpersonal or some combination of those three. That is based on the nature of the planets making the yod or boomerang, the signs involved, and the houses involved. The first four signs, houses, and the planets which rule them are considered personal, where we learn to meet our own needs, though the third and fourth sides of life are partly interpersonal. We become socialized there while growing up. The next four signs, houses, and the planets which rule them are considered interpersonal, dealing with face-to-face interactions, to meet our personal needs while respecting the needs of others. The last four signs, houses and the planets which rule them are considered transpersonal, dealing with the "big scene," social issues, beliefs, the laws of life and the natural world, etc.

With signs and houses, quincunxes and oppositions can only occur across two of the major divisions of astrology's twelve sides of life. A yod may involve all three divisions. Only aspects between planets can produce a quincunx or opposition that is focused within a single division. Most configurations will be mixed, so you need to look for the emphasis.

Personal

This configuration, which may include Mars, Venus, Mercury, and the Moon, suggests inner conflict which needs to be resolved and integrated. Analysis is complicated by the fact that Mars and Venus are also rulers of the interpersonal signs Libra and Scorpio. Also, as adults, we frequently express Mercury and the Moon in relationships. The personal issues involve handling your personal needs. Separations involving your resources (including your home) and changing your sense of identity are possible. The ability to do as you please, satisfy your own desires, communicate comfortably or share easily with family could become a focus. You are learning to be number one, to go after what you want without going to the extremes of self-centeredness or of self-effacement.

Interpersonal

This configuration, which could involve the Sun, Pluto, Pallas, Juno, and Vesta where fellow-workers are concerned, implies inner conflict to be resolved. The focus revolves around relationships with others, whether at work, at home, or in intimate exchanges. Good-byes may need to be said to some people. The challenge is to interact comfortably and easily with others, while avoiding the extremes of accommodating too much to others, or expecting too much compromise from them. One-to-one exchanges are a fertile learning ground.

Transpersonal

This configuration, which could involve Jupiter, Saturn, Uranus, Neptune, and Chiron, points to inner conflict calling for resolution. The arena of focus is transpersonal: the greatest good for the greatest number, societal issues, the widest perspective, the "big picture." Separations are possible and could involve causes, organizations, your profession or ideas and ideals. The challenge is to understand a historical perspective, to be able to see the overview, without falling into the extreme of excessive detachment or impersonality. Large-scale issues offer growth opportunities, including moral principles, a search for meaning, and decisions on long-range values and goals.

Personal versus Interpersonal

This configuration highlights inner conflict between personal needs and interpersonal interactions. You may feel torn between assertion and accommodation. It may be difficult to decide how much to insist on what you want, and how much to adapt to what partners and other people in your life would prefer. Separations from people are possible. The challenge is to be able to satisfy yourself while still maintaining harmonious interactions with the people around you.

Personal versus Transpersonal

This configuration implies inner conflict between personal needs and transpersonal perspectives. You could feel an inner (and outer) tension between doing what you want just for yourself as an individual versus considering the widest viewpoint, the greatest good for the greatest number. Societal perspectives may vie with your personal point of view. Issues can include questioning how much to "fit in," versus "beating the system," versus just doing your "own thing." The challenge is to retain your individuality and to be able to enjoy life on your terms, while still able to function in a bigger world and make an important contribution to the whole.

Interpersonal versus Transpersonal

This configuration highlights inner conflict between interpersonal needs and transpersonal perspectives. You are likely to feel torn between relationship needs and societal demands. You may feel compelled to choose between time and energy for those near and dear to you versus people as a whole, or the larger, long-range and historical viewpoint of the world. Political, economic or social issues could emerge. The challenge is to be a meaningful member of society while still maintaining satisfying interpersonal exchanges with people who are emotionally close and important to you.

Mixed

This configuration denotes inner conflict. You are likely to feel tension between personal needs, interpersonal desires and transpersonal perspectives. You may feel torn about how much time and energy to devote to each, or feel that they compete with one another. The challenge is to keep room in life for all three, without sacrificing any of them. You need to make time for: personal desires and pleasures, gratifying one-to-one relationships, and a sense of higher purpose or contribution to the world at large. All three contribute to a full life.

CHAPTER NINE
MOON CHANGING HOUSES OR SIGNS

Due to the (relatively) fast motion of the progressed Moon, it will travel through each sign in about 2-1/2 years. The time to get through a house will average about that, but vary considerably, depending on the size of the house and whether interceptions are involved. The sizes of the houses in most house systems vary increasingly as we move away from the equator toward the poles. Changes of sign or house by the progressed Moon can point to a new cycle, but are not dramatic **by themselves**. The themes and issues will be repeated by other progressed factors when they are significant.

Although the progressed Moon is always a key to your emotional needs (including the desire for safety and close connections with other people), it also operates as a "timer" in a horoscope. The Moon's aspects will often pinpoint the two-month period within which significant events—or changes in your mind-set or emotional reactions and attitudes—occur. Such changes will be well reflected by other progressed aspects and patterns which are of longer duration. In those cases, the Moon is the symbolic "trigger" that pinpoints the time of action.

Moon into 1st House or Aries: Emerging Emotions

Emotional needs call for attention and dependency or nurturing issues may arise. Mothering instincts can be a current focus, whether your own or those of other people. Home and domestic concerns take more precedence. You may experience some conflict between inner emotional yearnings and free, outer self-expression. Neediness or moods could be experienced. Personal action may be tied to food, care taking or security needs. Your challenge is to be courageous and direct in your personal actions while still maintaining close, emotional ties. Don't neglect your personal needs to provide those of family members, but also avoid become so focused on your own desires that you neglect the bonds of love and blood.

The new period may involve personal courage (physical, mental, emotional, spiritual), a pioneering act, something you do **first**, or changes in your identity and action.

Moon into 2nd House or Taurus: Safety and Sensuality

You are likely to connect emotional security more strongly to money or material possessions or pleasures during this period. Urges for preservation of resources are more intense. You may wish to save more, or protect any existing nest eggs. Financial matters may be tied to domestic needs, your mother or your own nurturing instincts. Sensuality is strong. Tactile pleasures are essential, but avoid overindulgence. Your challenge is to gain increased comfort and security without overvaluing the material "things" in life. This is a time to solidify any gains, to "make real" the pioneering projects you may have begun with the Moon in Aries (or First House).

The new period will involve manifestation in some form—whether a literal, physical creation, or getting appropriate material (including financial) rewards for your efforts. You may reach a new level in terms of sensuality, ease within your own body, and capacity to just "be" and not try to "push the river."

Moon into 3rd House or Gemini: Environmental Emotions

Feeding your mind is a likely focus. You may seek emotional security through the intellect: listening, learning, reading or gathering information. The urge to learn and to "absorb" information is apt to be strong. Relatives could offer reassurance and a sense of protection or they could need your assistance. A logical approach to family members is possible and may be helpful. Intuition may be blended with logic more easily during the next couple of years. Emotions are a likely focus of conversation. Security is found through being nimble—fast on your feet (or quick with your hands and tongue). You may become more active, on the go physically as well as mentally. Your challenge is to take in masses of input and information—from a variety of people and sources—without being overwhelmed by it.

The new period may involve classes, writing, speaking, the media, work with your hands, transportation, siblings (or other relatives), or significant changes in your immediate environment.

Moon into 4th House or Cancer: Real Roots

Nesting urges are an issue. Home and domestic matters are important. Your mother, another mother figure, or your own mothering instincts may be a central focus in your life. Dependency and nurturing needs are predominant. Your basic sense of adequacy (or a lack of it) is highlighted. Food or physical security/ possessions may substitute for emotional reassurance. Concerns about the home itself as well as any inhabitants (including pets and plants as well as people) are emphasized. Caring and being cared for are important experiences now. Make sure your support system is solid. Your challenge is to listen more to your own feelings and to distinguish between what are your emotions and what is based on old familial (or societal) conditioning. You may need extra private time (sheltered) to do this inner work.

The new period could include a change of residence or altered relationships with the people (or pets) who share your domicile. Shifts are possible in your mothering connections (your own parents and anyone or anything you take care of). You may begin a new chapter in regard to blood ties or create a family of the heart if your family of origin is not supportive. (Changes could also relate to the homeland—patriotism and other national issues.) A new cycle will focus on emotional connections and unconditional love.

Moon into 5th House or Leo: Warm & Wonderful

Nurturing instincts are vital in love relationships. Those in the appropriate age range could be open to having a child. You may attract lovers who take care of you, or look to you to take care of them. Emotions are likely to be strong and passionate. Privacy versus public needs could be an issue, or pride versus shame. Warmth and compassion are often emphasized and love needs predominant with this combination. Mood swings are possible, associated with a need for emotional outlets. Creativity can offer a constructive expression for the intense emotions. You need to pour out from your own center—doing more than you have done before. This self-expressive essence could find outlets through drama, artistic pursuits, or anything which promotes you or provides an opportunity for positive attention from the world.

The new period could be very exciting. This will probably be a "push" for you—something which brings the rush of adrenaline. The new chapter is apt to entail taking a risk—in order to garner more of a return—whether in the form of love relationships, a child, investment (or gambling), acclaim for creativity, or applause for your daring, etc.

Moon into 6th House or Virgo: Sensible Support

Practical care taking is likely to be a focus. Health issues could become a center of attention, including diet and nutritional concerns. Nurturing is done in a pragmatic manner and must include physical results; words alone are not enough. Support from others should also be sought in sensible, tangible ways. You may criticize or be criticized as a function of caring and wanting to improve things. As much as possible, try to give and accept emotional support in your work. It is helpful to criticize the job, to do it more effectively, but to avoid judging and condemning yourself or other people. You may be inclined to carry more than your share of the load—physically and emotionally. Make sure that you take good care of yourself! Your challenge is to improve yourself (without succumbing to excessive self-criticism) and to increase your efficiency and skills in the material world.

The new period is likely to center around either work or health. You could make changes in either of those realms—including new jobs, new colleagues, a different state of physical well-being, etc. The key theme is enhancement. You will be motivated to make improvements wherever you can.

Moon into 7th House or Libra: Parenting Partners

This pattern suggests an increased need for emotional closeness through peer relationships. One option is choosing to get married. You may consciously want security and commitment in equalitarian relationships, but could end up taking care of a partner, or with one who plays parent to you. If peer relationships seem to be sliding into parent/child interactions, look for ways to take turns playing each of the roles. Compassionate instincts are likely to affect relationships, bringing empathic exchanges with other people, but excessive neediness is also possible. People can be a source of emotional support, but it is important to keep life a mutual give-and-take. You may also find more security through beauty and could become more involved with artistic efforts or with enhancing your own appearance. A more graceful attitude may prevail. Issues of justice, fair play, balance, and even-handedness are likely to be stimulated. Your challenge is to find the win/win solutions with other people.

The new period is likely to affect your one-on-one relationships. This can include new associations beginning as well as some ending. Marriage is a possibility, or any relationship which involves a very close, emotional bond. Competitive interchanges (including litigation) are also a potential. Look for beauty and balance and shared pleasure.

Moon into 8th House or Scorpio: Intensely Inward

This combination usually indicates a time of deep emotional needs, with intense feelings which are not easy to express. There is often a tendency to hold back and hold in emotionally. You may feel overwhelmed with the emotional needs of self or others. Learning to let go (whether of people, things, emotions) is often an issue. Avoid using emotional blackmail or manipulation—or being its target—by staying conscious of your feelings. Care taking could arise from compassion felt for a partner, or as an indirect way to control and take power. Nurturing and sexual needs may be mixed. Control of your emotions can be aided by a depth exploration of your psyche. Open up to facing yourself, and much healing and release of old garbage is possible. With self-scrutiny, assets can be strengthened and negatives transformed to positives. Part of your challenge is to guard your alone time so that you can do the inner work required, while still maintaining time for a deep commitment to intimacy with another person.

The new period may involve the elimination of something in order to move forward. Issues of endings and transformation could emerge. The sharing of power and possessions will probably be significant. You may be drawn to probe deeply into your own subconscious, or into the inner depths of others who are close to you, or into any of the mysteries of life.

Moon into 9th House or Sagittarius: Roots Versus Restlessness

Emotions are often exaggerated with this combination. Dependency or nurturing could be overdone, carried too far or fiercely resisted. Domestic needs are often at odds with a desire for change, adventure, exploration. Alternately, compassion, nurturing, home, mother or caring may be idealized. You may have to come to terms with unrealistic expectations regarding your mother (figure), home or your own care taking. Emotional security might be sought through education, travel, philosophy or religion. Roots may be carried into the world or sought in faraway places. Extravagance ("God will provide") may be at odds with saving instincts. But mostly feelings tend to be friendly and positive. You may be willing to break new ground emotionally, to explore new territory (literally or metaphorically). You are stretching your boundaries, going outside old comfort zones—and it can be very exciting!

The new period could include new travels (even a home in a foreign country), new studies, new philosophies, or just about any new adventure.

Moon into 10th House or Capricorn: Securing Stability

This combination tends to be cautious with emotions and practical about nurturing and dependency needs. A pragmatic approach to home, domestic needs, mother, and emotional security is common; a disciplined compassion. You may experience conflict between work and home responsibilities. A desire for safety and security is usually strong, with a tendency to save, protect, and avoid risks. Look for ways to satisfy your security needs; proving that you can cope will help you to gain or maintain a sense of adequacy. You will probably be motivated to solidify your gains in terms of career and reputation. You'll want your place in the world to be assured and ambitions could rise. Parenting motifs are accented, so you could become a parent, take on more responsibilities, or interact more with authorities or your own parent(s). You may decide to "go public" or "become more visible" in regard to certain feelings. Your capacity to be serious, to become an expert (an authority) is highlighted now. Your challenge is to avoid workaholism, depression or too much pressure to perform while appreciating that this is a time to achieve tangible results and seek the highest level in your accomplishments.

The new period could involve changes in terms of career, reputation, parents (or the parenting role), or activities which promote mastery and success on your part.

Moon into 11th House or Aquarius: Fond Friends

This combination can be expressed by nurturing and/or being nurtured by friends. It often marks a time for changing habit patterns. Security needs may be at odds with a desire for variety and change and domestic shifts are likely. Family issues may be seen with a widened perspective, including increased objectivity. Emotional commitments may be loosened to permit more freedom, turning family into friends. Erratic emotions and unpredictable responses may be expressed when freedom and closeness needs are at odds. This can be a time of sharing with people whose paths are parallel to yours. Your challenge is to become more secure in your individuality—to feed your uniqueness—without going to the extremes of anarchy or destructive behavior. Chaos and community are both options. You can expand your ability to clarify which rules should be broken and when security and safety should be reaffirmed.

The new period is likely to include a "radical" element of some sort. You may surprise the people around you with what you do. You may "come out" in some fashion—or simply stand out from the crowd. You could change your friendships, associations, or peer groups. A new attraction to the unusual, avant garde or unconventional is possible.

Moon into 12th House or Pisces: Cosmic Connections

During this period you may notice increased sensitivity (including physical) and tender emotions. A strong, subconscious yearning for oneness may invite mystical experiences. Where faith in a protective Higher Power is weak, food or drugs may be used for reassurance against a threatening world. A sense of inspiration is important. You may want to create beauty in your home or in our shared home, the Earth. Home, family, mothering, or motherhood may be idealized. It is possible to be overly dependent, or to play savior and attract people needing to be rescued. An inner sense of connection to all life helps offer a foundation for healthy interdependence. Now is a time to look within, to find inner wisdom and answers. The ability to tune into others (psychically and through compassion) is apt to increase. You will probably need more privacy to do inner work and to sort through all that you absorb. You are more open to the entire Universe now. Your challenge is to sort through everything that you have learned over the past 28-30 years (the full lunar cycle) and to discard what you no longer need—in preparation for a new and pioneering cycle to begin with Aries or the First House. Where personal, ego or security issues conflict with a greater, cosmic wisdom, you are learning to trust the latter. This is the lesson that each drop of water is an individual, yet all are part of the whole ocean. You are more fully pursuing the quest for infinite love and beauty, while knowing that the journey is endless. Perfection is a goal, but the journey is eternal.

The new period is likely to affect your handling of spiritual and mystical urges, your physical and psychic sensitivity, and your personal faith, idealism, healing urges, and quest for beauty.

CHAPTER TEN
PROGRESSED ASPECTS BY SUN, MERCURY, VENUS AND MARS
(PLUS THE "BIG FOUR" ASTEROIDS)

Although we have emphasized the "hard" aspects (conjunction, square, opposition and quincunx), the "soft" aspects (sextile and trine) are also meaningful in progressions. Here we discuss the softer progressed aspects. In working with the outer planets, some aspect combinations must be considered long-term. That is noted in the text. In such cases, the themes and issues discussed will prevail for many years in your life.

When an aspect occurs in progressions between two planets which had an aspect in the natal chart, do take into consideration the natal framework. That is the foundation for everything, describing the basic character (habits) unless the person has changed. If, for example, the Sun and Mars were sextile at birth, and the Sun progresses to make a square to natal Mars, although challenges and conflicts are possible with the square (as well as just action or manifestation), the individual has the advantage of natal harmony between the Sun and Mars, so s/he is more likely to find a constructive way to integrate the conflicting desires symbolized by the progressed square. Similarly, a progressed trine shows potential harmony and talents, but if a natal square exists between those two planets, the individual must still resolve the issues of the square during the time the progressed trine is highlighting the basic desires symbolized by those two planets. Remember that harmony aspects can lead to excesses while conflict aspects can be integrated by finding a way to satisfy each of the different desires.

Harmony Aspects

Sun Sextile/Trine Moon

Private and onstage urges flow smoothly together. You can be comfortable both as the center of attention and in a background, supportive role. Domestic matters are favored. Nurturing, parental themes are in harmony. Emotional warmth and caring is likely. Agreement is suggested between your inner father and mother (and possibly the outer ones as well). You find it easier to express yourself within the nest and may become more creative at home. Your family provides support for your promotional instincts. You are each other's best cheer leaders and motivators.

Sun Sextile/Trine Mercury (and vice versa)

Your self-esteem and communicative skills are likely to support each other. Your capacity to shine, to be noticed, acknowledged and admired may be aided by intellectual abilities: talents for thinking, understanding, writing, or talking. Your mind may help you to be noticed and appreciated. Your exciting, passionate, risk-taking side may fuel your questioning, theorizing and seeking of information.

This aspect indicates potential harmony between your children and your siblings and other relatives. Loved ones are likely to be mutually supportive. Family members may assist one another.

Sun Sextile/Trine Venus (and vice versa)

The pursuit of pleasure is highlighted. Sensuality is likely to be marked, and overindulgence is possible. Any of the physical sense pleasures (eating, drinking, smoking, lovemaking) could have strong appeal. Extravagance (financially, materially, emotionally) is more likely, as you are drawn to the finer things in life. Pleasure may be sought through people as well—leading toward marriage, living together, or more focus on one-to-one interactions.

Artistic and aesthetic feelings may abound. Beauty can be a source of excitement, and you may become more active in the creative or performing arts. You might receive recognition through a higher salary—or other material demonstrations of your worth. Options also include spending more money on exciting activities—or on loved ones and children.

Your thrill-seeking side may blend easily with your comfort-oriented side. You can enjoy both the adrenaline rush and the relaxation of laid-back activities. You might, however, have to put a little effort into compromises between the drive for excitement, risk, passion and speculation versus the desire for security, stability, predictability and ease. A harmony aspect suggests that making time for both is relatively easy.

Sun Sextile/Trine Mars (and vice versa)

Drive and willpower are key themes here. With two fire planets supporting one another, the impetus is likely to be forward and outward. The primary urge is to get what **you** want. You may find new ways to shine in the world, achieving more recognition or applause. You may discover additional forums for self-expression and creativity—to truly flow from your own center. Directness and spontaneity are highlighted. Energy may be high, and sports or other physical activity can provide a good outlet. You need to express yourself—physically and emotionally.

Harmony between your actions and loved ones is suggested. Alliances with lovers and/or children probably flow more easily. You can promote your interests as well as the interests of those you love. People you cherish may help you to be more true to yourself.

If the "I'm number one" attributes of this aspect are carried too far, you might overreach into arrogance, rashness or selfishness. Some focus on the self and your desires is appropriate; just don't overdo. If you deny the fiery need for expression, you may find men in your lives or children or a lover who will overdo the willfulness and self-centeredness that is the key note. Healthy self-assertion and creative self-expression allows you to make the most of the potentials.

Sun Sextile/Trine Jupiter or Jupiter Sextile/Trine Sun (long-term)

Goals and dreams are highlighted. You are likely to be motivated to pursue your ideals with vim, vigor and vitality! Confidence and the willingness to take risks may support your quest for meaning, truth, and personal ideals. Your faith and values may strengthen your creative efforts and your desire to give and receive love.

If the double-fire of these two planets is carried too far, you may overreach or expect more than is possible. If it is positively channeled, you are likely to be full of energy for what you believe in. Your growth goals are strengthened and heightened by your ideals. You believe in yourself and are willing to "go for it" in life. This expansive combination suggests great enthusiasm, optimism and push toward the future. You are ready to do more than you have done before, to expand your boundaries, to increase your largesse in life.

Sun Sextile/Trine Saturn or Saturn Sextile/Trine Sun (long-term)

Productive accomplishments are quite possible with this pattern. Your enthusiasm, creativity, confidence and magnetism can assist your career ambitions to advance your position in the world. You may gain promotions or additional recognition or even renown through your work. Loved ones may assist you in your movement up the ladder of success.

This is a good time to work on any unresolved inner insecurities. Realistic success can build your self-confidence. If you have been reacting negatively to perceived blocks by authority figures or to "the rules of the game," look for a broader perspective that will let you work with the rules and the authorities. We fly planes that are heavier than air by working with the rules of gravity and air pressure. Don't overdo self-criticism or put excessive demands on yourself. Fear of failure that could lead to less risk taking and a spiral of lowered expectations is also possible, though less likely with a harmonious aspect between Sun and Saturn. Remember, this can be a period of great productivity if you believe in yourself and work realistically.

Sun Sextile/Trine Uranus or Uranus Sextile/Trine Sun (long-term)

Creativity, innovation, excitement and change are highlighted. Your inventive quotient is probably high. A unique perspective may come rather easily to you. You can be original and may be drawn to take some risks in order to break new ground and explore new possibilities. Passion and the intellect can support one another. Your emotional excitement feeds your urge to learn and to explore alternatives. Your rationality and detachment helps you to judge appropriate risks versus thrills that might be dangerous. Friends and loved ones are likely to support one another. Cooperation and teamwork can be quite constructive. You may find new ways to shine.

Sun Sextile/Trine Neptune
or Neptune Sextile/Trine Sun (long-term)

Romance is in the air! Intensified emotions are likely as your idealistic, imaginative, magic-seeking side supports your thrust toward love, admiration and positive attention. Artistic creativity is highlighted as a possibility. You may gain the limelight through your aesthetic talent, compassion, sensitivity, or healing abilities. (In a negative sense, attention is possible through victim or escapist behaviors.) Meditation, visualization and listening to your Higher Self can also add to the love and applause in your life (or lead to imaginary lovers if reality is not part of the picture). Creative projects (and children) may be assisted by your skill with illusions, fantasy, inspired beauty, and/or your faith.

Sun Sextile/Trine Pluto or Pluto Sextile/Trine Sun (long-term)

Power themes are highlighted. This pattern connects the power of a charismatic, dynamic individual wanting to reach out to gain love and attention from others with the inwardly-directed power of the adept who transforms the inner psyche and gains self-mastery. This aspect suggests harmony, indicating you achieve both outer and inner power.

Potential cooperation is also suggested between mates and children. Family teamwork is a real option. Approaches where everyone wins should be easier to come by. Your partner can be an asset to the children and vice versa, as well as cooperate with you to build deep mutual love.

If backed by other chart factors, this aspect may point to skill at financial management, or possible opportunities in terms of royalties, inheritance, return on investments, etc. Sensual needs are likely to be strong, although some tension between indulgence versus control is possible. Whether you focus more on sexual outlets, food, drink, smoking or other sensual involvements, there is a need to face the material world and enjoy its pleasures (without the extremes of denial or over-indulgence). Much gratification is possible.

Sun Sextile/Trine Ceres (and vice versa)

Parenting instincts are highlighted, along with the desire to shine through your tasks or work. Nurturing or procreation may take a center stage, with children entering the life through birth, marriage, adoption, or just playing an important role. More involvement with your own parent(s) is also possible. You will probably find it easy to give love, support, protection and assistance; being a caretaker may seem very natural.

Another option revolves around your work. Creativity may contribute to your efficiency. Sales or promotional skills might advance your career, or you may be working in a more creative field or fashion. You could achieve a bit more recognition or prominence in your field, or take some kind of leadership role. Children (your own or other people's) might contribute to or be involved in your job. Self-confidence and the willingness to take risks can be an asset in your work.

If outgoing, extroverted themes are not incorporated into your work, the frustrated need for recognition might contribute to physical stress or even illness. Finding something that you can do, in which you take pride, will be very helpful. You need applause and positive feedback for your productive accomplishments.

Sun Sextile/Trine Pallas (and vice versa)

Beauty and people are highlighted with this combination. Your perceptions may be creative, artistic and aesthetic. You could become more involved in the arts—especially the visual arts (photography, modeling, design, fashion, decorating, etc.) or the performing arts. Appearances could gain in importance and you might contribute to a "beautification" project with a partner or a child. Balance and harmony contribute to a loving, caring atmosphere.

Alliances are suggested between partners and children. Your kids may cooperate more easily with your partner and vice versa. The spirit of teamwork may be more in evidence. A partner may help you to shine or achieve more positive recognition. A creative project (or a child) may assist you toward a partnership. Mutual support is likely.

Light-heartedness and the desire for fun are suggested. Loving may be more natural, but life is not all fun and games, and things do not always come easily. A little effort will help consolidate the positive feelings suggested through sharing love, creativity, play, and an interest in beauty.

Sun Sextile/Trine Juno (and vice versa)

Closeness needs are in high focus, and your desire to give and receive love may be extra important. Marriage is one option. You can be particularly appreciative and admiring of a partner now, and may receive extra attention or positive feedback from a spouse. A mutual admiration society is possible, with each of you spurring the other on in terms of creativity and growth goals.

Feelings are likely to be more intense about sexuality and shared finances or resources. Commitments may deepen as emotions are very strong. This may be a golden opportunity to compromise on financial or sexual matters. Be sure both people's wishes are considered so that mutual pleasure and gain is the result.

This aspect can indicate potential harmony between partners and children. They may get along better with one another. Teamwork flows more easily. Encourage sharing and mutual understanding among family members.

Sun Sextile/Trine Vesta (and vice versa)

You have the potential of making noteworthy contributions to the world. Your creative, risk-taking, expressive talents may facilitate your work. Promotional or sales skills may contribute to your job. Children or a lover could enhance your productive efforts. Work and love should support each other.

Doing something which brings you positive feedback, attention or applause is likely to support good health as well as a sense of contribution. Expanding and enlarging your self-expression and your giving and receiving of love also helps to solidify and strengthen working accomplishments and general health. Careful planning, attending to details and disciplined efforts enable you to succeed at risk-taking, new ventures and creative projects.

Sun Sextile/Trine Chiron or Chiron Sextile/Trine Sun (long-term)

This pattern suggests a hunger for new knowledge or new experiences which can mark a time of creativity and exploration. Faith is encouraged, in yourself and/or in a Higher Power. If you are clear about what you want from life, you can move toward your personal goals. If you are searching for meaning and direction, this is a time to consciously evaluate possible options which will lead to an increased sense of self-worth. Overconfidence can be a hazard, so keep one foot on the ground. Optimism and questing urges may increase.

Sun Sextile/Trine Nodes or Nodes Sextile/Trine Sun (long-term)

The harmony aspects between your Sun and nodes suggest that you can be comfortable in combining your need to be creative and expansive with your capacity to nurture and be nurtured. The Sun represents our ability to procreate (among many other forms of creativity), while the Moon and its nodes represent our ability to care for dependents, whether kids, pets, or others who need help. This pattern shows emotional warmth with a need for interpersonal relationships as an important and valuable part of your life.

Mercury Sextile/Trine Sun (see Sun Sextile/Trine Mercury above)

Mercury Sextile/Trine Moon

This aspect suggests harmony between your nesting urges and your need for communication and mental stimulation. Family may support your intellectual pursuits, or encourage communication. Your objective side may assist building warm bonds of caring and assistance. You can harmonize thinking and feelings, bringing the best of both to situations. Relatives, neighbors or classes might contribute to your home and domestic satisfaction. Your nurturing or emotional support might prove helpful to the people in your immediate environment. You can be protective and nourishing, but also logical and reasonable.

Mercury Sextile/Trine Venus (and vice versa)

This pattern suggests that your pleasures and your reasoning mind support one another. Your earning capacity could be enhanced through thinking, communicating, dexterity, commerce or relatives. Your sensual, beauty-oriented side should blend easily with your seeking of information; you probably enjoy gathering data and exploring ideas. The combination implies a good ability to cope with everyday life and the material world. It also suggests open channels of communication in your relationships. Interchanges with partners are likely to be stimulating and varied. You can use words to build bridges to other people—with grace, charm, and empathy.

Mercury Sextile/Trine Mars (and vice versa)

Your assertiveness, courage, expressiveness and desire for action tend to flow in harmony with your intellect, communication skills and need for variety and new information. You can think before acting and act sensibly based on your perceptions. Your directness and integrity can assist your mental investigations and you may be able to think and speak quickly. You might have general harmony with siblings and other relatives and could possess good coordination and dexterity. Your communication will tend to be forthright and spontaneous, but at times you might need to guard against excessive bluntness. You can support your sense of identity through mental means and talents.

Mercury Sextile/Trine Jupiter
or Jupiter Sextile/Trine Mercury (long-term)

This is a highly mental combination, accentuating the capacity to learn, to think and to talk. You are likely to be articulate and could be increasingly intellectual during this period. Your mind may be far-ranging, with an instinct to learn from anything and everything, with interests as broad as the universe. An attraction to travel is quite possible, as your restless mind needs new vistas to explore. The focus is on constant mental activity, whether through learning, teaching, writing or traveling.

Mercury Sextile/Trine Saturn
or Saturn Sextile/Trine Mercury (long-term)

Your mind, coordination, dexterity, objectivity or relatives might contribute in some way to your career. Your ability to succeed, to master the physical world and to achieve professionally can be aided by your curiosity, communication skills or capacity for detachment. Likewise, your sense of responsibility, practical realism and orderliness can assist your mental explorations. Your father or authority figures might contribute to your learning, intellectual development or logic. You can put your mind to work in the world and wield your logic with authority and impact.

Mercury Sextile/Trine Uranus
or Uranus Sextile/Trine Mercury (long-term)

This combination is highly mental, with an original bent to the thinking. Equalitarian instincts are highlighted, with a focus on relating to everyone on the same level. Objectivity may be accentuated. Logic could be quite good, but might be seen by others as too cool and detached on occasion. Friends, groups, new age interests and anything on the cutting edge of change such as new technology may stimulate you mentally and provide good outlets. Communicative abilities can add to your capacity for networking, brainstorming and seeing the broad perspective in life.

Mercury Sextile/Trine Neptune
or Neptune Sextile/Trine Mercury (long-term)

This combination suggests the possibility of favorably blending your logic and your intuition. Bringing subconscious knowledge into conscious awareness can be done with the help of dreams, visualization, or other means, as well as by discussing and clarifying issues. Poetic language and music are possible talents to be explored. Guidance is available by listening to one's Inner Wisdom. When used to complement each other, the blend of rationality and psychic understanding is highly effective. However, wishful thinking, rationalizations or scattered, superficial mental activities are possible when not complemented by practicality. Look for ways to use your mind in an inspired fashion while keeping one foot on the ground.

Mercury Sextile/Trine Pluto
or Pluto Sextile/Trine Mercury (long-term)

This combination suggests that your interest in depth, complexities and hidden matters can be of assistance in your logical explorations, communication and intellectual understanding. Your thinking may be deep, probing and inclined to seek beneath the surface. Intimates, especially mates, may stimulate you mentally and encourage you to explore the arena of the mind. Relatives might contribute to your resources, financial backing or partnership prospects. You can utilize both passion and logic, both detachment and commitment.

Mercury Sextile/Trine Ceres (and vice versa)

Your intellectual capacities, communicative skills and mental openness to information could enhance and assist your work or your nurturing activities. You may stress mental development in terms of your parenting role. Perceptiveness, information, communicative abilities or intelligence could contribute to your competence and success on the job. Objectivity could be a career asset, or relatives or dexterity could be of assistance in your work. If your mother or a mother figure is still part of your life, she is likely to encourage your intellectual development. You can enjoy pure curiosity and gathering information for its own sake, as well as pursuing results and putting your mind to work to get a job done.

Mercury Sextile/Trine Pallas (and vice versa)

Your curiosity, intellectual openness or communication skills are likely to enhance your relationships, aesthetic abilities or capacity to meet people on an equal level. Talent for people and ideas is suggested, with an accent on fair play, objectivity and logic. You may be skilled at comparisons and contrasts, enjoying the give-and-take of different concepts and conceptualizations. You may be increasing your ability to see patterns through activity in some field of design. There is also the potential of harmony between your siblings and partners or among the people around you.

Mercury Sextile/Trine Juno (and vice versa)

Your curiosity, verbal skills or openness to learning could enhance your relationships. You might even develop a talent for diplomacy, soothing phrases or poetry. Your eye-mind-hand coordination might contribute to satisfying aesthetic endeavors. Balance and objectivity are suggested, yet a note of caring and emotional commitment is also present. This implies the capacity to blend mental and emotional needs, to be able to think clearly while still caring deeply. Harmony is suggested between your partner(s) and relatives. Relationships with people may flow rather easily, and you may become increasingly intuitive, able to sense their feelings.

Mercury Sextile/Trine Vesta (and vice versa)

Your curiosity, intellectual skills, and communicative abilities are likely to enhance your competence and ability to cope. You can use objectivity and thinking to deal with many of the necessities of life. Your mind will help you get the job done well. Health may also be assisted by an open mind and perceptive gathering of information. Mental achievements are supported by a sensible approach to your body, a reasonable regimen in terms of health habits, and a modicum of self-discipline. You may enjoy collecting information about ways and means of maintaining better health and/or increased productivity on the job. Relatives, dexterity or commerce may also contribute to your work efforts. Your discriminating, analytical eye can help you determine what information is most useful, winnowing out wheat from chaff.

Mercury Sextile/Trine Chiron
or Chiron Sextile/Trine Mercury (long-term)

This combination calls for mental adventures, whether in studies, teaching, writing, or traveling. Look for ways to expand your mind, with creativity and humor. One hazard might involve too much scattering of energy due to multiple interests and talents. This is especially a danger in charts which emphasize fire and air or cardinal and mutable factors. Try to be clear about primary goals and values which call for sustained attention and effort, and to take the rest of life more lightly. People with a fire and air emphasis may also need to remember that there are times for tact. But mostly, this combination encourages you to develop your mental abilities, both to satisfy personal curiosity and to make a contribution to the world.

Mercury Sextile/Trine Nodes
or Nodes Sextile/Trine Mercury (long-term)

Harmony aspects between Mercury and the Nodes are an indication of potential psychic talent. During this period, you can more easily bring the contents of the subconscious up into consciousness, to become aware of inner feelings and hunches. The pattern is also an indication that your ability to understand and communicate can help your personal relationships, or that family members may assist your drive to learn. There is a strong mental focus in the pattern, encouraging you to "live in the head." You can use this period both to learn and to share your knowledge with others. People close to you are likely to be important, including siblings and neighbors as well as your immediate family. Mutual cooperation can keep relationships comfortable.

Venus Sextile/Trine Sun (see Sun Sextile/Trine Venus above)

Venus Sextile/Trine Moon

This pattern suggests harmony between your nesting urges and your desire to enjoy the physical, sensual side of life. You may be quite comfortable with relaxing activities, and lean toward security and safety. You might contribute financially to your home, or profit from real estate. You may act to increase the beauty, comfort and pleasure connected to your home and family. Collecting possessions could be a form of reassurance, and food may be quite satisfying. This combination can be quite tactile, may enjoy cuddling and may be oriented toward sensual gratifications. Closeness urges are accented, with a desire to share with a partner. You can more easily combine the roles of parent and partner and could find more ease between your parents and your spouse. Affectionate exchanges are favored.

Venus Sextile/Trine Mercury (see Mercury Sextile/Trine Venus above)

Venus Sextile/Trine Mars (and vice versa)

This aspect blends the archetypal "masculine" and "feminine" images, suggesting support between your assertive, confident, expressive side and your receptive, comfortable, sensual side. Your personal action or courage can add to your gratification in life. Your ability to enjoy people, pleasure and beauty enhances your sense of identity or contributes to your self-expression. A certain amount of charisma with the opposite sex is likely. You may be more magnetic and attractive than usual—and more attracted to others. You probably have a good capacity for enjoying life, but might be tempted into over-indulgence at times. This is an excellent time for blending assertion and accommodation—for finding a good balance between your needs and the needs of other people.

Venus Sextile/Trine Jupiter
or Jupiter Sextile/Trine Venus (long-term)

This combination can point to making dreams come true. Your aspirations can lead to financial and material rewards. Your long-range goals and values may contribute to financial success or sensual gratification. Or you may simply enjoy the journey toward your personal vision. Beliefs, world views, travel, education, philosophy or religion might contribute to your income. Your material resources might also further your quest for the truth, for understanding, for seeking the meaning of life. The biggest hazard associated with this pattern is the potential for excessive indulgence. It is not necessarily true that if some is good, more will be better. Moderation is the ability to stop before the action becomes painful. This is an excellent time for sharing inspiration with a partner. A spouse may help you reach a long-term goal.

Venus Sextile/Trine Saturn
or Saturn Sextile/Trine Venus (long-term)

Harmony is suggested between your responsible, hardworking side and your desire for pleasure and gratification from life. You will be able to work as well as to play. You can be dedicated and disciplined, as well as laid-back and lazy—depending on the circumstances. You can enhance your financial resources through your career or careful attention to what is necessary. Mentors or authority figures might be of assistance. Placidity, an affectionate nature, a feeling for beauty, or a practical sense about resources might be helpful in your vocation. Now is a time when you can be well balanced between love and work. Your spouse or partner might assist your career or your work might contribute to your partnerships.

Venus Sextile/Trine Uranus
or Uranus Sextile/Trine Venus (long-term)

You may have good instincts for being individualistic and original while still maintaining a basic capacity for keeping security and stability in your life. This pattern encourages the ability to change without abruptness, and to maintain the status quo without feeling confined and hemmed in. Friends, groups or organizations may contribute to your financial resources or to your general enjoyment of life (or you may help support clubs, friends, networking financially). Your innovative outlook may generate a source of income. Openness and tolerance are likely. You can love with an open hand now, emphasizing freedom within relationships. Now is a great time to be best buddies with your spouse.

Venus Sextile/Trine Neptune
or Neptune Sextile/Trine Venus (long-term)

Beauty is highlighted here. You may have a strong feeling for aesthetics, with potential talent for creating beauty. Appearances could matter a lot to you. The general orientation is toward grace, ease and pleasure. If overdone, passivity is possible. You might expect life, and especially love, to flow more easily and smoothly than is reasonable; life might be viewed in soft-focus Technicolor. The potential exists for a gentle touch, a graceful approach, a contribution of more beauty and inspiration to the world. Your aesthetic talents might generate income as well as pleasure.

Venus Sextile/Trine Pluto or Pluto Sextile/Trine Venus (long-term)

You have the capacity to balance your sensual drives with your desire for self-knowledge and self-mastery. Though overindulgence remains possible, this aspect suggests that you can comfortably enjoy the material pleasures of life (eating, drinking, making love, enjoying money, etc.) while still maintaining a sense of self-control. This also implies a reasonable balance between personal pleasures and pleasures shared with a mate. The combination encourages the capacity for being able to give, receive, and share easily with a mate where money, sensuality, and sexuality are concerned. You also might profit from joint resources such as inheritance, returns on investments, pensions, or assistance from others.

Venus Sextile/Trine Ceres (and vice versa)

Your pleasure principle harmonizes well with your "mother earth" instincts. You may enjoy taking care of people, pets or plants. You may find gratification in being efficient and helpful. Your work might be assisted by your sensuality, artistic flair or easygoing attitude. You may receive financial rewards for nurturing/assisting activities, or simply enjoy being of service. You can appreciate efficiency and find pleasure in productivity. Mother or a mother figure might assist you financially, artistically, or in terms of increased pleasure and enjoyment (or you might contribute to her needs and pleasures). Harmony between parental and partnership roles is likely (including possible agreement between a spouse and a parent).

Venus Sextile/Trine Pallas (and vice versa)

This aspect accentuates people needs and beauty instincts. You may have a flair for artistic or aesthetic involvement. You are likely to be drawn toward activities involving ease, comfort, balance and harmony. If this is carried too far, you might be too other-directed, passive or unwilling to confront needed issues. Generally, this aspect suggests a talent for conciliation and compromise which facilitate getting along with others. It also encourages a feeling for equality and an instinctive appreciation of beauty.

Venus Sextile/Trine Juno (and vice versa)
This combination suggests that you can maintain a good balance between personal pleasures and shared pleasures. You are able to enjoy relationships and can bring gratification to yourself as well as to a partner. Your earning capacity or financial situation may be assisted by a partner, or there may simply be lots of mutual enjoyment. An aesthetic note is strong here, so interest in and talent for creating beauty is likely. In general, the picture is one accentuating love, harmony and comfort on both material and relationship levels.

Venus Sextile/Trine Vesta (and vice versa)
This aspect points to a good inner balance between work and play. You are able to be dedicated, disciplined and hard working, but also able to be relaxed, indulgent and find pleasure in life. You can be productive as well as passive, sensual as well as disciplined, and agreeable and accepting as well as critical when necessary. An eye for beauty or a comfortable attitude can enhance your work efforts. Your dedication may be rewarded materially, or bring you personal satisfaction. You can balance effort and ease. You also can divide time and energy between love and work in an equitable manner. Your spouse is apt to support your productive efforts and your efficient side will aid your relationships.

Venus Sextile/Trine Chiron
or Chiron Sextile/Trine Venus (long-term)
This combination suggests the ability to decide what you want and to go after it. The desires could focus on material possessions and appetites, on stimulating relationships, or on pleasure gained from intellectual pursuits. Harmony can be attained between aspirations/ideals and satisfactions in everyday life. One possible danger would be excessive indulgence with the feeling "if I want it, I should be able to have it." But with reasonable moderation, this pattern indicates a good potential to be clear about goals and to bring them into tangible manifestation in your life.

Venus Sextile/Trine Nodes
or Nodes Sextile/Trine Venus (long-term)
This combination points to harmony between your capacity for pleasure and your emotional security needs. Relationships are likely to be very important and can be very satisfying. You are able to be intuitive about your own needs and also the needs of others who are close to you. You may be helped by or be

helpful to others, whether financially or simply by emotional support. Other patterns in your chart may show stress and challenges, but this combination shows a support system that can help to handle the rest of life. The further development of artistic talents are another potential for this period. Also, the nodes, like all water factors, show the potential of contact with the subconscious, for inspiration and guidance.

Mars Sextile/Trine the Sun (See Sun Sextile/Trine Mars above.)

Mars Sextile/Trine the Moon

This pattern suggests the potential to harmonize your independent, active instincts with your desire for a nest and close, emotional attachments. You can blend freedom needs and closeness needs, creating a place in your life for both. The suggestion is that you are in harmony with your nurturing side; this can also indicate potential harmony between you and mother/nurturing figures. You can be yourself, and still make a caring commitment.

Since Mars represents a love of action, this pattern can indicate readiness to change your base of operations, to explore new surroundings or new associates. Or you may just let go of old attachments with grace.

Mars Sextile/Trine Mercury (See Mars Sextile/Trine Mars above.)

Mars Sextile/Trine Venus (See Venus Sextile/Trine Mars above.)

Mars Sextile/Trine Jupiter
or Jupiter Sextile/Trine Mars (long-term)

During this period, self-confidence is emphasized. You are likely to feel in touch with your own energy and enthusiasm and have a ready optimism. Indeed, if carried too far, the patterns can indicate rashness and overreach—trying for more than is possible. Your beliefs, values and goals will be central in what you achieve. You need to have something to reach for, a dream to seek, but one that is achievable. You are likely to be more courageous, open, honest, forthright and pioneering than usual. You can also inspire others.

Mars Sextile/Trine Saturn
or Saturn Sextile/Trine Mars (long-term)

This period shows a strong potential for achievement. You have the capacity to direct yourself and to put your energy into accomplishments. You are probably motivated to support your career or ambitions in the outer world. It is potentially a time of working your way up the ladder of success. Excessive ambition and overdrive (trying to carry the whole world) can be a hazard, along with the opposite reaction, self-blocking (reluctance to try for fear of failing or falling short). But you can realize a high potential by combining initiative and endurance, enthusiasm and practicality, speed and caution, confidence and capability.

Mars Sextile/Trine Uranus
or Uranus Sextile/Trine Mars (long-term)

Freedom is in the air! The accent is on openness, risk-taking and a fresh, pioneering spirit. You may break new ground in many areas. You are likely to resist being tied down, hemmed in or limited in any way. Circulation is vital. You need to explore. You may initiate action with friends, groups or anything that is new and different. New technology could attract you. Inventiveness is accentuated, as well as the potential to expand mechanical skills. You can make a contribution to the future, can aid the cutting edge of change.

Mars Sextile/Trine Neptune
or Neptune Sextile/Trine Mars (long-term)

You have the potential to move closer toward your ideals, visions and dreams. This could mean taking actions that increase beauty in the world, that contribute to healing, that accent spirituality or otherwise aid the quest for perfection. You may be inspired spiritually, receive insight through artistic avenues, or energetically pursue worthy causes or philanthropic concerns. If idealism is overdone, victimization is possible. Wanting perfection does not guarantee realism. But generally this should be a time when your inner wisdom and intuition can lead you to inspired action.

Mars Sextile/Trine Pluto or Pluto Sextile/Trine Mars (long-term)

Strong emotions are highlighted, and your passions may be more intense during this period. The potential of an important sexual/sensual bond is present. Relationship issues are likely, especially revolving around money and pleasures, but you have the ability to balance your own needs and desires with those of a mate, to help and to be helped. This is a positive configuration for balancing personal power ("mine") with shared power ("ours"). Physical endurance and stamina may well be good and you can both initiate and follow through and finish up on projects. Will power is accented; be willing to compromise.

Mars Sextile/Trine Ceres (and vice versa)

You have the potential of channeling much energy and vitality into your work or into nurturing, assisting activities. You may build self-confidence through being efficient and productive. You may find nourishing, protecting or helpful activities exciting and vitalizing. You could also gain support from a mother or mother figure. You are harmonizing self-expression and care taking instincts.

Mars Sextile/Trine Pallas (and vice versa)

You have the capacity to meet both personal and interpersonal needs. Harmony is suggested between your independent side and your desire to share the world with others. You can operate alone and together. You can meet your need for self-expression as well as your desire for partnership. You may be willing to expend energy on behalf of relationships, equality, justice or balance. You are likely to support fair play. A partner or relationship may also be of assistance or aid to you and you should be able to balance your wants with the desires of another. You may become actively involved in artistic/aesthetic pursuits, especially active ones like dancing or sports which express grace in action.

Mars Sextile/Trine Juno (and vice versa)

Potential harmony is suggested between you and partners (especially marriage or committed relationships). This is a period when you can more easily blend personal and interpersonal needs and pleasures, so agreement between self and other should flow more naturally. You may also energetically create beauty (perhaps in a physical form or with such physical actions as dancing, yoga or gymnastics). Passion could be increased and partners may offer support or assistance to you (and vice versa). You have the opportunity to fully be yourself while sharing life with another and encouraging his/her full flowering.

Mars Sextile/Trine Vesta (and vice versa)

This aspect points to potential productivity. Your energy flows easily into competence and doing the job well. You may also feel a natural attraction toward physically healthy activities. The urge for efficient functioning (on the job and in your body) harmonizes with and supports your basic energy and self-confidence. Your actions are aimed toward practical results. You may find it easier to be organized.

Mars Sextile/Trine Chiron
or Chiron Sextile/Trine Mars (long-term)

This pattern encourages confidence and spontaneous action. Physical activity can be a good outlet for the energy, including any kind of sport that allows free movement. Increased knowledge could also be a major goal; gaining it or giving it to others. You are likely to be clear about what you want, and eager to go after it. Sometimes impatience and over-confidence can be a hazard, but if you can stay realistic about goals, including the time and effort needed to reach them, you have the potential for considerable success. If some of your goals are distant in time and/or space, try to stay realistic about the small steps which will eventually attain the desired ends. The fire emphasis of this combination would prefer to be there in one leap, but most goals take both the fire willingness to try something new and the earth willingness to keep on trying until we get there. This aspect encourages optimism and a willingness to "go for it."

Mars Sextile/Trine Nodes or Nodes Sextile/Trine Mars (long-term)

This combination shows a capacity to integrate the need for both freedom and closeness, for independence and dependence, for change and stability/ security. Though life should be big enough for these polarities, a great many people have trouble making a place in their lives for both ends. During this period, you can also expand your psychic openness. Often, with Mars aspects to water factors, the inner guidance will flow directly into instinctive action without any conscious decision. You may do the right thing at the right time without consciously understanding why.

Ceres Sextile/Trine the Sun (See Sun Sextile/Trine Ceres above.)

Ceres Sextile/Trine Moon
Mothering and nurturing themes are accented. The emphasis in on contact with a mother (figure), activities in or around the home or with family members, and caretaking pursuits—whether toward pets, plants, people, handicrafts or other concerns. A balance between giving and receiving protection and support could be achieved. Parental motifs are highlighted. Your skills at managing both tasks and emotions are accented. You can accomplish much and also help people to feel good about what gets done. Warmth and family focus are likely.

Ceres Sextile/Trine Mercury (See Mercury Sextile/Trine Ceres above.)

Ceres Sextile/Trine Venus (See Venus Sextile/Trine Ceres above.)

Ceres Sextile/Trine Mars (See Mars Sextile/Trine Ceres above.)

Ceres Sextile/Trine Jupiter
or Jupiter Sextile/Trine Ceres (long-term)
This period holds the potential of successfully grounding your dreams. You may come closer to your ideals in terms of work or nurturing issues. Your goals and values are likely to reinforce your urge toward competence and clear analysis may assist your visions. Nurturing figures may contribute to your confidence, enthusiasm or faith in life, or you may uplift and energize others.

Ceres Sextile/Trine Saturn
or Saturn Sextile/Trine Ceres (long-term)
This period highlights competence and the achievement of tangible results. Facing facts and applying effort should be easier. Nurturing figures may assist your career or you may contribute to the support of others. Parenting archetypes are emphasized, so you may have more contact with your own parents, or play a parenting role to others. You can balance bottom-line realism with gentle compassion and have the best of both. You have a good potential for seeing what needs to be done and doing it. The focus is on work, with a caring flavor. Practicality and humane concern are emphasized. You need a sense of accomplishment and can be effective in areas where you can see tangible results.

Ceres Sextile/Trine Uranus
or Uranus Sextile/Trine Ceres (long-term)
This period could include innovation in your work, health or patterns of nurturing. Children could move toward a more equalitarian role; friends might assist your career; you might put your originality to work or otherwise open up your

options in terms of productivity and caretaking. Intellectual insights could be applied to produce practical accomplishments. Tolerance and open-mindedness are likely to be assets with both family and coworkers. You can be pragmatically inventive.

Ceres Sextile/Trine Neptune
or Neptune Sextile/Trine Ceres (long-term)

This period holds the potential of visionary accomplishments. You have the capacity to blend idealism with practicality, imagination with discipline and compassion with competence. You may be drawn to create handicrafts or other objects that are both useful and beautiful. You could turn aesthetic talents into a professional role. You might become more involved in nurturing, care taking activities. Suggested talents include capable caring and adept artistry.

Ceres Sextile/Trine Pluto or Pluto Sextile/Trine Ceres (long-term)

This period suggests the potential of harmonious cooperation between your desire for intimacy and your drive to work competently and to assist others. Family members may support each other. Your work may be enhanced by a mate, or you may serve your partner in a practical way. You are likely to exhibit good organizational skills and may expand a talent for details. You might tune in to family members partially on an intuitive level. On a broader scale, you might be involved in a service or a profession like social work which uses public funds. Or you could work with joint resources in fields like accounting or investments.

Ceres Sextile/Trine Pallas (and vice versa)

This combination points to harmony between your parenting instincts and your equalitarian needs. There are times to be strong, capable, pragmatic, responsible and assist others, as well as times to share responsibilities, take turns and let others do their part. Balancing relationship needs with work needs allows room for both. Relative harmony is likely between your partners and your family, with mutual support and caring. You may choose to work with people in a service profession, or your family may pull together on tasks.

Ceres Sextile/Trine Juno (and vice versa)

Closeness and competence are highlighted during this period. This pattern suggests a good capacity for handling work, a nurturing role, and committed relationships. You can be parental as well as equalitarian, assisting as well as cooperating, balancing intimacy needs with the desire to do a good job. Caring is emphasized, but productivity is also important. Mentoring figures may assist your relationships; you may cooperate in parenting ventures; partners may contribute to your vocation or assist you with tasks. A harmonious exchange is implied between close sharing as a protector and as an equal, as well as competent attainments.

Ceres Sextile/Trine Vesta (and vice versa)

Competence is highlighted for this period. You have a strong urge to do things well, to achieve, to work for measurable results. A good capacity for discipline, effort and dedication is also suggested. Practicality may be marked. You could be particularly focused on achieving excellent health, or on improving and furthering your work in the world. The pattern is good for working with details, or for putting the pieces together to produce a useful and helpful whole. You may feel inclined to assist others, but the major emphasis is on productive accomplishment.

Ceres Sextile/Trine Chiron
or Chiron Sextile/Trine Ceres (long-term)

This combination supports the ability to use personal initiative and self-confidence or faith in a Higher Power to help people. The action could focus on family members or could be directed into service and assistance for many people. Some form of healing would be especially appropriate, whether physical, mental, or spiritual. The pattern is excellent for expanded knowledge which could be applied in practical ways. Work could involve teaching, writing, traveling, etc. Clarity about goals and values can contribute to effective work in the world.

Ceres Sextile/Trine Nodes
or Nodes Sextile/Trine Ceres (long-term)

Parent-child relationships are often highlighted with this pattern. Great emotional warmth, attachment, and mutual assistance are possible. If the scope of the life is broadened beyond the immediate family, there is considerable ability to play parent to the world. Such action could range from raising foster children to working for or contributing to social causes which help children, animals, ecology, etc. Emotional security is important and there may be much satisfaction from nurturing and being nurtured.

Pallas Sextile/Trine Sun (See Sun Sextile/Trine Pallas above.)

Pallas Sextile/Trine Moon

Closeness urges are accented. You have an opportunity to balance relationship urges and nurturing needs. You can bring together partners and children or activities which involve teamwork and cooperation as well as those requiring you to be more parental or protective. Issues of justice and fair play can be blended with family needs. Your wisdom function proves valuable within the nest. A partner may be more supportive or you may strengthen the emotional foundation of your relationship(s). Beauty could lend extra security to your psyche.

Pallas Sextile/Trine Mercury (See Mercury Sextile/Trine Pallas above.)

Pallas Sextile/Trine Venus (See Venus Sextile/Trine Pallas above.)

Pallas Sextile/Trine Mars (See Mars Sextile/Trine Pallas above.)

Pallas Sextile/Trine Jupiter
or Jupiter Sextile/Trine Pallas (long-term)

This period invites you to use your dreams to gain more balance and equality in your life. Aspirations, confidence, faith or optimism may assist your relationships with others or your aesthetic pursuits. An outgoing, expressive, exploratory attitude is likely to be an asset in your dealings with others. A partner may positively contribute to your faith or beliefs or to the achievement of personal goals. Issues of justice, equality and fair play are emphasized. You might want to offer knowledge or inspiration as a counselor, consultant, or lawyer, or study toward such a goal.

Pallas Sextile/Trine Saturn
or Saturn Sextile/Trine Pallas (long-term)

Power and equality are potentially in harmony during this time. You have the possibility of a good balance between your executive, controlling side and your desire for balance, harmony and equal sharing. You can instinctively know when to cooperate and when to take charge. There is the potential of mentors or authority figures assisting your relationships or teamwork, or of partners aiding your career. The theme is harmony between working and relating. You could be attracted by social causes, including political involvement, or counseling, or be drawn to fields which produce structures that are both artistic and functional. Products can be both beautiful and useful.

Pallas Sextile/Trine Uranus
or Uranus Sextile/Trine Pallas (long-term)

A feeling for people may be evident during this period. This patterns suggests that you have the capacity to balance emotional attachments with a light touch, to be involved, but to maintain your own independence and encourage the uniqueness of the other person. A friendly spirit is likely to enhance your associations with others. You may be more drawn to groups, causes, networking, politics, consulting or other forms of people contact. Your inventiveness might spark a new aesthetic approach. Detachment and objectivity are likely to be easier than usual as well as an instinct for justice, fair play and seeing both sides of issues.

Pallas Sextile/Trine Neptune
or Neptune Sextile/Trine Pallas (long-term)

A feeling for beauty is highlighted by this combination. Artistic or aesthetic talent may come easily to you during this period. Grace, ease and harmony are apt to appeal. You may also find it easy to see the best in relationships. Your idealism may assist your capacity for balance, justice, fair play and sharing, or attract you toward spiritual counseling. A partner or associate could assist your dreams, aspirations or spiritual path. You may enjoy sharing art, inspiration, healing/helping activities or mystical leanings.

Pallas Sextile/Trine Pluto or Pluto Sextile/Trine Pallas (long-term)

Relationships are highlighted by this combination, especially close, one-to-one encounters with others. The potential exists for satisfying interactions which can include intense, intimate sharing as well as open, intellectual, objective interactions. Logic and emotions can be blended well in your exchanges with others. Joint efforts could range from personal to concern with the needs of society. Activity as a counselor or consultant could be fulfilling and successful.

Pallas Sextile/Trine Ceres (See Ceres Sextile/Trine Pallas above.)

Pallas Sextile/Trine Juno (and vice versa)

The emphasis in this aspect centers on associations with other people. Inner agreement is suggested in the goal of seeking close exchanges with others. You may experience some ambivalence between an intense, absorbing emotional bond and a more objective, intellectual connection, but you can probably find a reasonable compromise. Equality is highlighted with a good capacity for meeting people on their level, for sharing comfortably with partners. Themes of justice and fair play are likely to be important to you; evenhandedness is emphasized.

Pallas Sextile/Trine Vesta (and vice versa)

You have the capacity to achieve a good balance between a "look for flaws and fix-them" orientation and the capacity to accept people and things as they are. Relative harmony is suggested between your desire to improve and your willingness to observe and understand without trying to change things. You can choose when to be a spectator in life and when to work to make something over, to find the flaws and improve upon them. Criticism can be balanced with acceptance; equality (taking turns) can be balanced with the need to do it yourself, and work can be balanced with relationships.

Pallas Sextile/Trine Chiron
or Chiron Sextile/Trine Pallas (long-term)

This pattern points to your ability to blend your peer relationships with your knowledge and ideals. You can build lasting friendships and partnerships with people who share your interests and values and goals. Work in fields such as counseling or consulting could be satisfying and successful. You can expand and share your knowledge. You may choose to develop skills in the graphic arts, and travel is possible. Concern with fair play and justice may attract you into work for social causes. You might also wish to enlarge your social circle or just become more socially active. In general, you are being encouraged to use your intelligence and objectivity to strengthen interpersonal relationships and to heal the planet.

Pallas Sextile/Trine Nodes
or Nodes Sextile/Trine Pallas (long-term)

This pattern suggests that you can maintain harmony between your partner(s) and your parents or children to build a cross-generational support system. The peer relationships could include associates in your job, with teamwork contributing to feelings of mutual security. Fields such as counseling or consulting are possible, where awareness of the feelings of others is an asset. You could expand your empathy to include humanity or other forms of life, playing a nurturing role or receiving help from others. You might also be drawn into artistic activity as a source of personal well-being.

Juno Sextile/Trine Sun (See Sun Sextile/Trine Juno above.)

Juno Sextile/Trine Moon

Intimacy is highlighted. You may move toward more closeness with other people. This could include giving and receiving more support from a partner or moving toward more equality with your children. A spouse and kids may get along better. You can balance parental and partnership roles. You can shift more easily between dependency and teamwork. Beautification efforts involving the home or family members may go well. Sharing and caring are the goals.

Juno Sextile/Trine Mercury (See Mercury Sextile/Trine Juno above.)

Juno Sextile/Trine Venus (See Venus Sextile/Trine Juno above.)

Juno Sextile/Trine Mars (See Mars Sextile/Trine Juno above.)

Juno Sextile/Trine Jupiter
or Jupiter Sextile/Trine Juno (long-term)

Mythologically, this aspect represents a marriage made in heaven (or, at least, on Mount Olympus). Positively, this can indicate a sense of faith, trust, optimism, hope, confidence and humor contributing to a successful relationship (especially marriage). It can also suggest a partner assisting your dreams, aiding your beliefs, or furthering your values and long-range goals. You also might use your knowledge to increase financial security for yourself or others. An extroverted combination, this suggests a good sense of fun, expressiveness, emotional intensity, and a strong sense of justice.

Juno Sextile/Trine Saturn
or Saturn Sextile/Trine Juno (long-term)

This period highlights a balance between relationships and career. You may find it easier to blend love and work—your accomplishments in the world and your ties to other people. A marriage or other partner could assist your career or your practical efforts might be helpful to a partner. Beauty instincts or talents might contribute to your work. The pattern suggests you can manage a good balance between cooperating with others in a team and taking charge as an executive.

Juno Sextile/Trine Uranus
or Uranus Sextile/Trine Juno (long-term)

This period suggests an inner ability to balance your freedom side with your desire for committed relationships (especially marriage). This can point to more openness, friendship and camaraderie within an already-established relationship. It could show a friendship turning into something deeper, or a new interpersonal development. The focus is on sharing intimacy while still maintaining a firm sense of personal independence and individuality. Innovative artistic activities are also encouraged during this period.

Juno Sextile/Trine Neptune
or Neptune Sextile/Trine Juno (long-term)

This combination emphasizes a feeling for beauty and a desire for grace and harmony in relationships. The potential exists for sharing ideals, aesthetics, inspirations or dreams with a committed partner. Excessive idealism is also possible, inviting savior/victim relationships or just reluctance to acknowledge the misery in the world. It is possible to accentuate the positive, to encourage the best in people, while still being fully aware and accepting of human frailties. It is possible to work to create the best possible relationship while enjoying what we have already.

Juno Sextile/Trine Pluto or Pluto Sextile/Trine Juno (long-term)

Intimacy is the focus with this combination. You are likely to be in inner agreement around issues of depth, self-mastery, emotional bonding and shared possessions and pleasures. This includes the possibility of a clarity in terms of what you want in and from a mate. You might also be concerned with issues of insight and self-control. Discipline and endurance are encouraged, along with a retentive memory which could make forgiveness and/or resentment into an issue. Willpower is emphasized, almost to the point of dogged determination to do what you feel is necessary. Compromise may be needed at times, or learning how to let go. You may be more psychically open to a partner, and could use your intuition in fields such as counseling, research, psychotherapy or hypnosis. On the highest level, you and a mate share souls with one another.

Juno Sextile/Trine Ceres (See Ceres Sextile/Trine Juno above.)

Juno Sextile/Trine Pallas (See Pallas Sextile/Trine Juno above.)

Juno Sextile/Trine Vesta (and vice versa)

This aspect focuses on themes of harmony between love and work. You have the potential to balance intimacy instincts with your drive for competence and tangible achievements. Partners may support your career (or you support theirs), and practical efforts may enhance your relationships. Effort and ease should be in reasonable balance. You may work with joint resources, personally or professionally, dealing with investments, taxes, accounting, etc., or incorporate artistic elements into your job.

Juno Sextile/Trine Chiron
or Chiron Sextile/Trine Juno (long-term)

This pattern indicates that you can harmonize your search for something more in your life with your desire for a close, caring partnership. You and the people who are close to you can share the quest for knowledge, the goal of creating a better world, the urge to heal the wounded. You can explore both the heights and the depths of the human psyche with your mate. The most enduring relationships are those built on shared values and goals where people journey together toward their mutual ideals.

Juno Sextile/Trine Nodes or Nodes Sextile/Trine Juno (long-term)

This period offers potential harmony between mate and family, strongly supporting a life centered around relationships. Mutual empathy may be emphasized, as you share life with people you love. It is important to be able both to give and receive support to achieve interdependency, to avoid one-sided dependency. The desire for security may be very strong, with a tendency to hold on, sometimes too long. Don't make your whole security depend on other people or on possessions. You can stay in touch with your own power partly through helping others. Now is the time to practice giving and receiving comfortably with loved ones.

Vesta Sextile/Trine Sun (See Sun Sextile/Trine Vesta above.)

Vesta Sextile/Trine Moon

Practical and emotional caretaking are likely to be in harmony. You can nurture people while accomplishing tasks in the real world. You can look after people's feelings while making sure that the job gets done. Family members may assist you in regard to chores or your job. You may take steps to improve the health or nutritional status of yourself or loved ones. A good balance is likely between time and energy for emotional ties and time and energy for achievement. You may more easily compromise between family and work duties.

Vesta Sextile/Trine Mercury (See Mercury Sextile/Trine Vesta above.)

Vesta Sextile/Trine Venus (See Venus Sextile/Trine Vesta above.)

Vesta Sextile/Trine Mars (See Mars Sextile/Trine Vesta above.)

Vesta Sextile/Trine Jupiter
or Jupiter Sextile/Trine Vesta (long-term)
This pattern shows a good potential for harmony between aspirations and effort. This period highlights confidence and reaching for more as well as practical competence. You have the potential of being clear about what you want and then working hard to achieve your dreams, to manifest long-range goals. Perfectionism, standards set too high, could bring dissatisfaction, but the steady achievement of small goals will carry you to the bigger ones.

Vesta Sextile/Trine Saturn
or Saturn Sextile/Trine Vesta (long-term)
Efficiency and accomplishment are highlighted with this aspect. The focus may center around your body and good health, or around tasks, or your career. Competence is important. You have the potential of much dedication, discipline, organization, thoroughness and willingness to pay your dues, to do what it takes to get the job done. These drives might be overdone, producing workaholism or too much criticism (of yourself or others), but they support the capacity to work hard and to accomplish much. Just remember to also make room for other parts of life.

Vesta Sextile/Trine Uranus
or Uranus Sextile/Trine Vesta (long-term)
You have the capacity to blend logical analysis with sudden flashes of insight. This period highlights both intellectual overviews and pragmatic, piece-by-piece understanding. Your originality and inventiveness can assist your work and further your accomplishments, while your discipline and focus on details can ground and make useful your "instant insights." Friends may assist your work or networking could further your attainments. You may make useful, practical changes in what you do or in the associations you choose and your work could contribute to the well-being of the society and humanity.

Vesta Sextile/Trine Neptune
or Neptune Sextile/Trine Vesta (long-term)
This could be a time when you bring together hard-headed facts and the most beguiling of fancies. You have the potential of a partnership between logic and intuition, discipline and compassion, unity and details. You can approach subjects from a holistic viewpoint as well as analyzing all the pieces in a linear fashion. A strong urge toward service or assistance is likely, or you might become involved in handicrafts that are both useful and attractive. You may be drawn toward inspirational work, or your work may be central in giving meaning to your life.

Vesta Sextile/Trine Pluto or Pluto Sextile/Trine Vesta (long-term)

A capacity for details, thoroughness, discipline, endurance and organization is implied by this pattern. You may find it easier to plan and to accomplish. Your work efforts could be assisted by a close intimate, or you might make material contributions to the achievements of a mate. Your tasks and relationships can support one another. Your emotions and practicality should both contribute to success. Increased self-knowledge and self-mastery are also possible, sometimes tending toward over-asceticism. Don't get so caught up in a tunnel vision focus that you lose your broad perspective.

Vesta Sextile/Trine Ceres (See Ceres Sextile/Trine Vesta above.)

Vesta Sextile/Trine Pallas (See Pallas Sextile/Trine Vesta above.)

Vesta Sextile/Trine Juno (See Juno Sextile/Trine Vesta above.)

Vesta Sextile/Trine Chiron
or Chiron Sextile/Trine Vesta (long-term)
This pattern supports a successful integration between your goals and ideals and your work in the world. You are able to bring your vision into practical form in the material realm. Some form of helping/healing work is especially appropriate, but many forms of service are possible. Continuing learning can contribute to your effectiveness in your job. Alternately, travel or distant areas might be involved. Basically, it is clearly defined values and willingness to work in practical ways which can combine to produce success in the world.

Vesta Sextile/Trine Nodes
or Nodes Sextile/Trine Vesta (long-term)
This pattern suggests that you are able to harmonize your work and your relationships. There can be a good balance between practicality and emotional warmth, though security issues may be emphasized to the detriment of light-hearted fun. You may work in a service profession including some form of healing. Nutrition might become a strong interest. You could also work with or for your family. In general, this period is likely to involve work which will provide security to you and your close relationships.

Chiron Sextile/Trine Nodes (See Chapter Two.)

Conflict Aspects

(Include octiles and trioctiles with squares.)

Sun Square/Opposite/Quincunx Moon

You may feel a push/pull between public (onstage) urges and the desire for privacy. Introversion could vie with extroversion until you achieve a reasonable balance. Conflict or competition could occur with loved ones in regard to who gets attention (and how much) and who provides the nurturing versus the ones receiving the care taking. Disagreements in regard to domestic matters are possible. Parental demands or duties may be difficult to handle. Separations are possible—with people pulling apart from one another or going in different directions. Compromise can make this a period of building more warmth and caring with those near and dear to you. With mutual empathy, bonds can be strengthened and deepened.

Sun Square Mercury (and vice versa)

There is the potential of conflict between your passionate, risk-taking, creative side and your logical, reasoning, objective capacities. You may feel torn between rationality and emotional reactions or between seeking excitement and seeking information. The needs or demands of siblings (and other relatives) may compete with the needs and demands of children (or lovers). Ego needs (your own or other people's) may present challenges in terms of communication and sharing knowledge. Pride, shame, the need to shine, or the desire to be special may challenge clear communication (in speaking and/or writing) and the rational collecting of data. With integration, you can find excitement in learning and communicating and share the limelight.

Sun Square Venus (and vice versa)

Sensuality and passion are highlighted. The appetites may be strong, whether expressed primarily through food, smoking, drinking, sensuality or sexuality. You are likely to be drawn toward the finer things in life and your taste may be excellent. Some ambivalence is suggested, however, in the realm of finances and the pursuit of life's pleasures. Challenges in love relationships are possible if hedonistic tendencies are out of balance between you and loved ones. Conflicts might relate to money or sensuality.

One side of your nature is oriented toward excitement, passion, intensification of emotions, grandstanding, and thrill-seeking. Another side wants comfort, ease, predictability, security, and smooth sailing. You may feel torn between consolidation and creative expansion; between enjoying and hanging on to what you have now and risking for more in the future. Personal pleasures may need to be balanced against the needs and desires of children (and/or lovers).

A positive synthesis can be attained through artistic creativity, or you can take steps to manifest more resources or more love in your life, or you can focus on enjoying what is possible.

Sun Square/Opposite/Quincunx Mars (and vice versa)

Energy, drive, vitality, assertion and "me first" needs are highlighted. With two fire planets involved, emotions may be fierce. The challenge calls for getting some of what **you** want—while still maintaining love relationships with other people. Conflicts, clashes and anger are possible. Facing issues directly is most likely to be constructive. Sitting on the fire won't help. Blocked assertion usually just leads to feeling tired, or, if carried on too long, the stress can contribute to physical illness. Alternately, we may project our power and attract others who attack us.

Physical activity (including sports) can be a healthy channel for the energy and emotion that are represented. You need ways to assert yourself, to be admired and recognized, to express your inner essence, while still respecting and appreciating the rights of others (especially those nearest and dearest to you). If you deny your own personal power, children and/or a lover might express the energy to an extreme of aggressiveness, selfishness or impatience. If you overdo your need to move, to do, to be exactly who you are, rashness or impatience could short-circuit constructive relating or even lead to accidents. With integration, you can creatively define and enlarge your own identity, while still leaving room for loved ones to be special and have their own areas to shine.

Sun Square/Opposite/Quincunx Jupiter
or Jupiter Square/Opposite/Quincunx Sun (long-term)

Growth goals are highlighted, but some ambivalence or conflict is possible. Perhaps ego needs or the desire for attention and recognition compete with the quest for meaning, education, understanding or a spiritual path. Perhaps the needs of children and loved ones compete with the drive to travel, to explore, to adventure and to pursue goals wherever they take you.

This aspect combines two fire planets, indicating a focus on confidence, zest, enthusiasm, energy, vitality and extroversion. If these attributes are overdone, you might be rash, self-righteous, too sure of yourself or inclined to want/expect too much, too fast or too easily. If your energy and enthusiasm are blocked (due to inner conflicts), you may inhibit your dynamism, sit on your confidence, and hold back on your inner fire, perhaps even to the point of attracting other people who overdo it, or feeling tired or even ill from the energy that doesn't have an outlet. The goal is a positive manifestation of your need to expand, to do more, to increase your creativity and expression from your own center without overdoing or acting against your own sound judgment and ethical principles.

Sun Square/Opposite/Quincunx Saturn
or Saturn Square/Opposite/Quincunx Sun (long-term)

Ambition is one possible focus for this period. You may want to achieve something noteworthy and are capable of great determination in your efforts to reach the heights. You need to avoid two extremes. One is impatience—expecting to "leap tall buildings with a single bound"—to "make it" immediately. There are realistic limits and structural rules in life that demand some discipline and practicality. The other extreme is overdoing the restraints you place on yourself. You might be too judgmental and harsh in your self-assessments, and stop yourself from trying things that **are** achievable, or hold yourself back with self-criticism. A reasonable blend of confidence and practicality allows you to achieve much.

Love needs might be at odds with work needs during this period. You are likely to feel competing demands (for time and energy) between your career and those nearest and dearest to you. Both are important; the challenge is to avoid neglecting one for the other. The same principles can be experienced as a need to balance work versus play, or discipline versus relaxation and fun.

Sun Square/Opposite/Quincunx Uranus
or Uranus Square/Opposite/Quincunx Sun (long-term)

This combination suggests an "electric" feeling in the air. The impetus is toward creativity, change, risk-taking, thrills and the urge to "live life on the edge"—to go beyond where one has gone before! This can be a period of expansion, growth, constructive change and progress. If overdone, however, chaos, dangerous thrills or sudden upsets are possible. The goal is to open up options where needed, without totally destroying life's essential order.

Conflict is possible between your intellectual, detached side and your emotional, loving side. This could be a push/pull between friendship and passion, or the head and the heart. You may be ambivalent in terms of love relationships or children—wanting the emotional ties, yet not wanting to be tied down. Closeness may vie with freedom within your psyche. If some of this is out of consciousness awareness, it could be lived out by those near and dear to you. Relationship shifts or even breaks are possible if freedom needs break out suddenly after long repression. The challenge is to create loving commitments that are loose enough to allow everyone's individuality to flourish within them.

Sun Square/Opposite/Quincunx Neptune
or Neptune Square/Opposite/Quincunx Sun (long-term)

Love, romance, beauty and imagination are highlighted. Dreams and visions may facilitate the pursuit of love or imagination may assist creativity. If carried too far, being "in love with love" is possible. You might place so much importance on an ideal image of love that you deceive yourself (or allow others to deceive you) in matters of passion. Savior/victim relationships are also possible, with one partner attempting to "play God" or be **everything** for the other person. Disillusionment is likely when unrealistic dreams are pursued. Ego needs or expectations of applause, attention and admiration may be grandiose or encouraged by infinite imaginings. Expectations for love or for loved ones may be beyond the reach of human beings. One positive expression is the capacity to see the best in those we love. If combined with practicality and realistic assessment, this ability to encourage the positive and the higher potentials of those we love can be an asset.

An alternative form of the conflict is to experience spiritual/compassionate/ rescuing instincts as being at odds with the desire to be special, applauded and admired. Overdoing the sacrificial instincts can result in squelching necessary self-confidence and capacity to shine. Overdoing the desire for positive feedback or being "King of the Mountain" may result in insufficient empathy, sympathy and concern for the Whole of life. Balance requires some of both.

Sun Square/Opposite/Quincunx Pluto
or Pluto Square/Opposite/Quincunx Sun (long-term)

Power and passion tend to be highlighted by this aspect, but you may feel torn between inwardly-directed power (toward self-knowledge and self-control) and outwardly-oriented power (toward attaining attention, recognition, acknowledgment and love in the world). Swings are possible between withdrawal to work on your self and a zestful plunge into exciting relationships. Or, you may express one side, while a partner expresses another. Managing a reasonable balance can be a challenge.

Shared possessions, pleasures and finances are likely to be an important focus. Learning to give, receive and share equally with another person may be another challenge. Intimidation, power plays, and emotional manipulation (from you toward others or from others toward you) might occur over sex, power and money until integration is achieved.

Issues of willpower and control may also surface between your mate and children. Rather than feeding any competition, look for opportunities to encourage cooperation and teamwork. Arranging family matters as joint projects (rather than parents telling kids what to do) can help ameliorate matters. Getting input from everyone and making a place for differing opinions will be helpful where teamwork is appropriate. The competitive spirit can be expressed in competition with other teams. Sports and business provide appropriate outlets.

Sun Square/Opposite/Quincunx Ceres (and vice versa)

Parental instincts may be prominent, although a focus around appreciation for efforts (on the job, in the family, etc.) is quite likely. The desire to serve, to work humbly and efficiently, to be dedicated and modest may conflict with a desire for attention, recognition, applause and power.

Two extremes are possible. You might feel overworked and under appreciated. This could be in terms of family members, or in terms of your job. You may feel as if you are stuck with the boring details and other people get the excitement and positive attention. If this seems to be happening, you need to create avenues for more recognition and applause. Perhaps you have been taking on the drudgery because you feel others will not do a good enough job; if so, you can let up a bit on your standards and be willing to delegate. Perhaps you have been too supportive and protective, and need to let others chip in a little, to do their share.

The opposite extreme involves reluctance to work at unexciting details. You may prefer the limelight and seek out jobs with thrills or an adrenaline rush, but every occupation has some nitty-gritty, boring or "plain hard work" aspects to it that also need attention. Productivity requires effort as well as thrills.

If parenting and family are the major focus, a balance still needs to be found between service and appreciation. If pregnancy is a goal, ambivalence may exist—fear of being tied to a routine or drudgery perhaps or concern about losing out on passion, creativity and excitement. Of the financial necessity to work at a demanding job might make it hard to do justice to both family and job. Facing these issues can help facilitate positive parenthood.

Sun Square/Opposite/Quincunx Pallas (and vice versa)

The theme involves a need to balance equalitarian instincts with the drive to be special, noticed and superior in some way. You may feel that relationship compromises do not leave you room to be a leader, onstage in some way, or admired and appreciated. Or, the demands of exciting others, being magnetic, larger-than-life or involved in creative projects may seem to take you away from simple sharing or peer relationships. The challenge is to manage relating as an equal as well as standing out from the crowd.

Conflict between partners and children or partners and parents is possible. You may feel torn about how much time and energy to devote to children, a spouse, or parents. Loved ones may seem to have competing agendas and alliances. Seek out win/win solutions and ways to encourage teamwork among everyone. Beauty and a spirit of fun may be ways to connect people. Objectivity and a sense of fair play may be important.

Sun Square/Opposite/Quincunx Juno (and vice versa)

Emotions are likely to intensify in the arenas of committed relationships, sexuality and shared possessions and finances. Strong feelings are probable, but there may be tension between safety instincts and the desire to take a risk for greater gain.

If the ambivalence between safety and excitement/expansion needs is played out internally, you may swing from one to the other—whether around sexuality, money, or relating. Or you might identify with one side and attract a partner (often spouse) who lives out the other side. Then, you can confront one another on the issue. The outer power struggle often mirrors the inner ambivalence, but can help you to reach a compromise which leaves room for both positions. If power needs get out of hand, guilt-tripping, intimidation, power plays, withdrawal or emotional blackmail are possible. This pattern may also mark a time for learning "when is enough" and "how to let go." By focusing on the capacity for deep love and intense commitment, you can find ways to share the pleasures, power and possessions.

There is also the potential of some power struggles between a partner and children. Arrange situations so that teamwork is the best avenue for people to get what they want. Seek out win/win alternatives and use the power of positive feedback and attention to encourage the best in everyone concerned. Though the aspect is most often manifested through close relationships, it may also be expressed in competitive work or in counseling interactions.

Sun Square/Opposite/Quincunx Vesta (and vice versa)

A potential conflict is indicated between drives for excitement, attention, applause and passion and the need for productivity, pragmatic planning, detailed analysis and painstaking efforts.

If the fire side wins out, you may seek the adrenaline rush, move toward more and more excitement, dynamism and thrill-seeking. Details could be overlooked; discipline could be ignored and effort could be scorned. If the earth side wins out, you may be dedicated, hardworking and fading into the wallpaper. Others gain the kudos, while you do the work. Or your job could be too routine and repetitive, denying your need for more variety or to have more control. A compromise is necessary, where you can offer dedicated service and receive positive recognition for your efforts. If there is no way to bring creativity into your work, you need to find a hobby that lets you combine creativity with a sense of achievement.

Conflict between work and love is also possible. Time and energy demands may pull you between dedication to your job and loving commitment to your family. Or, duties and responsibilities may vie with playfulness and the fun-loving spirit. Sex may conflict with ascetic tendencies. Life should not be a forced choice; having room for both sides is essential. In the best integration, you can be creative, productive, and receive recognition for your accomplishments.

Sun Square/Opposite/Quincunx Chiron
or Chiron Square/Opposite/Quincunx Sun (long-term)

A period of conflict between two fire factors often indicates a desire for more than is possible. We might want something bigger, or easier or sooner than is realistically possible, and just need to enjoy the process of moving toward our goals. Alternately, we may be unsure of what we want and need to clarify personal values and goals, to have a clear value hierarchy on which to base our choices. Your sense of self-worth is connected to your faith, so try to be practical in your expectations of yourself and life. This is the time to clarify your dreams and then pursue them—one step at a time.

Sun Square/Opposite/Quincunx Nodes
or Nodes Square/Opposite/Quincunx Sun (long-term)

Conflict aspects between the Sun and the nodes of the Moon suggest a need to make room in your life for both your expansive, creative, power-seeking side and your ability to be empathic and sensitive to the needs of others. Fire (Sun) is instinctively independent in the sense of wanting to be in control. Water (the Moon and its nodes) is instinctively dependent or nurturing. Life should be big enough for both. Successful integration involves finding an appropriate way to shine, be admired and express your power while also allowing softness and vulnerability, your own and that of others.

Progressed Moon Aspects, see Chapter Eleven.

Mercury Square Sun (See Sun Square Mercury above).

Mercury Square/Opposite/Quincunx Moon

Potential conflict is implied between your dependency/nurturing urges and your logical, rational side. Emotions might vie with reason, or subjectivity be at odds with objectivity. You are probably learning to balance thinking and feelings. Another potential clash lies between care taking or dependent instincts versus the desire to relate as an equal and a peer. You are learning to blend your inner parent and inner sibling (and this could play out externally as conflict between those individuals in your life).

Parental demands (or your own parental role) might seem at odds with the desire to casually and comfortably share with relatives, neighbors and people who do not require caretaking. Emotional or domestic needs may compete with your urge to learn, to add variety to your life, to explore the immediate environment and exchange ideas with the people in your area. The best expression of this combination is to make your home more lively and mentally stimulating and to combine head and heart in your decisions.

Mercury Square Venus (and vice versa)

There is potential stress between your urge for pleasure and your objective, information-seeking side. Your mind might vie with your senses, intellectual needs competing with physical ones. Conflict is possible with relatives over issues of money, possessions or gratification. Tact may vie with honesty. Communication blocks with a partner may develop. Your desire for variety, changes of scene and adaptability may be at odds with a preference for stability and security. Generally, however, this is an easygoing combination that can readily be integrated by making room for both the mental and the material sides of life.

Mercury Square/Opposite/Quincunx Mars (and vice versa)

Your assertiveness, courage, independence and need for action may sometimes clash with your thinking, communicating and objectivity. You might act before thinking or rush into impulsive speech. Verbal clashes (arguments, irony, sarcasm) are possible if you overdo the need for directness and expressing your personal will and desires. The aspect can signal the mind of a debater and a tongue like a sword. Alternately, you might be afraid to say what you really feel, holding back on communications that would be healthy to express. If too much anger or irritation is held in, it could break out as small accidents (cuts, burns) by interfering with coordination and your attention focus. You might feel at odds with relatives and sibling rivalry is possible. With integration, you can think and react quickly, but also sensibly.

Mercury Square/Opposite/Quincunx Jupiter
or Jupiter Square/Opposite/Quincunx Mercury (long-term)

Mental restlessness is suggested by this combination, and you may be eager to learn, to teach, to talk, to write, to travel or to understand. The urge for knowledge could lead you to be scattered and overextended, if you try to master all topics. You may have to establish some priorities. Curiosity for its own sake might vie with knowledge which contributes to your sense of meaning in life and helps you formulate a world view. You might sometimes leap to conclusions, or generalize beyond the available data. Immediate environmental or family concerns may vie with long-range goals, values and aspirations. The most common form of expression is a conflict between ideals and the ordinary world around us. With integration, we meet both short-range and long-range goals, enjoy lighthearted learning as well as deep, significant philosophical/spiritual discussions, and enjoy the journey toward our ideals. A clear value hierarchy permits choices that keep us on the path to a final destination while still handling the world immediately around us.

Mercury Square/Opposite/Quincunx Saturn
or Saturn Square/Opposite/Quincunx Mercury (long-term)

Your curiosity, light-heartedness, relatives or verbal skills might compete or be at odds with your achievement drives, sense of responsibility, authority role or desire for tangible results. Knowledge for its own sake might vie with "practical" applications. An equalitarian approach of meeting everyone on the same level might be at odds with the desire to lead, to be in control and to run the show. This aspect can also play out as feeling misheard or misunderstood by authorities. Self-doubt, critical judgments, or a focus on limits/constraints could inhibit your thinking or verbal expression. Until integrated, you could feel torn between siblings and father, casual fun and hard work, pure curiosity versus accomplishing something, or multiple interests versus a firm focus. Trust your intellectual abilities and use them to further your accomplishments while balancing carefree and competent urges within yourself.

Mercury Square/Opposite/Quincunx Uranus
or Uranus Square/Opposite/Quincunx Mercury (long-term)

This combination is highly mental, but it might encourage tangential thinking or unusual offshoots. Although originality and inventiveness is likely, excesses can produce rebelliousness, eccentricity or simply off-the-wall concepts. Freedom of thought could be carried to an extreme. Objectivity could be overdone to the point of callousness. Friends might vie with relatives or group/organizational demands compete with your personal learning and intellectual development. Thinking may be brilliant or erratic. Use your unique perspectives wisely. Flashes of genius are possible and can offer major gifts to the world if they are backed up by some earth practicality.

Mercury Square/Opposite/Quincunx Neptune
or Neptune Square/Opposite/Quincunx Mercury (long-term)

This combination suggests conflict between your logical, rational, objective and "linear" side and your global, intuitive, non-rational and subjective side. Life can be a seesaw between the two, if they are not integrated or you might live out one side while someone close to you expresses the opposite extreme. The goal is to make room for both, to allow them to be complementary rather than competitive. Then, language can be used to beautify and to heal. Compassion can be backed by thinking and planning. Inspiration can be based on both instincts and intelligence. Rather than succumbing to confusion or information overload, you can bring beauty and grace into the world through your mind, hands, or communication skills.

Mercury Square/Opposite/Quincunx Pluto
or Pluto Square/Opposite/Quincunx Mercury (long-term)

This combination implies competition between depth pursuits and an eagerness to sample everything. Curiosity and a restless need to explore the world of the mind may vie with the desire to finish up, to complete whatever is undertaken. Detachment could be at odds with intensity or emotions could war with logic. Compulsivity could compete with variety needs, unless room is made for both in life. The best integration expresses as an investigative bent, research skills, and enough mental focus and patience to pursue goals to a reasonable (not obsessive) conclusion.

Mercury Square/Opposite/Quincunx Ceres (and vice versa)

Your intellectual capacities, communicative skills and curiosity may be at odds with your urge for efficiency or your nurturing activities. You may feel torn between theory and applications—knowledge pursued for its own sake versus knowledge put to work in the world. Work efforts could be hindered by communication blocks, conflicts with relatives, lack of dexterity or coordination or issues around objectivity. If a mother or mother figure is still part of your life, she could be at odds with you in terms of mental issues, communication needs, or detachment. Family squabbles are possible, with different ideas vying for support. Combining the intellect with practicality can open channels of communication and encourage shared mental stimulation without acrimony, while still getting important tasks accomplished.

Mercury Square/Opposite/Quincunx Pallas (and vice versa)

Your curious, lighthearted variety-loving side may conflict with your desire for partnership, aesthetics or justice. Relationships with others are highlighted, but you may be torn between a casual relationship and a deeper commitment. You might experience competing demands on your time and energy between relatives and a partner. Or, beauty needs might vie with intellectual demands. Usually, however, this combination is rather easy to integrate, with a shared focus on objectivity, ideas and people, including various forms of the graphic arts.

Mercury Square/Opposite/Quincunx Juno (and vice versa)

Your casual, variety-loving mind may sometimes be at odds with your desire for intimacy and a committed relationship. Communication gaps with a partner are possible, or you may face an inner war between thinking and feeling. Detachment might be at odds with intensity, or siblings (or other relatives) could be at odds with your partner. Your lighthearted and flirtatious side might vie with your desire for an enduring emotional connection. You and a partner might differ in ideas about sharing sexual, sensual pleasures or financial and physical resources. Integration allows you to reach comfortable, equalitarian sharing—physically, mentally and emotionally—with the significant people in your life.

Mercury Square/Opposite/Quincunx Vesta (and vice versa)

Your curiosity, intellectual needs or communication skills may be somewhat at odds with your urge for efficiency, productivity and getting the job done well. Theory may seem at odds with applications, as you try to balance the collection of pure knowledge and information versus putting such understanding to work in the world and getting results. Health issues might surface. Curiosity about anything and everything must be integrated with the need to do something really well and thoroughly. Issues with relatives, business demands or coordination may present barriers to success in your practical, working endeavors, or you might be overly critical of your mental or communicative abilities and block yourself from realizable achievements. Keep a balance between openness and analysis, naive acceptance of all input versus critical rejection of most input. A middle ground works well. You can enhance your communications and use your mental skills well on the job and for good health. With clear priorities, you can do one or two things well and take the rest of life lightly.

Mercury Square/Opposite/Quincunx Chiron
or Chiron Square/Opposite Quincunx Mercury (long-term)

The tension in this pattern is often experienced as conflict between high aspirations and ideals versus living comfortably in an ordinary world. The tension can be eased by maintaining high goals, but enjoying the process of moving toward them. Alternately, the challenge may involve a need to be clear about what is trusted and valued. We can't do everything well, and we can't expect perfection from small parts of life; in ourselves or from a job, a mate, a parent, etc. There are times to "take things lightly," with humor and detachment. Look for ways to expand your mind, in studies, teaching, writing, or traveling. The quest for knowledge is a driving force in this pattern and should be a source of personal satisfaction.

Mercury Square/Opposite/Quincunx Nodes
or Nodes Square/Opposite/Quincunx Mercury (long-term)

This combination shows tension between mental attitudes and close relationships. Possible issues include ambivalence over being dependent or nurturing versus being an equal, or feeling pulled between rational objectivity versus emotional sensitivity. Conflict aspects usually call for compromise. We need to make room for both thinking and feeling, for both helping and being helped and for operating as an equal. Usually, Mercury-Node conflicts involve close relationships: parents, siblings, children, mates, but any "nearby" associates may be part of the issue. By developing both the capacity for objective logic (Mercury) and for empathy for the feelings of others (nodes), we can work out compromises which are fair to all concerned. Increased psychic ability is also possible during this period, and can be cultivated by paying attention to feelings and hunches. Sometimes dreams can be revealing. Ask questions of your subconscious and then listen.

Venus Square Sun (See Sun Square Venus above).

Venus Square/Opposite/Quincunx Moon

Potential conflict is suggested between your nesting side and your desire for pleasure. Perhaps family responsibilities (particularly in terms of nurturing) seem to eat into your time to enjoy life in your own way. There may be ambivalence over relying on others versus meeting your personal needs yourself. Perhaps the home itself consumes a lot of your financial or physical resources. Perhaps earning a living takes you away from home more than you would like. Competition may exist between parental and partnership tasks (or adversarial attitudes between a parent and your spouse). The challenge is to be able to enjoy emotional attachments (being vulnerable as well as able to care for others) and also have time to indulge in personal pleasures.

Venus Square Mercury (See Mercury Square Venus above).

Venus Square/Opposite/Quincunx Mars (and vice versa)

This aspect suggests possible competition between personal action or self-expression and the pursuit of beauty and pleasure. Your urge for independence or pioneering spirit or just the desire for periodic change, may vie with your desire for stability, safety and comfort or your quest for a partnership. Ease, receptivity and beauty instincts may be at odds with your courageous, fighting spirit. There is a time both for physical action and to relax and smell the flowers. Small changes may satisfy, and avoid really disruptive ones. This combination suggests an inner "male versus female" conflict which could manifest as tensions in relationships with the opposite sex. Integration requires some of both sides. If we identify with and express only one side of our nature, we are likely to meet other people who overdo the other side. By being both receptive (empathic) and assertive (in the appropriate contexts), you can have harmonious (and exciting) relationships and other sources of pleasure in the world.

Venus Square/Opposite/Quincunx Jupiter
or Jupiter Square/Opposite/Quincunx Venus (long-term)

This combination suggests the need to integrate the material and the spiritual sides of life. Your quest for meaning and understanding in life may be difficult to achieve or expensive or use up material resources needed for prosaic necessities. Your spiritual aspirations may vie with sensual desires and your quest for enjoyment. Your urge to do something bigger, better, and more exciting could conflict with your desire for security, safety, hanging on to what you have, or just relaxing. Expectations for love and love relationships may be too high. Peace must be made between these various needs, in order to find a compromise position with a bit of each. It is important not to allow a small part of life to become so important that happiness depends on it. High goals are not a problem as long as we enjoy the journey toward them. You can aim toward creating the best in love and pleasure, while able to enjoy what is at the moment.

Venus Square/Opposite/Quincunx Saturn
or Saturn Square/Opposite/Quincunx Venus (long-term)

You are probably learning to balance work needs with pleasure needs or with love. You may be torn between responsibility, discipline and dedication versus ease, passivity, pleasure, indulgence and love relationships. Blocks or limits around sensuality, finances, or affection are possible if you subconsciously feel "undeserving" or as if you haven't "earned it" yet. Judgmental attitudes might interfere with pleasure, or a lackadaisical approach could undermine effectiveness. Life needs a reasonable blend of both willingness to work and the capacity for love and pleasure. Another way to say it is that you can learn to enjoy what is possible and to at least tolerate what is necessary for survival in a physical world and to be at peace with your conscience.

Venus Square/Opposite/Quincunx Uranus
or Uranus Square/Opposite/Quincunx Venus (long-term)

You are probably learning to balance your desire for security and stability with your urge for risks, surprises and change. Your innovative side may be at odds with your comfortable, complacent side. You could feel torn between consolidation and breaking new ground. Friends, groups or organizations could be at odds with you financially or in terms of sensuality or material resources. You might compare (to your own dissatisfaction) your material well-being with that of associates and friends. You could sometimes feel hemmed in and want to break out, or be upset by sudden changes, until an armistice is negotiated between these two very different sides of life. Financial or relationship disruptions are possible. The most positive expression is bringing more freedom, stimulation and excitement into your love relationships and appreciating variety in your material and sensual indulgences. The mutual acceptance and enjoyment of differences can work wonders in relationships. A variety of pleasures saves us from being too dependent on a single one that we require to be happy.

Venus Square/Opposite/Quincunx Neptune
or Neptune Square/Opposite/Quincunx Venus (long-term)

A focus on beauty is indicated. You could develop potential talent for aesthetics, but may have to handle carefully or guard against excesses with issues of beauty, ease, passivity, gentleness or the desire to keep things "looking good" and seeming pleasant. Ideals, dreams, rose-colored glasses or savior/victim instincts might affect your financial resources. Overindulgence or over idealism is possible. You may see what you want to see (rather than what is there) in other people and end up hurt and disillusioned in love relationships. Be realistic about finances, material goods, and people. Moderation is likely to be helpful, along with an outlet for artistic interests and spiritual aspirations.

Venus Square/Opposite/Quincunx Pluto
or Pluto Square/Opposite/Quincunx Venus (long-term)

You are probably learning to balance self-indulgence with self-control. This aspect implies you might have a seesaw tendency between appetite indulgence and appetite mastery. This can point to "feast versus famine" all-or-nothing tendencies in regard to eating (dieting), drinking (not drinking), smoking (not smoking), sex (celibacy), spending (saving), etc. Alternately, you might attract significant partners who overdo in one area (while you underdo) and the two of you could nag each other about weight, finances, sex, etc. The more you can achieve an inner balance by enjoying moderation in a variety of pleasures, the easier the outer balance is likely to become. Questions are also possible regarding who earns the money and how it is spent. Interdependency lets each partner contribute in his or her own area of skills, with differences over handling the resources managed by compromise.

Venus Square/Opposite/Quincunx Ceres (and vice versa)

Your pleasure principle may be at odds with your "mother earth" instincts. You may find duties take you away from what you enjoy. Your need to be of service or to nurture (people, pets, plants, etc.) may vie with your desire to kick back, indulge and seek sensual gratification. Or caretaking responsibilities could compete with partnership goals. You may feel that nurturing or assisting activities are too costly in financial terms (or in terms of enjoying life or a love relationship). You may be at odds with your mother (or a mother figure) in issues involving finances, sensuality, beauty, or your partner(ship). When integrated, this combination inclines toward stability, comfort and tangible results. Gratification comes through **doing.**

Venus Square/Opposite/Quincunx Pallas (and vice versa)

This aspect suggests that pleasure from people might be at odds with pleasure from physical, sensual areas. Financial conflicts with partners are possible. Differing approaches to sensuality and pleasure are possible. An instinct for beauty is accented, but you may be torn between a more tactile approach to aesthetics versus a more visual approach, a preference for a bit of space which allows a wider perspective, arts with a focus on line and form. Your relationships may sometimes be at odds with physical, material demands, but there really is room in life for both. You can enjoy relating to others and still maintain room for your personal, individual forms of gratification.

Venus Square/Opposite/Quincunx Juno (and vice versa)

You may be learning to balance personal pleasures with shared pleasures. Relationships are a likely focus, with the need to integrate what you enjoy with what the other party enjoys, or issues may involve indulgence versus restraint. Financial, sensual or sexual conflicts are possible if one person's gratification is given priority over the other's. Love needs are strong, but equality is essential. Beauty is also highlighted by this pattern, and the further development of artistic or aesthetic talent is quite possible.

Venus Square/Opposite/Quincunx Vesta (and vice versa)

This aspect suggests that you are learning to balance work and play. You may be torn between your dedicated, disciplined, hardworking side versus your relaxed, indulgent, pleasure-loving potential—or between a career and a partner. Until integrated, passivity could vie with productivity, and puritan instincts may war with the pleasure principle. Extremes include working too hard for insufficient remuneration or refusing to work because it is not easy enough or sufficiently enjoyable. By balancing effort with ease and love with work, you can have some of each and reach a constructive synthesis.

Venus Square/Opposite/Quincunx Chiron
or Chiron Square/Opposite/Quincunx Venus (long-term)

This combination points to possible tension between aspirations and ideals versus a comfortable acceptance of everyday life. Finances or other reality factors connected to coping with the material world might limit desired education or travel. Achieving goals may seem to take an unreasonable amount of time or effort. Expectations from relationships may be higher than can be realized. Associates may hold differing beliefs and values that need to be resolved. Compromise is the name of the game. It is possible to have high aspirations, to pursue knowledge, to value freedom, and to still enjoy human companionship and the little "ordinary" pleasures of life.

Venus Square/Opposite/Quincunx Nodes
or Nodes Square/Opposite/Quincunx Venus (long-term)

This combination suggests tension between your security needs and your potential for pleasure, whether from the material world or from people in your life. Usually, the challenges involve close relationships. Personal needs and power may conflict with the power and desires of others. Parental urges may vie with equality instincts. Issues may involve finances or the handling of possessions and appetites or the handling of dependency. Compromise is usually needed to make room in the life for conflicting desires. You can find ways to take turns between various needs and increase the pleasure (on all sides) in your close associations.

Mars Square/Opposite/Quincunx Sun

(See Sun Square/Opposite/Quincunx Mars above).

Mars Square/Opposite/Quincunx Moon

This aspect implies a need to integrate your independent, assertive side with your vulnerable, supportive side. You may experience a sense of tension between doing your own thing versus being closely tied to another person—either taking care of them or being taken care of by them. This could also express as ambivalence in your relationship with your mother—blowing hot/cold, or pulling away when she wants to be close, or feeling she pulls away when you want to be close. You might also have mixed feelings about being a parent—wanting be involved in a caring way, but concerned about being trapped or tied down. You may be changing your home or associates, and feeling ambivalent about the change. Your spontaneous, outgoing, impulsive side could vie with your reticent, protective, inward side—until balance is achieved. Mood swings are possible until you manage to make room for spontaneous expression as well as for holding in when security is at stake. With integration, emotional warmth is likely. Feelings are strong and deep.

Mars Square/Opposite/Quincunx Mercury
(See Mercury Square/Opposite/Quincunx Mars above).

Mars Square/Opposite/Quincunx Venus
(See Venus Square/Opposite/Quincunx Mars above).

Mars Square/Opposite/Quincunx Jupiter
or Jupiter Square/Opposite/Quincunx Mars (long-term)
This is a time when the issues revolve around action, excitement and risks. Confidence and courage may be marked, but foolhardiness (or acting against your better judgment) is also possible. You may be willing to take risks; be sure they are reasonable and that the reward justifies the risk. Issues of faith are often present with this pattern. Too little faith leaves one afraid to act, but too much faith can lead to the "true believer" who pushes his/her version of reality and values aggressively onto others. Incorporate beliefs, values, ethics and morality into your actions in realistic ways. You may make shifts in terms of religion, philosophy, spiritual goals or simply what you want from life. Personal freedom and a desire for change are likely to be very important during this period.

Mars Square/Opposite/Quincunx Saturn
or Saturn Square/Opposite/Quincunx Mars (long-term)
You are facing a challenge between self-will and the limits to self-will presented by the rules of the game of life. If self-will (Mars) is carried to an extreme, you are likely to feel blocked, frustrated, hemmed in, that the world won't let you do all that you want to do. Or, your own health may prove one cannot do **everything**. You may push too hard, trying to control it all—only to discover that there are limits in life. The opposite extreme (overdoing the Saturn side) can find you giving up before you even start—afraid to express any confidence, energy or drive—for fear of falling short, not measuring up, being stopped, put-down, etc. Between these two extremes is the productive middle ground of figuring out what you **can** do (within the rules of the game) that you **want** to do—and doing it! If you manage the integration, this can be a period of great productivity and accomplishment.

Mars Square/Opposite/Quincunx Uranus
or Uranus Square/Opposite/Quincunx Mars (long-term)
"Don't fence me in!" could be a watchword for this period. Your sense of identity is encouraged in a more free-wheeling, independent direction. This can be an innovative, original time period. However, if the resistance to limits is overdone, this aspect can point to the runaway: "If I don't like it, I'll leave!" Not looking before one leaps can also contribute to accidents (as can denying and repressing one's freedom needs—until they burst forth in an uncontrolled fashion). You can be an inventive risk-taker and make a real contribution to the future if your originality is positively expressed. Be true to yourself within reason!

Mars Square/Opposite/Quincunx Neptune
or Neptune Square/Opposite/Quincunx Mars (long-term)

You are facing the issue of self-assertion versus self-sacrifice in this period, or lofty ideals versus the personal ability to reach them. If realism is not maintained, delusions, escapism or other forms of victimization are possible. You could aim for more than is humanly possible and stay frustrated. Or you could swing between trust in your own personal action versus trust in a Higher Power. A constructive balance can include an active pursuit of beauty (including through your own body and actions), and/or doing helping or healing activities, including fighting for causes/ideals in which you believe. Inspired actions are a true possibility, but you must be able to distinguish between inner wisdom and wishful thinking, between your own power and Cosmic Power.

Mars Square/Opposite/Quincunx Pluto
or Pluto Square/Opposite/Quincunx Mars (long-term)

Emotions are likely to be intense and passions strong during this period. Issues around independence and dependence may need to be resolved. Your will is strong, and the handling of power is likely to be important. Constructive sharing of pleasures, finances and resources is essential. Otherwise, power struggles, arguments, fights or abuse, misuse or manipulation are possible (you to others and/or others to you). A goal of this period is to learn to understand yourself through the mirror of another person (especially a mate). Through jockeying for power, each of you potentially gains some self-mastery, partly out of respect for the rights of the other person. That, at least, is a goal of this period. With discrimination, you can engage in healthy competition in sports and business while working out compromises with members of your own "team," your close personal relationships.

Mars Square/Opposite/Quincunx Ceres (and vice versa)

You may feel torn between doing your own thing versus taking an assisting or nurturing role. Independence may vie with being dependent or taking care of others. Your spontaneous, eager side may feel at odds with your careful, discriminating, exacting side that is willing to be practical and to handle details. You will need to integrate the preference for immediate decisions with hesitation to move without due deliberation. You may feel competition between your personal needs and the demands of work or the needs of those you care for. Life can include it all. Be creative in combining your different drives.

Mars Square/Opposite/Quincunx Pallas (and vice versa)

You are facing the polarity of self versus other. You may overdo assertion or accommodation in learning to balance personal needs, wants and desires with those of other people. You may feel torn between being on your own versus sharing with another. Some conflict is possible between you and partners or peers, until issues of equal sharing are resolved. Balance is the key. "Healthy" competition may be helpful, with a "game-playing" attitude that can win or lose and play again. This can occur in sports, games, or business. There are times to compete and times to cooperate. You may begin (or end) a significant relationship as you learn to deal with this "self-other" issue that is so common in the western world when basic material needs have been met.

Mars Square/Opposite/Quincunx Juno (and vice versa)

There is the potential of conflict between personal needs and relationship desires. You may feel somewhat at odds with a partner (especially marriage or committed relationships). Interpersonal strife is possible, until true equality of sharing is achieved. Conflicts might emerge over shared resources (money and possessions), sex, power, or the issue of what is fair. You could also experience inner tension between the desire to be on your own and the urge to share your life with another. This aspect signals an intense form of the "freedom-closeness" dilemma which is very common in the western world once basic material needs have been met. The goal is to make room for both.

Mars Square/Opposite/Quincunx Vesta (and vice versa)

The challenge of this period is to integrate spontaneous self-expression with your need to be productive, to do something practical and do it well. Criticism and/or self-criticism might be overdone in the urge to do things right. You might stop yourself from certain accomplishments because you don't feel you could do them well enough—or push yourself into a workaholic role by trying to do it all! If health challenges occur, they are likely to be related to your feelings about work. Your sense of self-confidence, personal power and good health are strongly related to personal satisfaction with your accomplishments. This can be a highly productive time if you sidestep the extremes of working **too** hard, or giving up too soon, or being only willing to work on your own terms. A successful synthesis can produce major accomplishments when you are working at what you want to do in ways that make the work uniquely yours.

Mars Square/Opposite/Quincunx Chiron
or Chiron Square/Opposite/Quincunx Mars (long-term)

There is a strong fire theme in this combination, usually with some tension between aspirations and goals versus personal power and desires. We may be seeking goals which are difficult to reach, or feel that we should attain them more quickly or more easily. Realism and patience should help resolve the problem. High ideals are fine as long as we enjoy the journey toward them. If we wait until we reach them to be happy, we may stay frustrated for much of our lives. Look for physical outlets which let you build your muscles and your self-confidence, and look for mental outlets which let you gain knowledge or give it to others. Travel may be a stimulating part of your life. If you are ambivalent or unclear about what you really want out of life, this aspect represents an opportunity to clarify what you trust and value so you can make choices based on what is really important to you. Once the important goals are decided, then allow some space for variety and impulse, to satisfy the need to keep moving.

Mars Square/Opposite/Quincunx Nodes
or Nodes Square/Opposite/Quincunx Mars (long-term)

Conflict aspects from Mars to the Moon or to its nodes indicate a possible freedom-closeness or independence-dependence issue. It is normal to want the freedom to do what we please but also to need some sort of emotional support system. For most people, the latter is provided by close human relationships, though it is possible to substitute pets, a home, food, etc. for people connections. Normally, a compromise offers the best solution: emotional ties which allow some space. Individuals who have been overly dependent may need to learn to function more on their own. Individuals who have been reluctant to accept any limits on personal freedom may need to discover that emotional sharing can be rewarding even though it requires compromises.

Ceres Square/Opposite/Quincunx Sun

(See Sun Square/Opposite/Quincunx Ceres above).

Ceres Square/Opposite/Quincunx Moon

Challenges around nurturing are possible. You may have to balance competing needs between various family members or your own desire for emotional protection and safety with that of other people. Separations from home or changes within the nest—or the people occupying it—are possible. You may take steps to manifest the home environment you desire. Interactions with parents, your own parenting duties, or other care taking responsibilities could increase. Your best course is to focus on making your support system as healthy and interdependent as possible.

Ceres Square/Opposite/Quincunx Mercury

(See Mercury Square/Opposite/Quincunx Ceres above).

Ceres Square/Opposite/Quincunx Venus

(See Venus Square/Opposite/Quincunx Ceres above).

Ceres Square/Opposite/Quincunx Mars

(See Mars Square/Opposite/Quincunx Ceres above).

Ceres Square/Opposite/Quincunx Jupiter
or Jupiter Square/Opposite/Quincunx Ceres (long-term)

Conflicting themes may require integration during this period. One side suggests idealism, high expectations and an exploratory quest for answers. Another side suggests pragmatism, facing facts and the details of daily life whether helping others or being helped. Family must be balanced with freedom, and dreams with reality. Expectations, if unreasonably high, could create havoc in relationships at home and at work. Aspirations are healthy if balanced with practicality, if we are satisfied to reach small goals on the way to big ones.

Ceres Square/Opposite/Quincunx Saturn
or Saturn Square/Opposite/Quincunx Ceres (long-term)

This period highlights the need for tangible results. You will feel most satisfied working on projects which end in something physically real or measurable. You need to see, touch, experience the results of your labors. Changes in your career or the details of your job are possible. It is important to be realistic, to avoid trying to do too much (being overly responsible) or seeking to escape all responsibility. There may be tension between work demands and domestic duties with a need for compromise. This aspect could also imply tension between the parenting archetypes: the disciplinarian father archetype versus the more nurturing, supportive mother archetype. Stress between your parents is possible, and could provide an example to help you learn to handle these two sides of life. Parents can teach us what to do (when they have it together) or what not to do (when they have not learned to handle the problem). You can find satisfaction in helpful service and measurable achievements.

Ceres Square/Opposite/Quincunx Uranus
or Uranus Square/Opposite/Quincunx Ceres (long-term)

This period is focused on the integration of theory and practice, of family and friendships. You might feel torn between an abstract overview or intellectual understanding, versus practical hands-on experience. You may experience competing demands from family and friends. Your desire for independence may battle your wish for attachments and accomplishments. Flashes of insight may vie with a cautious, step-by-step approach. By maintaining a place for all, you can make your different desires and talents support and assist one another.

Ceres Square/Opposite/Quincunx Neptune
or Neptune Square/Opposite/Quincunx Ceres (long-term)

The challenge of this period revolves around integrating aspirations and essentials. Expectations of "heaven on earth," whether from one's family, a job, or whatever, invite disillusionment or disappointment. You might want more than is possible or lack clear goals. You need to satisfy your inspired side in a realistic fashion, achieving measurable results as you work toward your dreams. You could be drawn toward and find a measure of fulfillment in artistic activities, helping/healing pursuits, or anything that brings your ideals into everyday reality.

Ceres Square/Opposite/Quincunx Pluto
or Pluto Square/Opposite/Quincunx Ceres (long-term)

Tension is possible between your urge for intimacy and your drive for efficient functioning. Domestic duties or job routines might compete with partners for your time and energy. Work might seem at odds with relationships. You may feel torn between being an equal versus being in a parenting association (as either parent or child in the interaction). You may have good organizational skills, but be susceptible to overly critical judgment. Keep the criticism aimed at the job, not at other people. This can be a very productive period both materially and emotionally if you maintain some degree of moderation and flexibility.

Ceres Square/Opposite/Quincunx Pallas (and vice versa)
During this period, tension is possible between your parenting instincts and your equalitarian needs. You may feel pulled between being strong, helpful, assisting and supportive, versus taking turns with others, looking to someone else to do their part, to share the load. You could feel that relationship and career demands compete in your life. You might experience friction between a partner and your family. It may take time and effort and compromises to get the people in your life working together and pulling in the same direction.

Ceres Square/Opposite/Quincunx Juno (and vice versa)
Themes of attachment and competence are highlighted. You may feel pulled between roles as a parent, a partner, or a worker. Time and energy demands connected to a job could compete with domestic duties and desires. You may feel a spouse or partner takes you away from nurturing tasks or vice versa. A parent may vie with other relationships. Children could compete with a spouse (and vice versa). It is necessary to compromise to make time to be a caretaker, a peer, an achiever, and for mutual needs to be met.

Ceres Square/Opposite/Quincunx Vesta (and vice versa)
Efficient functioning is in high focus during this period. You may be involved with health or healing issues. You could be searching for the best way to maintain physical well-being. Work challenges are also possible. An overly critical attitude could be a problem, especially with colleagues or family. You need to find a useful outlet for your urge to repair, fix and make-over things or people. This can be a highly productive period if you keep your critical side focused on your work. The capacity to organize, to be practical, and to work hard are the keys to success, but remember that life includes more than one's work.

Ceres Square/Opposite/Quincunx Chiron
or Chiron Square/Opposite/Quincunx Ceres (long-term)
This pattern suggests tension between goals/values/aspirations and the realities of obligations in a material world. The urge to escape, to be free to pursue high ambitions or just to do what you please, may be in conflict with the need to earn a living or to care for family members. A compromise calls for allowing some space for studies, travel, or just being part of the wider world while still working effectively in an ordinary job, on unexciting daily tasks. Life should have room

for the visions of something more and better, while not neglecting the necessity of coping with survival in a physical world.

Ceres Square/Opposite/Quincunx Nodes
or Nodes Square/Opposite/Quincunx Ceres (long-term)

This pattern suggests tension centered around material and/or emotional security. Pressures may stem from work demands which conflict with family obligations. There may be questions about dependency versus nurturing and a need to work out an equitable sharing of the load. With mutual sensitivity to the feelings of all concerned, it should be possible to build a support system that offers joint protection.

Pallas Square/Opposite/Quincunx Sun

(See Sun Square/Opposite/Quincunx Pallas above).

Pallas Square/Opposite/Quincunx Moon

Equalitarian instincts are competing with nurturing, protective drives. You may feel torn between devoting yourself to children or family members versus a spouse or devoted partner. There could be conflicts between parents and a partner or children and a partner. You might be working on the balance between the objective intellect and your feeling nature. Competitive urges may vie with your desire to succor others. Your beauty instincts could pull you away from safety and security. The goal is to find a way to take turns caring for others and being cared for, to reach a degree of equity with loved ones, to share in many different ways.

Pallas Square/Opposite/Quincunx Mercury

(See Mercury Square/Opposite/Quincunx Pallas above).

Pallas Square/Opposite/Quincunx Venus

(See Venus Square/Opposite/Quincunx Pallas above).

Pallas Square/Opposite/Quincunx Mars

(See Mars Square/Opposite/Quincunx Pallas above).

Pallas Square/Opposite/Quincunx Jupiter
or Jupiter Square/Opposite/Quincunx Pallas (long-term)

This period focuses on the interaction between dreams/ideals and justice/equality. You could be active in pursuing fair play or social causes. It is also possible that excessively high expectations (from you to others or from others to you) could affect your interpersonal relationships. Other people may challenge your faith, values or goals. The urge to explore a wider world might war with your desire to stay put to share life with a close associate. Keenness of mind and wit are often emphasized with this aspect, along with fun and liveliness, but tact might be needed at times. Don't let your aspirations or rigid beliefs and values disturb your sense of balance and ability to see both sides of issues. Do encourage the best through your relationships and/or through involvement with larger, social concerns such as the law, politics, and working as a consultant.

Pallas Square/Opposite/Quincunx Saturn
or Saturn Square/Opposite/Quincunx Pallas (long-term)

You may be working on the resolution of power drives versus the urge to be equal. If there is tension with authorities or with partners over the question of when to be in charge and when to cooperate on a peer basis, try to clarify the limits of your responsibility and authority. Alternately, you might feel pulled between work demands and relationship needs. With integration, you can choose appropriate times for teamwork and togetherness and other times for responsible effort in an executive role. You might find satisfaction from producing things that are both beautiful and useful. Or you may be drawn into working for social causes. Stay conscious of the realistic limits of power, of individuals, groups, and the laws of life.

Pallas Square/Opposite/Quincunx Uranus
or Uranus Square/Opposite/Quincunx Pallas (long-term)

This could be a sociable period, including much activity with other people. You may, however, feel a bit of tension between casual friendships and more committed relationships. You could feel ambivalent about the degree of closeness you seek with other people. Objectivity is likely to be stronger than usual, and you may find it easy to see alternate points of view. You may innovate in relationships or in artistic pursuits. You may make changes in your interactions with others, but are likely to seek an intellectual understanding of it all. Involvement in social causes is possible, including law and politics.

Pallas Square/Opposite/Quincunx Neptune
or Neptune Square/Opposite/Quincunx Pallas (long-term)

Grace and beauty are highlighted, but may bring challenges. Personal idealism or aspirations could be at odds with the ideals of other people. More than is possible might be sought in relationships, leading to savior/victim associations or an escape into fantasy if real people do not measure up to an inner dream. Harmony (or competitiveness) could be overvalued and overdone in the life. A downside potential is running away into fantasy, passivity or chronic dissatisfaction because people or society or life are not ideal enough. More constructively, you can make room in your life for aesthetics and the quest for inspiration—sharing both with others.

Pallas Square/Opposite/Quincunx Pluto
or Pluto Square/Opposite/Quincunx Pallas (long-term)

Relationship issues are emphasized by this aspect. You may feel pulled between a deep, intense, absorbing bond versus a more casual, intellectual connection that allows some separation and space between. Your intense emotional side might vie with a more detached, logical side. You may feel torn in different directions in terms of partnership goals and needs. Integration calls for bringing together the objective and the subjective, the more casual and the intense, your mind and gut into a harmonious whole. Despite the tension (or sometimes because of it), this can be a good period for expanding your understanding of the human psyche. You may function as a counselor or consultant or work to support social causes.

Pallas Square/Opposite/Quincunx Ceres
(See Ceres Square/Opposite/Quincunx Pallas above).

Pallas Square/Opposite/Quincunx Juno (and vice versa)
This combination is centered on associations with other people. Some inner conflict is implied between different desires. You may feel pulled between seeking an intense, emotional, absorbing bond versus a friendly, intellectual, objective connection. Friendships or other associations, including concern with the needs of society, may compete with a primary partnership. Heart and mind may vie with one another in regard to your interpersonal interactions. You may perceive a lack of equality, fair play, balance or harmony in your life and strive to rectify it. As usual, solutions are likely to require compromise.

Pallas Square/Opposite/Quincunx Vesta (and vice versa)
This aspect suggests tension between a "fix-it" (repairing) orientation and the capacity to accept people and things as they are. You could feel pulled between the desire to improve situations and merely observing or understanding them. Tolerance could vie with criticism. Equality and taking turns might compete with your desire to do things yourself (to insure they get done right). Time and energy demands of your work might compete with time and energy needs for relationships. You are learning to balance openness, objectivity and observation with critical judgment, the desire to **do**, and personal effort: partly learning when to do which.

Pallas Square/Opposite/Quincunx Chiron
or Chiron Square/Opposite/Quincunx Pallas (long-term)
This combination suggests tension between ideals and comfortable, peer rela-
tionships. You may want more than is possible in a partner or be dealing with another person who expects too much of you. There may be differences in beliefs, values, or goals between you and close associates. Your need for freedom to pursue knowledge or personal ideals may make it difficult to establish a close relationship. Compromise is the name of the game. Life should be big enough to include a mutually accepting, caring partnership as well as opportunities to explore a wider world. With some willingness to compromise on both sides, you can enjoy both close relationships and participation in new

adventures of the mind and spirit. The latter could include increased involvement in social causes, law or politics, or just making new friends.

Pallas Square/Opposite/Quincunx Nodes
or Nodes Square/Opposite/Quincunx Pallas (long-term)

This combination suggests tension connected to relationships and security issues. Compromises may be necessary to achieve equality while still satisfying the need to nurture or to be nurtured. It may seem difficult to satisfy both children and a mate. Or family obligations may interfere with artistic expressions, with pleasure with friends, or with the desire to play a role in the transpersonal realm working for social causes. You have the capacity to be both sensitive and empathic to the feelings of others but also intellectually logical and objective. The best compromise usually leads to interdependence where everyone can both give and receive.

Juno Square/Opposite/Quincunx Sun

(See Sun Square/Opposite/Quincunx Juno above).

Juno Square/Opposite/Quincunx Moon

Differing drives for closeness may compete with one another: attachment to a home and/or family members, sharing with a spouse, and caring connections with parents and/or children. Family members may vie with one another for your time and attention. You may feel torn between relating as a vulnerable child (requiring protection), an equal partner, or protective parent. How resources are shared could come up for discussion and resolution. Now is the time to be clear in your closest associations—to get and give the love and support you need.

Juno Square/Opposite/Quincunx Mercury

(See Mercury Square/Opposite/Quincunx Juno above).

Juno Square/Opposite/Quincunx Venus

(See Venus Square/Opposite/Quincunx Juno above).

Juno Square/Opposite/Quincunx Mars

(See Mars Square/Opposite/Quincunx Juno above).

Juno Square/Opposite/Quincunx Jupiter
or Jupiter Square/Opposite/Quincunx Juno (long-term)

Trouble in Paradise? Dreams, values, goals, aspirations or beliefs are likely to rouse conflicts in relationships. You or a partner (often marital) may expect more than is humanly possible. Differing goals, philosophies or life directions may create conflict. Questions of justice are likely to arise, especially concerning the fair allocation of resources, money and pleasures. A sense of humor will help lighten any conflicts and seeing the best in one another can help to work out compromises.

Alternately, it is possible that freedom needs, educational aspirations, or spiritual pursuits may conflict with commitment in human relationships. Life can make room for both unless we choose to be religious celibates. This is a time to find visions and objectives you can share with a partner.

Juno Square/Opposite/Quincunx Saturn
or Saturn Square/Opposite/Quincunx Juno (long-term)

This period highlights the need to balance relationships and career, or equality and power. You may feel torn between time and energy demands by a partner versus by your work. Conflicts with a partner (especially marital) could revolve around basic reality issues and what each of you sees as the necessary limits or rules in life. If either of you tries to dominate the other, tension is likely. You are learning when to take charge in life and when to cooperate as an equal. Beauty and pleasure might seem at odds with life's necessary demands and duties. The key to a more satisfying life is make room for both.

Juno Square/Opposite/Quincunx Uranus
or Uranus Square/Opposite/Quincunx Juno (long-term)

This period suggests the need to balance intimacy instincts with your desire for freedom and change, always wanting something better. You (or a partner) may look for a bit more space in a committed relationship. You could make some changes, shake up the status quo, or move toward more tolerance and acceptance of one another. If debating a relationship, the ambivalence is still accentuated; you need to be sure you keep room in your life for both intense involvement and independent action. If either person tries to dominate or coerce or possess the other, intense power struggles are possible. Will power and resistance to control are emphasized. Friends might seem to compete with lovers, or intellectual demands with emotional needs, but it is possible to keep room for both!

Juno Square/Opposite/Quincunx Neptune
or Neptune Square/Opposite/Quincunx Juno (long-term)

The quest for infinite love and beauty may conflict with your human desire for intimacy and sharing with another person. This could indicate unrealistic expectations on the part of you or your partner. It might point to subconscious attraction toward savior/victim scenarios. It might indicate over-romanticism, reluctance to see what is really there, or the placing of too much faith in a human being, which could lead to deception and/or disillusionment. If you keep one foot on the ground, your search for something higher in life (through religion, spirituality, art, causes, etc.) can be shared with a partner for mutual support and benefit.

Juno Square/Opposite/Quincunx Pluto
or Pluto Square/Opposite/Quincunx Juno (long-term)

Issues around depth emotions, mate relationships, shared resources, finances and pleasures are likely in this period. You may feel ambivalent about when and where to exercise discipline and self-control. You may experience power struggles (or manipulation/intimidation) with a spouse or mate. Conflicts over sexuality, sensuality or money and possessions are possible until all concerned learn to compromise. One goal is for both individuals to learn to control and master themselves out of respect for the rights of the other. Tuning in to one another's feelings can assist the process; you are likely to be more intuitively open to a partner's emotions during this period. Expanded empathy and awareness can also be used in fields such as counseling, psychotherapy and hypnosis.

Juno Square/Opposite/Quincunx Ceres

(See Ceres Square/Opposite/Quincunx Juno above).

Juno Square/Opposite/Quincunx Pallas

(See Pallas Square/Opposite/Quincunx Juno above).

Juno Square/Opposite/Quincunx Vesta (and vice versa)

This aspect focuses on learning to integrate love and work. You may feel that your job takes you away from relationships, or vice versa. You could feel pulled between the time and energy needed for a career, versus the time and energy devoted to a spouse or partner. Criticism could be an issue in your exchanges with other people. A practical approach to shared resources (including money and sexuality) may require extra effort in order to achieve a compromise. Balance requires both effort and ease, accomplishments and intimacy, tangible results and emotional attachments.

Juno Square/Opposite/Quincunx Chiron
or Chiron Square/Opposite/Quincunx Juno (long-term)

This combination suggests tension between the desire for close relationships and the desire for something more ideal. Sometimes, the expectations are too high. Conflicting beliefs and values may be a problem in relationships. One individual in a partnership may want more space to explore while the other wants a closer bond: wider horizons versus more intense intimacy. If either partner tries to control the other, there are likely to be serious problems, including power struggles. A compromise solution is possible if both partners are able to respect the individuality of the other; to have a commitment without trying to possess the other. Mutual faith and trust are essential to permit mutual pleasure.

Juno Square/Opposite/Quincunx Nodes
or Nodes Square/Opposite/Quincunx Juno (long-term)

This combination suggests possible tension around security issues and relationships. There may be friction between family and a mate. Issues of dependency and power are possible. Seek interdependency with each individual able both to give and to receive. Strong emotions and sensitivity are likely with this pattern. If security is too tied to one or more relationships, it may be hard to let go when it is time to focus more on personal self-reliance. Try to enjoy emotional ties and closeness, but do not make your happiness depend on them.

Vesta Square/Opposite/Quincunx Sun

(See Sun Square/Opposite/Quincunx Vesta above).

Vesta Square/Opposite/Quincunx Moon

Conflicts may develop between family needs and work demands. You might feel burdened, as if you have to take care of everyone. Emotional as well as practical duties may weigh heavily upon you. Health concerns (for you or loved ones) could arise or criticism or alienation could become a challenge. Now is the time to mobilize family members to help you out, to aim for cooperative, mutually supportive pursuits. Common sense steps to add to your security are appropriate along with setting up emotional ties that will aid you in your accomplishments.

Vesta Square/Opposite/Quincunx Mercury

(See Mercury Square/Opposite/Quincunx Vesta above).

Vesta Square/Opposite/Quincunx Venus

(See Venus Square/Opposite/Quincunx Vesta above).

Vesta Square/Opposite/Quincunx Mars

(See Mars Square/Opposite/Quincunx Vesta above).

Vesta Square/Opposite/Quincunx Jupiter
or Jupiter Square/Opposite/Quincunx Vesta (long-term)

The potential exists of stress between aspirations and accomplishments. Although both energy and competence are highlighted, extremes are possible. You might succumb to perfectionistic standards—always wanting a little bit more, better, faster—never quite satisfied. You might inhibit or hold back from starting projects or be dissatisfied with results due to excessive criticism or nit-picking. You might go overboard with faith and trust, reaching for an impossible dream. Analyze your goals. Look for small steps that will take you closer to bigger aspirations. Then try to enjoy the journey as you channel your optimism and confidence into capable and productive attainments.

Vesta Square/Opposite/Quincunx Saturn
or Saturn Square/Opposite/Quincunx Vesta (long-term)

Efficient functioning and facing reality are highlighted in this period. The issues might revolve around bodily health and well-being, or around your work or tasks in the world. Frustration connected to work can be one of the causes of health problems, so it is important to find something that will give you a sense of accomplishment, something that you feel is worth doing that you can do well. Guard against overwork or too much nit-picking, including self-criticism that can lead to giving up or never being satisfied. Organizational skills are emphasized by this aspect, and you could be quite thorough and persevering. Power drives (and relations with authorities) may conflict with the willingness to offer humble service. You may need to budget time and know when to say "no"—to let someone else do the job. If you are clear about what is possible and what is necessary, and working voluntarily, you can turn this period into one of considerable accomplishments.

Vesta Square/Opposite/Quincunx Uranus
or Uranus Square/Opposite/Quincunx Vesta (long-term)

You may experience some tension between your free-wheeling, inventive and innovative side versus your careful, linear, discriminating side. Sudden insights may vie with step-by-step analysis. Abstract, intellectual overviews could compete with a pragmatic, hands-on approach to problems. Friends may seem to compete with your work (or vice versa). Changes, new technology or something unusual or different may threaten your job unless you learn new skills and adjust to the shifts and freedom. An experimental, open-minded but also practical attitude will help you make the most of your possibilities.

Vesta Square/Opposite/Quincunx Neptune
or Neptune Square/Opposite/Quincunx Vesta (long-term)

You are dealing with polarized issues during this period: parts versus whole; material versus spiritual; effort versus passivity; discipline versus receptivity; and realism versus idealism. If you are able to integrate these opposites, you can get the best from both sides. You may be drawn toward artistic creations (especially of a practical nature), toward helping/assisting activities, toward health enhancement, or toward work which is inspirational and uplifting.

Vesta Square/Opposite/Quincunx Pluto
or Pluto Square/Opposite/Quincunx Vesta (long-term)

This period emphasizes the need to bring together intense emotional drives toward intimacy with the desire to do a good job, to be competent and get things done. Your work might seem to compete with relationship needs or vice versa. A critical attitude might interfere with loving closeness (from you to others or others to you). If you remember that we can only change ourselves, not others, this could be a time when you improve, repair, make-over or transform your intimate associations for the better. You could also work with joint resources, in fields such as accounting, taxes, or investments, or be drawn toward research, the past, or hidden areas. Your primary power can be used to increase personal discipline and self-mastery, and to achieve productive results.

Vesta Square/Opposite/Quincunx Ceres
(See Ceres Square/Opposite/Quincunx Vesta above).

Vesta Square/Opposite/Quincunx Pallas
(See Pallas Square/Opposite/Quincunx Vesta above).

Vesta Square/Opposite/Quincunx Juno
(See Juno Square/Opposite/Quincunx Vesta above).

Vesta Square/Opposite/Quincunx Chiron
or Chiron Square/Opposite/Quincunx Vesta (long-term)
This combination points to tension between ideals and practical necessities. You may just want to do more than is humanly possible. Or your job may fail to use your talents, may be too routine and repetitive, may offer few opportunities for independent judgment and action, or may contribute less than you would like to the well-being of the world. Life always demands compromise, but if a job is too frustrating, there is some danger of illness produced by the subconscious mind to get us out of the frustration. If work is necessary (as it is for all except the very wealthy), it is important to find something that seems worth doing that we can do well without demanding a perfect job or expecting ourselves to do it perfectly. With a reasonable compromise, this pattern can bring the intellect and ideals into productive action in the world, to provide you with a sense of accomplishment and to make the world a little better as a result of your presence in it.

Vesta Square/Opposite/Quincunx Nodes
or Nodes Square/Opposite/Quincunx Vesta (long-term)
This combination points to tension involving work and security issues. Available jobs may fail to satisfy your physical or emotional needs. Or they may conflict with your family obligations. Illness is a hazard when we become too frustrated with our work, as the subconscious enables us to escape the job. Sometimes an earth-water emphasis is a sign that we are taking ourselves and life too seriously and we need to lighten up. Practical realism and emotional sensitivity are both emphasized in this pattern, so you have the capacity to cope with the situation by combining your ability to work and your ability to be aware of the feelings of others. An effective integration of the principles calls for balance between handling your share of the responsibility and allowing others to do their share.

Chiron Square/Opposite/Quincunx Nodes (See Chapter Two).

CHAPTER ELEVEN
ASPECTS OF PROGRESSED MOON

This section examines aspects from the progressed Moon. The Moon is a key to our basic need for emotional security. We may seek this through home and family, with pets, by caring for other people, or looking to others to care for us, from food, or from other sources of reassurance.

Progressed Moon aspects are shorter than those involving other progressed planets, but they are still important. In terms of timing, people are most likely to take action or experience changes during the period when the progressed Moon forms aspects to other planets in a configuration or network of aspects.

Aspects from the progressed Moon to other planets or angles indicate that our emotional security needs are interacting with other desires and needs in our lives. Sextiles and trines normally suggest that we can easily combine these various drives. Conflict aspects (squares, oppositions and quincunxes) imply tension between different needs and desires and normally call for compromise.

The natal chart pictures our fundamental nature unless we have changed dramatically. Natally, the Moon might have had a conflict or harmony relationship (or no aspect) with the planets featured currently. We may have shifted from natal harmony to progressed conflict or from natal conflict to progressed harmony, but the natal pattern always colors the current situation.

Integration means expressing all sides of ourselves (symbolized by the different astrological factors)—either taking turns or compromising by being moderate in our manifestation of the different parts of life.

As mentioned in Chapter 9, the progressed Moon also operates as an important "timer" in the chart. With each of the aspects interpreted below, you can also view the Moon as merely "highlighting" the issues of the planet it is aspecting, saying: "This is important." Rulerships can also be relevant. Thus, the progressed Moon activating any planet which rules the 2nd house can be emphasizing the matter of money, resources, pleasures, and possessions for that two-month period of the aspect. So, consider both the nature of the planet being aspected by the Moon and the nature of the houses which that planet occupies and rules.

When outer planets aspect the natal Moon—for long periods of time—they highlight similar issues as the progressed Moon aspecting them, but those issues remain in focus for a much longer time. Where long-term aspects are possible, the first paragraph gives a summary pertinent to the progressed Moon aspect, while later paragraphs cover some of the potentials which last for years with outer planets aspecting the natal Moon.

Conjunctions

Progressed Moon Conjunct Natal Sun

(Progressed Moon Conjunct Progressed Sun is a New Moon—discussed in Chapter 4.)
Emotional security needs and warmth are in high focus. Family feelings may be strong, with procreative and nurturing instincts emphasized. Attachments to loved ones are important. Emotional support is a desired goal; mutual admiration is quite possible. You may feel a bit torn between expressing your feelings versus holding them in, or between holding on to the past versus reaching out to create a new future. You have the opportunity for a new beginning, particularly where emotions, loved ones and self-esteem are involved.

Progressed Moon Conjunct Natal Moon

This period suggests a strong focus on emotional needs. You may be more nurturing, more dependent, or more involved in the search for emotional security. Home, family, mother(ing), food, land or the public could be highlighted. You may be more intuitive/psychic. You could face yourself and your emotional needs through women (females) in your life. Provide a sense of safety, nourishment and protection for yourself.

(The remainder of aspects discussed are from progressed Moon to either natal **or** progressed planets and asteroids.)

Moon Conjunct Mercury

You may naturally blend thoughts and feelings, bringing together logic and intuition in your life. Family or relatives could be an important focus, as you seek to communicate in the realm of feelings. An adaptable, flexible attitude about domestic issues can be quite valuable. Current activities could involve studies, writing, travel or developments in the neighborhood.

Moon Conjunct Venus

You are likely to experience a more sensual period, with more of a "touchy feely" orientation. Pleasure might center on food, family, safety or emotional attachments. The known, the secure and the predictable are likely to appeal. You might make money (or gain gratification) through the land, public, women or close, feeling ties. You may channel some of your emotions into art or into loving and being loved. A focus on comfort is likely.

Moon Conjunct Mars

Strong feelings are suggested, with potential push/pull between expressing versus holding in. If you sit on your emotions, personal outbursts are possible, or other people around you may be explosive. Strive for constructive outlets, for regular expressions of what is going on inside without going to extremes. Much personal focus on family, emotional needs, home, safety and security is likely. You are learning to balance your assertive and your protective instincts; your "me first" tendencies with your desire for emotional attachments. With integration, much emotional warmth is likely and you can achieve a good balance between being yourself and assisting others.

Moon Conjunct Jupiter

You may look to religion, philosophy, education, travel, metaphysics or faith for a sense of safety, security and assurance. You might experience some tension between your desire for roots and your quest for ideals which can take you to the ends of the Earth. You might question the beliefs and values held by your family. Alternately, you might idealize your home and/or family and need to accept human limitations. You are striving to combine your emotional needs with your intellectual expansion, keeping room for protection and support along with adventures and exploration, looking for something better.

Jupiter Conjunct Moon (long-term)

Security issues are confronting the drive for adventures and exploration, searching for an ideal. Which side wins out—or if a balance prevails—depends on the bulk of your nature (as shown by the rest of the horoscope). One option is finding your security in exploration. This could lead to travel, living abroad, adventuring with emotions and turning the world into your home. Another option is finding your adventures in the home. This could lead to bringing lots of books, intellectual discussions, foreigners, philosophy or religion into your home.

The freedom/closeness ambivalence over settling down versus searching for something better may also affect feelings about motherhood (nurturing). One person may see nurturing as an ultimate value and want lots of children. Another person may avoid parenting if they cannot be the perfect parent of perfect children, brought into a perfect world. That individual is likely to have zero children. Since the security needs of small children also threaten the freedom needs represented by Jupiter, having a family or settled home life may be put off until some distant "perfect" time.

It is not uncommon for a high value to be placed on the home, but the individual may still spend a lot of time away, seeking answers and whatever they define as ultimately important in life. High expectations for family, mother and mothering are also common. There can be mutual idealization (each seeing only the highest potential in the other) or mutual dissatisfaction with the lack of perfection in the other party.

Integration and a moderate, middle ground approach allows individuals to value their homes and families (without everything having to be ideal), to enjoy domesticity and still get out and about a lot, to have a permanent home but be able to travel, to have standards and ethics and principles, but realize life is a process growing toward perfection and no one has reached that exalted stage yet.

Moon Conjunct Saturn

Your emotional needs may center more around safety, not rocking the boat, basic survival and dealing with the limits/rules of the world. Productive work which encourages a sense of accomplishment and confidence in your ability to cope with the world can counteract the danger of anxiety or depression. It is important to also maintain an emotional support system with family or friends. Events during this period are like a report card, providing feedback on how you are doing in handling the "rules of the game." Handle your share of the responsibility and allow other people to handle their own. Do what is within your power and then let go. A sense of humor also helps.

Saturn Conjunct Moon (long-term)

This period emphasizes a polarity in your nature. Like any potential seesaw, we need both ends. The challenge is to make a place for both, in moderation, so that our life is richer. In this case, the polar opposites involve compassion, warmth, protection, home, family and emotions versus pragmatism, responsibility, rules, facing facts, career, status and the bottom line. One might also call this the "mother versus father" polarity. These are the themes you are seeking to balance.

One extreme overdoes the "father" role—too strong, dominating, controlling, practical, over-responsible. Another extreme overdoes the "mother" role—too gentle, over-protective, supportive and caring. Or, you might attract people into your life who are eager to play "Mom" or "Dad" to your "child" role. These issues can be played out with your own parents or in your interactions as a parent. You could bounce between home versus career, compassion versus control, or other extremes in this seesaw.

Integration requires creating time and space for feelings, emotional needs and family interactions, while also making time and space for career demands, common sense, survival needs and the practical necessities of life. Competent caring, compassionate capability, and loving limits contribute to your success-ful balancing of both family and success in the career world.

Moon Conjunct Uranus

This may be a period of unanticipated change. Your emotional support may be based on friends, the new, the unusual, or anything on the cutting edge. You may be pulled between a desire for freedom, uniqueness and independence versus an urge for close, caring attachments in a secure nest. Or you may feel pulled between the past and the future, between the intellect and the emotions. Try to find ways to care and be cared for which still cherish the individuality of everyone concerned.

Uranus Conjunct Moon (long-term)

This period suggests a time when you are striving to combine two very different drives. One part of your nature is concerned with security, protection, nurturing, emotional vulnerabilities, home, family, safety and the past. Another part is drawn toward change, risks, the new, the different, the unusual, the intellect, friends, and freedom. Doing a bit of both can be a challenge.

If you flip from one extreme to the other, you could cling to people and then break loose when you start to feel trapped. You might swing from absorption in the past to fascination with the future; from being a "super-supportive" parent to "I'm just your objective friend"; from protecting or being protected to being defiantly independent, etc. Or, you could express one end of this seesaw, while someone near and dear to you lives out another side. You could feel pulled between friends and family, social organization and children, individuality and your domestic role.

Emotions could change suddenly as you deal with these issues. You may also experience intuitive flashes. By using your capacity to tune in to other people, you have an additional talent to help you achieve balance. You can nurture friends, be friends with family and still have room in life for both independence and dependence, risks and safety.

Moon Conjunct Neptune

Intuitive perceptions are closer to the surface at this time. You may have richer dreams, visions, fantasies. You can tune in to the subconscious, and may be inspired by your Higher Self. But psychic openness can also be experienced as vulnerability. Faith in a higher power is essential during this period, to counter-act the danger of anxiety or depression over the contrast between high ideals and actual life. You seek an atmosphere of beauty and grace, of harmony and peace. If you overidealize what human relationships can provide, you may want more than is reasonable from family members. Appreciate and support the best in the people who share your life, but look to a higher power for ultimate faith and security.

Neptune Conjunct Moon (long-term)

This aspect marks a time of extreme sensitivity. You may feel drawn toward experiences that are soft, subtle, mysterious, gentle and flowing. With two water planets conjuncting, the inner world is important. Emotions are likely to be stronger than average, but you may also be inclined to keep things inside and not reveal them. (If the rest of your chart is strongly fire, you could get involved with people who express this water reticence and sensitivity for you.) Psychic insights are possible, but you may not realize how much you know, just instinctively "going with the flow."

Some idealization of home, family, mother(ing) is possible. This can range from beautifying the home, dealing with a victim in the family, idealizing mother(ing), looking for the perfect home/family/parent or seeking the best in all those areas. If rose-colored glasses are not overdone, family members can use this time to support one another's highest potentials. Insecurity and lack of faith can lead to escapist activities, to running away from an "ugly" or threatening reality. Shared faith can work wonders, and inspirations from art, nature, beauty or religion build the sense of emotional protection and safety.

Moon Conjunct Pluto

Your psychic ability and your emotions are intensified, but you are likely to internalize much of what you are feeling. Now is an appropriate time to think in therapy terms: figuring out your deeper feelings and channeling them in constructive directions. You may probe at buried emotions and use this period to open up and clean up old garbage (including forgiving yourself and/or others and remembering that everyone is human). You may wish to investigate and deal with the state of your shared finances and resources, anything coming from or owed to others, to ensure a greater degree of security.

Pluto Conjunct Moon (long-term)

Psychological depths are highlighted by this aspect. The issues revolve around intense feelings. This can be a time of emotional transformation, with a depth commitment to another person and a caring confrontation of one's own inner drives and motives. It can also be a time of emotional withdrawal, a retreat from perceived threats and a sense of being overwhelmed by the demands of others. Feelings can be so intense that "smothering" is experienced.

Buried issues with mother (or one's own feelings about parenting) may emerge. Commonly, there is a psychic link with the mother or mother figure, and many of her subconscious needs/drives have been picked up (without awareness) by you. You could be living out some of her "scripts" for life; getting a handle on what you want to keep and what you want to throw away of her "stuff" would be very helpful. Where mothering is concerned, emotional boundaries may be breached, invaded and overwhelmed. In such cases, withdrawal is a necessary and self-protective measure. (In severe situations, actual abuse is involved.)

Once you achieve a sense of inner security and power, there is likely to be a desire for an intense, intimate connection with a mate. Mutual support becomes very important, but the two of you must balance nurturing so that one does not end up playing "parent" all of the time while the other remains in the child role. You have a tremendous capacity for intimacy and could get involved with someone who moves you very deeply. Psychic attunement with a mate is possible. You may understand one another without words.

Moon Conjunct Ceres (and vice versa)

A double focus on nurturing and closeness issues suggests a time when family matters may be paramount. Involvement with children, nurturing or caretaking activities is likely. You are capable of emotional and practical support (or might look to others for it). Parents or your role as a parent may be a focus. Helpful, compassionate instincts are likely to be highlighted.

Mother(ing) is the watchword for this period. The focus revolves around issues of nurturing, support, dependency, vulnerability and emotional security needs. You may face these issues primarily through interactions with your own mother (or mother figure), through your role as a parent, through nurturing/assisting activities in which you participate (at work, in hobbies, etc.), or through being taken care of by others.

Generally, you are likely to be drawn toward a parenting role during this period—if at all possible (given age, life circumstances, etc.). If you are female and biologically fertile, pregnancy is very possible during this whole period. If you do not want to get pregnant (or, if a male, to "father" a child), be very careful in your precautions! If you are outside the age of pregnancy, children could come into your life through adoption, marriage, grandparenting, etc. Other nurturing activities are also possible, including caring for pets and plants.

If you are not comfortable with your own dependency needs, illness could be a subconscious mechanism for receiving a little "TLC." By taking turns being vulnerable and protected versus cherishing and caring for others, you encourage balance and health in your life.

Moon Conjunct Pallas (and vice versa)

You are apt to be emotionally focused on relationships. Interdependence is important now—to be able to care for others and to be cared for. You particularly need a sense of nurturing in your partnership(s) during this period. You may also find emotional support through beauty or aesthetic activities. You have the potential of blending logical perceptions and emotional impressions for the fullest understanding.

Closeness is a featured theme for this period. Emotional security is connected to relationships and balance. Usually this correlates with a strong desire for partnership. This can include marriage, or simply a significant emotional commitment. You are likely to want a relationship which features strong emotional support and caring. Mutual nurturing is appropriate. If this theme is out of balance, one partner may fall into the role of "baby," with the other playing the role of "mother." Equality might take a bit of work, but the desire for balance and fairness makes the effort worthwhile.

You may feel the urge to beautify your home or domestic environment. Your emotional reactions are more strongly attuned to beauty and aesthetics. Surrounding yourself with harmony helps to maintain your inner security. You can nurture yourself (and your family) through creating beauty.

Moon Conjunct Juno (and vice versa)

Sharing, commitment, attachments and closeness are central themes now. You may be ready for a deeper level of association. You may further explore interdependency, especially in your partnership(s). Emotional support from and to a spouse/partner becomes more central. You may also get sustenance from beauty/artistic activities.

Commitment is a central theme for this period. With the asteroid of marriage and the planet of home and family joining forces, thinking about "domestic bliss" is extremely likely. Usually, the urge is for a permanent love relationship, or for strengthening and deepening already-existing bonds. If the rest of your chart is very freedom-oriented, you could subconsciously attract a partner to express this very family-oriented side for you. Generally, this aspect suggests a strong focus on love, caring, emotional support and a solid home life.

Security, fidelity, commitment, support and protection are part of the picture. This can be a time when one spouse (or partner) depends a bit more than usual on the other (perhaps due to illness or other stress in the life). If carried too far, the partnership can become more like a parent/child association. If the spouses are able to take turns caring for one another, it is healthy, human interdependency. Each has something to give that the other can receive.

An urge to bring more beauty, grace, pleasure or aesthetic activities into the home is also possible. The desire for harmony and balance may be satisfied through artistic endeavors or "house beautiful" activities. In general, this is a time to explore the concept that "Love means being there for each other."

Moon Conjunct Vesta (and vice versa)

This period may be a time when you find your security in hard work and doing something **really** well. You might choose to focus more intently on your job, or take up a regimen to improve your health. Apply your critical ability to your work to avoid self-criticism or alienation from other people. Tangible results are important now, but you also need to share emotional connections with others.

This period highlights a productive focus connected to emotional issues. You may do repair work on close relationships, especially those involving nurturing and dependency issues. Flaws are likely to be spotted, with an impetus for fixing them. Efficiency of emotions is one of the themes. If these motives are misdirected, home and family (including mother or mother figure) could be the source of (or recipient of) criticism, judgment and nit-picking. You (or Mom, or the family) might seem impossible to please. There is a danger of alienation from personal relationships. A contributing factor can be the focus on work. If feelings are seen as inefficient, a person may turn to the work for a sense of satisfaction and productivity. The work becomes more and more important because it shows measurable results, which family relationships often do not. This excessive concentration on a job further contributes to emotional stress in the home.

If the work is frustrating and the individual lacks a sense of inner emotional security, health problems are possible. Chronic frustration and feelings of not measuring up, not accomplishing enough, take their toll on the body. It is urgent that you have a constructive outlet, something you can do (preferably of a helpful and assisting nature) which gives you a sense of competence, of making a contribution, of being useful. Sometimes family projects (particularly of a physical sort such as repairs, refurbishing, redecorating, painting the house) can help to constructively channel nit-picky drives into the physical world rather than into emotional exchanges with those we love. Any of the helping professions can provide a positive outlet.

Moon Conjunct Chiron
Your emotional security needs may center around a desire to reach out to the world, to seek the truth, to explore, to heal and to go further. This could create a push/pull between safety instincts and risk-taking tendencies, so that a compromise is essential. You may gain emotional support and sustenance through learning, through faith or through optimism. You could nurture understanding or you could idealize home and/or family.

Chiron Conjunct Moon (long-term)
Your need for emotional security is connected to your search for faith and meaning in life. Personal reactions to this combination can range from making home and family into the source of ultimate value (which means that if they are threatened, your faith is shaken), to being willing to give up rootedness (a nest, personal attachments) to be able to pursue your search for the Absolute wherever it takes you. Try to find a balance between valuing emotional attachments but not making them the only source of security versus rejecting them because they are not perfect or because they are too limiting. With love and faith, this period can be one of deeper understanding, and healing, for yourself and/or for others in your life.

Moon Conjunct/Opposite Nodes
Aspects between the Moon and its nodes emphasize our need for emotional security, but conflict aspects suggest tension in satisfying that need. We may be unwilling to accept our own dependency needs, fighting feelings of vulnerability. Or we may feel unable to satisfy the demands of others. We may be too empathic, too open to feeling the moods of other people. Home and family are likely to be important, whether we are looking for a closer support system or

wanting to escape a confining, even suffocating, nest. With any conflict aspect, compromise is usually the best solution, though it is possible to take turns, alternately satisfying the different drives in our nature. Whether we are involved in "mothering" or wishing we could be "mothered," a healthy life includes room to be interdependent; both to give and receive help. Increased psychic openness is also very possible during this period of Moon-node aspects. We need to pay attention to the inner guidance but also to be able to shut the psychic doors if we find ourselves too sensitive to the emotions of others. A focus on action, coping with the physical world, or detached analysis can shift us out of the water sensitivity. Use the talent but stay in control of it.

Nodes Conjunct/Opposite Moon (long-term)

Emotional security needs are in high focus. Analyze where and how you seek emotional safety, roots, protection and assurance. Your close attachments are likely to be highlighted, with a need to clarify when and how you nurture as well as when and how you can be nurtured by others. Family matters may come up for examination. Insecurity is possible. Empathy and psychic sensitivity are likely to be higher than usual, and emotions are usually strong. Stay conscious of your feelings and use wisdom as well.

For hard aspects between the progressed Moon and the angles (Ascendant, Midheaven, etc.), see Chapter 7.

Harmony Aspects

Moon Sextile/Trine the Sun

Your need for emotional security may encourage your desire for love, admiration and attention;, your procreative/creative urges, or your expression of emotional warmth. Family ties are highlighted; family feelings may be strong. You may be working on the balance between freely expressing your emotional reactions and holding back to protect yourself or others. Your drive for emotional safety may reinforce your desire to give and receive love, your involvement with children, or your search for admiration, applause and approval. Creativity may become central; emotional warmth is likely. You could feel torn between public (onstage) urges versus the desire for privacy, inwardness, and protection. Parenting instincts are strong, whether you care for others or are cared for.

Moon Sextile/Trine the Natal Moon

An increased focus on emotional security is likely during this period. Attention and action may center on your home or family, on your relationship with a mother figure or on your capacity to care for and protect others. You may wish to increase your own security, or you might direct your protective instincts into caring for pets, into gardening, into food and/or possessions associated with security and roots. On a wider scale, involvement is possible with the public, with one's homeland, with life (ecology), etc. Increased sensitivity (psychic openness) is also likely during this period. Watch your dreams and stay in touch with the subconscious side of your mind.

Moon Sextile/Trine Mercury

You have the potential to harmonize thinking and feeling, to bring together your head and your emotions. A balance between logical detachment and an emotional drive for safety is quite possible. You can be more objective in the realm of family, and you can include important feelings in your decision making. Current interests could range from studies or writing to travel or developments in the neighborhood. Lots of intellectual stimulation appeals.

Moon Sextile/Trine Venus

Your pleasure-loving and stability-seeking side is reinforcing your quest for emotional safety and security. The common bond is likely to incline toward physical and emotional grounding, protection and predictability. You may want to enjoy your family more, guard your resources or otherwise add to your sense of comfort. Loving relationships are likely to be pursued.

Moon Sextile/Trine Mars

This may be a period when you can make peace between personal needs for freedom and self-expression and interpersonal desires for emotional attachments and safety. You may find it easy to judge when to express your feelings openly and directly, and when to hold back to protect yourself or others. You may be able to put much energy into family matters and could find family members more willing to allow you to be independent and active.

Moon Sextile/Trine Jupiter

Your faith may offer inspiration and optimism for dealing with family and emotional matters. Or your close relationships may help you realize your highest dreams and goals. This is a time to clarify your values since your odds are good that you can move successfully toward them. Ideals may improve your domestic connections and emotional warmth may enlarge your perspective on life.

Jupiter Sextile/Trine Moon (long-term)

Roots and restlessness are highlighted, but with the suggestion of successful integration. You can find a way to have a nest and close, emotional attachments, while still exploring the wider world in a search for truth and meaning. Ideals, beliefs, values, moral principles, education, philosophy and spiritual quests can support and reinforce your secure home and sense of safety. Your emotional attachments (possibly including mother or mother figure and children) can support your seeking of more knowledge, understanding and insight into life's meaning, for a clear sense of what you trust, what is most important in your life.

Moon Sextile/Trine Saturn

Now is a time to make peace between work and home duties and demands. You can take turns between compassion and pragmatism, between vocational needs and family needs. Emotions and practicality will enhance each other, if you compromise between them. The tenor is serious, responsible and oriented toward caretaking. Don't overdo the parental role, and do remember to laugh along the way.

Saturn Sextile/Trine Moon (long-term)

The harmony aspect suggests you have the ability to easily balance this natural polarity. You can make room in life for both compassion and pragmatism; dependency and dominance; home and family as well as career; unconditional love and conditional love. On an outer level, your parents may relate fairly well. On an inner level, this suggests agreement between the archetypal mother and father principles within you. You can be empathic and caring as well as responsible and hardworking, sensitive as well as sensible, and deal well with both emotional and practical issues.

Moon Sextile/Trine Uranus

You may have the opportunity to balance your independent side with your desire for closeness and emotional attachments. This could include harmony between friends and family, or a smooth flow between your thinking and your feelings. You may find it easier to love openly, with tolerance and appreciation of each other's differences. You might take turns between your variety-oriented, risk-taking side and your security-oriented, protective side or find a reasonable compromise somewhere in the middle.

Uranus Sextile/Trine Moon (long-term)

This aspect implies that you can make an integration between the desire for security, roots and emotional closeness and the urge to take risks, change things, be independent. You can harmonize friends with family, and feeling commitments with intellectual freedom. You can keep room for both stability and change, security and risk. Your innovative, individualistic side can creatively contribute to your domestic life and your emotional attachments and caring involvements provide a secure base for your insights, brainstorming and inventiveness.

Moon Sextile/Trine Neptune

You may experience more psychic insights as you can tune into nonverbal understanding more easily during this period. You are apt to seek a sense of smooth, flowing beauty in your life. Aesthetic involvements can feed your psyche, but beware of overdoing rose-colored glasses, especially where family members are concerned. Serenity is an important goal; you need more alone time. You may want to take up or expand meditation or other practices, including analyzing your dreams, to help you "go with the flow" and connect to life's inspired rhythms.

Neptune Sextile/Trine Moon (long-term)

Feelings are highlighted, with an inward tendency—to feel deeply, but not reveal much on the surface. Potential psychic ability is indicated, with intuition a likely talent. Sensitivity is marked, with a real need to merge, to join, to be a part of something larger. Inspirational moods are possible, and you may be uplifted through nature, art or spiritual activities. You sometimes know things without knowing how you know. You are apt to be sensitive to the "vibes" of others and empathic to their feelings and needs. Your compassion could draw you into trying to rescue and take care of others. You need peace, harmony and serenity to use your talents and connect with your inner wisdom.

Moon Sextile/Trine Pluto

Feelings are highlighted, with a strong drive to merge with someone else. You may give and receive support from a mate, and could be involved in care taking roles that include financial or material assistance as well as emotional support. You have the opportunity to face deeply buried emotional issues, and to achieve catharsis and forgiveness. You may be more intuitive during this period.

Pluto Sextile/Trine Moon (long-term)

Intense feelings are highlighted, but many may be hidden from the world. Your inner depths are likely to be rich and imaginative, but you probably seek control of your emotions. Psychic talent is possible, and you probably can pick up well on people's subtle clues of inflection, body language, etc. You can "read" emotions. Lasting commitments are likely to be important, and you have an excellent capacity for blending partnership needs and family ties. This aspect can imply harmony between mates and children and between partners and parents. You want to commit to the very end. Your feelings tend to be equally enduring and you might sometimes have to learn to release and let go. Extreme caring is suggested, but you need some alone time as well, to do inner processing.

Moon Sextile/Trine Ceres

A strong focus on nurturing principles is indicated. You are likely to be in inner harmony where caretaking issues are concerned. You know how you want to nurture and be nurtured. There is inner agreement about blending your emotionally supportive side with your practical assessments of what would be most helpful. You can facilitate feelings as well as projects.

You may find it easy to put your energy into assisting activities. Parenting themes are accentuated; this might be more involvement with your own parent(s), your role as a parent or a general tendency to look after others emotionally and practically. The potential is strong for warmth, protective instincts, and a family focus.

Moon Sextile/Trine Pallas

Partnership and domestic issues are in focus here, with the suggestion of harmony between equalitarian instincts and the desire to care or be cared for in a more parental fashion. This can indicate harmony between a mother (or mother figure) and your partner, but it can also point to inner harmony between your partnership instincts and your own parenting energy. You may easily fill both the role of equal other and the role of parent (supportive, nourishing) or child (vulnerable, receiving assistance). Your aesthetic instincts might also contribute to a more satisfying home life, and your emotional warmth help build a more desirable partnership. Your equalitarian instincts could be helpful with people you care about. You can feed your soul through artistic/aesthetic involvement. Partners may offer emotional reassurance and support.

Moon Sextile/Trine Juno

A depth capacity for sharing and caring is suggested. Homing instincts are in harmony with the desire for a mate. Closeness and emotional commitment is sought at both ends, with the urge toward warmth with both a partner and a family. You can balance equality instincts with the caretaking and vulnerable sides of your nature, taking turns meeting on an equal level with being the one assisting or the one being assisted in a relationship. Potential harmony exists between partners and children and between partners and parents. You are open to making intense emotional attachments. You know when to give and when to receive support. An appreciation of or creation of beauty can also add to your emotional assurance.

Moon Sextile/Trine Vesta

Support and practicality are in harmony here. You have the capacity to be both warm and sensible, facilitating feelings as well as getting the job done right. Your work can help build a safer, more secure home and your domestic satisfaction can contribute to your success as a worker. The implication is that you can make a good integration of practical demands along with emotional needs. Your mother (or mother figure) may help you to develop competence and efficiency, or your work may involve service or caretaking of others. You have the potential to harmonize work demands and family duties. You may find compromises come more easily, or you instinctively take turns between emotional and physical caretaking. Your family may assist you in a new project, particularly of a "fix-it" or health focus. Your willingness to work, to be dedicated, and to improve things can be an asset in your domestic life.

Moon Sextile/Trine Chiron

This combination suggests that you have the capacity to integrate your need for emotional security with your search for faith and meaning in life. Mutual support may be present in your family for ideals and goals, possibly including education, teaching, writing, travel. You can maintain emotional roots without being trapped in the past by old dependencies or obligations to care for others. By continuing to deepen your own faith and empathy, you may be able to offer healing to others.

Chiron Sextile/Trine Moon (long-term)

You may be able to blend a drive for emotional security with a drive to explore, adventure and go beyond old limits. Your independent, maverick side could willingly take turns with your nurturing, protective, cautious side. You can make room for both roots and the open road, emotions and the wide reach of the mind. Your family may support your intellectual outreach and your idealism and your quest for the best may contribute to your domestic base.

Moon Sextile/Trine Nodes

Your drive for emotional assurance is primarily concerned with self/other relationships for this period. You may be reworking the balance between personal and interpersonal needs—between your desires and preferences and those of other people (especially partners). A caring support system is very important to you now. Interdependency is the key, letting you care for others and also accept their assistance in areas where you need it. You have the ability to move closer to people, to make stronger emotional commitments and connections.

Sensitivity, empathy, and care taking instincts are highlighted during this period. Your emotional needs for security and safety are emphasized. You may seek deeper emotional commitments and connections with other people. With a balance between nurturing and being nurtured, you can have a give-and-take relationship with others. Whatever contributes to your security (people, food, land, possessions, etc.) is a likely focus now. You can be extremely warm, helpful and protective.

Nodes Sextile/Trine Moon (long-term)

Aspects between the Moon and its own nodes reinforce the basic principle of emotional security and roots. Home and family are usually very important, though it is possible to widen one's scope and "mother" the world. With harmonious aspects, it should be possible for you both to help others and allow others to help you; to manage a healthy interdependency. You are also likely to be sensitive and empathic, open to the feelings of others and to inner inspiration and guidance. Some of the guidance could come through dreams. If you experience too much openness at times, it is possible to close the psychic door by moving into one of the other elements. We express fire by doing something active out of personal desire. We move into earth by doing something that produces tangible results, whether the results are practical or just for pleasure. We deal with air by functioning in the conscious side of the mind, observing and analyzing in a detached, logical way, as a spectator. Each of the elements is a valuable part of a whole life.

Moon Sextile/Trine Ascendant/Descendant (and vice versa)

An opportunity arises for ease between personal desires and nurturing needs. You may relate well with family members (parents, children, partners), or find it easier than usual to meet both your needs and those of loved ones. Emotions can be expressed rather smoothly. Your actions naturally incline toward domestic or care taking aims. Caring and sharing issues are highlighted.

Moon Sextile/Trine Midheaven/IC (and vice versa)

The potential of gaining more security is indicated. You may find more safety in your work or feel more ease in domestic circumstances. Keeping a balance between your public and private worlds is a bit easier than usual. You use both compassion and common sense in making decisions. Family members may contribute to your success or help to build a more satisfying nest. You may strengthen your emotional foundation, feel more centered and safe in the world.

Conflict Aspects

Moon Square/Opposite/Quincunx Sun

You may experience a clash between introversion and extroversion; between caution and enthusiasm, or between looking after others and being a star. Family matters are likely to be important. Intense feelings are highlighted, and you are capable of much warmth and caring. You might polarize between expressing emotions and holding back, between playing it safe and taking chances or between a protective, private focus and a public role with the potential for applause/admiration. Loved ones may be an important center of your attention. Feelings are likely to be strong, with the potential of much caring and strong attachments.

Moon Square/Opposite/Quincunx Natal Moon

This aspect points to possible tension around emotional security needs. A mother-figure may be an important part of the situation, or your role in caring for others may be highlighted. You may be concerned with children, pets, plants, food, or home and possessions. On a wider scale, you may be involved with the public, with your homeland, with life (ecology) etc. Try to allow interdependency, so that you can both give and receive nurturing support. You are likely to be more sensitive during this period, whether more aware of your own emotional needs or empathic, feeling the needs of others. Stay in touch with your subconscious. Dreams are one of the effective ways to become conscious of inner tensions and anxieties so at least a start can be made on handling the problems. A stable emotional support system is valuable. If family members are not available, friends can be a helpful substitute.

Moon Square/Opposite/Quincunx Mercury

You may experience some tension between your intellectual, rational side and your emotional, security-oriented side. You could feel torn between the familiar and a desire for variety, or between logic and intuition. Taking the best of both is advisable. Family members may present challenges, with the need to hear everyone's sides and make sure ruffled feelings are acknowledged and dealt with. Among other possibilities, current attention could focus on studies, writing, traveling, developments in the neighborhood or a wide variety of activities featuring intellectual stimulation or dexterity.

Moon Square/Opposite/Quincunx Venus

Safety or security needs may be challenging. Perhaps you are too concerned with protection and stability. Perhaps you have been ignoring necessary steps to solidify and look after your assets. You need to establish a sense of emotional assurance (but not complacency) and to enjoy the physical/sensual world without excessive hedonism or materialism. Relationships could be a concern—with tension between partnership and parental demands (your own roles or in-law issues). Caring and empathy on your part can strengthen the ties of love among all parties.

Moon Square/Opposite/Quincunx Mars

You are likely to face the push/pull between a desire to be on your own, answering only to yourself, versus a desire for home, family or emotional commitments. Compromising between personal assertion and the drive to nurture and assist others may be a challenge. You may also feel ambivalent about direct expression of what you feel, versus holding back to protect yourself or others. If you hold in emotions too long, personal temper outbursts are possible or you may be involved with other people who are explosive. With integration and compromise, you can be extremely warm and involved and still be true to your need for self-expression.

Moon Square/Opposite/Quincunx Jupiter

You are apt to be working on a balance between your desire for a nest, security, emotional connections and safety and your drive to explore, to expand, to adventure, to wander and to seek your personal ideals wherever the search takes you. Your risk-taking, optimistic side may vie with your cautious, protective instincts until you make room for both (or take turns comfortably between them). You also might expect too much from your home and/or family. Keep a secure foundation from which to reach out and explore the world and keep expectations reasonable.

Jupiter Square/Opposite/Quincunx Moon (long-term)

Roots may vie with restlessness, as you seek some form of integration. Your need for security, safety, a nest and emotional attachments must be balanced with your urge to explore, to adventure, to seek the truth, to travel and to go further in a quest for understanding higher principles and seeking what is most important to you. Until integrated, freedom needs may pull you away from home (or pull family members away) or family ties and security instincts may keep you in the domestic arena, but feeling confined. High expectations and (perhaps) perfectionistic ideals may affect your attitudes about home, family and nurturing activities. Values, ideals, ethics, moral principles or goals may be areas of conflict with your mother or mother figure or with your children. The challenge is to maintain reasonable aspirations, satisfying (yet not impossible) expectations and a warm, caring nest to come home to.

Moon Square/Opposite/Quincunx Saturn

You are dealing with polarity issues: the push/pull between home and family versus career; between tenderhearted compassion and hard-nosed pragmatism; between being the authority and being submissive. Life needs different actions at different times—choose wisely. An emphasis on stability and security is likely. Productive work which encourages a sense of accomplishment and confidence in your ability to cope with the world can counteract the danger of depression or anxiety. It is also important to maintain an emotional support system with family and/or friends. Judge your skill in dealing with the "rules of the game" by the feedback (events) occurring during this period. This is a time to be very realistic, but try not to take yourself or life **too** seriously. Remember that play and relaxation are important also.

Saturn Square/Opposite/Quincunx Moon (long-term)

This aspect reinforces the need to integrate a natural polarity: compassion versus pragmatism; dependency versus dominance; home and family versus career; unconditional love versus conditional love. On an outer level, there may be some stress (or even separations) between your parents, or you may be changing your job and/or your home. On an inner level, this aspect highlights the need to bring together your archetypal mother and father principles. Dangers include swinging from one extreme to the other, overdoing one, then overdoing the other, or identifying with one side and attracting people who overdo the opposite side. Finding a middle ground is important. With consciousness and effort, you can find a balance point, allowing both empathy and discipline, sensitivity and common sense, power in the world and emotional security in your home.

Moon Square/Opposite/Quincunx Uranus

This aspect suggests the need to integrate competing desires: the urge for security, roots and emotional closeness versus risk-taking instincts, the need for change and independence. Stability may seem at war with change, or emotions may battle intellectual detachment and aloofness. Friends may seem to compete with family (and vice versa). There is room in life for everything—with a little juggling. Part of the challenge is to maintain your sense of individuality and uniqueness while still maintaining close, caring connections with other people.

Uranus Square/Opposite/Quincunx Moon (long-term)

You are striving to achieve a sense of balance between very different needs. Part of you desires freedom, independence and to be uniquely yourself, while another part yearns for emotional connections, attachment and protection. Look for a compromise which allows for some of both. You are also striving to make peace between a security focus and a risk-taking orientation, between a desire for safety and the familiar versus an urge toward change and variety. Sensitive feelings could also confront the cool, detached intellect. A full life demands some of each.

Moon Square/Opposite/Quincunx Neptune

Feelings are highlighted, with an inward tendency—to feel strongly, but not to reveal much to the world. Psychic ability is possible, but it may not be handled easily, or could sometimes "spill through" in disruptive ways (e.g., being overwhelmed by impressions). Idealism or spiritual or escapist needs might compete with nurturing instincts and could be an issue with your own mother (or mother figure), or with your children. Running away from unpleasantness might seem the most appealing course. You are likely to seek peace, harmony and serenity, but may sometimes wish and hope for more than is possible, particularly in terms of home and family. It is important to nurture yourself, especially through art, nature or inspirational activities, and to seek faith in a higher power.

Neptune Square/Opposite/Quincunx Moon (long-term)

Sensitivities are apt to be accentuated during this period. You (and those about you) may feel more "touchy" than usual. Empathy can be helpful, but don't overdo it to the point of martyrdom. The need to rescue and assist could be carried too far into savior/victim entanglements. Artistic activity can provide an alternative way to make the world more ideal. Family members may influence your dreams, ideals and capacity to visualize the Highest in life. Faith in a Higher Power is important to counteract the danger of anxiety or depression over the contrast between high ideals and actual life. Support your psyche with meditation, alone time, affirmations, rituals, or other spiritual practices to provide a degree of support and serenity.

Moon Square/Opposite/Quincunx Pluto

Intense emotions are highlighted, and you may seek support or be tempted to withdraw. Security may be challenged in terms of a mate relationship, especially where money and shared possessions/pleasures are concerned. Try to achieve interdependency, to be able to give and receive nurturing, but be willing to compete if your rights are really attacked. With past struggles, look at old hurts and release them and let them go. Understanding hidden motives and probing the subconscious can help you avoid repeating old errors. Increased intuition can be helpful if you maintain a sense of your own power so the sensitivity is not experienced as increased vulnerability. Above all, stay conscious of your feelings and also of your strength.

Pluto Square/Opposite/Quincunx Moon (long-term)

Intense feelings are highlighted. Your emotional reactions are likely to be tenacious and enduring, so you may sometimes have to learn to forgive and let go (especially where resentments are concerned). Old conflicts with your mother or mother figure might continue to affect you presently, until resolved within you. Close emotional attachments are likely, but you could feel torn between being parental toward a partner, picking a partner who tries to play parent to you, or sharing on a more equalitarian basis. Sexuality, money and joint possessions could be a battleground for subtle intimidation, manipulation or power struggles until a comfortable compromise is reached. You can use emotions to gain power, so use them wisely!

Moon Square/Opposite/Quincunx Ceres

Nurturing principles are highlighted, but with the suggestion of an inner conflict. You may feel torn about how, when, and how much to nurture. Your own mother (or mother figure) may have presented a somewhat contradictory or ambivalent model of nurturing, and this is an appropriate time to work on any mixed feelings in this area. Emotions may vie with practicality, or unconditional caring with common sense. Resolving any inner stress allows you to be comfortable in the vulnerable position (being taken care of) as well as enjoying looking after others when appropriate. You may be inclined to take on too much of a parenting role, or be looking to others to protect and take care of you. Strive for interdependence, for a mutual give and take, and to balance compassion with common sense.

Moon Square/Opposite/Quincunx Pallas

Partnership and dependency/nurturing are highlighted here, with the suggestion of potential conflict between equality instincts and parent/child interactions. This could include an inner push/pull between relating on an equal level versus taking care of others or allowing them to take care of you. It might indicate competition between partner and children for your time and attention, or between parental figures and partners. Needs for beauty and pleasure might seem to vie with the urge for security and safety. The challenge is to keep room in your life for both partnership and a home/family, for equality and caretaking. You may be reworking the balance between an absorbing, intense connection and some space and room for individuality in relationships with loved ones. Or you may be dealing with competitive situations and need to be clear about personal rights and needs versus the rights of others. Putting together logical perceptions and emotional impressions can be helpful.

Moon Square/Opposite/Quincunx Juno

Emotional commitment is highlighted, but some potential ambivalence about its channels is possible. This aspect implies that your need to nurture and/or be nurtured might be at odds with your urge for an equalitarian peer relationship. Perhaps you feel torn between time/energy commitments to children or the home versus to a partner. Or, perhaps you feel competition between a parent and a partner. Issues surrounding joint resources, finances and sexuality may affect domestic harmony (or lack of). Learning to give, receive and share comfortably is an issue. Life should have room for both cooperation and healthy competition, but it is important not to compete against team members. If competition is involved, stay aware of both your personal rights and needs and the rights of others. Aim for healthy interdependence, where both parties can give in their areas of strength and receive in their areas of weakness.

Moon Square/Opposite/Quincunx Vesta

You may feel as though your practical and emotional sides are at odds with each other. If you focus too much on work and "efficiency," you could end up feeling alienated from people close to you. If you are too concerned with emotional attachments and safety, your capacity to do things well, to be practical and accomplish, might suffer. By taking turns, you can do your best in both areas and help create mutual support between your job and your family or other sources of emotional support. It could be that your work takes you away from your home more than you would like (or vice versa). Your nurturing instincts might seem to clash with your common sense or urge to improve things. Your mother (or mother figure) or your own nurturing urges could vie with your need to be productive and achieving in the world. Critical judgment and a focus on the flaws of other people could lead to alienation and threaten emotional closeness. Feelings could overwhelm practicality. The goal is to take the best of both practicality and sensitivity and to express them when they are appropriate. You need to do something well, but you also need to share emotional warmth and closeness.

Moon Square/Opposite/Quincunx Chiron

This combination shows tension between your need for emotional security and your hunger for something more in life. Your personal faith, values and goals may conflict with family traditions or obligations. Life should be big enough to include a nest, but also the freedom to leave it periodically. If expectations can be kept reasonable, we can maintain our emotional attachments but also play a role in the larger world. It is important to be clear about basic beliefs and values, and to be willing to compromise.

Chiron Square/Opposite/Quincunx Moon (long-term)

You may feel some ambivalence between your concern with emotional safety and your quest for broader horizons and expanded knowledge. Roots may vie with exploration, or the emotions compete with intellectual understanding. Life, of course, demands some of each—in their proper spheres. With mind and heart in harmony, empathy may contribute to a truer understanding of life's meaning and an openness to the new can bring more possibilities and choices to those near and dear to you. Guard against expecting too much from close relationships. Shared ideals can strengthen love bonds. Where close relationships hold conflicting beliefs and values, compromise and mutual tolerance can help.

Moon Square/Opposite/Quincunx Nodes

Relationships are a probable focus in your quest for emotional safety. You may do some bouncing back and forth in terms of self/other interactions. Challenges are suggested in balancing your desires with those of other people. You might assert too much—or too little. Empathy can be an asset in the search for compromises. You may feel ambivalent about being on your own versus sharing with others, yet both are necessary for fullest satisfaction. You may experience some conflict in your quest for emotional security. Perhaps you have been depending on people/things that are no longer so stable. Perhaps you have been overdoing dependency **or** nurturing. Perhaps you want a greater level of commitment in your close connections to others. In this period, you need to deal with issues of emotional warmth, caring, empathy and involvement with others. If you balance your giving and receiving in this area, rewarding interactions are possible. This may also be a time to release old dependencies.

Nodes Square/Opposite/Quincunx Moon (long-term)

Aspects between the Moon and its nodes emphasize our need for emotional security, but conflict aspects suggest problems in satisfying that need. We may be unwilling to accept our own dependency needs, fighting feelings of vulnerability. Or we may feel unable to satisfy the demands of others. We may be too empathic, too open to feeling the moods of other people. Home and family are likely to be important, whether we are looking for a closer support system or wanting to escape a confining, even suffocating nest. With any conflict aspect, compromise is usually the best solution, though it is possible to take turns, alternately satisfying the different drives in our nature. Whether we are involved in "mothering" or wishing we could be "mothered," a healthy life includes room to be interdependent; both to give and receive help. Increased psychic openness is also very possible during this period of Moon-node aspects. We need to pay attention to the inner guidance, but also to be able to shut the psychic doors if we find ourselves too sensitive to the emotions of others. A focus on action, coping with the physical world, or detached analysis can shift us out of the water sensitivity. Use the talent but stay in control of it.

For hard aspects between the progressed Moon and the angles, see Chapter 7.

CHAPTER TWELVE

EXAMPLES

A few examples help illustrate the principles, so this chapter covers a few sample charts. In each case example, we will follow the outline which was presented in Chapter One to search for the most significant factors. The charts are presented in a format of two concentric circles. The inner ring (which also sets the house cusps) is the natal chart (the basis for everything). The outer ring is the progressed chart for a particular date. (The full horoscope is provided so you can look at indicators above and beyond the outline on your own.)

A few technical notes. The Midheaven is progressed by the solar arc method. We have checked a number of events with the RA of Mean Sun method for progressing the Midheaven. (Sometimes the RA of Mean Sun is very striking, as with Ms. A for whom the RA of Mean Sun progressed Midheaven was opposite Neptune—its ruler—for the time in question.) Although we believe the RA of Mean Sun is valid, we do get a clearer picture **more often** with the solar arc method.

You will note that the significant event for two of these individuals happened around age 30. In addition to being the end of a Saturn Return (by transit), around age 30 everything in the horoscope semi-sextiles itself in the system of forecasting called Solar Arc Directions. Similarly, everything octiles (semi-squares) itself around age 45 and everything sextiles itself around age 60. Those ages are worth noting with clients as they often highlight important events or feelings.

Case Studies

Ms. A

Long-term aspects: Chiron trine Jupiter; Neptune sextile Pluto; Uranus sextile Jupiter, Ceres quincunx Saturn; Saturn octile/trioctile the Nodes, Mercury conjunct Jupiter and Mercury trine Chiron, Vesta octile Neptune. [We see a mental focus with the many aspects involving Mercury, Jupiter, Uranus and Chiron. We note a career versus domesticity clash with Saturn at odds with both Ceres and the Nodes.]

` **Cycle changes**: Sun changing signs (from Gemini to Cancer)—and Venus will change signs in another year as well. [The fact that there is a cycle change marks this as an important year. The cycle could affect self-esteem and creativity—the natural meaning of the Sun. It might also involve communication and media (Sun rules 3rd house natally) or financial matters and pleasure (Sun also rules the Leo occupying the 2nd house).]

Conjunctions to angles: Progressed Mercury and progressed Uranus conjunct progressed East Point (auxiliary Ascendant). Progressed Moon conjunct natal East Point. [A change in personal action is likely since the East Point is similar to an Ascendant. We expect movement toward more variety, independence, intellectual stimulation—involvement of Mercury and Uranus. A change in the home or family circumstances is also possible with the Moon in one of the conjunctions.]

Hard aspects to angles: Progressed Midheaven octile Sun [should involve career ambitions]. Progressed Ascendant quincunx Node [separations in regard to family or close relationships]. Progressed Ceres conjuncts the natal Antivertex (an auxiliary Ascendant) and progressed Vertex (auxiliary Descendant) quincunxes natal Ceres [new work or domestic circumstances]. Progressed Mars trioctile Midheaven [challenge or manifestation regarding personal action and career, authority figures, status].

Aspect configurations: Progressed Ceres activating natal T-square between Pluto (in Leo), Venus (in Taurus) and Juno (in Aquarius). [Since the natal T-square is in fixed signs and includes Venus and Pluto—two major fixed planets—we would expect the activity to center around self-indulgence versus self-control issues or the question of sharing power, possessions, and pleasures with other people. Financial changes are possible. Since progressed Ceres is the trigger, nurturing or domestic matters—or work—could be in focus.]

Hard aspects to planets/asteroids: Progressed Venus conjunct progressed Sun (combining houses 2/3, 4/5, and 11/12 in natal chart). Progressed Mercury conjuncts progressed Uranus (blending houses 3/4, with 8/9, or 12 with 8/9 in natal chart). Progressed Sun square Pallas. Progressed Venus square Pallas. Progressed Pallas octile Venus. Progressed Pallas quincunx Vesta. Progressed Ceres quincunx Neptune. Progressed Ceres square Pluto. Progressed Juno trioctile Saturn. [Changes in relationships are likely with all the Venus, Pallas,

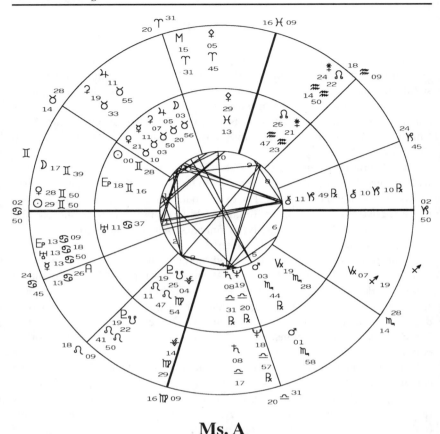

Ms. A

Juno activity. Love may compete with work with conflicts between relationship factors and Saturn and Vesta. Two separative aspects to Ceres could indicate domestic shifts.]

Progressed Moon aspects: Progressed Moon just finished square to natal Midheaven and is conjunct the East Point (personal action).

What happened?

The "event" was a new job which involved a change of residence, leaving a partner behind, and a substantial raise in income.

Ms. B

Long-term aspects: Chiron semi-sextile Jupiter, Pluto conjunct Node, Mars quincunx Jupiter, Sun trine Neptune, Venus trine Uranus, Vesta octile Jupiter. [Strong idealism is likely with Jupiter and Neptune emphasized. We also suspect some freedom versus closeness issues with the intense, emotional

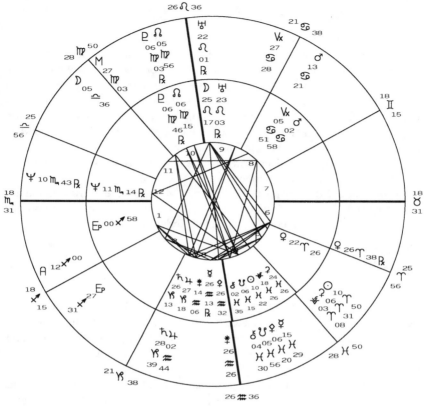

Ms. B

committed conjunction of Pluto and Node vying with the independence needs of Mars, Jupiter and Uranus.]

Cycle changes: Progressed Juno moving into 4th house. [A new chapter in terms of relationships and/or domestic or parental matters.]

Conjunctions to angles: Progressed Juno conjunct IC [accenting relationships, endings, and family]. Progressed Antivertex conjunct Jupiter [personal idealism and faith].

Hard aspects to angles: Progressed Ascendant octile Jupiter. Progressed Midheaven quincunx Pallas. Progressed Ascendant octile Saturn. Progressed Vesta octile Ascendant. Progressed Ascendant trioctile progressed Venus. Progressed Ceres square Vertex/Antivertex. [Personal action and identity are primarily affected with all the aspects to the Ascendant.]

No natal **aspect configuration** is triggered. However, a yod is present among the current patterns. The progressed Midheaven in Virgo is quincunx progressed Juno (and natal Mercury and Pallas) in Aquarius and quincunx progressed Venus in Aries on the other side. [Yods are often keys to major forks in the road, particularly when separations are involved.]

Hard aspects to planets/asteroids: Progressed Pallas conjunct South Node. Progressed Vesta square Mars. Progressed Juno conjunct Mercury and Pallas. Progressed Ceres quincunx Node. Progressed Ceres quincunx Pluto. Progressed Sun quincunx Neptune. Progressed Sun octile Mercury. Progressed Venus square Saturn. Progressed Sun trioctile Moon. Progressed Venus square Jupiter. Progressed Sun octile Pallas. Progressed Pallas opposite Pluto. Progressed Mars quincunx Juno. [Relationships are accented with an emphasis on Pallas and Juno, while family or domestic matters are in focus with Ceres involved repeatedly. Separation is possible with all the quincunxes.]

Progressed Moon aspects: Progressed Moon square Vertex (auxiliary Descendant). Progressed Moon quincunx South Node. [Our deepest emotional connections are usually a concern when the Nodes are in the picture.]

What happened?

Ms. B's mother passed away.

Ms. C

Long-term aspects: Ascendant trine Chiron, Mars semi-sextile Jupiter, Mercury quincunx South Node, Saturn trine Pluto, Midheaven quincunx Uranus, Pallas conjunct Jupiter, Moon trine Uranus, Vesta square Jupiter, Ceres square Nodes, Juno trine Pluto, and Sun trine Uranus. [A theme of much harmony and talent is suggested with all the trines. Perseverance is likely with Pluto in harmony to Saturn and Juno. Freedom needs work well on a personal level with Uranus in harmony to Sun and Moon but may be challenging professionally with Uranus quincunx Midheaven and Vesta (work/health) square Jupiter.]

Cycle changes: None (although Venus only entered Aquarius a bit over one year previously).

Conjunctions to angles: Progressed Midheaven conjunct Venus [classic for marriage or increased money or pleasure in career].

Hard aspects to angles: Progressed Vertex (auxiliary Descendant) square Venus, progressed East Point square Mercury, progressed Vertex quincunx Ceres, progressed Pallas (just left) quincunx to Vertex, progressed Venus (just finished) trioctile Vertex. [Relationships are featured with the self-other axes prominent along with Venus and Pallas.]

Aspect configurations: Progressed Juno triggering natal T-square involving Ceres and Mars square the Nodes. [This mutable T-square by signs and most of the houses suggests a dilemma regarding ideas and ideals. The progressed Juno square Ceres repeats the theme of progressed Moon square progressed Pallas: nurturing/mother principles at odds with equalitarian/partner principles.]

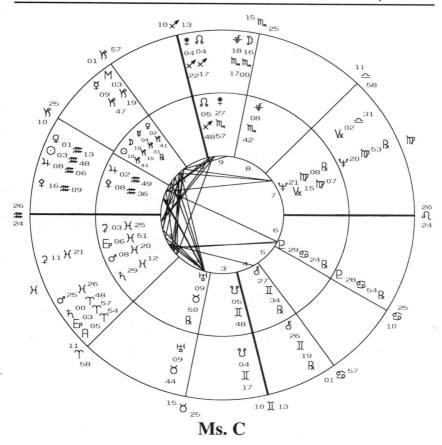

Ms. C

Hard aspects to planets/asteroids: Progressed Mercury conjunct the Moon, Progressed Vesta octile Venus, progressed Mars octile Uranus, progressed Mercury conjunct Sun, progressed Juno square Ceres, progressed Juno conjunct progressed Node, progressed Sun conjunct Jupiter (and progressed Venus approaching conjunction to Jupiter). [The aspect theme emphasizes conjunctions, suggesting cohesion or blending.]

Progressed Moon aspects: progressed Moon sextile Vertex [harmonious relationships], square progressed Pallas [peer associations], and approaching a conjunction to Vesta [focus on job or health].

What happened?

Ms. C got married. (With the progressed Moon square progressed Pallas and progressed Juno square Ceres, the Earth Mother asteroid, guess who was totally in charge of the wedding—Mom!)

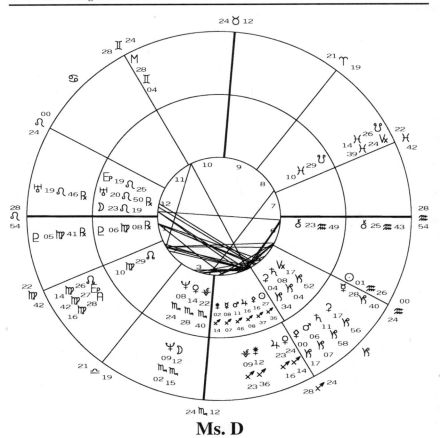

Ms. D

Ms. D

Long-term aspects: Moon trine Jupiter. Neptune octile Jupiter. Mars semi-sextile Saturn. Ceres trioctile Uranus. East Point conjunct Uranus. Chiron sextile Jupiter. Vesta semi-sextile Jupiter. Mercury semi-sextile Neptune. Midheaven quincunx Jupiter. Saturn sextile Neptune. [A strong theme of idealism and questing comes through with almost every aspect involving Neptune or Jupiter—the two "looking for God" planets.]

Cycle changes: Pallas into new sign (Capricorn). [A new cycle in regard to relationships—Pallas—and possibly parents or parenting since Capricorn is a parental sign.] Also, since progressed Mercury is rather rapid at this point, it will be entering a new sign (Aquarius) in less than a year. Since Mercury rules the (Virgo in the) 1st, 2nd, 10th and 11th, a new cycle in personal action (or appearance or health), or in finances, or in friends and associations, or in career, status or relationships with authority figures is possible.

Conjunctions to angles: Progressed IC conjunct Sun. Progressed Ascendant conjunct Node (and progressed East Point). Progressed Ceres conjunct Vertex (auxiliary Descendant). [With the IC, Node and Ceres all involved, we suspect home/ family/ parental/ domestic matters are emphasized.]

Hard aspects to angles: (Progressed Midheaven opposite Sun—see above IC conjunct). Progressed Ascendant (and progressed East Point) square Sun. Progressed Venus quincunx Midheaven. Progressed Mercury quincunx Ascendant. [We suspect a separation—voluntary or involuntary—is possible with two quincunxes and an opposition.]

Aspect configurations: Progressed Ascendant and progressed Midheaven activating natal T-square between Sun and Nodes of the Moon. [The T-square is in mutable signs indicating issues of balancing idealism and realism. The houses involved show challenges in regard to feast versus famine tendencies and handling monetary matters as well as family concerns. Ms. D's personal action is probably important in the situation as the Sun rules her natal Ascendant. Since the Sun also rules the 12th house, matters could involve escapism, spiritual quests, beauty, or sheltered places.]

Hard aspects to planets/asteroids: Progressed Juno conjunct Mars. Progressed Sun octile Jupiter and Pallas. Progressed Mars octile Uranus. Progressed Ceres octile Juno. Progressed Pallas octile Venus. Progressed Venus octile Neptune. [The aspect theme is an octile—suggesting stress, challenge, conflict or the need to make manifest. Relationships are accented with Pallas, Venus, and Juno prominent.]

Progressed Moon aspects: Progressed Moon octile Sun. [This is a highly emotional combination, harks back to parents or family issues.]

What happened?

The "event" was that Ms. D's mother became seriously ill. (It was a life-threatening ailment.) Ms. D moved across the country to help take care of her. Her mother did recover.

Ms. E

Long-term aspects: Chiron square Neptune, Pluto sextile Neptune, Uranus square Neptune, Pluto semi-sextile Jupiter, Neptune square Chiron, Mars quincunx Uranus, Neptune square Jupiter, Pallas sextile Uranus, Chiron opposite Jupiter, Jupiter conjunct Uranus, Mars trine Pluto, Uranus semi-sextile Pluto, Ascendant quincunx Saturn. Chiron quincunx Pluto. [The Neptune in Libra in the 7th is under siege from almost everything. We'd suspect important challenges in regard to the quest for "made in Heaven" relationships.]

Cycle changes: None.

Conjunctions to angles: Progressed Juno conjunct Vertex (auxiliary Descendant). [Focus on marriage, commitment, or elimination.]

Hard aspects to angles: Progressed East Point (auxiliary Ascendant) trioctile Venus, progressed Ascendant quincunx progressed Vertex (auxiliary

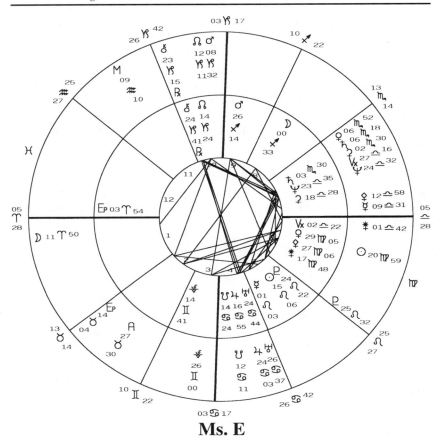

Ms. E

Descendant), progressed East Point (almost to) square to Sun. [Self-other issues predominate.]

Aspect configurations: Her T-square is a long-term one involving progressed Jupiter and natal Uranus (in Cancer in 4th) square to Neptune in the 7th and opposite Chiron in the 10th. None of the inner planets or asteroids were triggering it, although progressed Vesta (key to work and health) had been quincunx Chiron for several previous years.

Hard aspects to planets/asteroids: Progressed Venus conjunct progressed Saturn; progressed Mercury square progressed Mars, progressed Sun octile progressed Venus, progressed Sun octile progressed Saturn, progressed Mercury octile Pluto, progressed Vesta opposite Mars, progressed Ceres octile Juno, progressed Mars trioctile Pluto. [The Venus/Saturn suggests facing facts about relationships, with other Venus and Sun aspects suggesting love relationships are a focus. The involvement of some Mars and Pluto aspects could show an indomitable spirit or issues around personal power versus shared power with abuse or violence as negative options.]

Progressed Moon aspects: Progressed Moon squares the progressed Nodes and is approaching the opposition to progressed Pallas. [Again, we suspect the matter involves people who push our deepest emotional buttons with the Nodes in the picture.]

What happened?

Ms. E left an abusive marriage and moved a long distance.

Mr. G

Long-term aspects: Vesta quincunx Jupiter, Jupiter trine Uranus, Moon trine Saturn, Uranus trine Chiron, conjunct progressed Mean Node, Ascendant opposite Neptune, Mars conjunct Pluto, Venus conjunct North Node, Saturn quincunx South Node. [There is a strong emphasis connecting relationships and

Mr. G

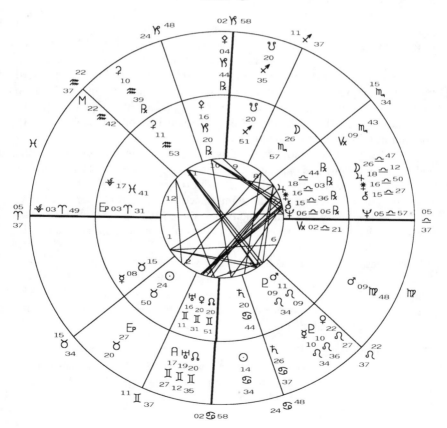

career to harmony, helping, and spiritual ideals with Venus, Jupiter, and Neptune. Uranus/Node/Venus connects relationships to expanding knowledge.]

Cycle Changes: There were no changes of signs, though progressed Moon changed signs about 3 months after the event. Progressed Venus and progressed MC were both changing houses, moving into the 6th and 12th respectively, connecting the event to work.

Conjunctions to angles: Progressed Venus was conjunct the progressed IC as they entered the 6th house, progressed Ascendant had completed a conjunction to natal Uranus but was on the midpoint of natal and progressed Uranus. Often such a pattern shows an extended time period from the time the factor reaches one degree before the natal planet until it moves one degree beyond the progressed position of the planet. [With Uranus and the Ascendant, we expect changing personal action, which could include new knowledge, non-traditional areas of interest, new people in the life, etc.]

Hard aspects to angles: Progressed Ascendant squares Vesta, progressed East Point opposes Moon and is quincunx progressed Moon. Progressed Antivertex squares Pluto and progressed Mercury. Progressed Pallas squares Ascendant. [These aspects suggest changes in the work (Vesta the details of the job and Pallas in the 10th house), and in the home/family activity (Moon), and in finances (East Point in the sign and house of Taurus and natal Moon in the sign and house of Scorpio, Antivertex in Taurus and Pluto the ruler of Scorpio).]

Aspect configurations: Progressed Mercury, progressed Pluto, progressed Ceres, and progressed Antivertex were aspecting the natal T-square of Ceres, Mercury, and Pluto-Mars. [Possible changes could include finances (Taurus and Pluto), family (Leo-5th house, Ceres), personal action (Mars, Antivertex), communication (Mercury, Aquarius).]

Hard aspects to planets/asteroids: Progressed Mercury conjunct natal and progressed Pluto and opposite progressed Ceres, progressed Mars quincunx progressed Ceres. [Work is highlighted with progressed Mars in the sign and house of Virgo and Ceres with its significance of a mix of Cancer and Virgo. Venus entering the Virgo house and opposite the MC supports this interpretation, while its placement in Leo suggests possible power and a position in the limelight.]

Progressed Moon aspects: Progressed Moon square progressed Saturn, quincunx progressed East Point, and semisextile natal Moon, having just finished a quincunx to natal Sun and an octile to progressed Mars while activity was occurring which led to the event. [Major focus on security issues involving finances and relationships.]

What Happened?

The "event" was accepting a job offer which made Mr. G the manager of a business in his field of interest, disseminating new age knowledge, with a sizable increase in power and income.

Mr. H

Long-term aspects: Venus octile Saturn, Ascendant trine Jupiter, Juno quincunx Jupiter, Saturn trioctile Jupiter; North Node quincunx Saturn; Antivertex square Chiron, Moon conjunct Uranus, Neptune conjunct progressed south Node; Mercury sextile Pluto, Pluto trine North Node. [Career and relationships are connected to ideals, possible conflict between freedom and closeness, or relationships with either work or ideals.]

Cycle changes: There were no major sign changes, though Ceres will change signs within a year. Progressed Jupiter recently reached the 5th house cusp for a possible change in creativity, whether personal (in love relationships) or in career/authority figures (Capricorn).

Conjunctions to angles: Progressed Antivertex conjunct progressed Venus (and progressed Ascendant for the place of residence conjuncted natal Venus). [Personal pleasure is highlighted, whether love, finances, sensuality, beauty, etc.]

Mr. H

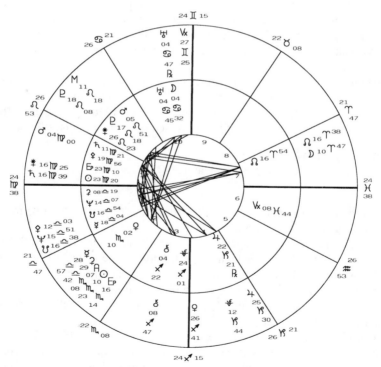

Progressed Relocated Asc 2 ♏ 58

Hard aspects to angles: Progressed East Point quincunx Node, about to start square to Pluto, progressed Ascendant about to start octiles to Sun and East Point, progressed MC trioctile progressed Venus. [Relationship changes are emphasized.]

Aspect configurations: Progressed East Point moved into a sextile to progressed Juno (which is conjunct progressed Saturn) to form a yod to the North Node, suggesting a new direction in status and close relationships. All factors except the progressed East Point were in orb of aspects to Pluto, to bring it into the network, confirming the emphasis on intimacy and relationships.

Hard aspects to planets/asteroids: Progressed Juno conjunct progressed Saturn, quincunx Node, progressed Mars square Chiron, progressed Mercury conjunct progressed Ceres. [Close relationships are connected to status/role and taken seriously and idealized (Virgo in the 12th house), relationships and finances are emphasized (Libra in the 2nd house).]

Progressed Moon aspects: Progressed Moon was trine progressed MC. [It had moved into a new house and sign in the preceding year, showing the urge to change the handling of security. Its placement in Aries pointed to personal action and in the 7th house to peer relationships, potentially dealing with the basic freedom-closeness dilemma shown in the natal chart.] Progressed Moon was quincunx Saturn and progressed Sun, forming a yod. [Separation from a previous status/role and changes in joint resources (progressed Sun in the 2nd house in Scorpio).]

Though not emphasized in a focus on events, there were also significant harmony aspects, including progressed Venus trine Juno and the progressed Antivertex had just finished a trine to Juno. Progressed Mars was sextile Moon-Uranus, progressed MC was sextile progressed Pallas and semisextile Saturn.

What happened?

Mr. H married for the first time, at age 47.

Mr. I

Long term aspects: Uranus trine Jupiter; MC square Saturn, trioctile Chiron, Pallas semisextile Saturn; Mercury square Chiron; Ascendant trine Uranus; East Point sextile Neptune; Saturn trine Pluto; Juno trine South Node. [Mental activity is emphasized with aspects between the mental planets as well as to other factors. Relationships look relatively harmonious.]

Cycle changes: Progressed Mars will change signs in less than a year. [Movement from Sagittarius into Capricorn suggests bringing dreams down to earth, making visions real.]

Conjunctions to angles: There were no conjunctions to the angles for the birthplace. Using the angles calculated for the location of the event, progressed Ascendant was conjunct progressed Jupiter, progressed East Point was conjunct Saturn, progressed Saturn was conjunct the Antivertex, progressed birthplace

MC was (almost) conjunct the local Ascendant. [Career, personal action, ideals, and knowledge are connected.]

Hard aspects to angles: Progressed local Antivertex quincunx Pluto, octile progressed local Ascendant and progressed Jupiter, progressed local MC quincunx Moon, square Saturn, octile Uranus, birthplace progressed MC square progressed Uranus, Antivertex, octile progressed Mercury and progressed Ceres, progressed Ascendant octile Pallas, progressed East Point octile Ceres and progressed Mars. [Separations involving work and/or home are suggested.]

Aspect configurations: Progressed Vesta squared (progressed) Pluto, while natal Pluto opposed Moon to complete a T-square. Progressed Pallas formed a T-square to the progressed true Nodes. [The major emphasis is on interpersonal involvement.]

Hard aspects to planets/asteroids: Progressed Venus conjunct Sun, progressed Mars conjunct Ceres, progressed Mercury conjunct progressed Ceres, progressed Vesta square progressed Pluto, progressed Juno conjunct Pallas, progressed Sun octile Moon. [Vesta and sometimes Ceres point to work change while Pluto, Juno, Pallas, Sun, and Moon emphasize interpersonal activity. The Venus/Sun combination can be romantic and marriage-oriented or emphasize monetary gain. Venus rules the 5th house (creativity, speculation, children) and the 10th (career, status) while the Sun rules the 8th (joint finances). All the conjunctions suggest union or cohesion.]

Progressed Moon aspects: The event was in process over a period of six months, so a variety of Moon aspects occurred. The date selected is the one on which a legal document was signed. Progressed Moon was trine the progressed MC and local Ascendant and quincunx the birthplace Ascendant, semisextile progressed Uranus, trioctile progressed Vesta, just coming to the octile to progressed Pluto. [A major move in a new direction is suggested, especially involving personal action.]

What happened?

Mr. I bought a company, and was making plans for a move of his home and/or another business.

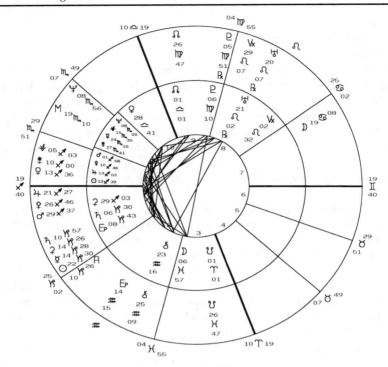

Mr. I

Progressed Relocated Angles		Relocated Angles	
p. MC	6 ♎ 34	MC	27 ♌ 43
p. ASC	20 ♐ 55	Asc	20 ♏ 24
p. EP	5 ♑ 32	EP	2 ♐ 00
p. ⊗	5 ♒ 45	⊗	10 ♑ 26

Conclusion

We hope that this tour of the possibilities inherent in progressions has proven
enlightening and wish you the very best in your journey through life and in
exploring the fascinating field of astrology!

Create YOUR FUTURE!

Progressed Profile

You have the power to create your own future — to take control of seemingly random events. Astro's Progressed Profile gives you a look at the year ahead using Secondary Progressions; it analyzes the year as a whole and provides dates and interpretations for astrological patterns that will form. The themes that are most emphasized during the year are discussed in terms of possible events and your underlying psychological needs. This outstanding report will help you to understand the choices you are likely to face so that you can maximize your opportunities and create the life you have always imagined.

Progressed Profile Report 11-25 pages PRP-BKUYF   **$21.95**

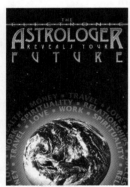

SOFTWARE:
The Electronic Astrologer Reveals Your FUTURE

Full of insights, encouragement and suggestions to make the most of any aspect, this outstanding program will help you to see the future of your love life, spirituality, career, travel and more. Incorporating the two most popular methods of forecasting - transits and secondary progressions, this easy to use program will help you to pinpoint the best times to make those important decisions and be prepared for upcoming events. For details and to view report samples, visit Astro's web site at www.astrocom.com. **IBMWEAF-BKUYF $69.95**

Day-by-Day Progressions

See how your progressed planets unfold as they form aspects to your natal planets and to each other. This easy to read listing includes positions and aspects of your progressed planets as of January 1st, and the exact dates of:

- Aspects to natal and progressed planets
- Progressed planets changing signs or houses

Please specify starting year.

5 years   PROG5-BKUYF $6.95
10 years   PROG10-BKUYF $9.95
85 years   PROG85-BKUYF $41.95

```
   PROGRESSED JAN 1 POSITIO
** 55 YEARS OLD IN 1986** *
Sun 12-CA- 8  22-N-54   2
Moo 10-PI-57   9-S-41  11
Mer 18-CA-29  23-N-53   2
Ven 24-GE-29  22-N-54   1
Mar 13-VI-36   7-N-15   5
Jup 27-CA-19  21-N- 5   3
Sat 20-CP-34R 21-S-43   9
Urn 19-AR-12   6-N-55  11
Nep  3-VI-41  10-N-50   4
Plu 20-CA-12  22-N-14   3
Asc 22-CA-36  21-N-33   3
Mc   4-AR- 0   1-N-36  11
Nod  9-AR-25R  3-N-44  11

E - ENTER 1 DEGREE ORB.   X
Jan 06 Moo X    0 Moo R
Jan 14 Sat L  135 Asc R
Jan 23 Moo X   30 Mc  R
```

1-800-888-9983
Astro Communications Services, Inc.
5521 Ruffin Road, San Diego, CA 92123
Operators available Monday through Friday, 8 am to 5 pm Pacific Time.
Prices subject to change.   Shipping & handling will be added.